尾田栄一郎

Eiichiro Oda

My staff and I often go to a very noisy Japanese restaurant where a lot of people take their children. There are TVs at each table. If you go there on Sunday nights at 7:30, you'll see the children staring at the TV screens with their mouths wide open, looking silly.

They're watching *One Piece*.

When I see that, I never want to let them down.

–Eiichiro Oda, 2001

E iichiro Oda began his manga career at the age of 17, when his one-shot cowboy manga **Wanted!** won second place in the coveted Tezuka manga awards. Oda went on to work as an assistant to some of the biggest manga artists in the industry, including Nobuhiro Watsuki, before winning the Hop Step Award for new artists. His pirate adventure **One Piece**, which debuted in **Weekly Shonen Jump** in 1997, quickly became one of the most popular manga in Japan.

ONE PIECE VOL. 17
BAROQUE WORKS PART 6

**SHONEN JUMP Manga Edition**

This graphic novel contains material that was originally published in English in
**SHONEN JUMP** #59–62. Artwork in the magazine
may have been slightly altered from that presented here.

STORY AND ART BY EIICHIRO ODA

English Adaptation/Lance Caselman
Translation/JN Productions
Touch-up Art & Lettering/Vanessa Satone
Additional Touch-up/Rachel Lightfoot
Design/Sean Lee
Editors/Urian Brown, Yuki Murashige

Printed in the U.S.A.

Published by VIZ Media, LLC
P.O. Box 77010
San Francisco, CA 94107

10 9 8 7 6 5 4
First printing, March 2008
Fourth printing, January 2012

www.viz.com

THE WORLD'S
MOST POPULAR MANGA

www.shonenjump.com

SHONEN JUMP MANGA

# ONE PIECE

## Vol. 17

## HIRILUK'S CHERRY BLOSSOMS

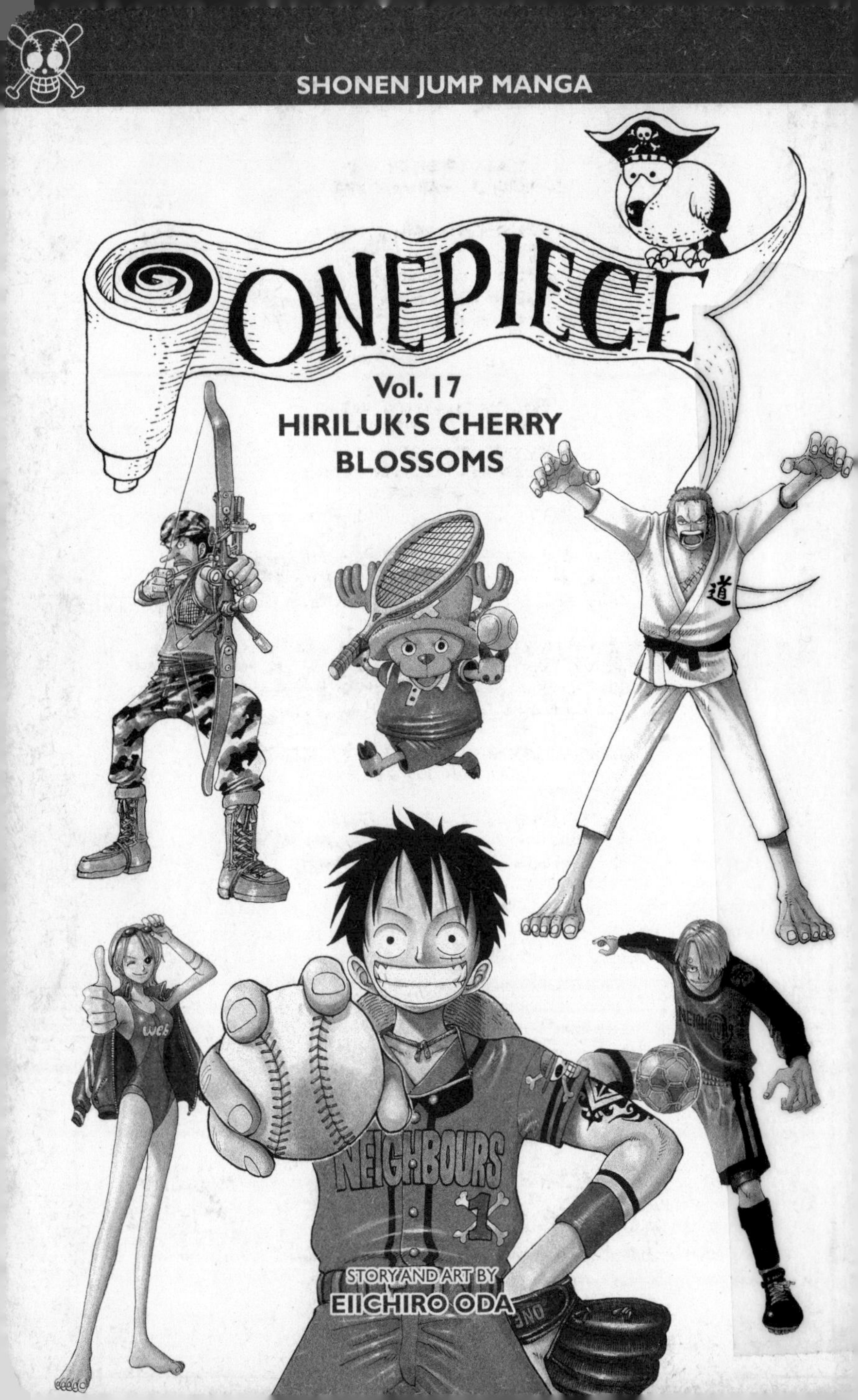
NEIGHBOURS

STORY AND ART BY

EIICHIRO ODA

# THE STORY OF

Volume 17

# ONE PIECE

Dr. Kureha

Karoo

Dr. Hiriluk

Wapol

CHOMP

KRAK

KRAK

Dalton

Kuromarimo & Chess

Monkey D. Luffy started out as just a kid with a dream—and that dream was to become the greatest pirate in history! Stirred by the tales of pirate "Red-Haired" Shanks, Luffy vowed to become a pirate himself. That was before the enchanted Devil Fruit gave Luffy the power to stretch like rubber, at the cost of being unable to swim—a serious handicap for an aspiring sea dog. Undeterred, Luffy set out to sea and recruited some crewmates: master swordsman Zolo, treasure-hunting thief Nami, lying sharpshooter Usopp, and Sanji, the high-kicking chef.

Having reached the Grand Line, Luffy and crew promise to take Princess Vivi to Alabasta in order to prevent Baroque Works from taking it over. But after a fierce battle on the island of Little Garden, Nami suddenly comes down with a high fever. In search of a doctor, the crew arrives at Drum Island where they encounter Chopper, a blue-nosed reindeer that walks on two legs and even talks! Fascinated by this living marvel, Luffy tries to recruit him as one of the crew. Meanwhile, Wapol, the former king of Drum Island with a very unusual appetite, has returned to reclaim his throne and his castle—and only the Straw Hat pirates stand in his way!

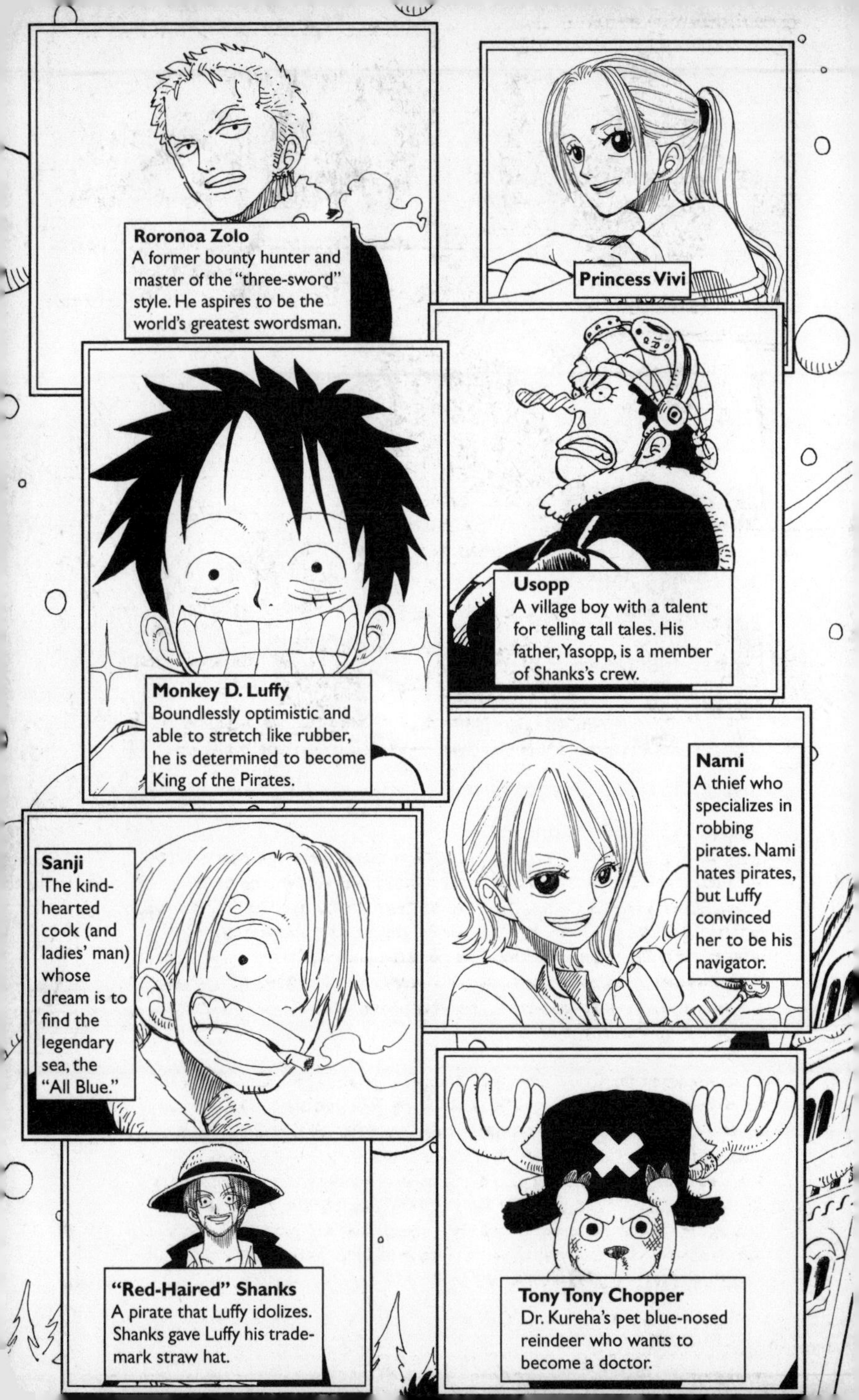
Princess Vivi
Roronoa Zolo
A former bounty hunter and master of the "three-sword" style. He aspires to be the world's greatest swordsman.
Usopp
A village boy with a talent for telling tall tales. His father, Yasopp, is a member of Shanks's crew.
Monkey D. Luffy
Boundlessly optimistic and able to stretch like rubber, he is determined to become King of the Pirates.
Nami
A thief who specializes in robbing pirates. Nami hates pirates, but Luffy convinced her to be his navigator.
Sanji
The kind-hearted cook (and ladies' man) whose dream is to find the legendary sea, the "All Blue."
Tony Tony Chopper
Dr. Kureha's pet blue-nosed reindeer who wants to become a doctor.
"Red-Haired" Shanks
A pirate that Luffy idolizes. Shanks gave Luffy his trade-mark straw hat.

BAROQUE WORKS

# ONE PIECE

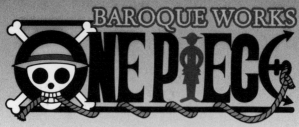

## Vol. 17
## Hiriluk's Cherry Blossoms

## CONTENTS

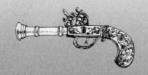

# Chapter 146:
# BATTLE TO DEFEND THE KINGDOM

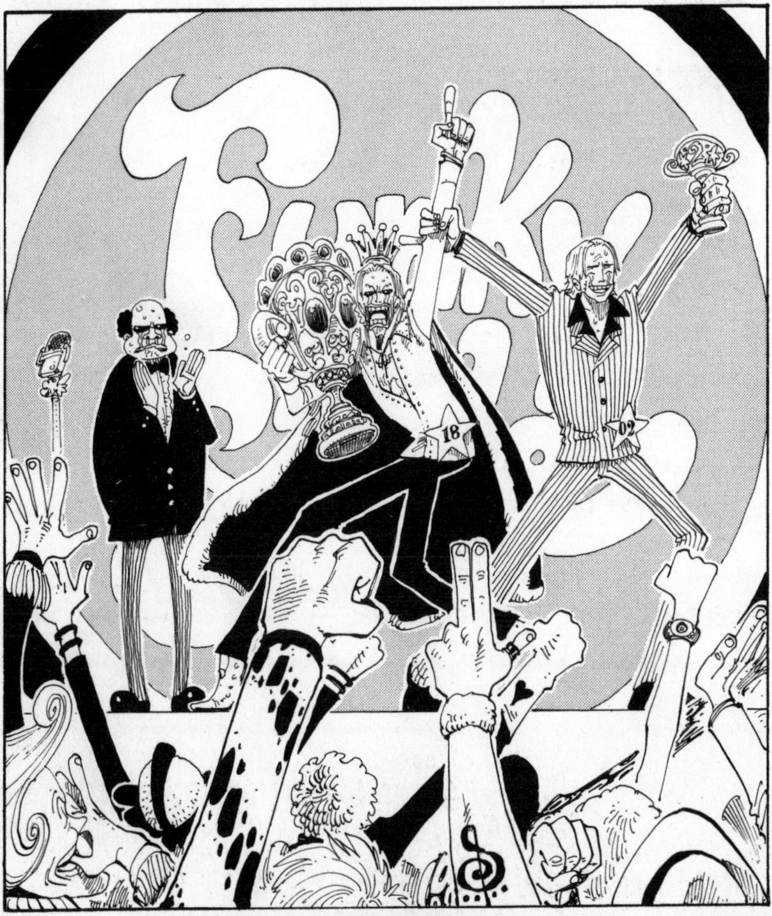

18
02


DJANGO'S DANCE HEAVEN, VOL. 16:
"LORD OF THE DANCE"

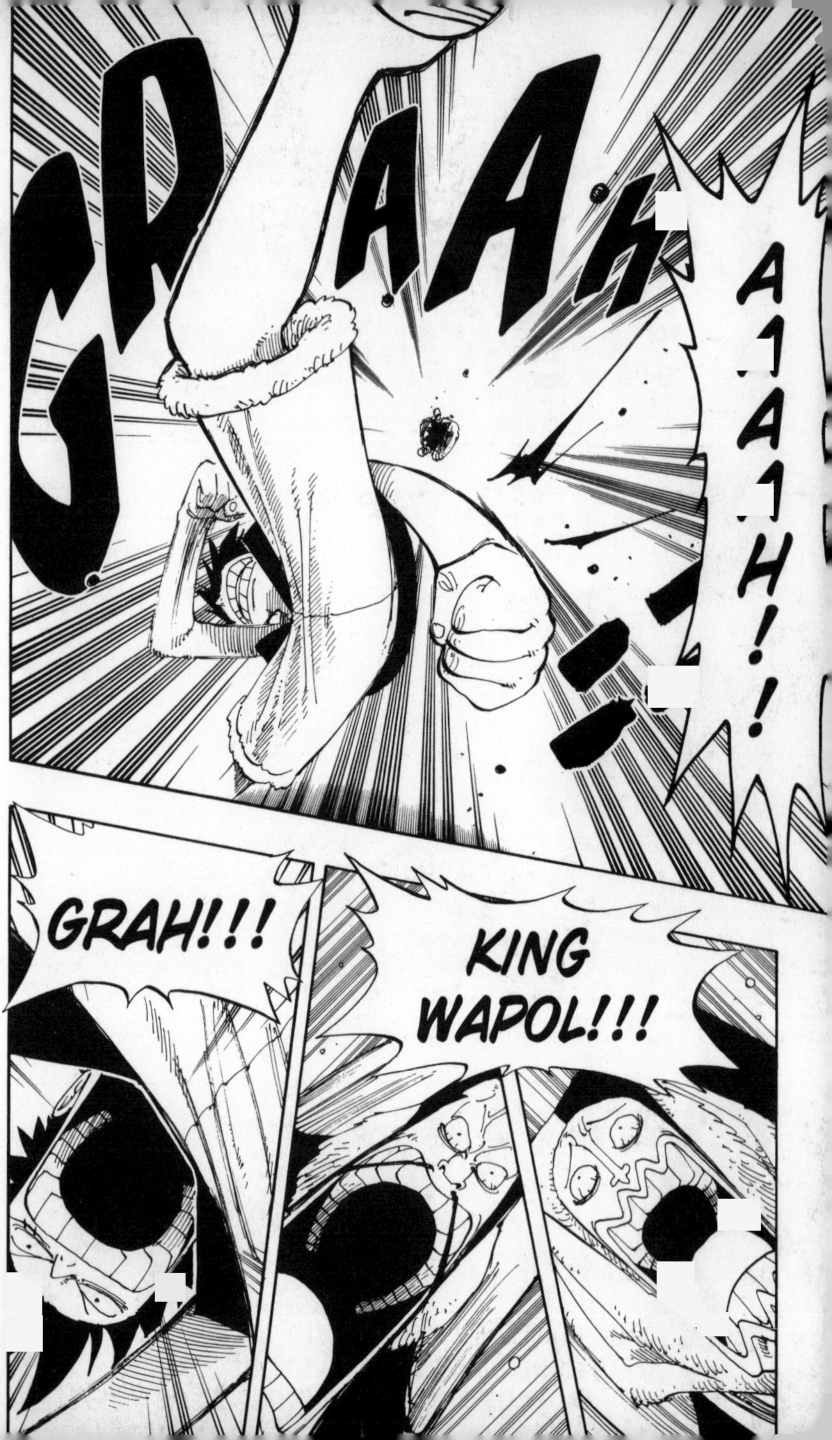
CRAAA
AAAAH!!
KING WAPOL!!!
GRAH!!!

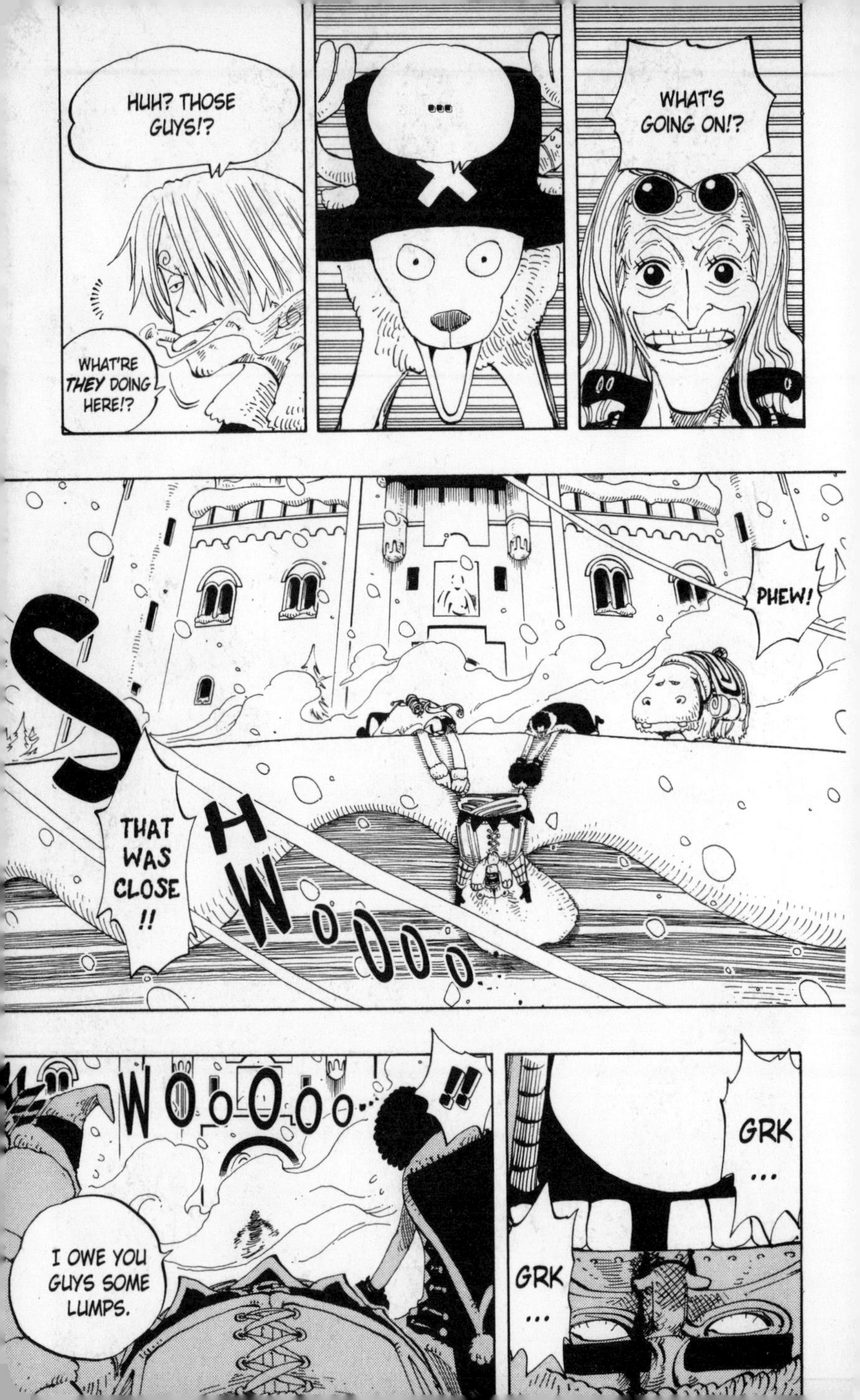
WHAT'S GOING ON!?
...
HUH? THOSE GUYS!?
WHAT'RE *THEY* DOING HERE!?
PHEW!
SHWOOOOO
THAT WAS CLOSE !!
GRK ...
GRK ...
WOOOOOO..!!
I OWE YOU GUYS SOME LUMPS.

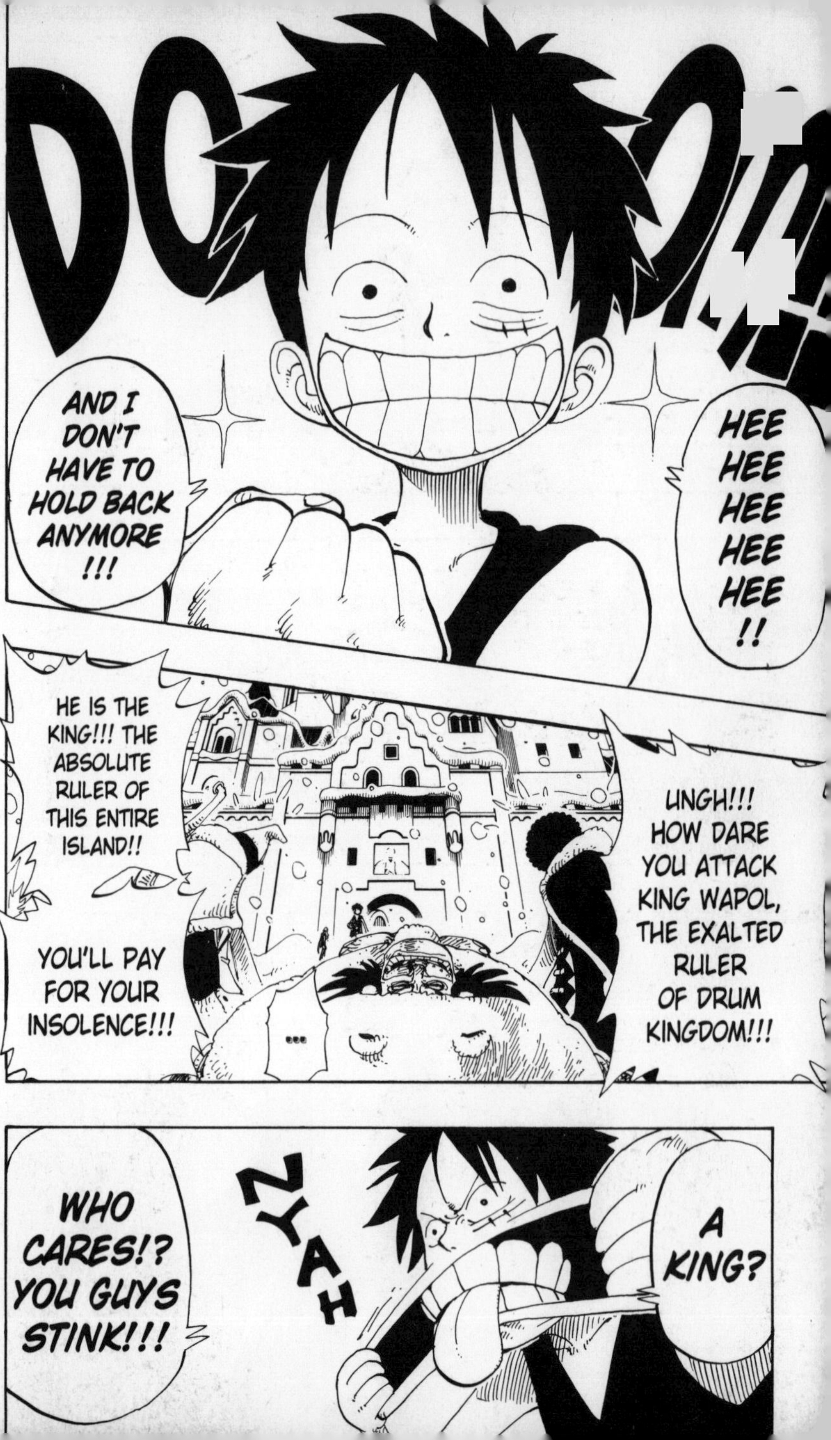

DO
HEE HEE HEE HEE HEE!!
AND I DON'T HAVE TO HOLD BACK ANYMORE!!!
UNGH!!! HOW DARE YOU ATTACK KING WAPOL, THE EXALTED RULER OF DRUM KINGDOM!!!
HE IS THE KING!!! THE ABSOLUTE RULER OF THIS ENTIRE ISLAND!!
YOU'LL PAY FOR YOUR INSOLENCE!!!
...
A KING?
ZYAH
WHO CARES!? YOU GUYS STINK!!!

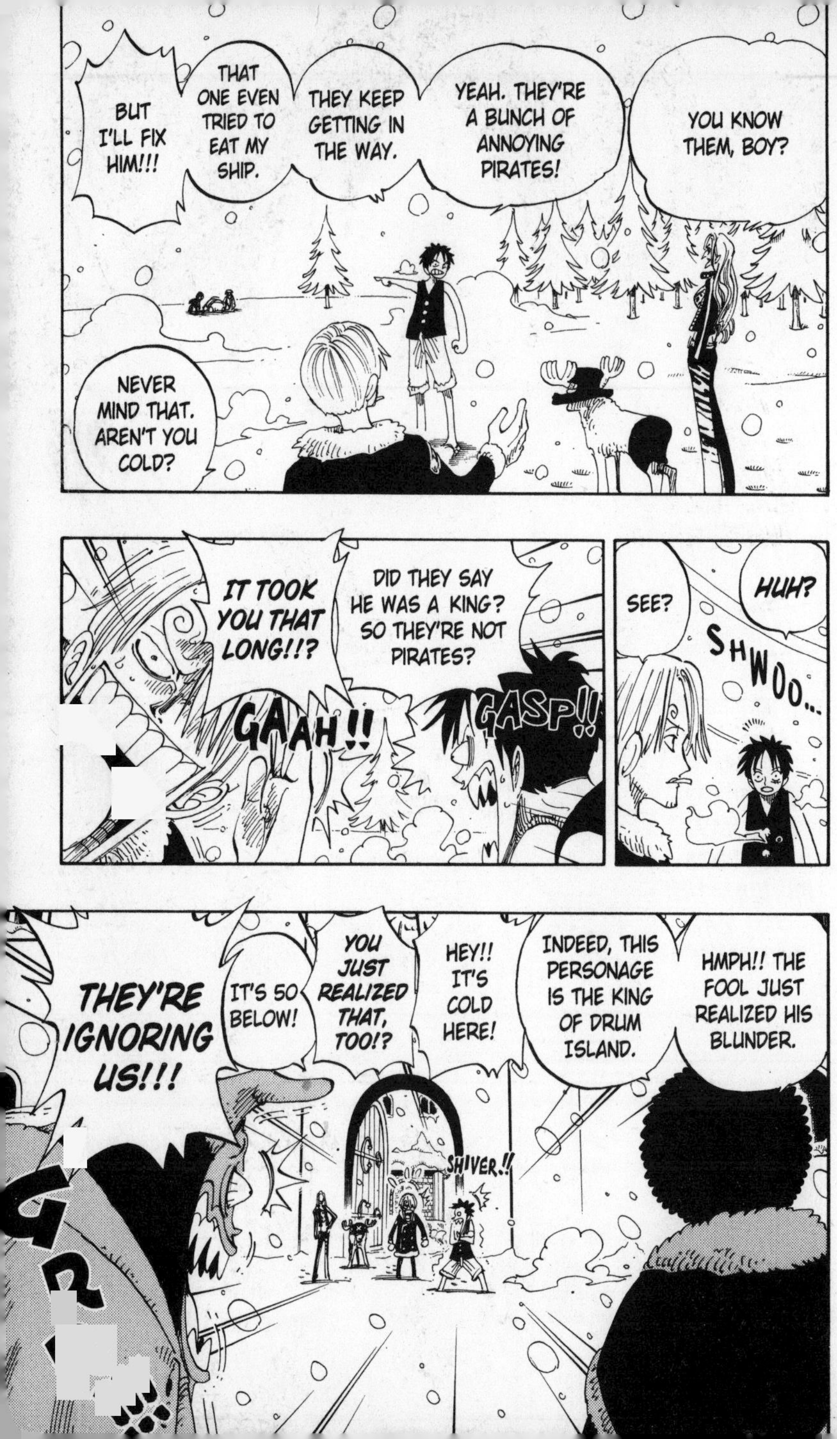
YOU KNOW THEM, BOY?
YEAH. THEY'RE A BUNCH OF ANNOYING PIRATES!
THEY KEEP GETTING IN THE WAY.
THAT ONE EVEN TRIED TO EAT MY SHIP.
BUT I'LL FIX HIM!!!
NEVER MIND THAT. AREN'T YOU COLD?
HUH?
SEE?
SHWOO...
DID THEY SAY HE WAS A KING? SO THEY'RE NOT PIRATES?
GASP!!
IT TOOK YOU THAT LONG!!?
GAAH!!
HMPH!! THE FOOL JUST REALIZED HIS BLUNDER.
INDEED, THIS PERSONAGE IS THE KING OF DRUM ISLAND.
HEY!! IT'S COLD HERE!
YOU JUST REALIZED THAT, TOO!?
IT'S 50 BELOW!
SHIVER.!!
THEY'RE IGNORING US!!!

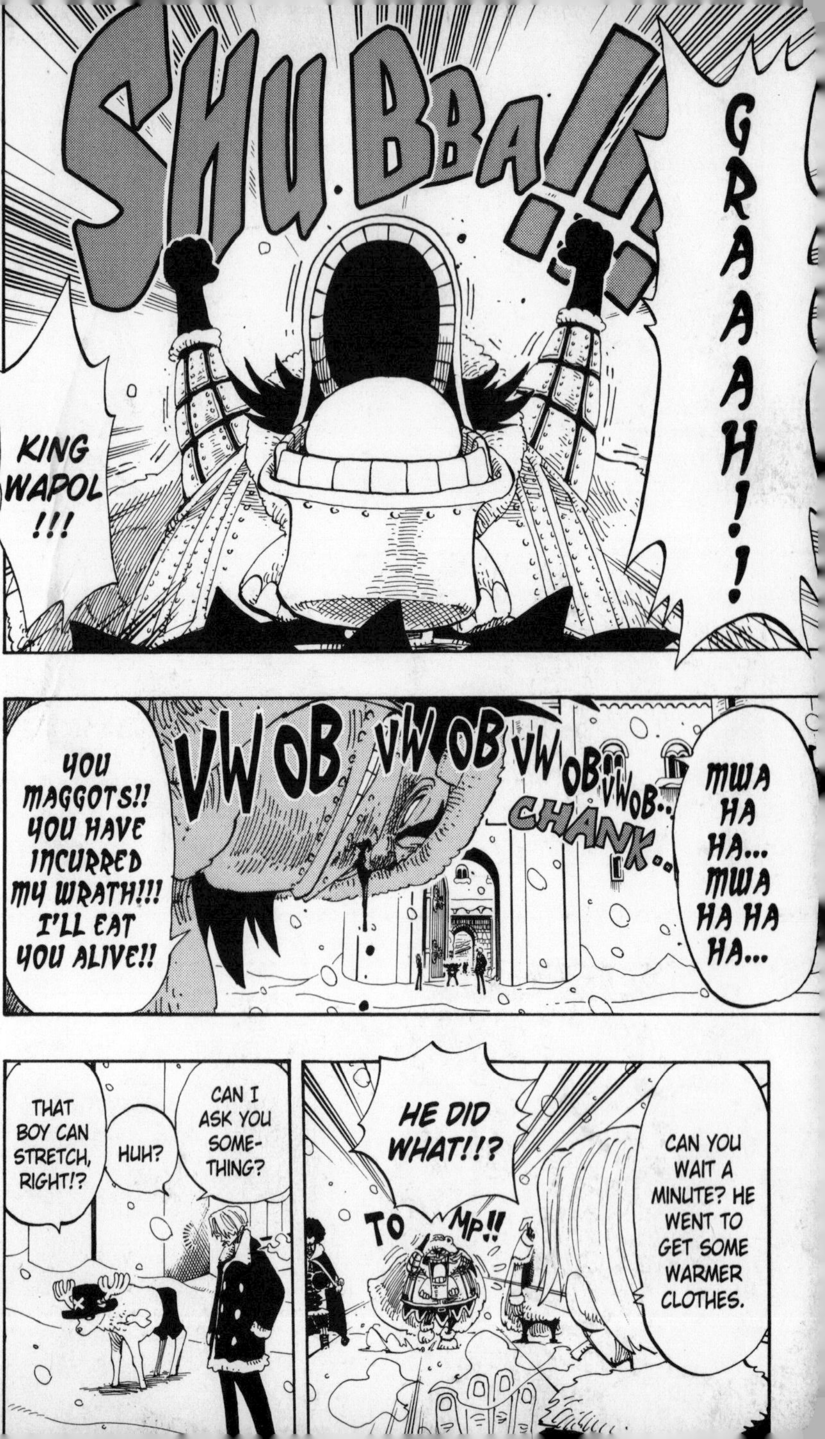
SHUBBA!!!
GRAAAAH!!!
KING WAPOL!!!
MWA HA HA... MWA HA HA HA...
VWOB VWOB VWOB VWOB...
CHANK...
YOU MAGGOTS!! YOU HAVE INCURRED MY WRATH!!! I'LL EAT YOU ALIVE!!
CAN YOU WAIT A MINUTE? HE WENT TO GET SOME WARMER CLOTHES.
HE DID WHAT!!?
TOMP!!
CAN I ASK YOU SOMETHING?
HUH?
THAT BOY CAN STRETCH, RIGHT!?

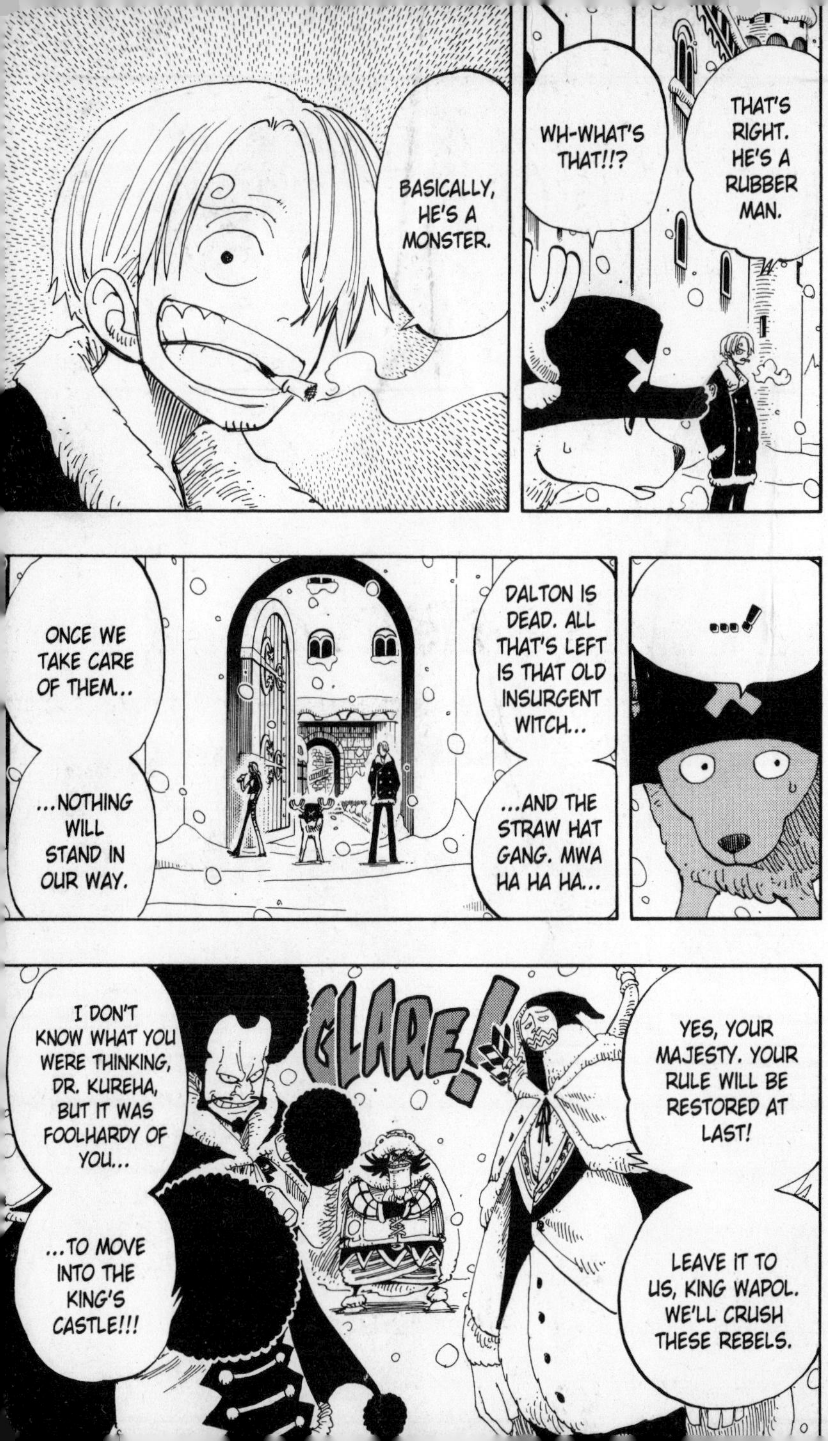

WH-WHAT'S THAT!!?
THAT'S RIGHT. HE'S A RUBBER MAN.
BASICALLY, HE'S A MONSTER.
...!
DALTON IS DEAD. ALL THAT'S LEFT IS THAT OLD INSURGENT WITCH...
...AND THE STRAW HAT GANG. MWA HA HA HA...
ONCE WE TAKE CARE OF THEM...
...NOTHING WILL STAND IN OUR WAY.
YES, YOUR MAJESTY. YOUR RULE WILL BE RESTORED AT LAST!
LEAVE IT TO US, KING WAPOL. WE'LL CRUSH THESE REBELS.
GLARE!
I DON'T KNOW WHAT YOU WERE THINKING, DR. KUREHA, BUT IT WAS FOOLHARDY OF YOU...
...TO MOVE INTO THE KING'S CASTLE!!!

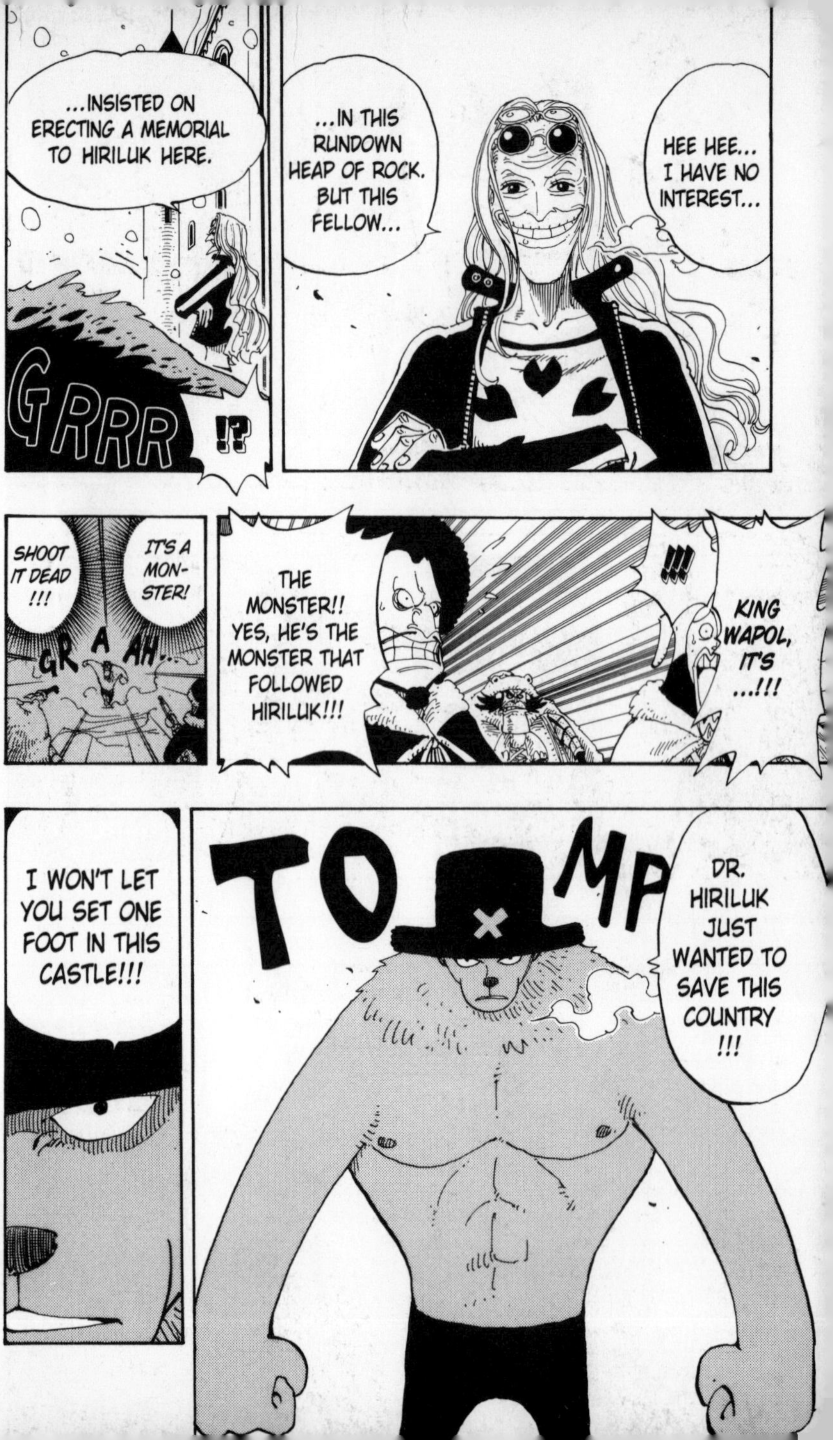
HEE HEE... I HAVE NO INTEREST...
...IN THIS RUNDOWN HEAP OF ROCK. BUT THIS FELLOW...
...INSISTED ON ERECTING A MEMORIAL TO HIRILUK HERE.
GRRR
!?
!!!
KING WAPOL, IT'S ...!!!
THE MONSTER!! YES, HE'S THE MONSTER THAT FOLLOWED HIRILUK!!!
IT'S A MONSTER!
SHOOT IT DEAD!!!
GRAAH...
TOMP
DR. HIRILUK JUST WANTED TO SAVE THIS COUNTRY!!!
I WON'T LET YOU SET ONE FOOT IN THIS CASTLE!!!

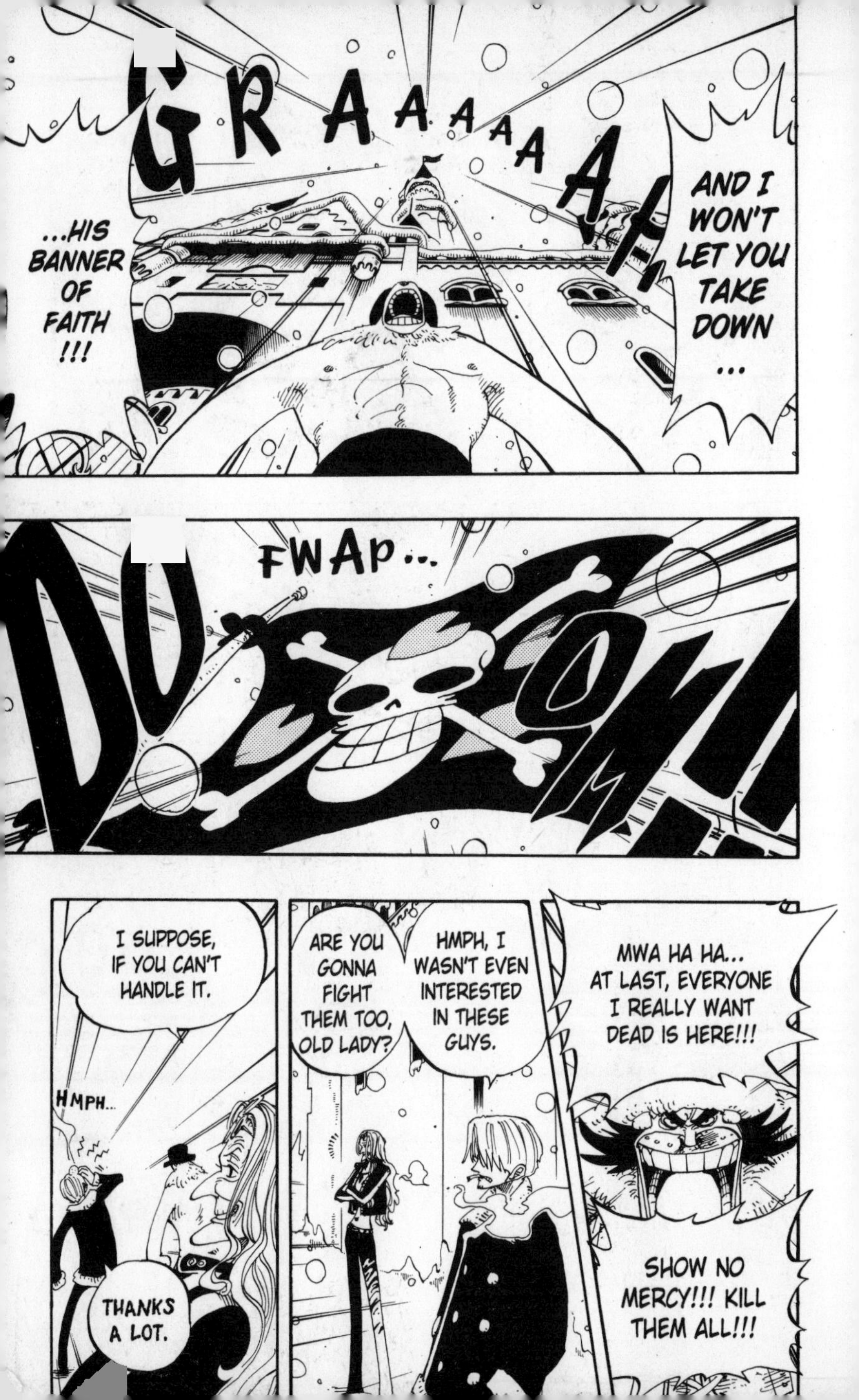
AND I WON'T LET YOU TAKE DOWN...
...HIS BANNER OF FAITH!!!
GRAAAAAAH
FWAP...
MWA HA HA... AT LAST, EVERYONE I REALLY WANT DEAD IS HERE!!!
SHOW NO MERCY!!! KILL THEM ALL!!!
HMPH, I WASN'T EVEN INTERESTED IN THESE GUYS.
ARE YOU GONNA FIGHT THEM TOO, OLD LADY?
I SUPPOSE, IF YOU CAN'T HANDLE IT.
HMPH...
THANKS A LOT.

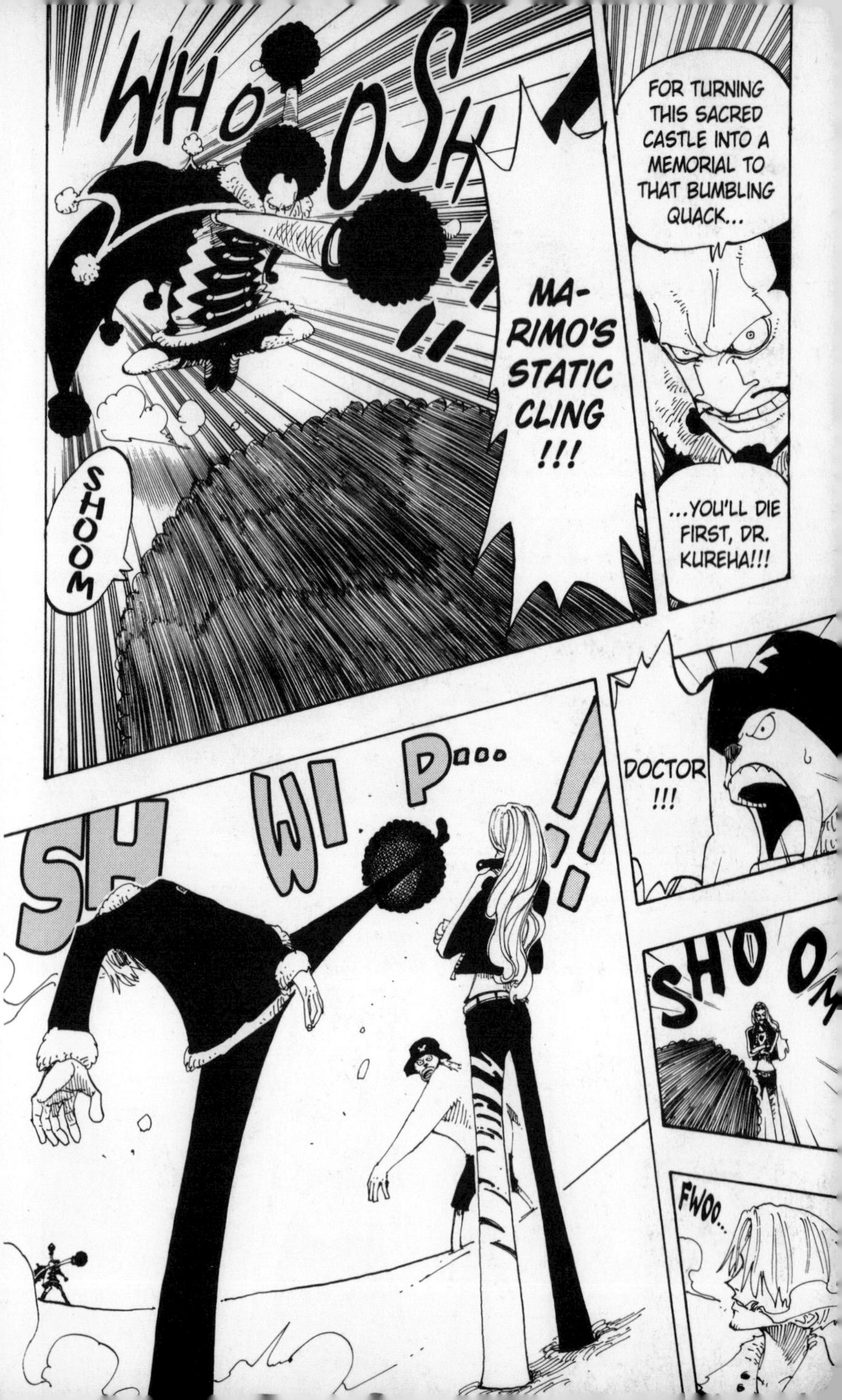
FOR TURNING THIS SACRED CASTLE INTO A MEMORIAL TO THAT BUMBLING QUACK...
...YOU'LL DIE FIRST, DR. KUREHA!!!
WHOOSH
MA-RIMO'S STATIC CLING!!!
SHOOM
DOCTOR!!!
SHOOM
FWOO...
SHWIP...

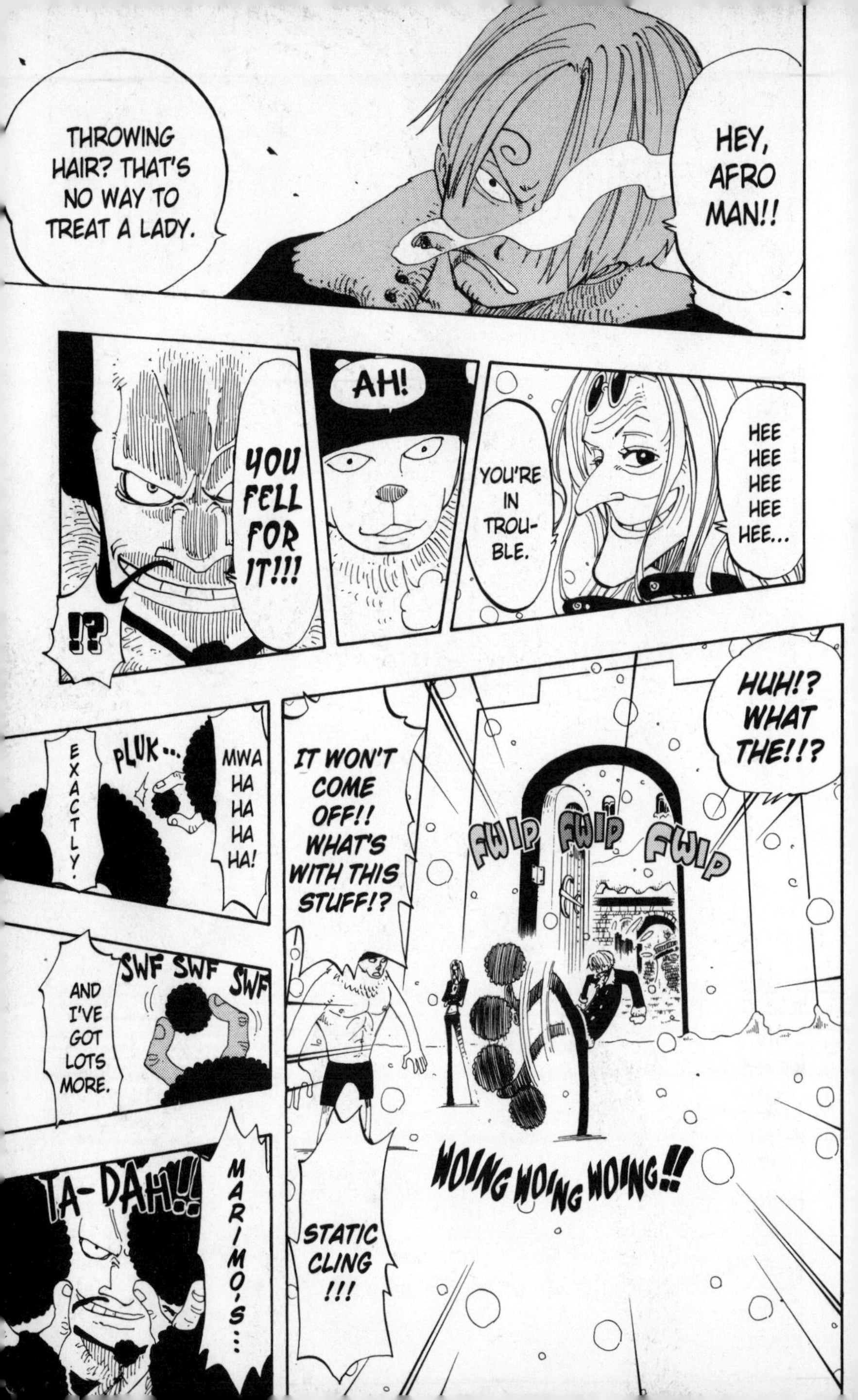
HEY, AFRO MAN!!
THROWING HAIR? THAT'S NO WAY TO TREAT A LADY.
HEE HEE HEE HEE HEE...
YOU'RE IN TROU-BLE.
AH!
YOU FELL FOR IT!!!
!?
HUH!? WHAT THE!!?
FWIP FWIP FWIP
IT WON'T COME OFF!! WHAT'S WITH THIS STUFF!?
WOING WOING WOING!!
STATIC CLING!!!
MWA HA HA HA HA!
PLUK...
EXACTLY.
SWF SWF SWF
AND I'VE GOT LOTS MORE.
MARIMOS...
TA-DAH!!

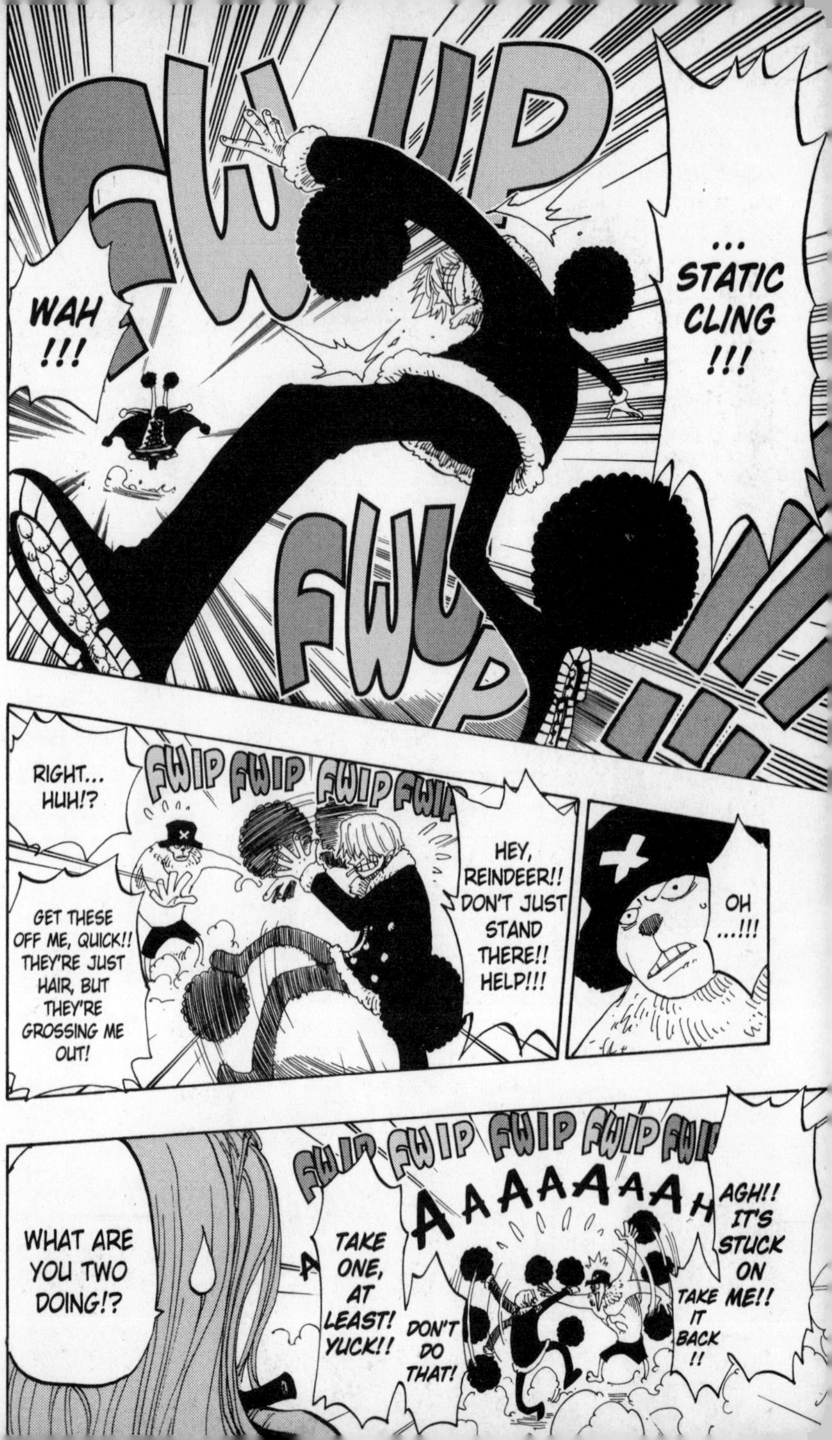
FWUP
... STATIC CLING !!!
WAH !!!
FWUP
RIGHT... HUH!?
FWIP FWIP FWIP FWIP
OH ...!!!
HEY, REINDEER!! DON'T JUST STAND THERE!! HELP!!!
GET THESE OFF ME, QUICK!! THEY'RE JUST HAIR, BUT THEY'RE GROSSING ME OUT!
FWIP FWIP FWIP FWIP FWIP
AGH!! IT'S STUCK ON ME!!
TAKE IT BACK !!
AAAAAAAH
DON'T DO THAT!
TAKE ONE, AT LEAST! YUCK!!
WHAT ARE YOU TWO DOING!?

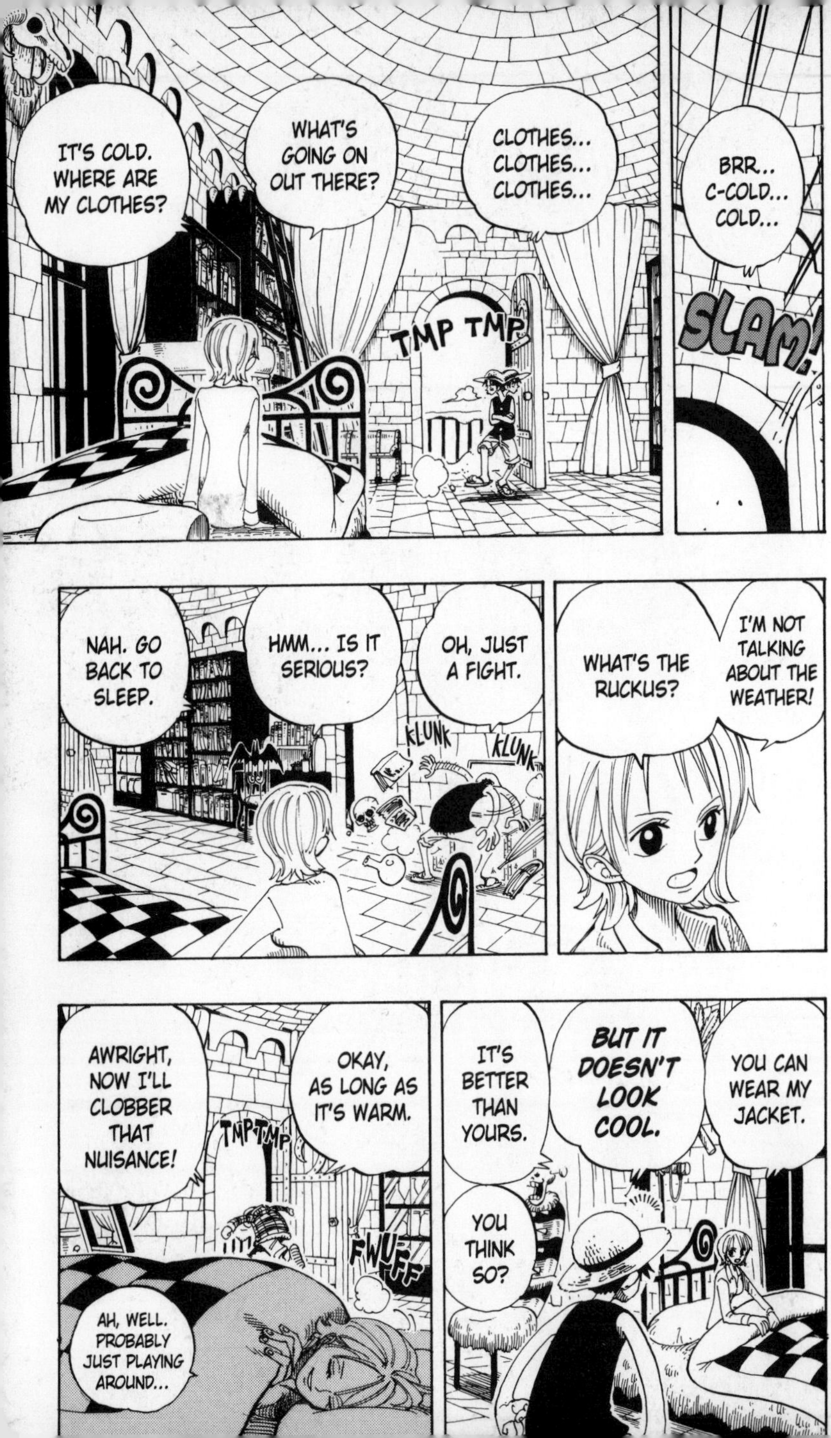
BRR... C-COLD... COLD...
SLAM!
CLOTHES... CLOTHES... CLOTHES...
TMP TMP
WHAT'S GOING ON OUT THERE?
IT'S COLD. WHERE ARE MY CLOTHES?
I'M NOT TALKING ABOUT THE WEATHER!
WHAT'S THE RUCKUS?
OH, JUST A FIGHT.
KLUNK
KLUNK
HMM... IS IT SERIOUS?
NAH. GO BACK TO SLEEP.
YOU CAN WEAR MY JACKET.
BUT IT DOESN'T LOOK COOL.
IT'S BETTER THAN YOURS.
YOU THINK SO?
OKAY, AS LONG AS IT'S WARM.
AWRIGHT, NOW I'LL CLOBBER THAT NUISANCE!
TMPTMP
FWUFF
AH, WELL. PROBABLY JUST PLAYING AROUND...

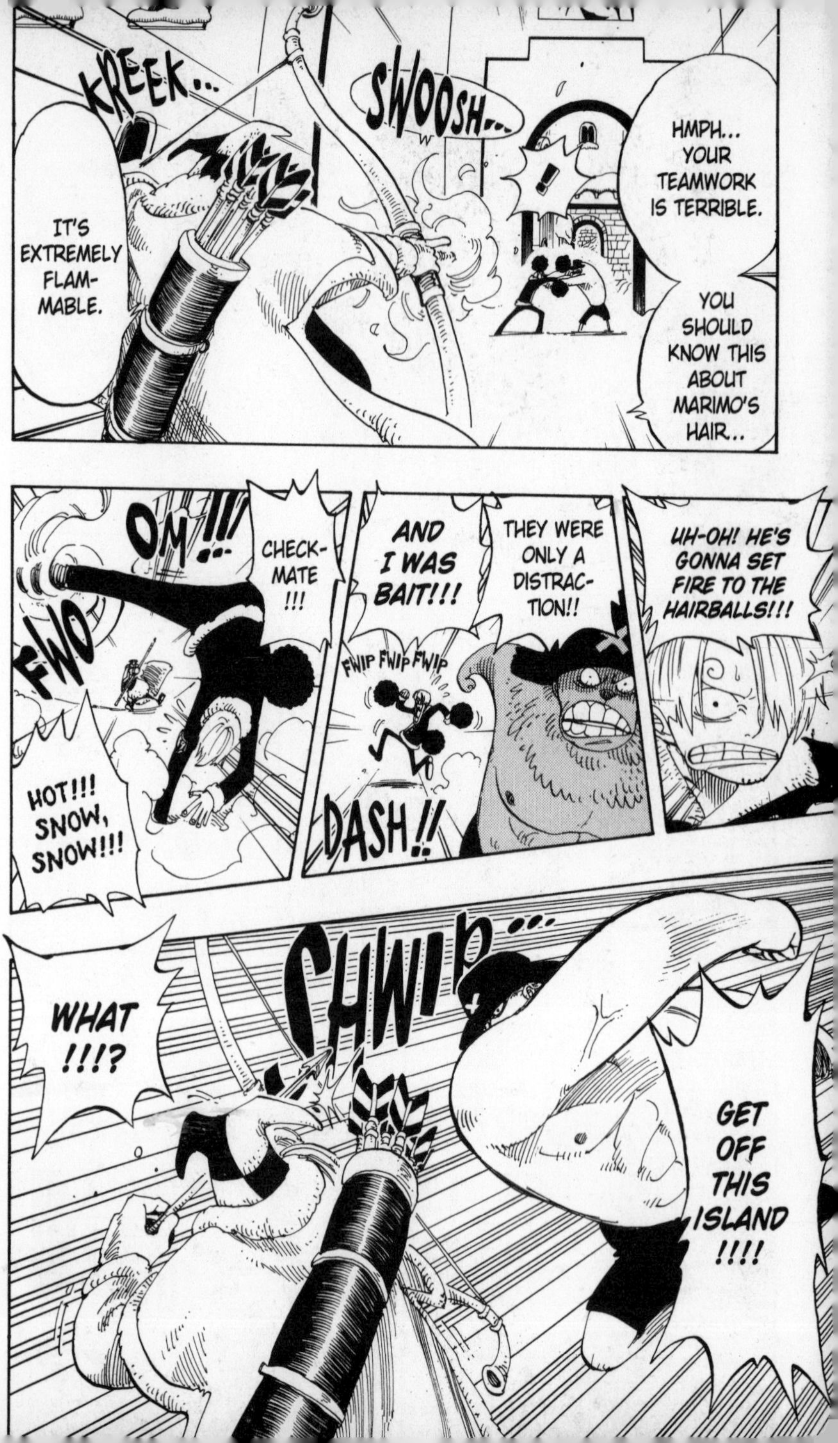
HMPH... YOUR TEAMWORK IS TERRIBLE.
YOU SHOULD KNOW THIS ABOUT MARIMO'S HAIR...
!
SWOOSH...
KREEK...
IT'S EXTREMELY FLAM-MABLE.
UH-OH! HE'S GONNA SET FIRE TO THE HAIRBALLS!!!
THEY WERE ONLY A DISTRAC-TION!!
AND I WAS BAIT!!!
FWIP FWIP FWIP
DASH!!
CHECK-MATE!!!
FWOOM!!!
HOT!!! SNOW, SNOW!!!!
GET OFF THIS ISLAND!!!!
CHWIP...
WHAT!!!?

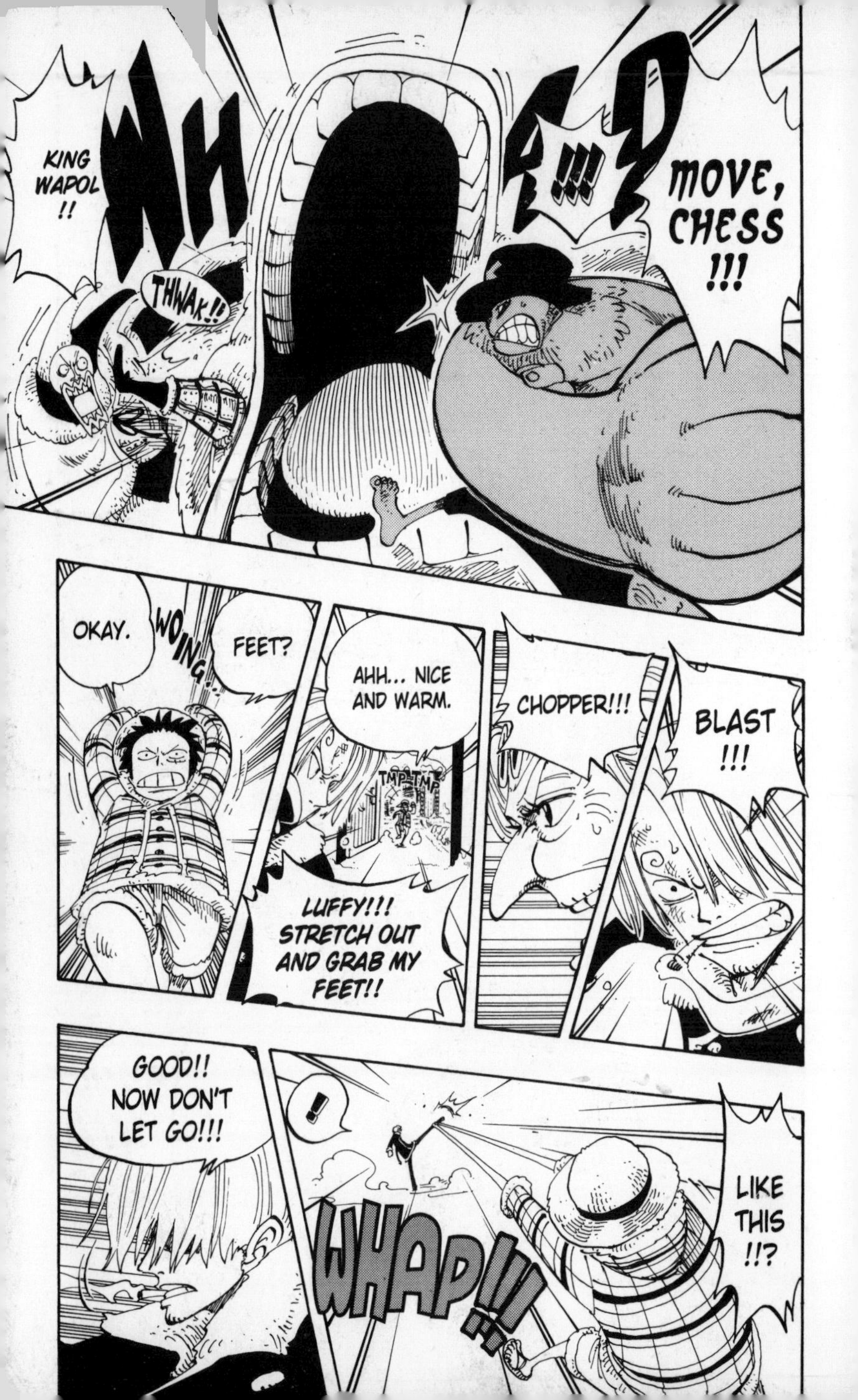
MOVE, CHESS!!!
THWAK!!
KING WAPOL!!
BLAST!!!
CHOPPER!!!
AHH... NICE AND WARM.
TMP TMP
LUFFY!!! STRETCH OUT AND GRAB MY FEET!!
FEET?
WOING..
OKAY.
LIKE THIS!!?
!
WHAP!!!
GOOD!! NOW DON'T LET GO!!!

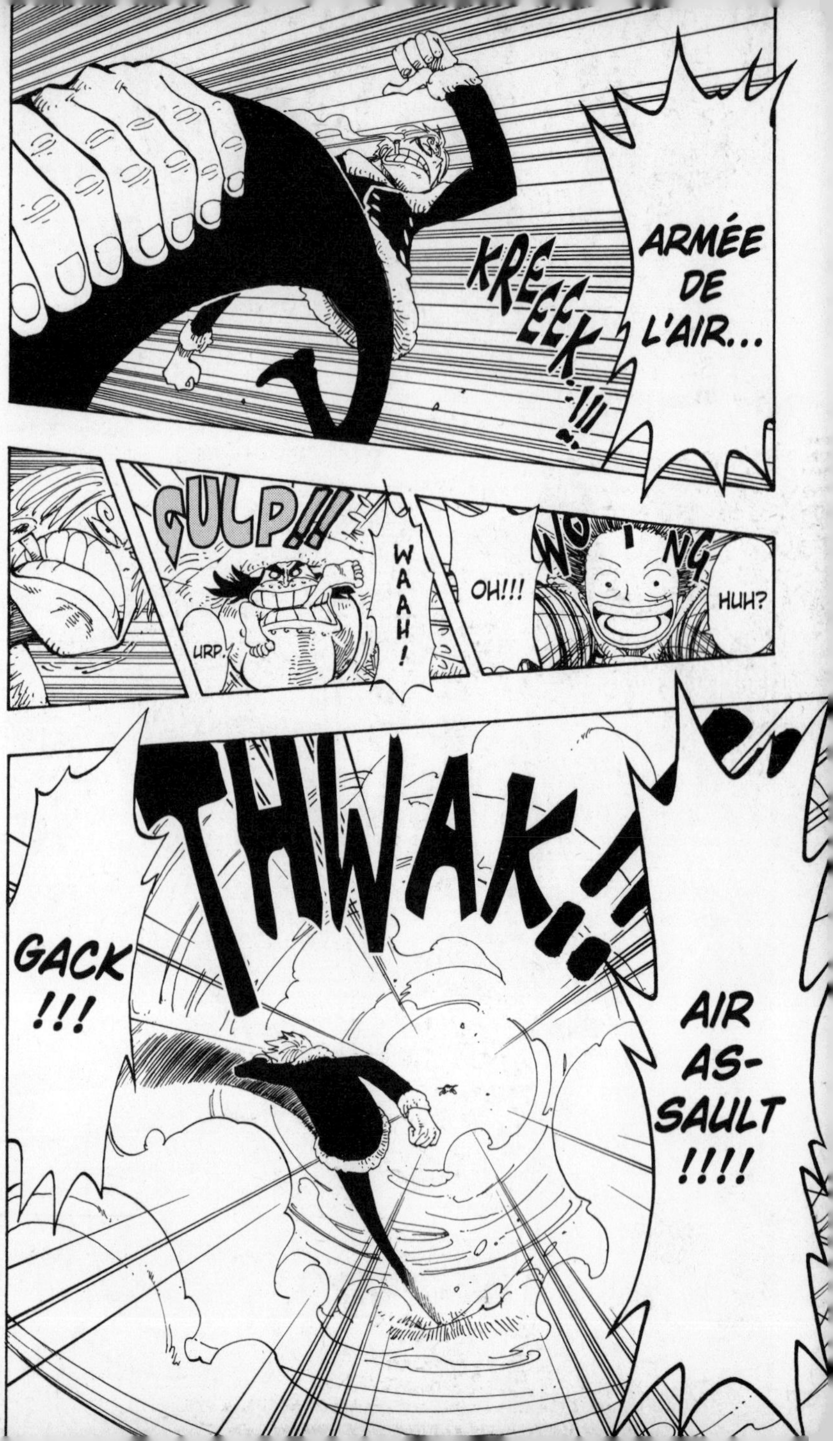
ARMÉE DE L'AIR...
KREEEK!!!
HUH?
WOING
OH!!!
WAAAH!
GULP!!
URP.
AIR AS-SAULT!!!!
THWAK!!
GACK!!!

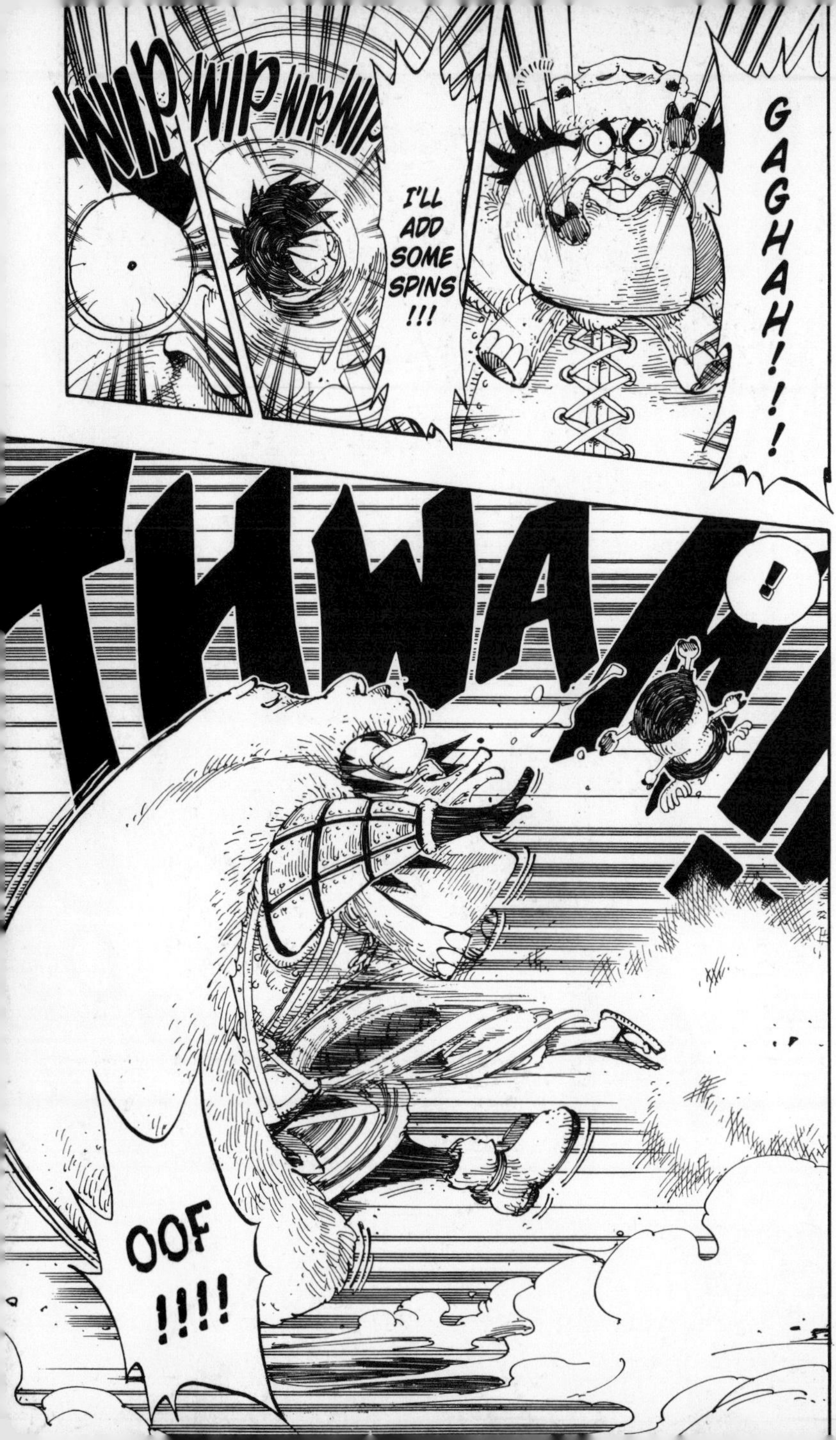
GAGHAH!!!
I'LL ADD SOME SPINS!!!
WIP WIP WIP WIP
THWAM!!
!
OOF!!!!

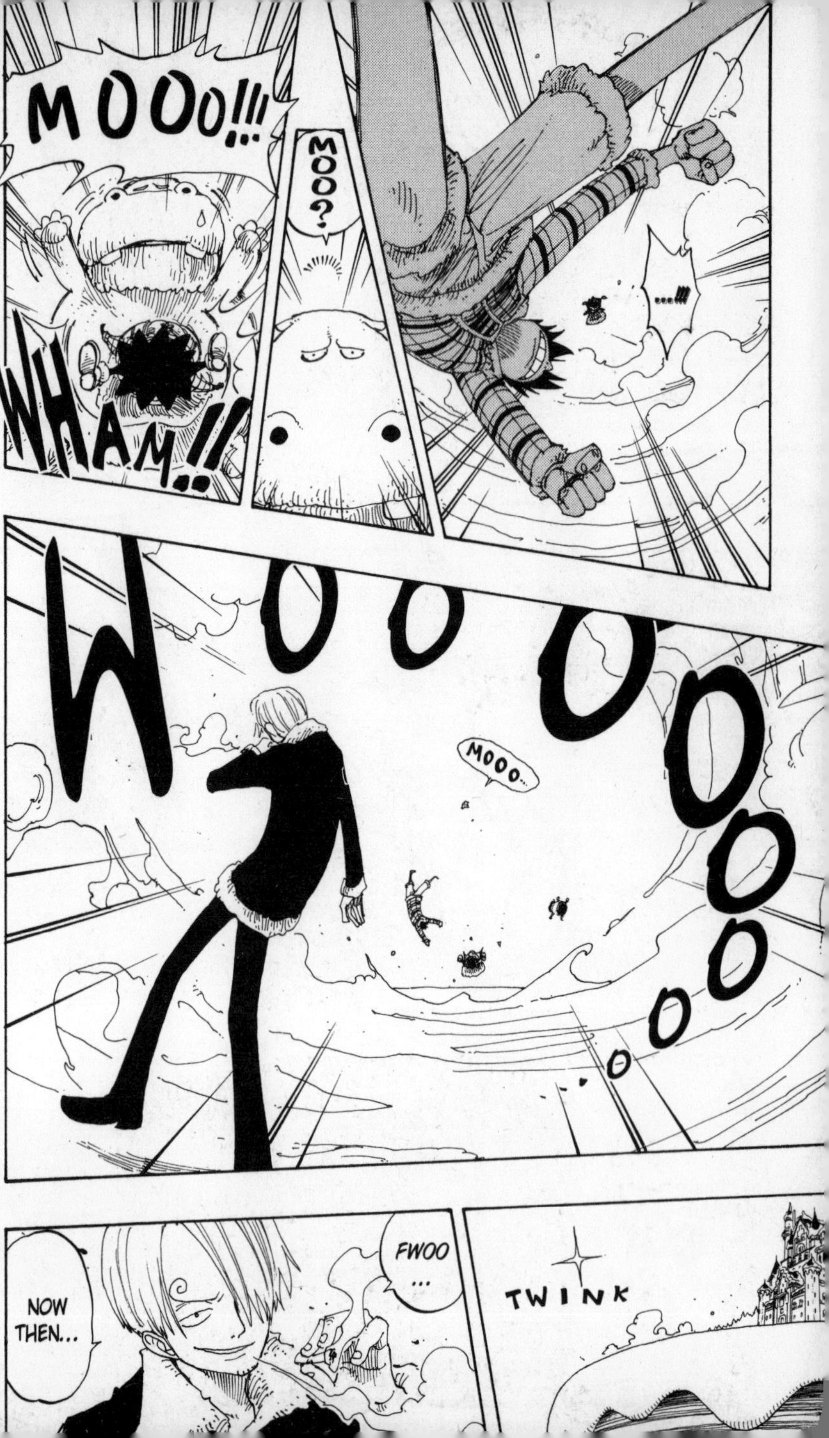

...!!!
MOO?
MOOO!!!
WHAM!!
WHOOOOOOOOO
MOOO...
TWINK
FWOO...
NOW THEN...

...!!!
TH-THANK YOU!
YOU GUYS ARE AMAZ-ING.
HEY, LUFFY!! THAT'S NAMI'S JACKET!!
HMM... LOOK!! HE'S STILL ALIVE!!
POKE
POKE
THE HIPPO FLEW OFF SOME-WHERE THOUGH.
TAKE IT OFF!!
KING WAPOL, ARE YOU HURT!!?
THEY'RE STRONGER THAN WE THOUGHT!!
I'LL KILL THEM.
AH!
HISS
IT'S TIME FOR...
...THE MUNCH-MUNCH FAC-TORY!!!

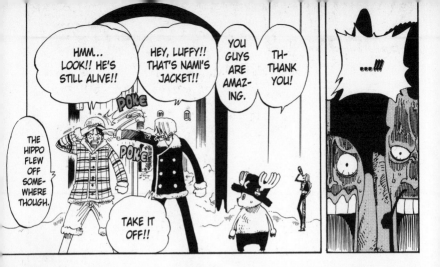

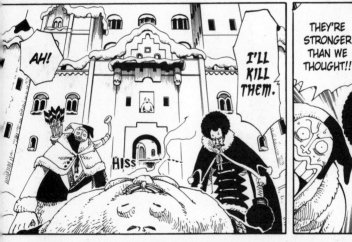

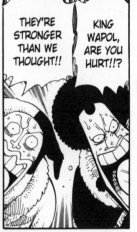

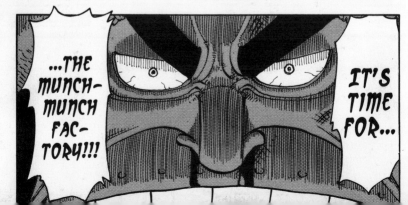

# Chapter 147: FRAUDS

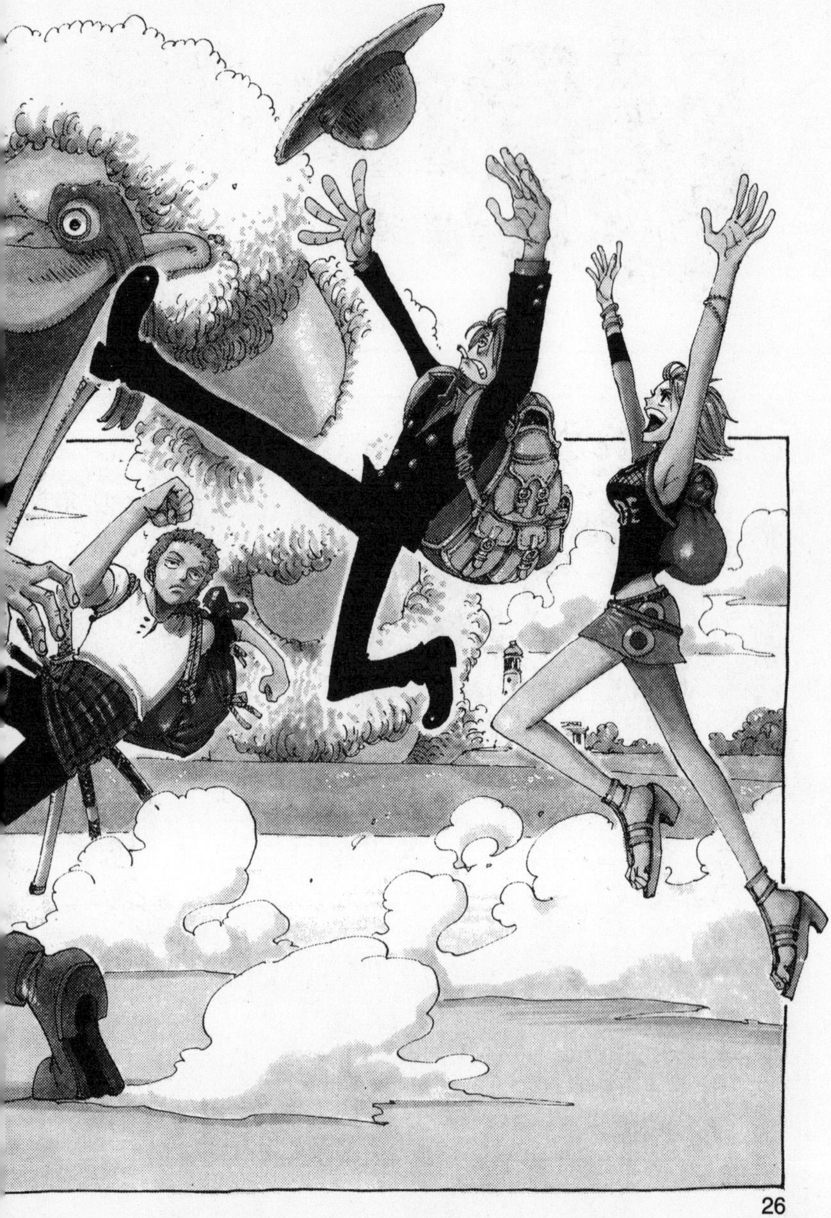

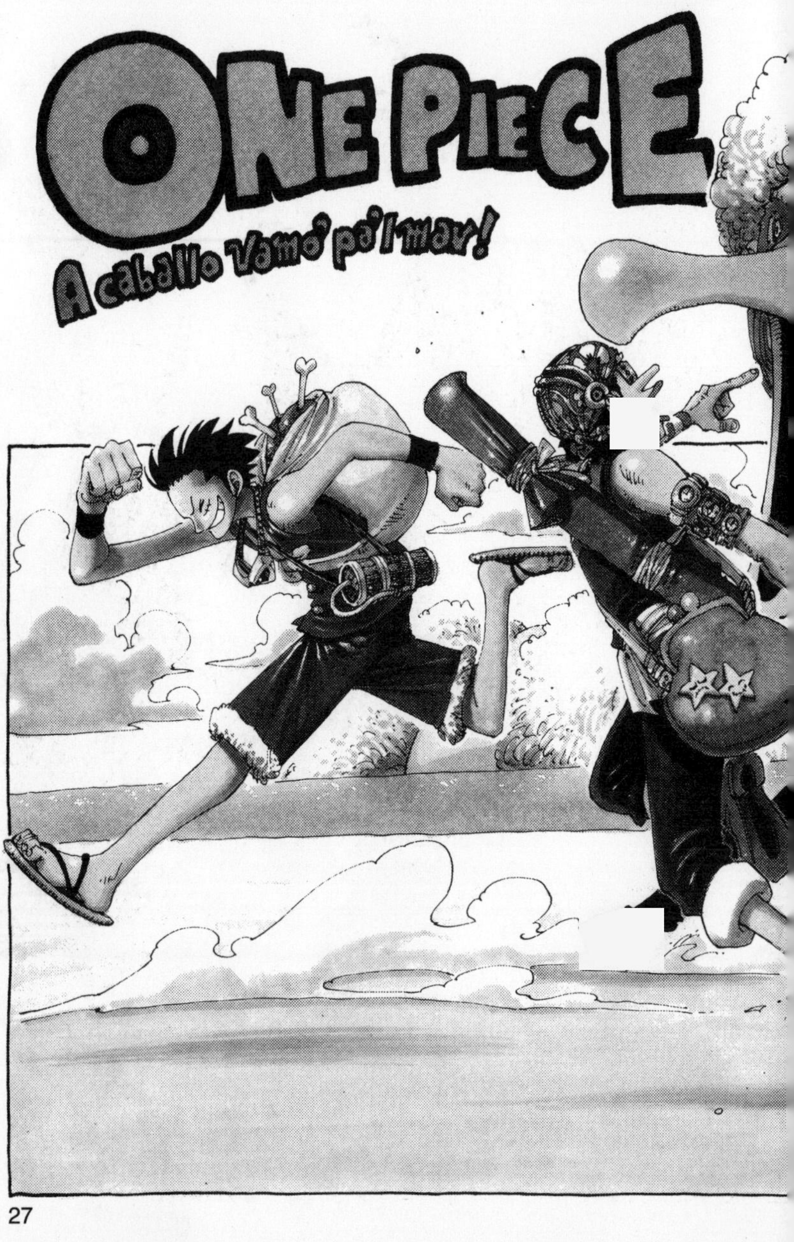
ONE PIECE
A caballo vamo' pa'l mar!

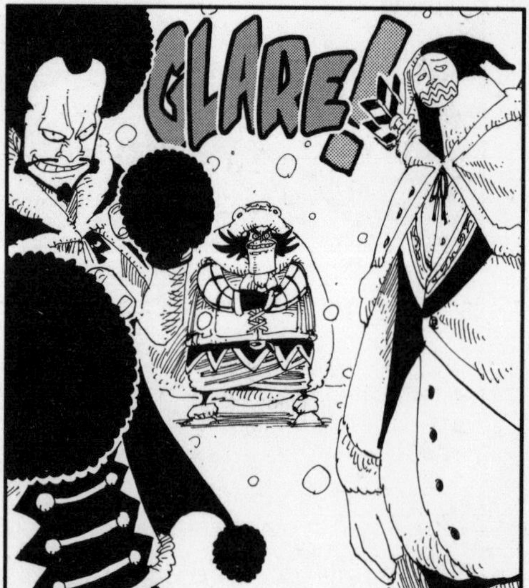
GLARE!

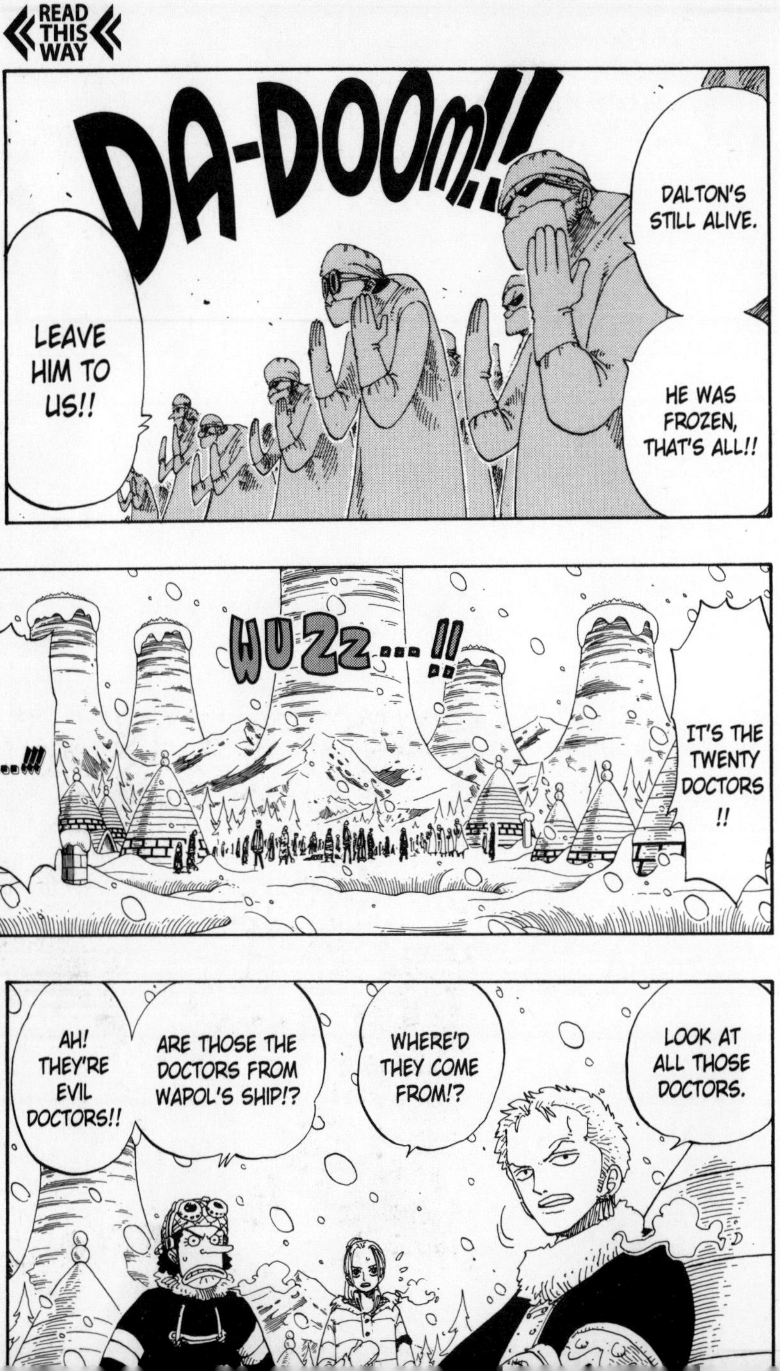
READ THIS WAY
DA-DOOM!!
DALTON'S STILL ALIVE.
HE WAS FROZEN, THAT'S ALL!!
LEAVE HIM TO US!!
IT'S THE TWENTY DOCTORS !!
WUZZ... !!
...!!!
LOOK AT ALL THOSE DOCTORS.
WHERE'D THEY COME FROM!?
ARE THOSE THE DOCTORS FROM WAPOL'S SHIP!?
AH! THEY'RE EVIL DOCTORS!!

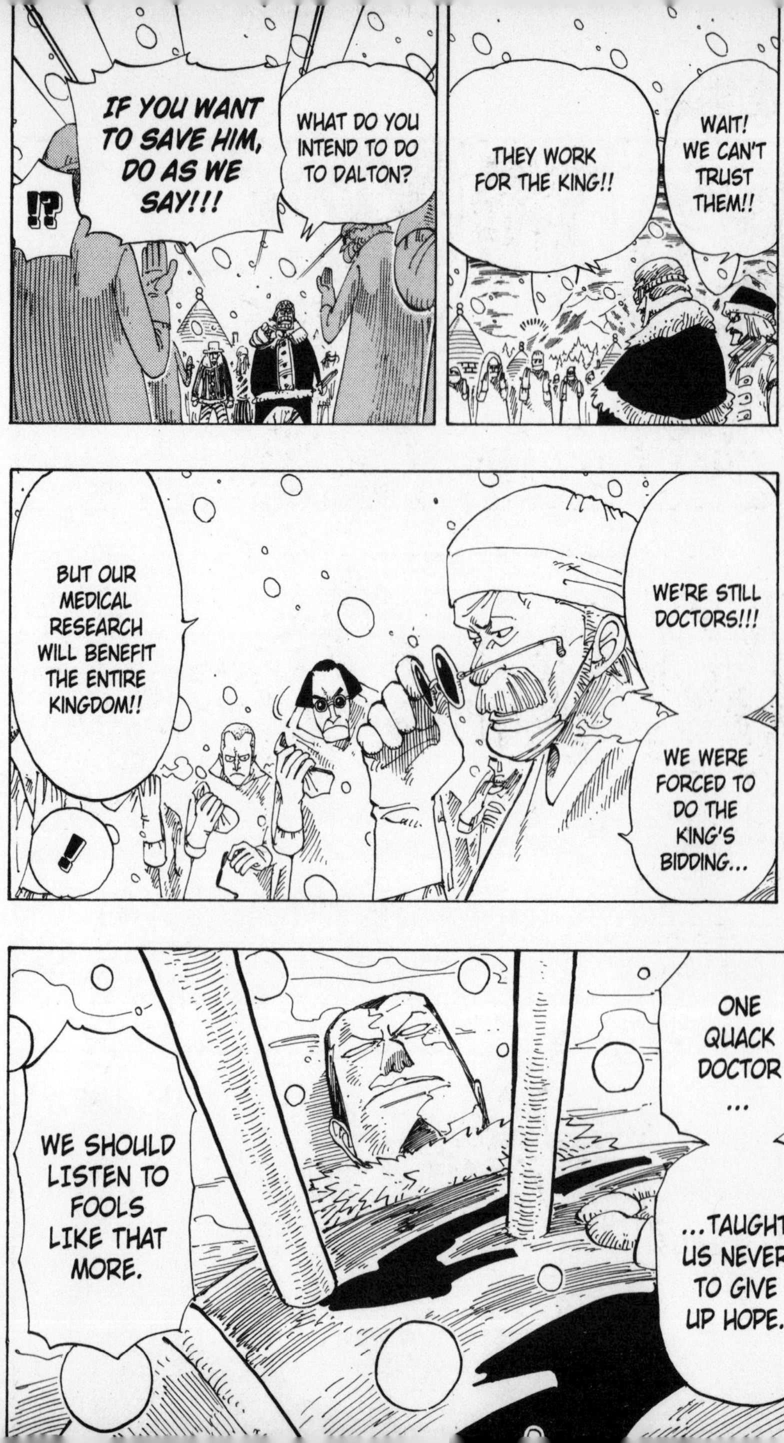
WAIT! WE CAN'T TRUST THEM!!
THEY WORK FOR THE KING!!
WHAT DO YOU INTEND TO DO TO DALTON?
IF YOU WANT TO SAVE HIM, DO AS WE SAY!!!
!?
WE'RE STILL DOCTORS!!!
WE WERE FORCED TO DO THE KING'S BIDDING...
BUT OUR MEDICAL RESEARCH WILL BENEFIT THE ENTIRE KINGDOM!!
!
ONE QUACK DOCTOR ...
...TAUGHT US NEVER TO GIVE UP HOPE.
WE SHOULD LISTEN TO FOOLS LIKE THAT MORE.

READ THIS WAY

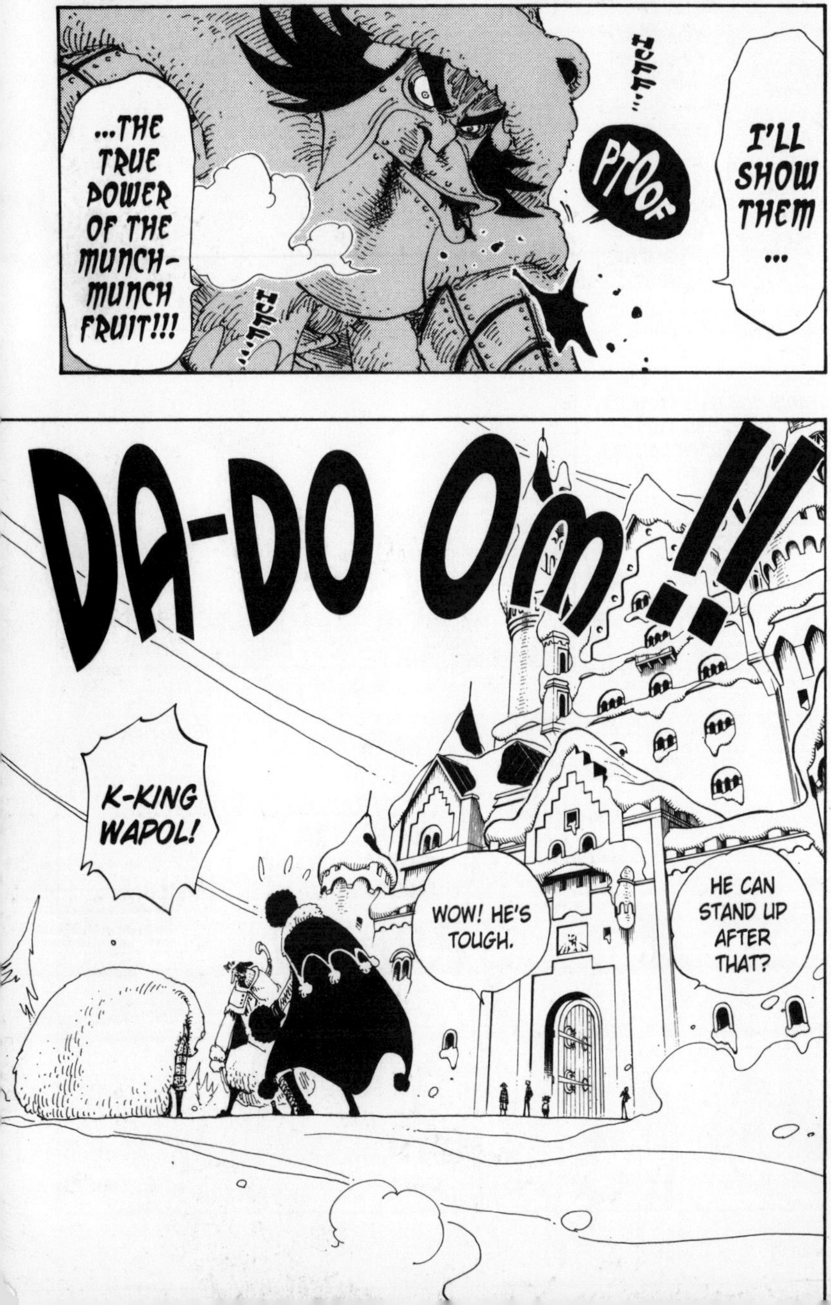

I'LL SHOW THEM ...
HUFF...
PTOOF
...THE TRUE POWER OF THE MUNCH-MUNCH FRUIT!!!
HUFF...
DA-DO OM!!
HE CAN STAND UP AFTER THAT?
WOW! HE'S TOUGH.
K-KING WAPOL!

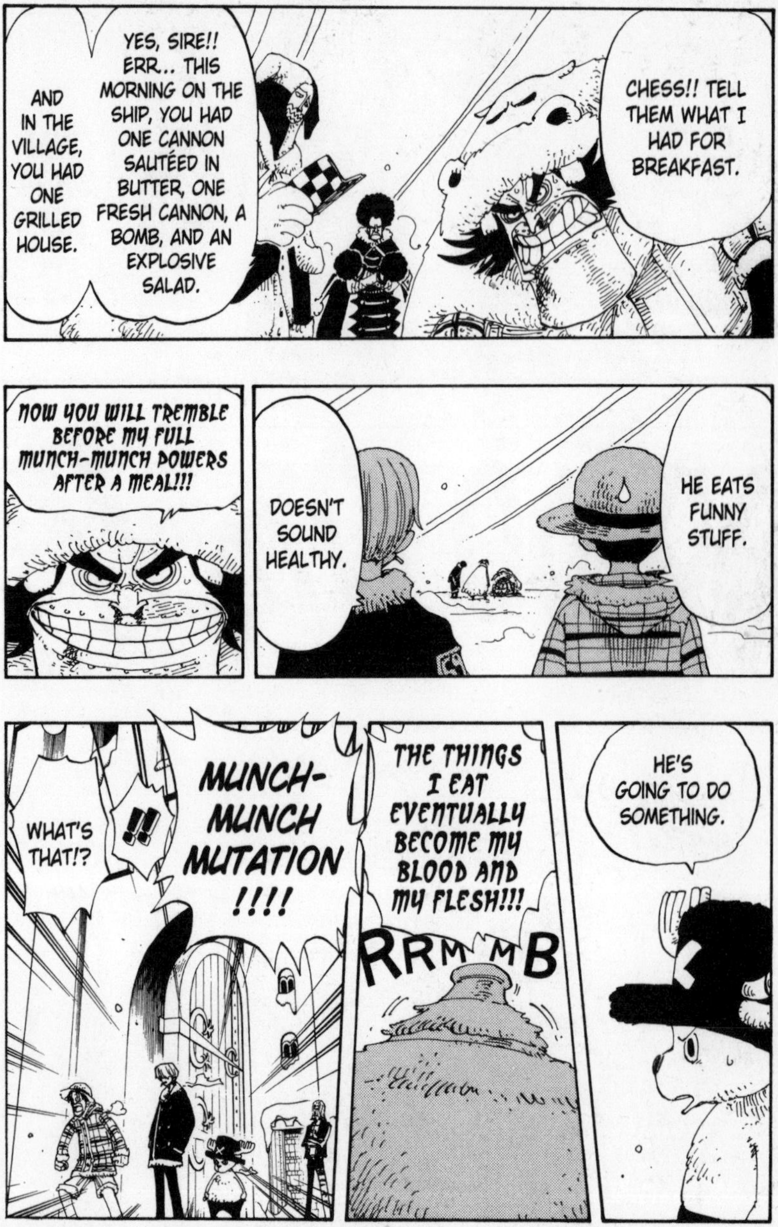
CHESS!! TELL THEM WHAT I HAD FOR BREAKFAST.
YES, SIRE!! ERR... THIS MORNING ON THE SHIP, YOU HAD ONE CANNON SAUTÉED IN BUTTER, ONE FRESH CANNON, A BOMB, AND AN EXPLOSIVE SALAD.
AND IN THE VILLAGE, YOU HAD ONE GRILLED HOUSE.
HE EATS FUNNY STUFF.
DOESN'T SOUND HEALTHY.
NOW YOU WILL TREMBLE BEFORE MY FULL MUNCH-MUNCH POWERS AFTER A MEAL!!!
HE'S GOING TO DO SOMETHING.
THE THINGS I EAT EVENTUALLY BECOME MY BLOOD AND MY FLESH!!!
RRM MB
MUNCH-MUNCH MUTATION!!!!
!!
WHAT'S THAT!?

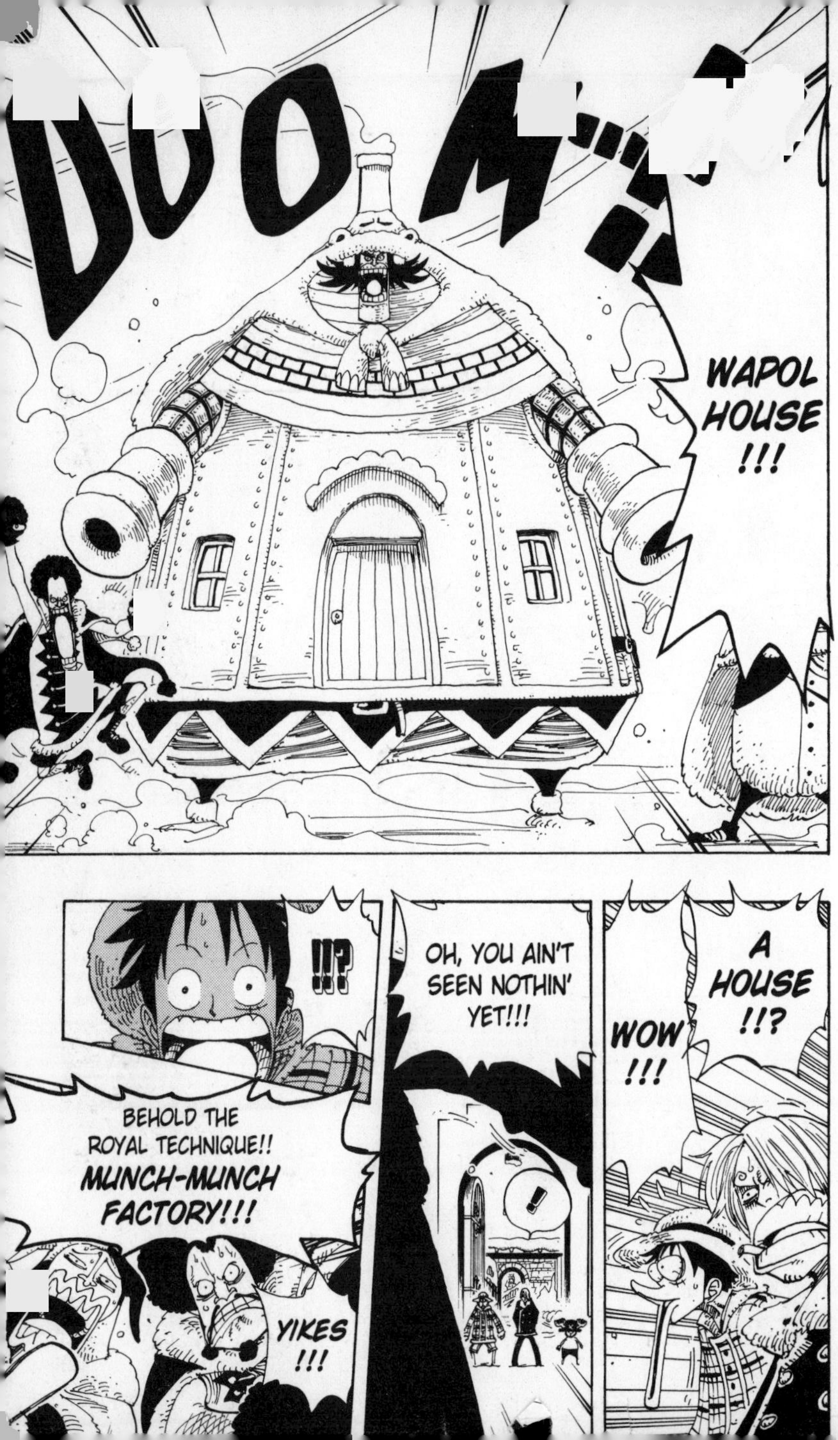
WAPOL HOUSE!!!
A HOUSE!!?
WOW!!!
OH, YOU AIN'T SEEN NOTHIN' YET!!!
!!?
BEHOLD THE ROYAL TECHNIQUE!! **MUNCH-MUNCH FACTORY!!!**
YIKES!!!

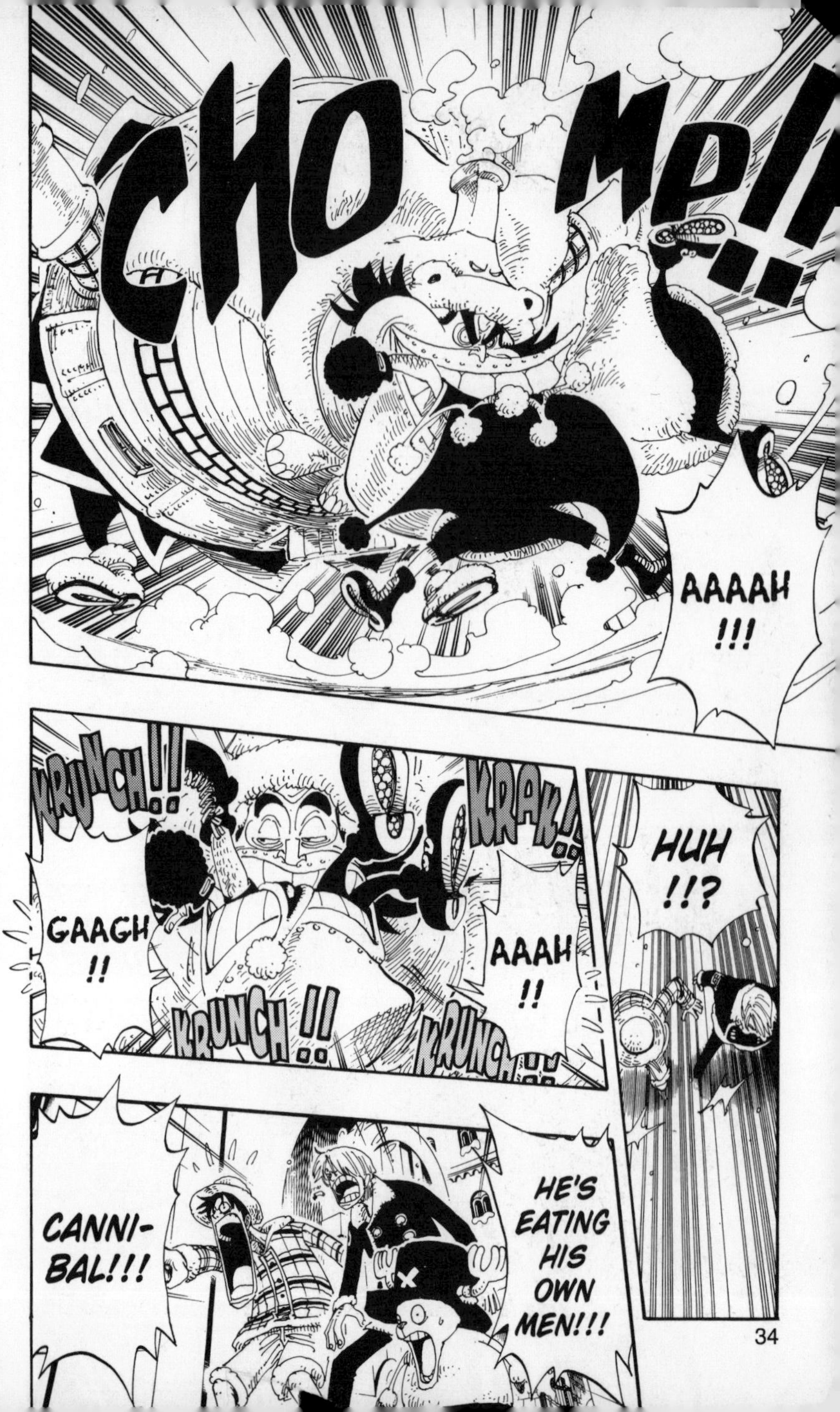
CHOMP!!!
AAAAH!!!
HUH!!?
KRAK!!
KRUNCH!!
AAAH!!
GAAGH!!
KRUNCH!!
KRUNCH!!
HE'S EATING HIS OWN MEN!!!
CANNI-BAL!!!

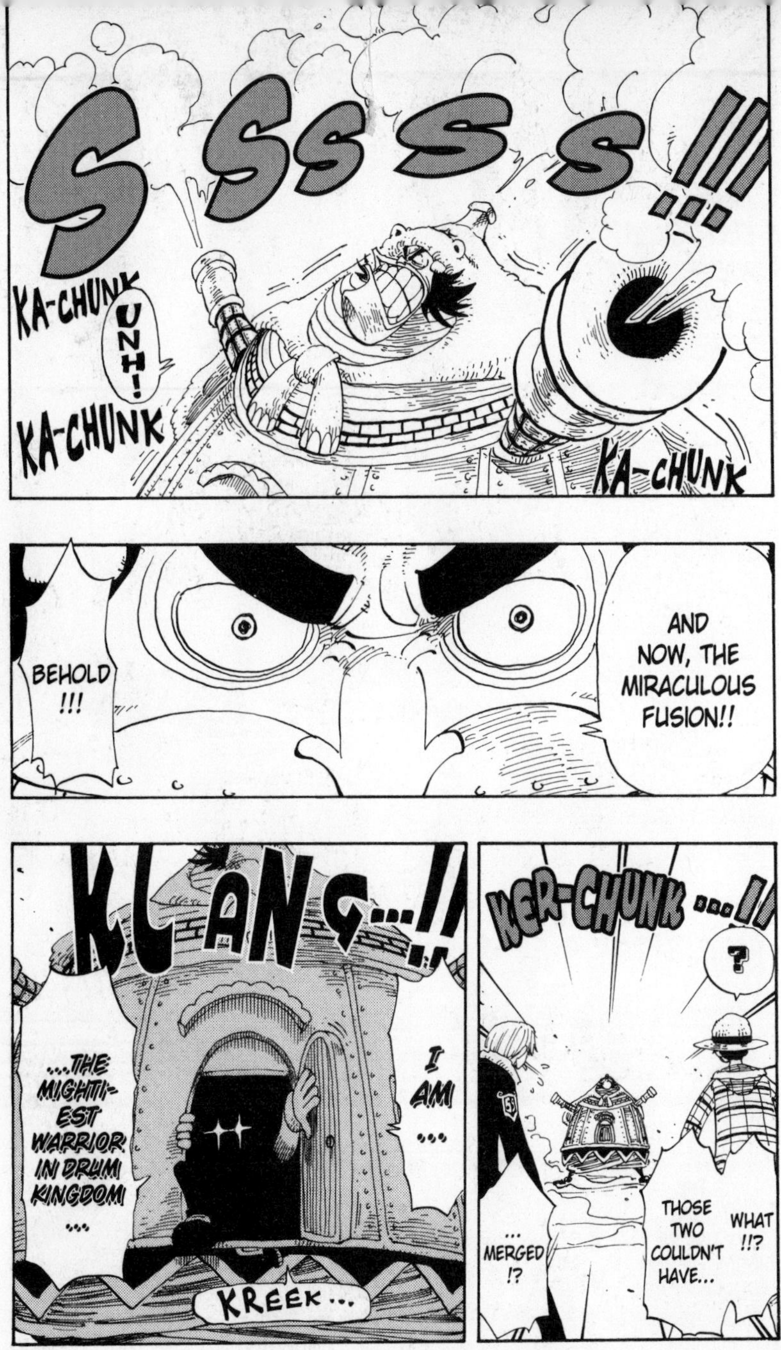
SSSSS!!!
KA-CHUNK
UNH!
KA-CHUNK
KA-CHUNK
AND NOW, THE MIRACULOUS FUSION!!
BEHOLD!!!
KER-CHUNK...!!
?
WHAT!!?
THOSE TWO COULDN'T HAVE...
...MERGED!?
KLANG...!!
I AM...
...THE MIGHTI-EST WARRIOR IN DRUM KINGDOM...
KREEK...

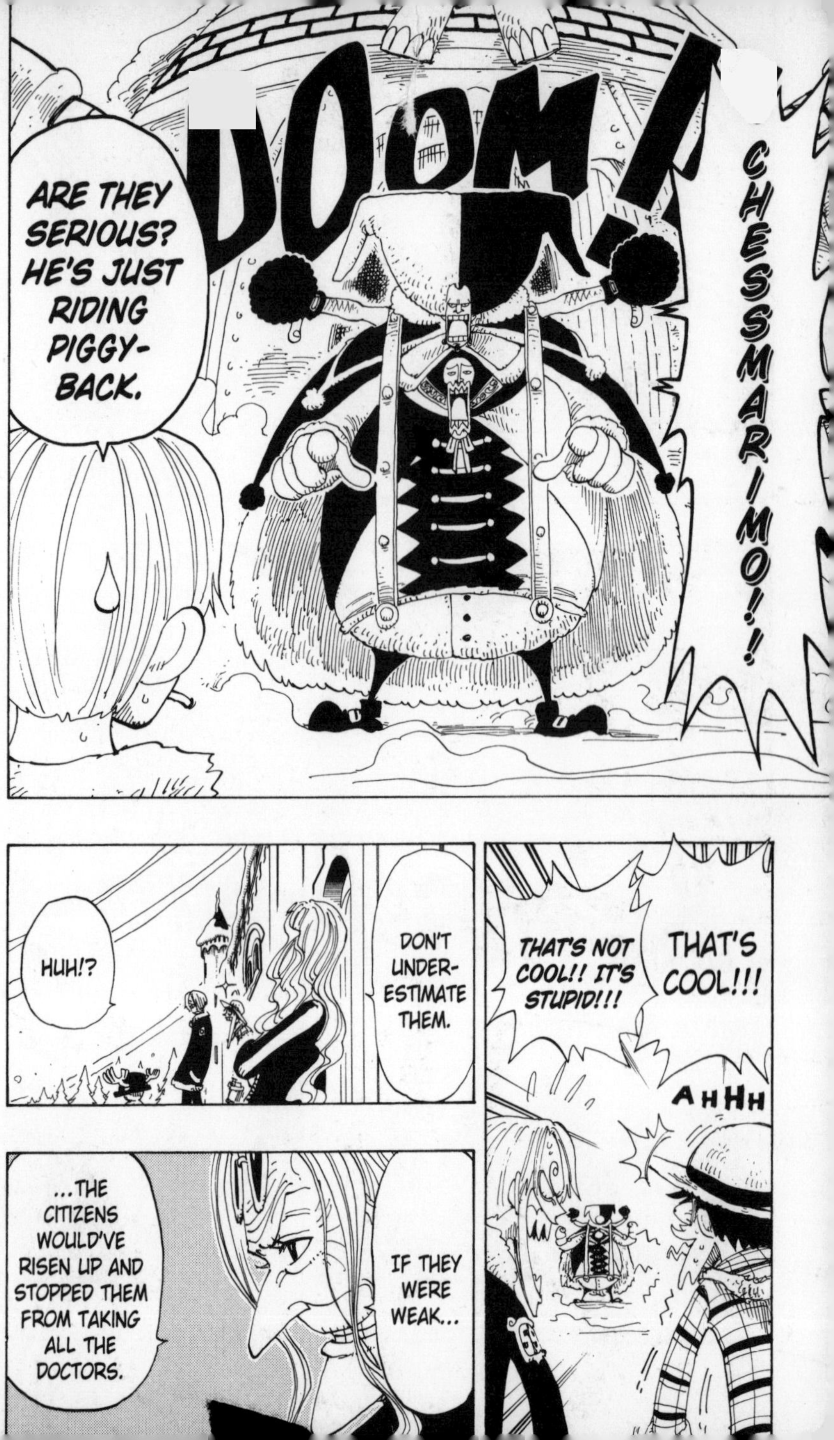
DOOM!
CHESSMARIMO!!
ARE THEY SERIOUS? HE'S JUST RIDING PIGGY-BACK.
THAT'S COOL!!!
THAT'S NOT COOL!! IT'S STUPID!!!
AHHHH
DON'T UNDER-ESTIMATE THEM.
HUH!?
IF THEY WERE WEAK...
...THE CITIZENS WOULD'VE RISEN UP AND STOPPED THEM FROM TAKING ALL THE DOCTORS.

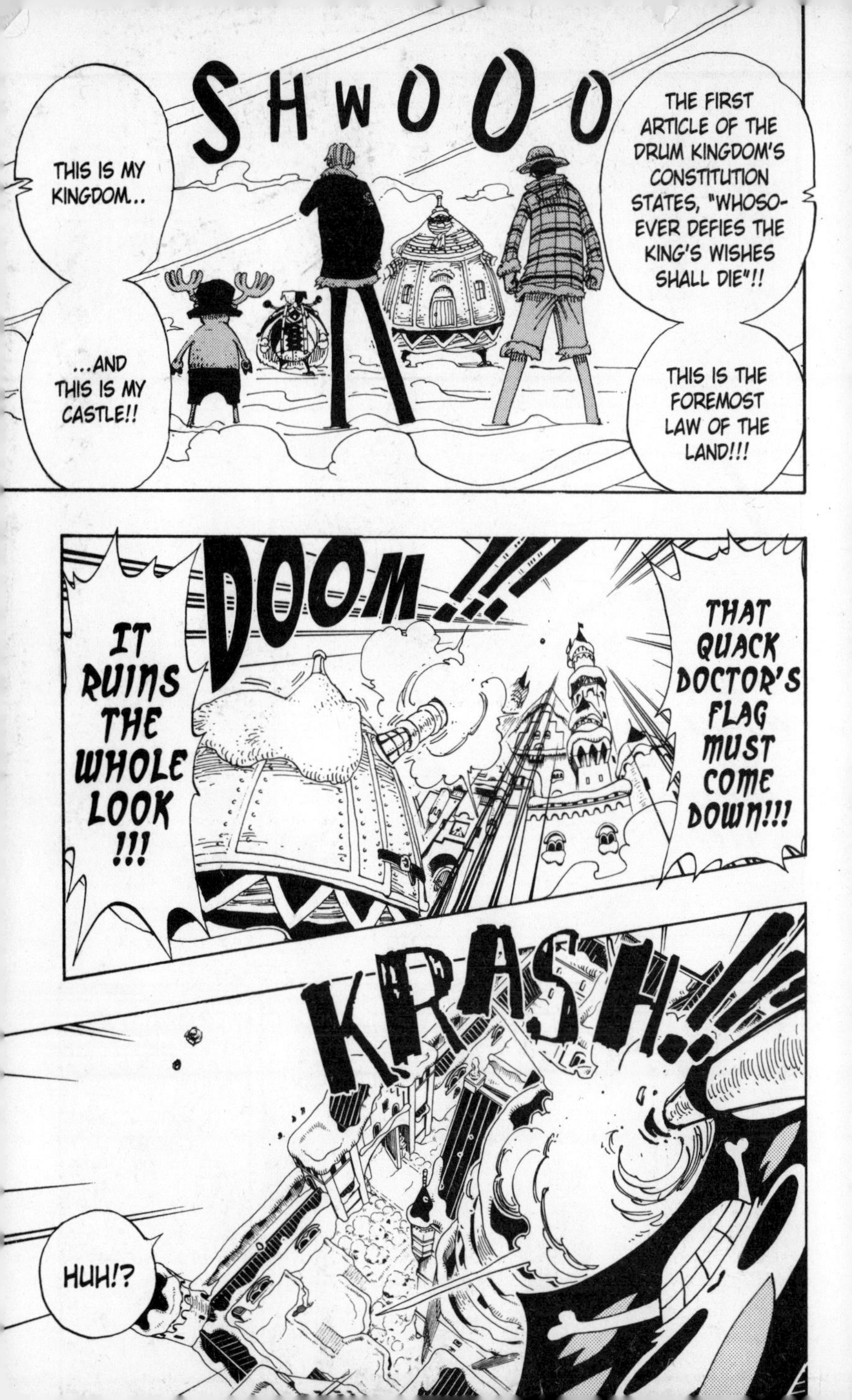
SHWOOO
THE FIRST ARTICLE OF THE DRUM KINGDOM'S CONSTITUTION STATES, "WHOSOEVER DEFIES THE KING'S WISHES SHALL DIE"!!
THIS IS THE FOREMOST LAW OF THE LAND!!!
THIS IS MY KINGDOM..
...AND THIS IS MY CASTLE!!
DOOM!!!
THAT QUACK DOCTOR'S FLAG MUST COME DOWN!!!
IT RUINS THE WHOLE LOOK!!!
KRASH!!
HUH!?

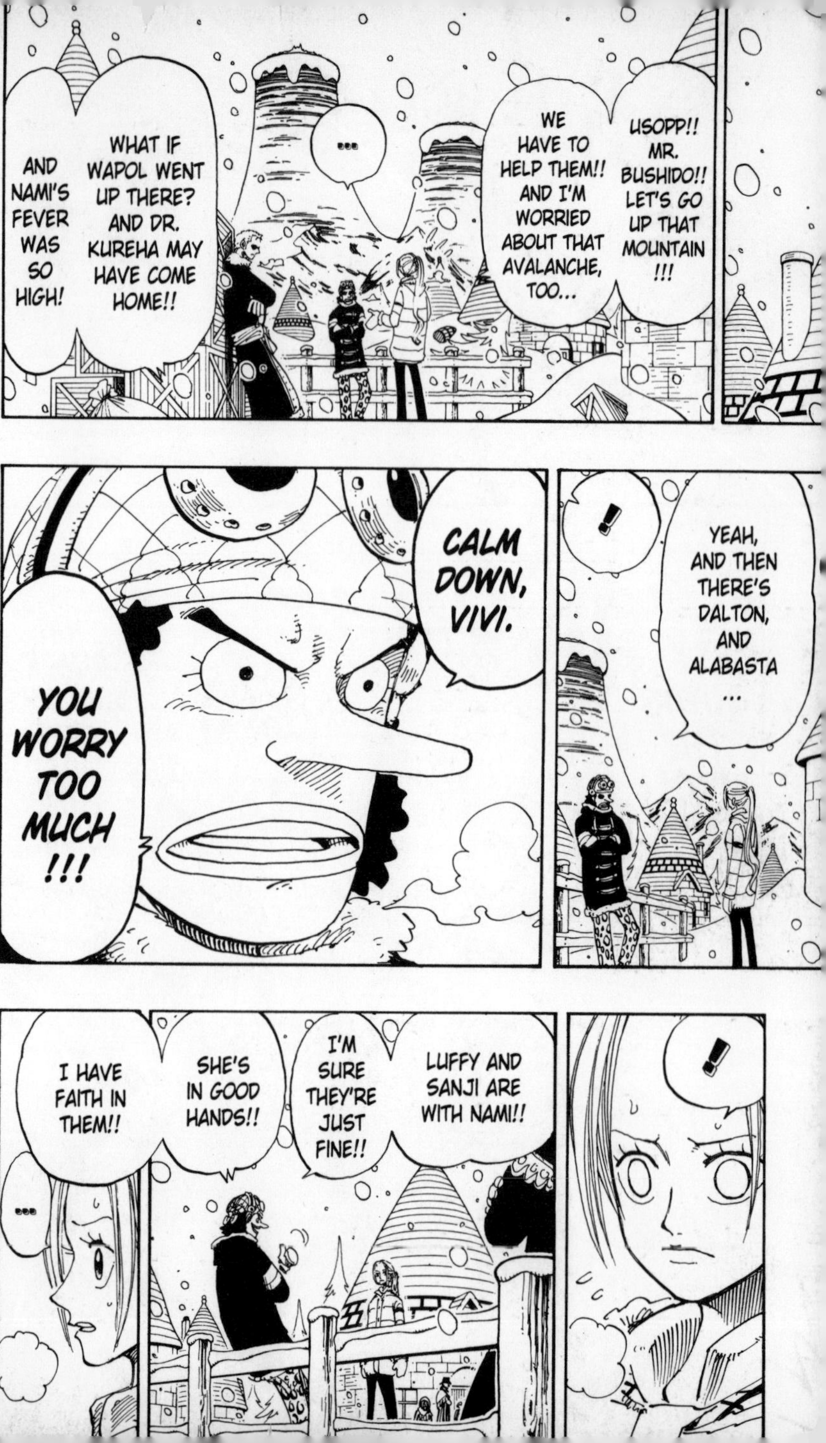
USOPP!! MR. BUSHIDO!! LET'S GO UP THAT MOUNTAIN!!!
WE HAVE TO HELP THEM!! AND I'M WORRIED ABOUT THAT AVALANCHE, TOO...
...
WHAT IF WAPOL WENT UP THERE? AND DR. KUREHA MAY HAVE COME HOME!!
AND NAMI'S FEVER WAS SO HIGH!
YEAH, AND THEN THERE'S DALTON, AND ALABASTA ...
!
CALM DOWN, VIVI.
YOU WORRY TOO MUCH!!!
!
LUFFY AND SANJI ARE WITH NAMI!!
I'M SURE THEY'RE JUST FINE!!
SHE'S IN GOOD HANDS!!
I HAVE FAITH IN THEM!!
...

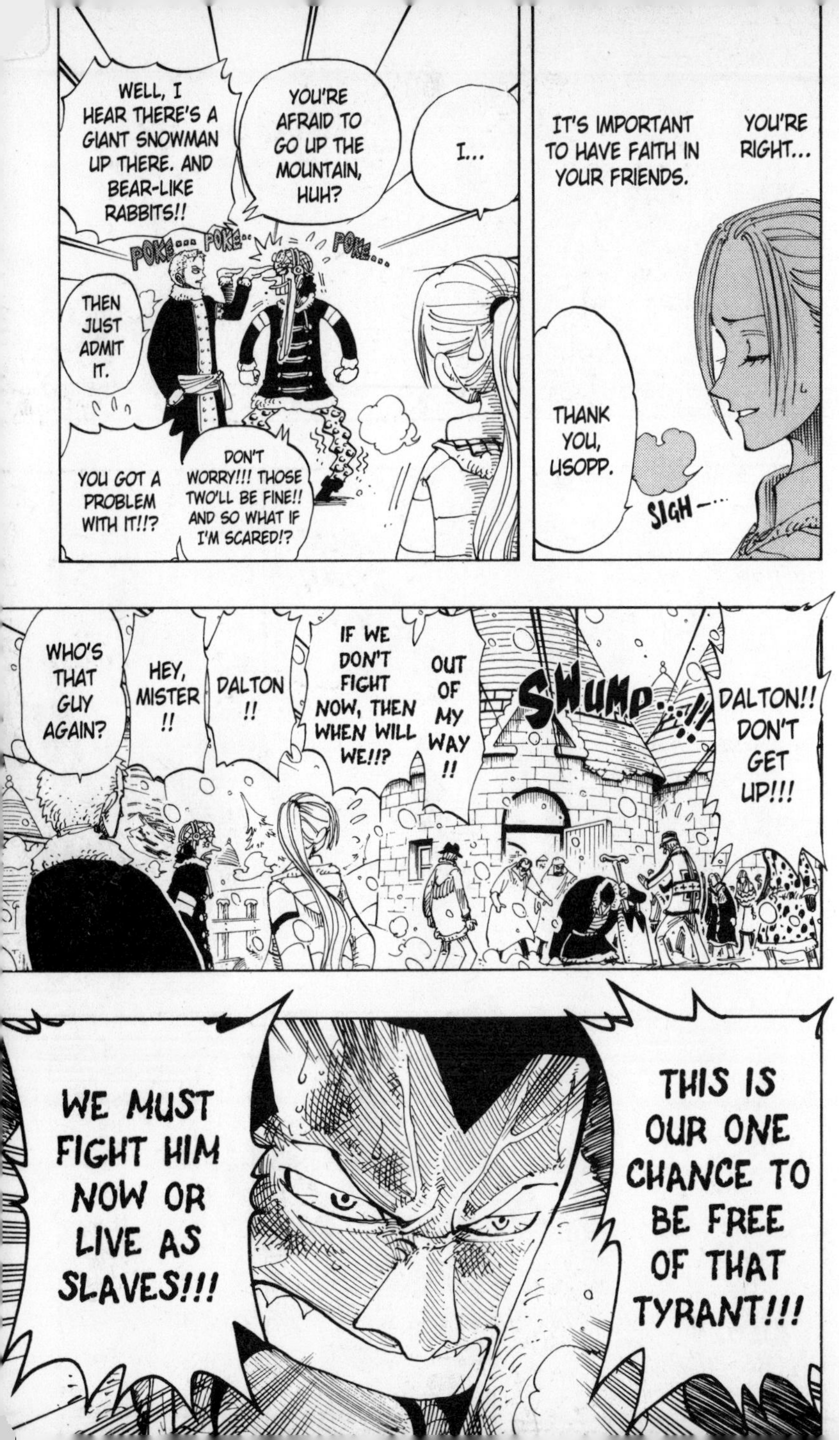
YOU'RE RIGHT...
IT'S IMPORTANT TO HAVE FAITH IN YOUR FRIENDS.
SIGH—...
THANK YOU, USOPP.
I...
YOU'RE AFRAID TO GO UP THE MOUNTAIN, HUH?
WELL, I HEAR THERE'S A GIANT SNOWMAN UP THERE. AND BEAR-LIKE RABBITS!!
POKE... POKE... POKE...
THEN JUST ADMIT IT.
DON'T WORRY!!! THOSE TWO'LL BE FINE!! AND SO WHAT IF I'M SCARED!?
YOU GOT A PROBLEM WITH IT!!?
DALTON!! DON'T GET UP!!!
SWUMP...!!
OUT OF MY WAY!!
IF WE DON'T FIGHT NOW, THEN WHEN WILL WE!!?
DALTON!!
HEY, MISTER!!
WHO'S THAT GUY AGAIN?
THIS IS OUR ONE CHANCE TO BE FREE OF THAT TYRANT!!!
WE MUST FIGHT HIM NOW OR LIVE AS SLAVES!!!

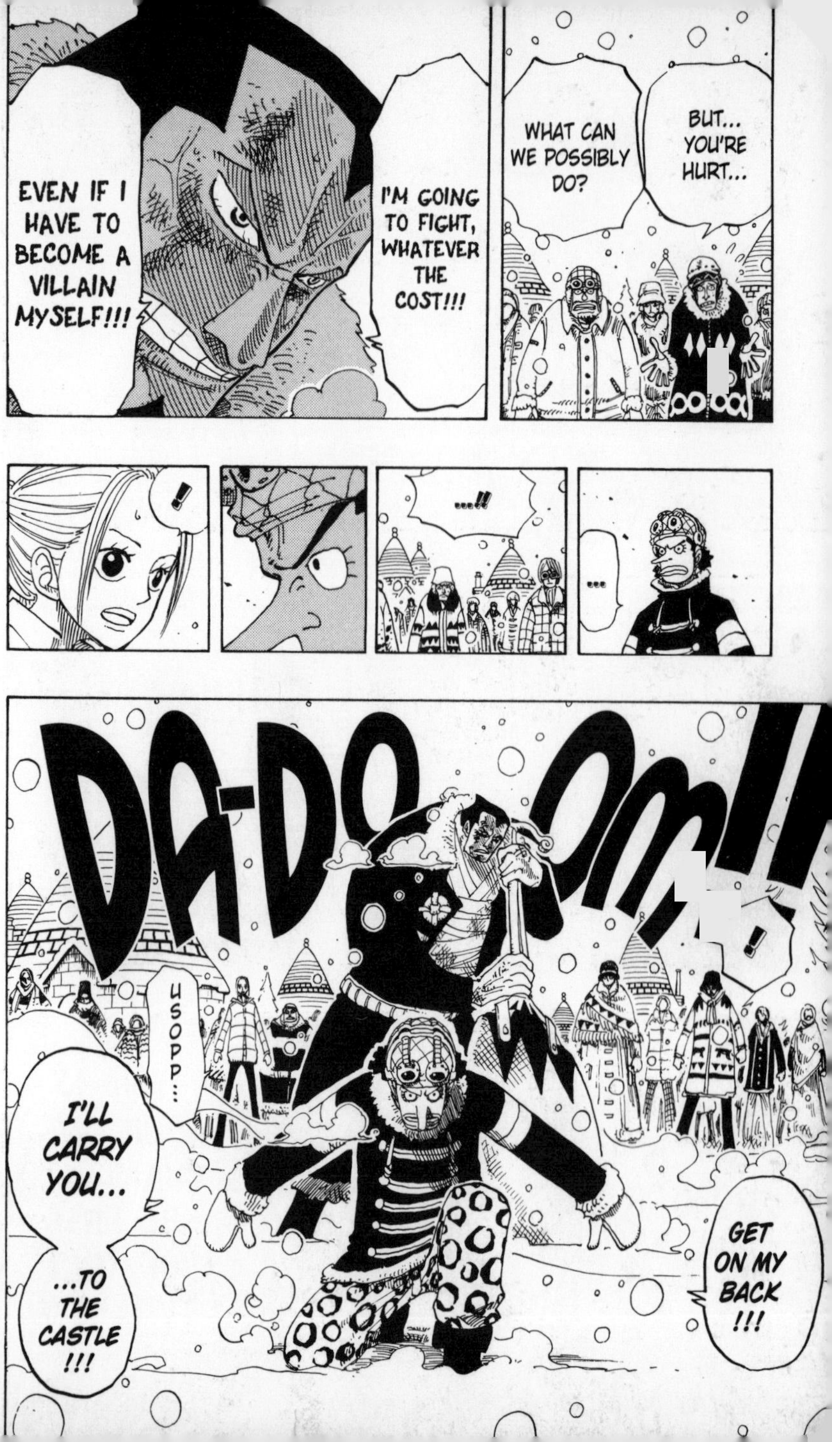
BUT... YOU'RE HURT...
WHAT CAN WE POSSIBLY DO?
I'M GOING TO FIGHT, WHATEVER THE COST!!!
EVEN IF I HAVE TO BECOME A VILLAIN MYSELF!!!
...
...!!
!
DA-DOOM!!
!
USOPP...
GET ON MY BACK!!!
I'LL CARRY YOU...
...TO THE CASTLE!!!

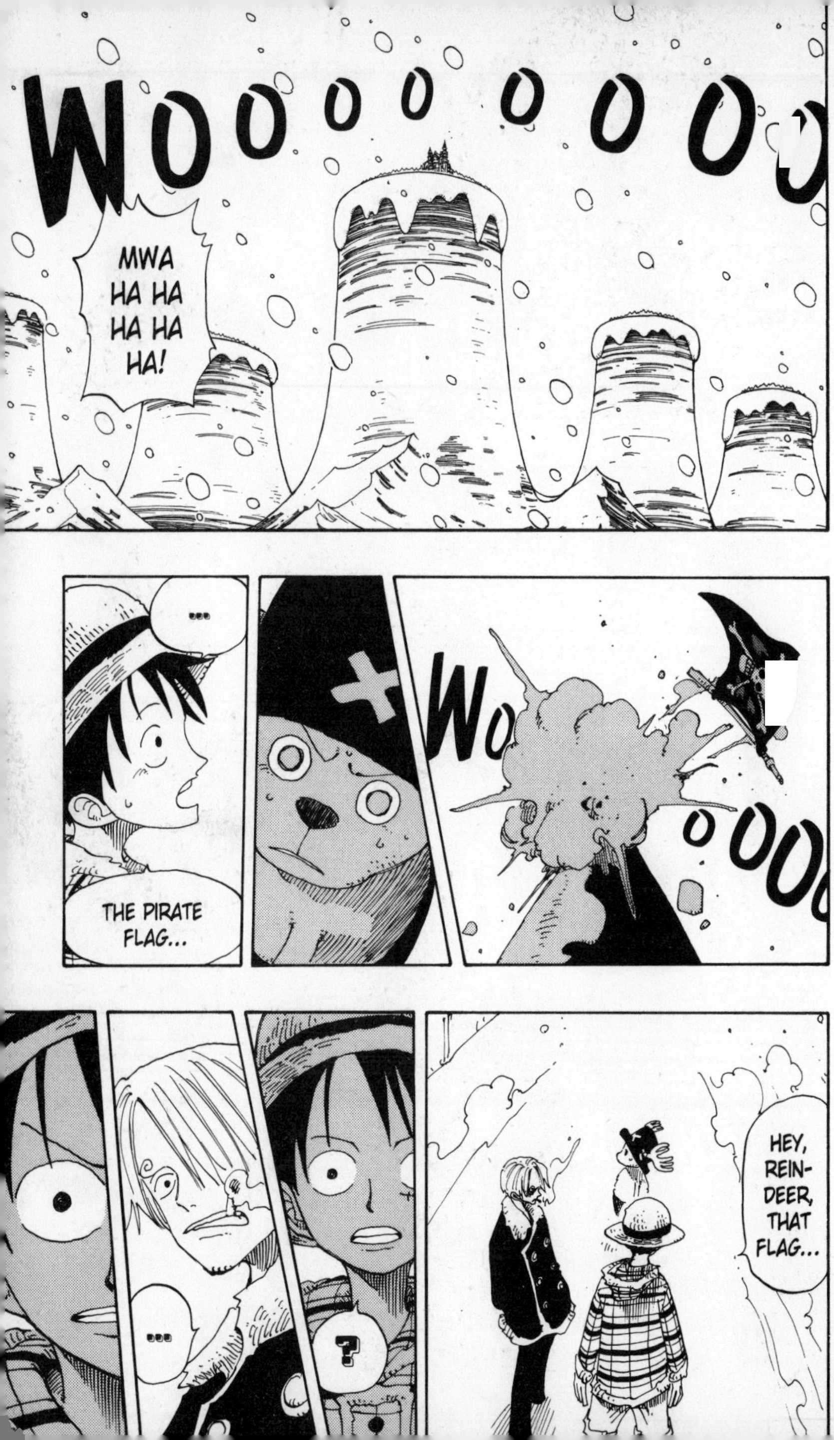
WOOOOOOOO
MWA HA HA HA HA HA!
WOOOOO
...
THE PIRATE FLAG...
HEY, REIN-DEER, THAT FLAG...
?
...

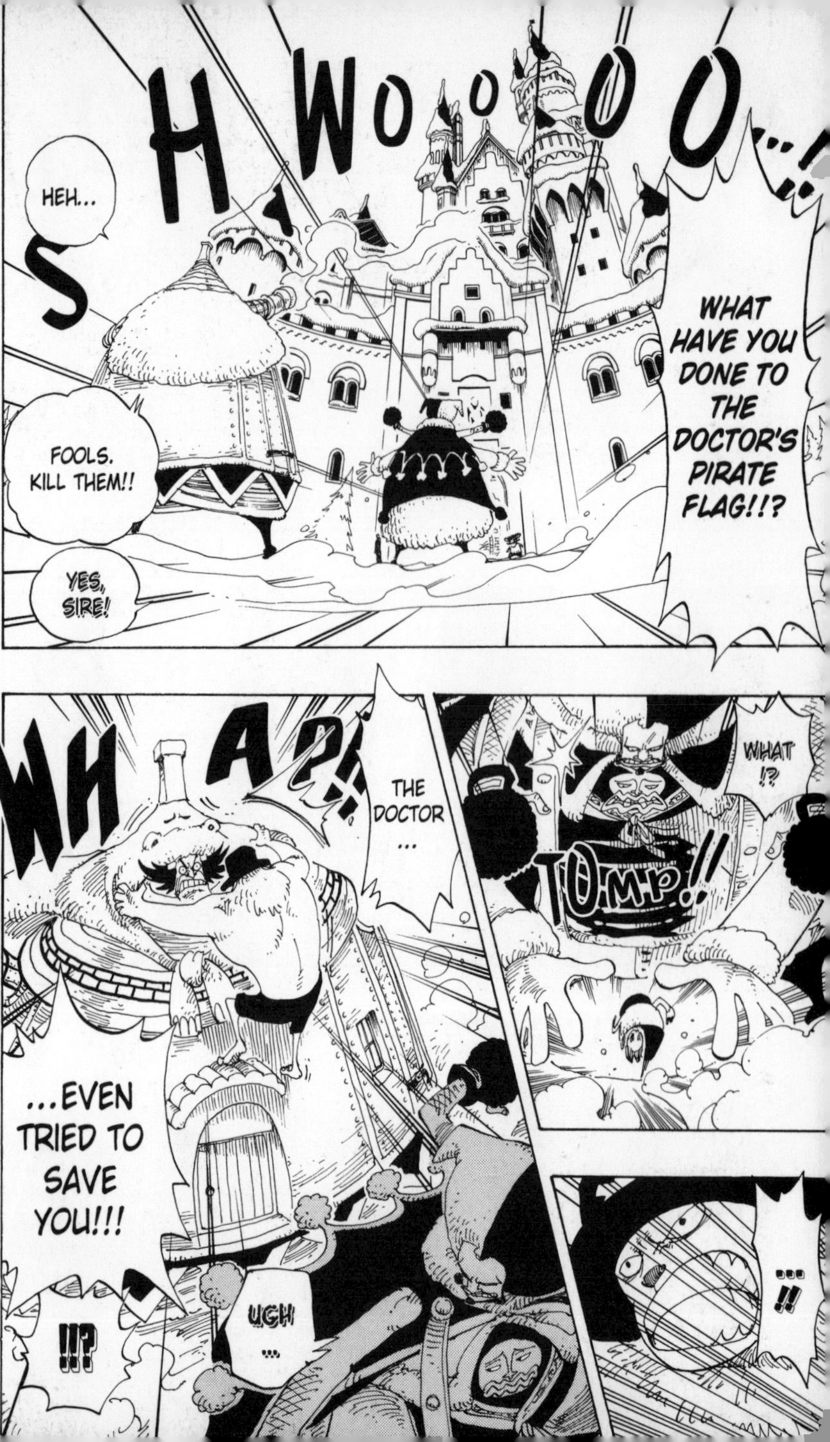
SHWOOOOO...!!
WHAT HAVE YOU DONE TO THE DOCTOR'S PIRATE FLAG!!?
HEH...
FOOLS. KILL THEM!!
YES, SIRE!
WHAT !?
TOMP!!
...!!
WHAP!!
THE DOCTOR ...
...EVEN TRIED TO SAVE YOU!!!
!!?
UGH ...

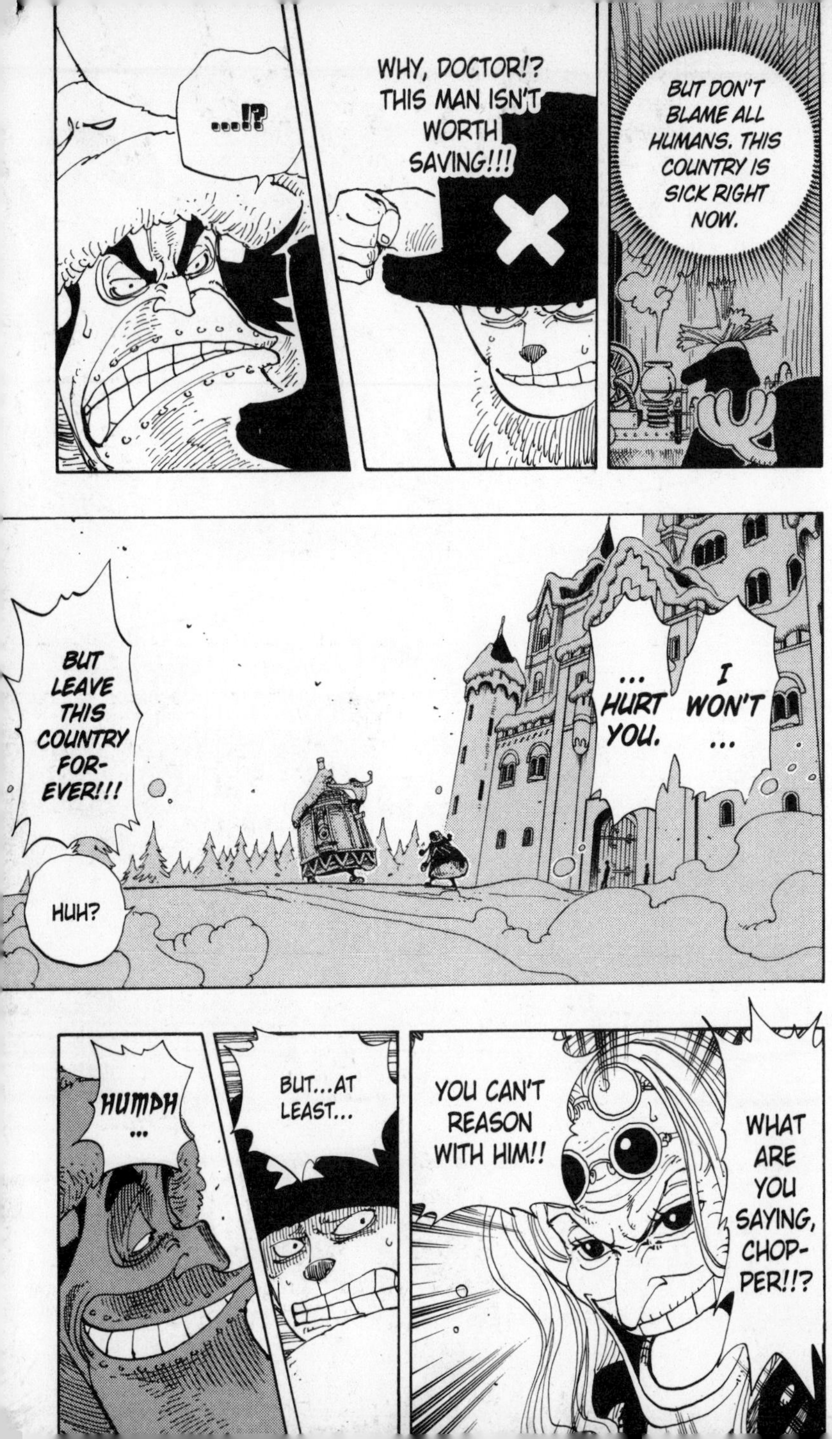
BUT DON'T BLAME ALL HUMANS. THIS COUNTRY IS SICK RIGHT NOW.
WHY, DOCTOR!? THIS MAN ISN'T WORTH SAVING!!!
...!?
I WON'T ...
... HURT YOU.
BUT LEAVE THIS COUNTRY FOR-EVER!!!
HUH?
WHAT ARE YOU SAYING, CHOP-PER!!?
YOU CAN'T REASON WITH HIM!!
BUT...AT LEAST...
HUMPH ...

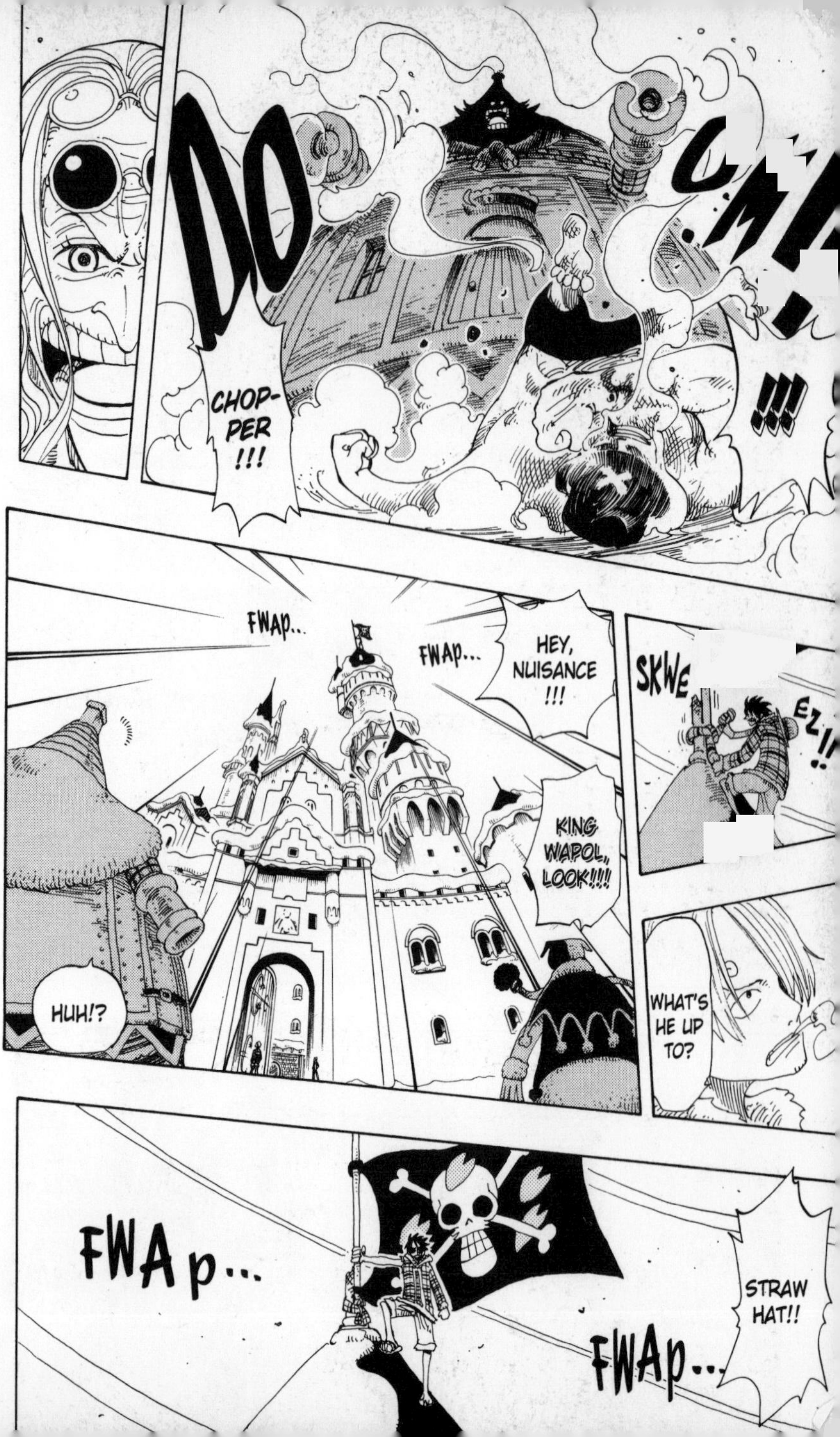
DO
CHOP-PER!!!
SKWE
EZ!!
WHAT'S HE UP TO?
HEY, NUISANCE!!!
FWAp...
FWAp...
KING WAPOL, LOOK!!!!
HUH!?
STRAW HAT!!
FWAp...
FWAp...

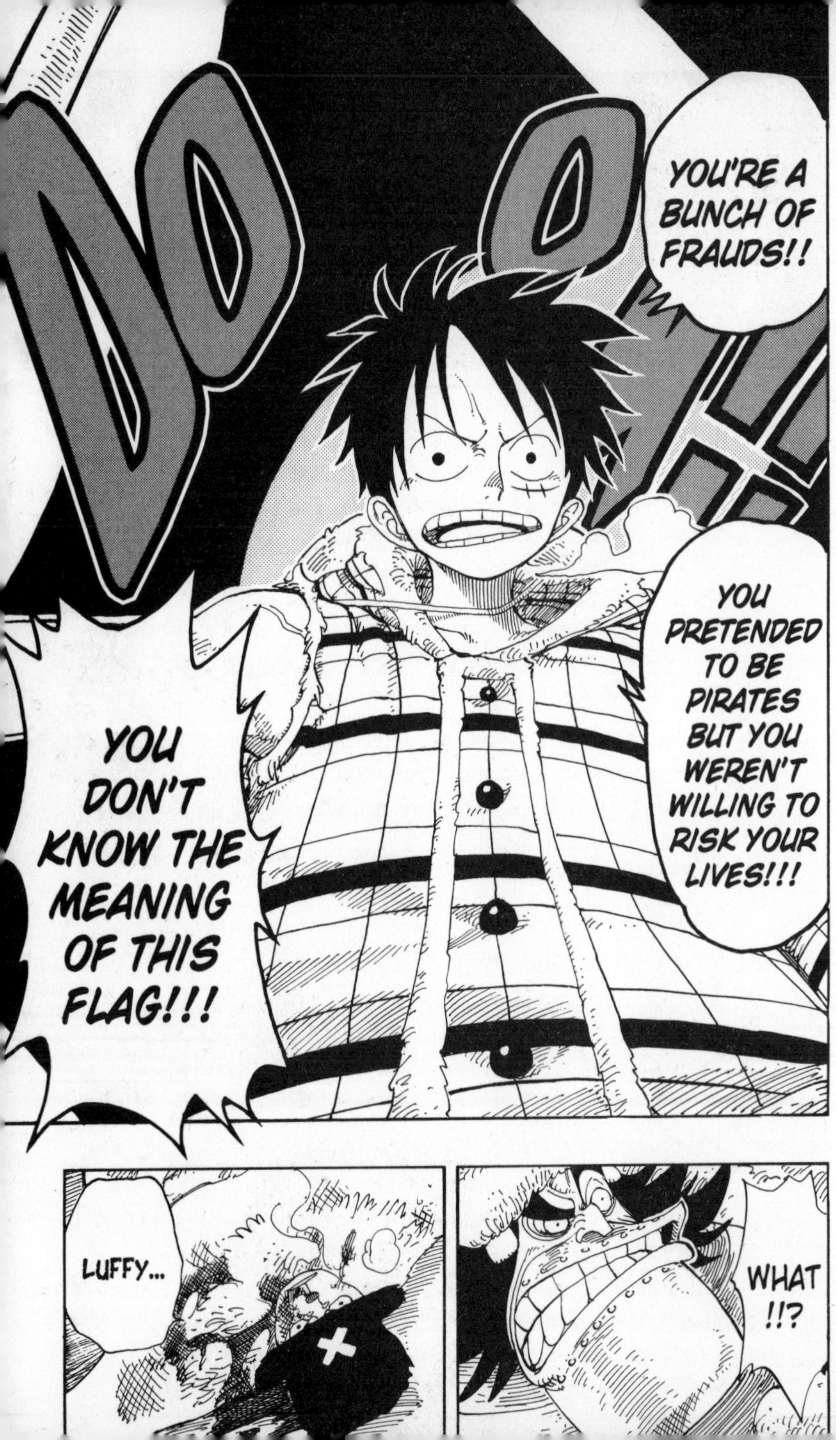
YOU'RE A BUNCH OF FRAUDS!!
YOU PRETENDED TO BE PIRATES BUT YOU WEREN'T WILLING TO RISK YOUR LIVES!!!
YOU DON'T KNOW THE MEANING OF THIS FLAG!!!
WHAT !!?
LUFFY...

Question Corner
S
B
S
MATSU

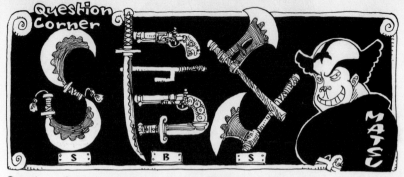

Oda: Before we begin the SBS corner... We have the S (some) S (small) M (mistakes) Corner!! This is for everyone who purchased the first printing of Volume 16.
First, about Chopper's name:
"Tony Tony Chopper" is what it says, but this was a typo. It should really be "TonyTony Chopper," so please remember that. What? It doesn't matter!? Oh well, I just thought I'd bring it up. All right, on to the Question Corner!

Reader: Hello, Oda Sensei. Recently, a lot of people have been wanting to shout out the start of the SBS Corner. Actually, I'm one of them. But I'm sure you want to say it, too. So, let's each do half. Ready?
"SBS will now be--"

Oda: "--gin." Um... Huh!?

Reader: Where is Oh Come My Way? Is it near my house?

Oda: Hmm... Oh Come My Way? Well, this is a difficult question, but, it's a place where people who have "come out" go to walk. And I think it exists anywhere. ♡ Yeow!!

Reader: Oda Sensei, a question about the helmets worn by the giants Broggy and Dorry. One resembles a Celtic horned helmet and the other seems to be from the Swedish Vendel Period (not sure when that was). Am I correct?

Oda: Well, the inspiration for the "Warriors of Elbaph," the tribe of giants, was my favorite pirates of the north, the Vikings, so you are absolutely right. Banzai to those intrepid spirits!

# Chapter 148:
# UNBREAKABLE

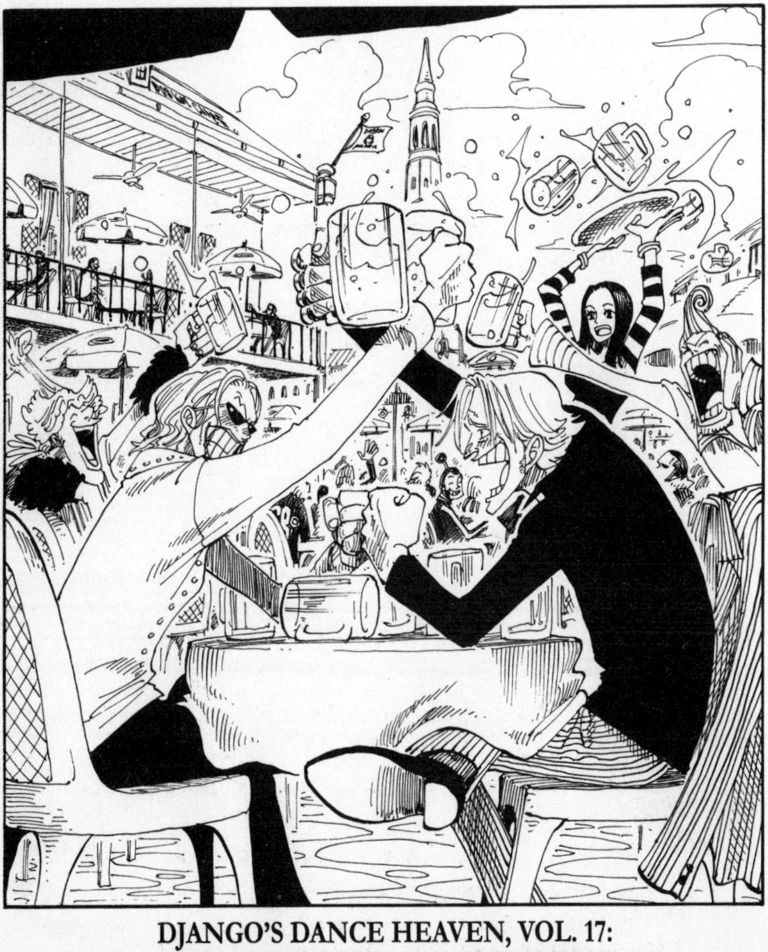

DJANGO'S DANCE HEAVEN, VOL. 17:
"THE POST-BATTLE CELEBRATION"

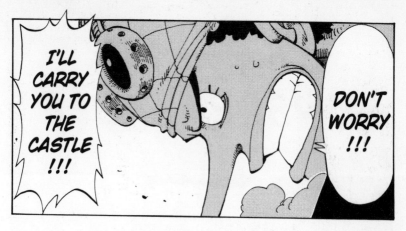

I'LL CARRY YOU TO THE CASTLE !!!

DON'T WORRY !!!

...!!

USOPP!!

...

YES, IT WILL!!!

KRUNCH...

IT WON'T WORK, USOPP.

KRUNCH...

...

I'LL CARRY YOU ALL THE WAY!!!

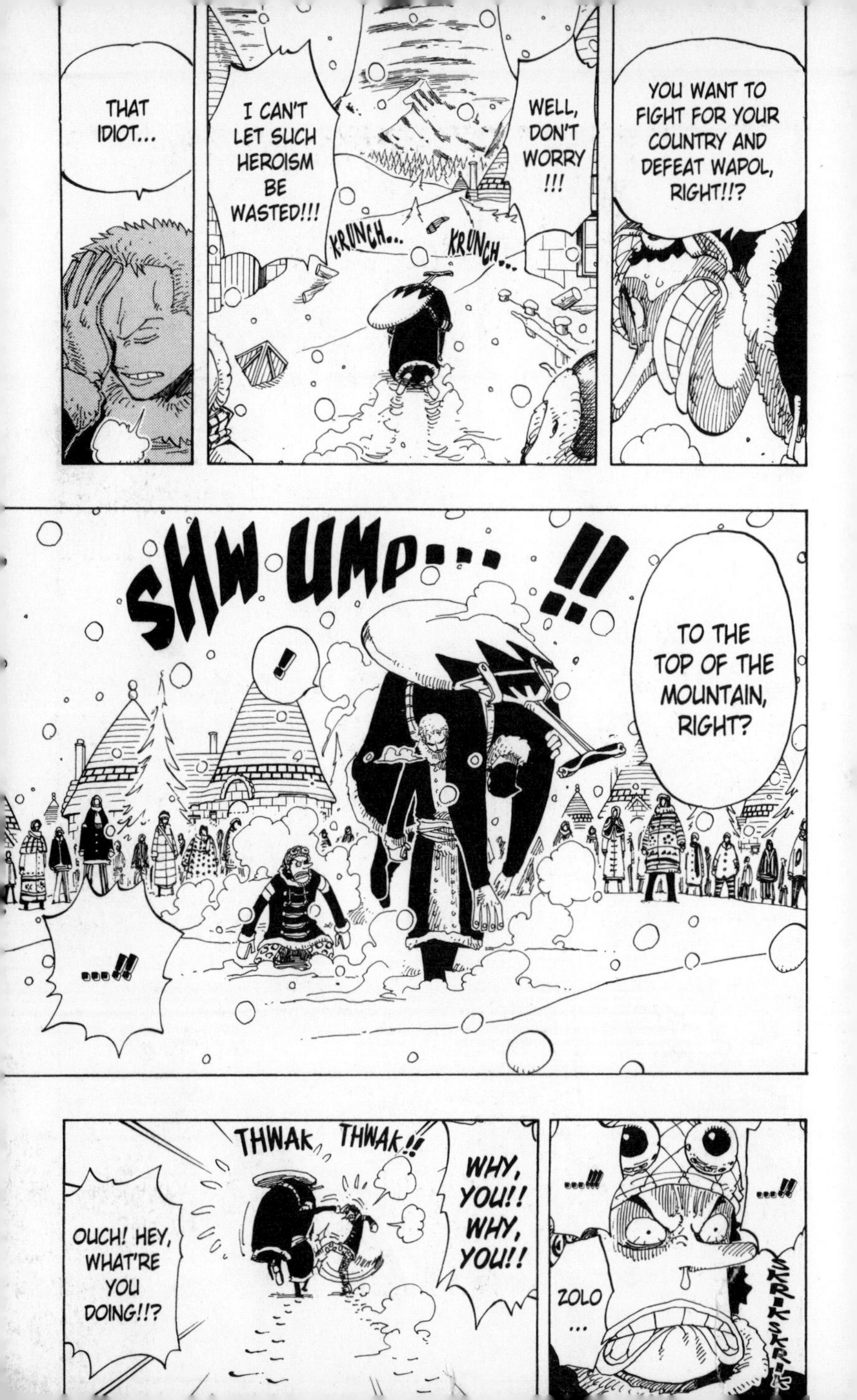
YOU WANT TO FIGHT FOR YOUR COUNTRY AND DEFEAT WAPOL, RIGHT!!?
WELL, DON'T WORRY!!!
I CAN'T LET SUCH HEROISM BE WASTED!!!
KRUNCH... KRUNCH...
THAT IDIOT...
TO THE TOP OF THE MOUNTAIN, RIGHT?
SHWUMP...!!
!
...!!
...!!
...!!!
SKRIKSKRIK
ZOLO...
THWAK THWAK!!
WHY, YOU!! WHY, YOU!!
OUCH! HEY, WHAT'RE YOU DOING!!?

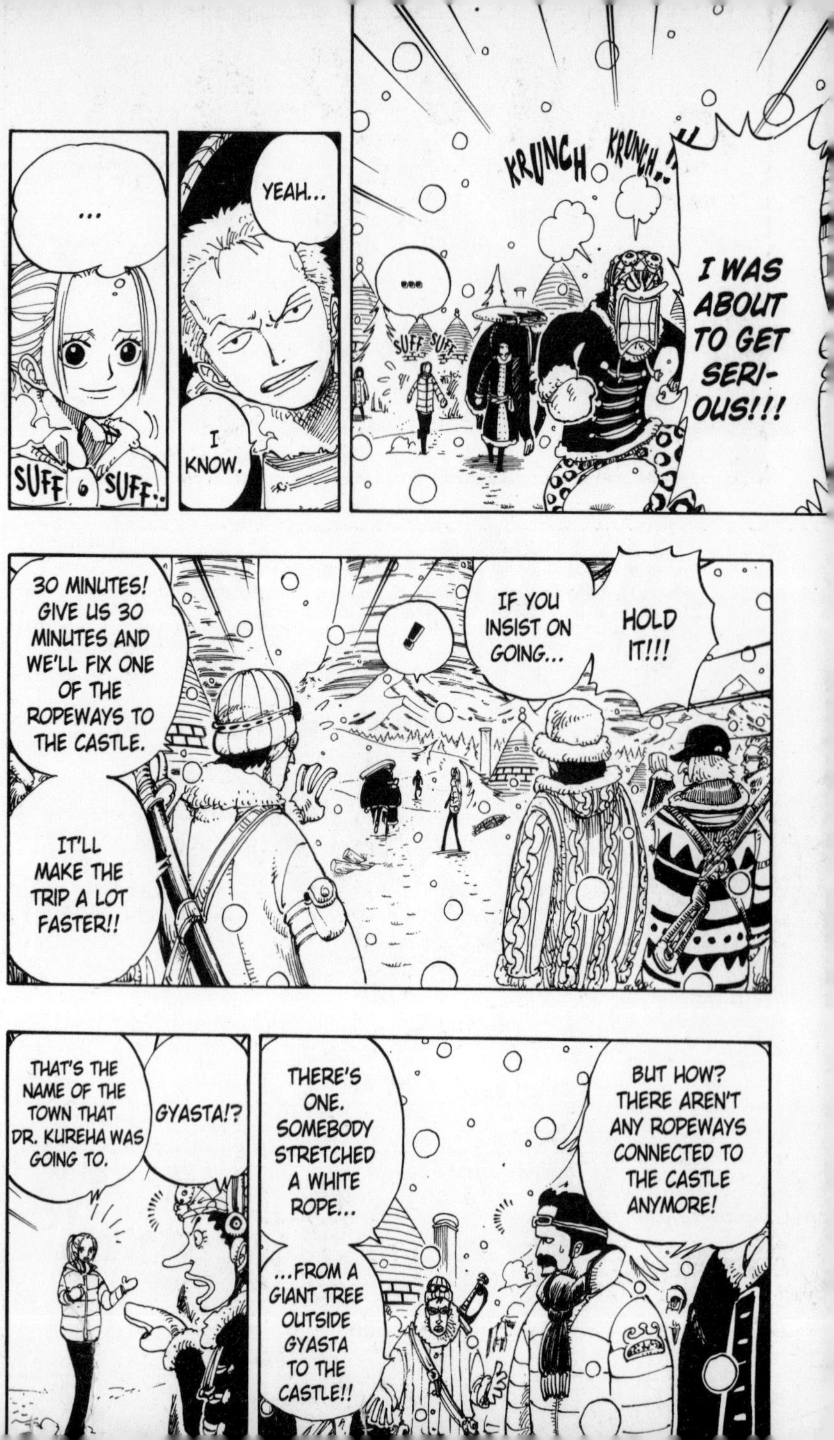
KRUNCH KRUNCH..!!
I WAS ABOUT TO GET SERI-OUS!!!
...
SUFF SUFF
YEAH...
I KNOW.
...
SUFF SUFF..
HOLD IT!!!
IF YOU INSIST ON GOING...
!
30 MINUTES! GIVE US 30 MINUTES AND WE'LL FIX ONE OF THE ROPEWAYS TO THE CASTLE.
IT'LL MAKE THE TRIP A LOT FASTER!!
BUT HOW? THERE AREN'T ANY ROPEWAYS CONNECTED TO THE CASTLE ANYMORE!
THERE'S ONE. SOMEBODY STRETCHED A WHITE ROPE...
...FROM A GIANT TREE OUTSIDE GYASTA TO THE CASTLE!!
GYASTA!?
THAT'S THE NAME OF THE TOWN THAT DR. KUREHA WAS GOING TO.

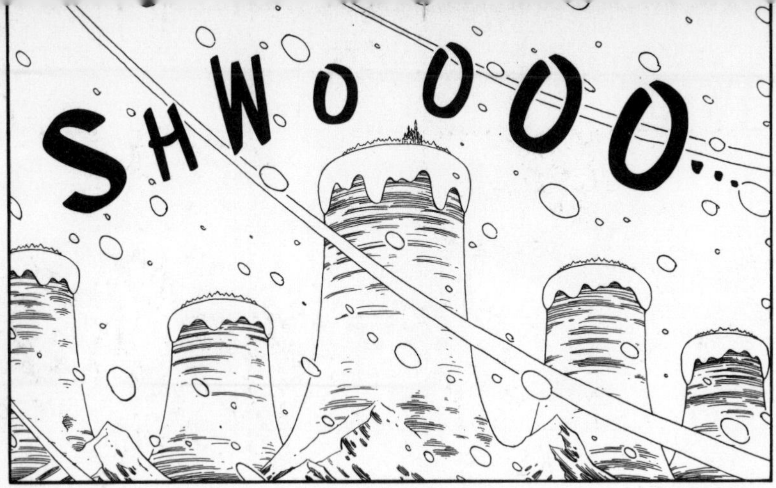
SHWOOOO...

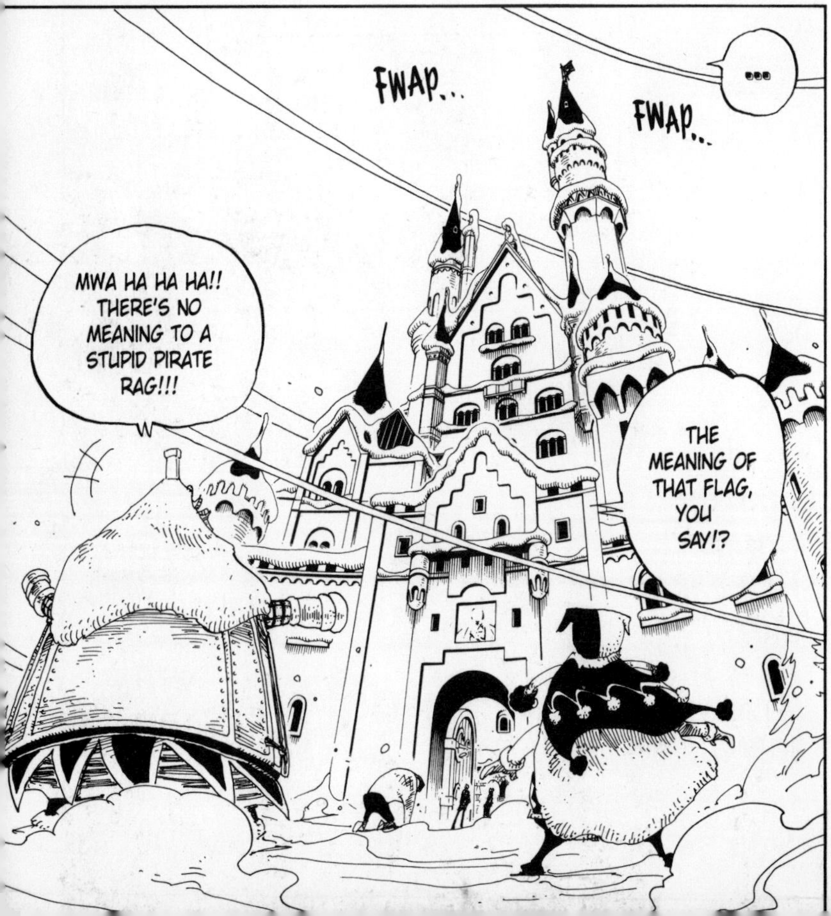
...
FWAP...
FWAP...
MWA HA HA HA!! THERE'S NO MEANING TO A STUPID PIRATE RAG!!!
THE MEANING OF THAT FLAG, YOU SAY!?

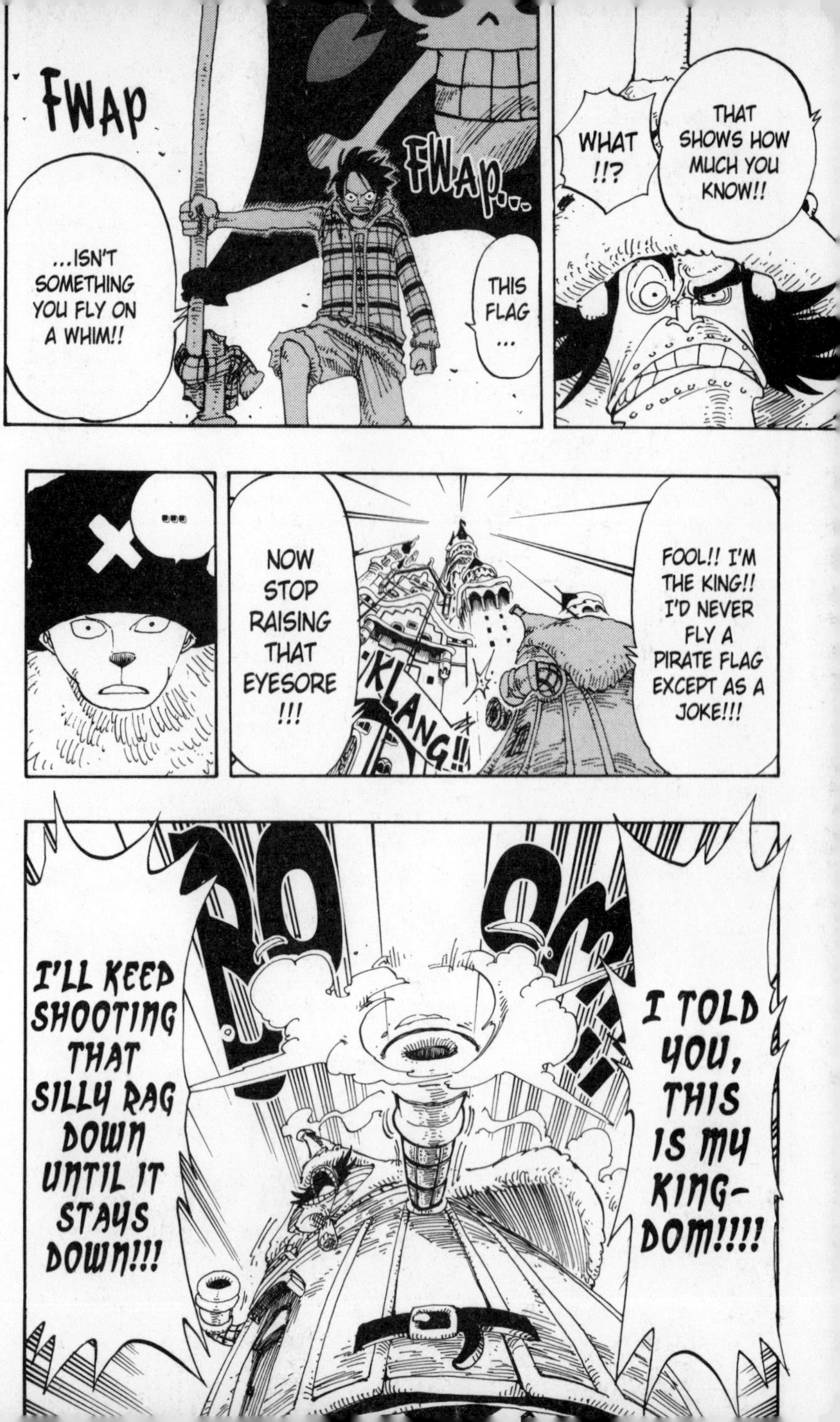
THAT SHOWS HOW MUCH YOU KNOW!!
WHAT !!?
FWAP
FWAP..
THIS FLAG ...
...ISN'T SOMETHING YOU FLY ON A WHIM!!
FOOL!! I'M THE KING!! I'D NEVER FLY A PIRATE FLAG EXCEPT AS A JOKE!!!
KLANG!!
NOW STOP RAISING THAT EYESORE !!!
...
I TOLD YOU, THIS IS MY KING-DOM!!!!
BOOM!!
I'LL KEEP SHOOTING THAT SILLY RAG DOWN UNTIL IT STAYS DOWN!!!

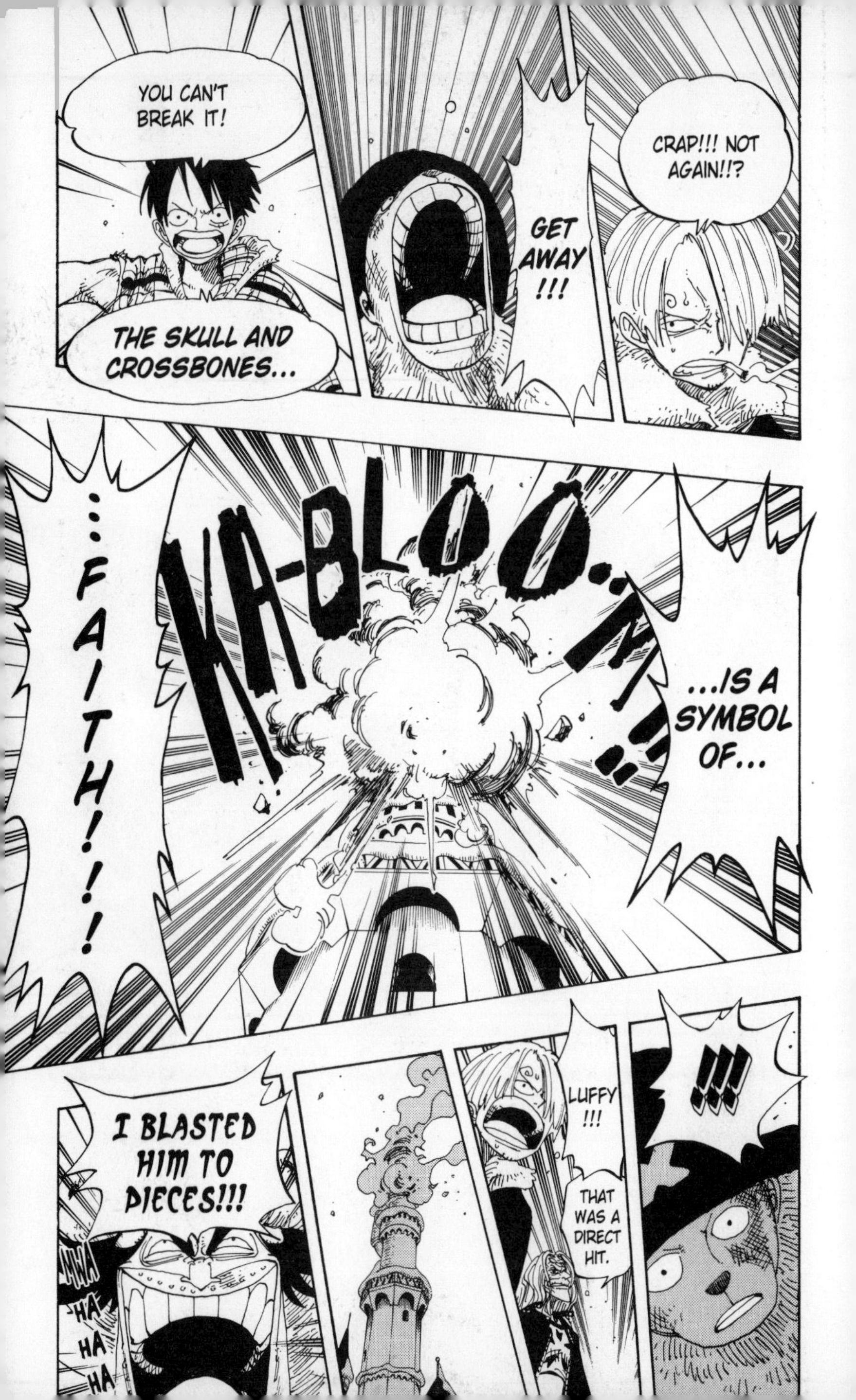
CRAP!!! NOT AGAIN!!?
GET AWAY !!!
YOU CAN'T BREAK IT!
THE SKULL AND CROSSBONES...
...IS A SYMBOL OF...
KA-BLOOM!!!
...FAITH!!!!
!!!
LUFFY !!!
THAT WAS A DIRECT HIT.
I BLASTED HIM TO PIECES!!!
WHA -HA HA HA HA

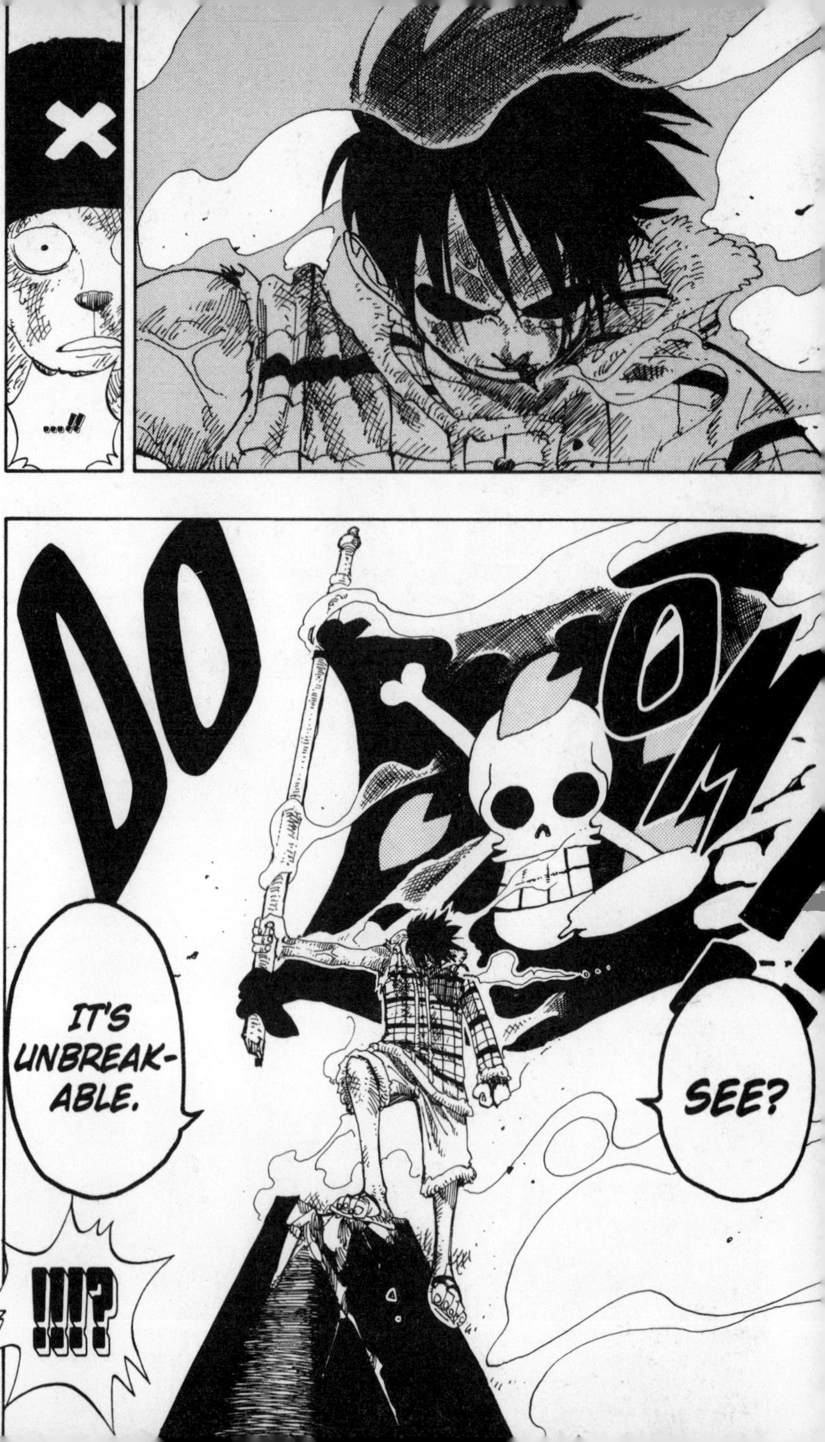
...!!
DOOM!
SEE?
IT'S UNBREAKABLE.
!!!?

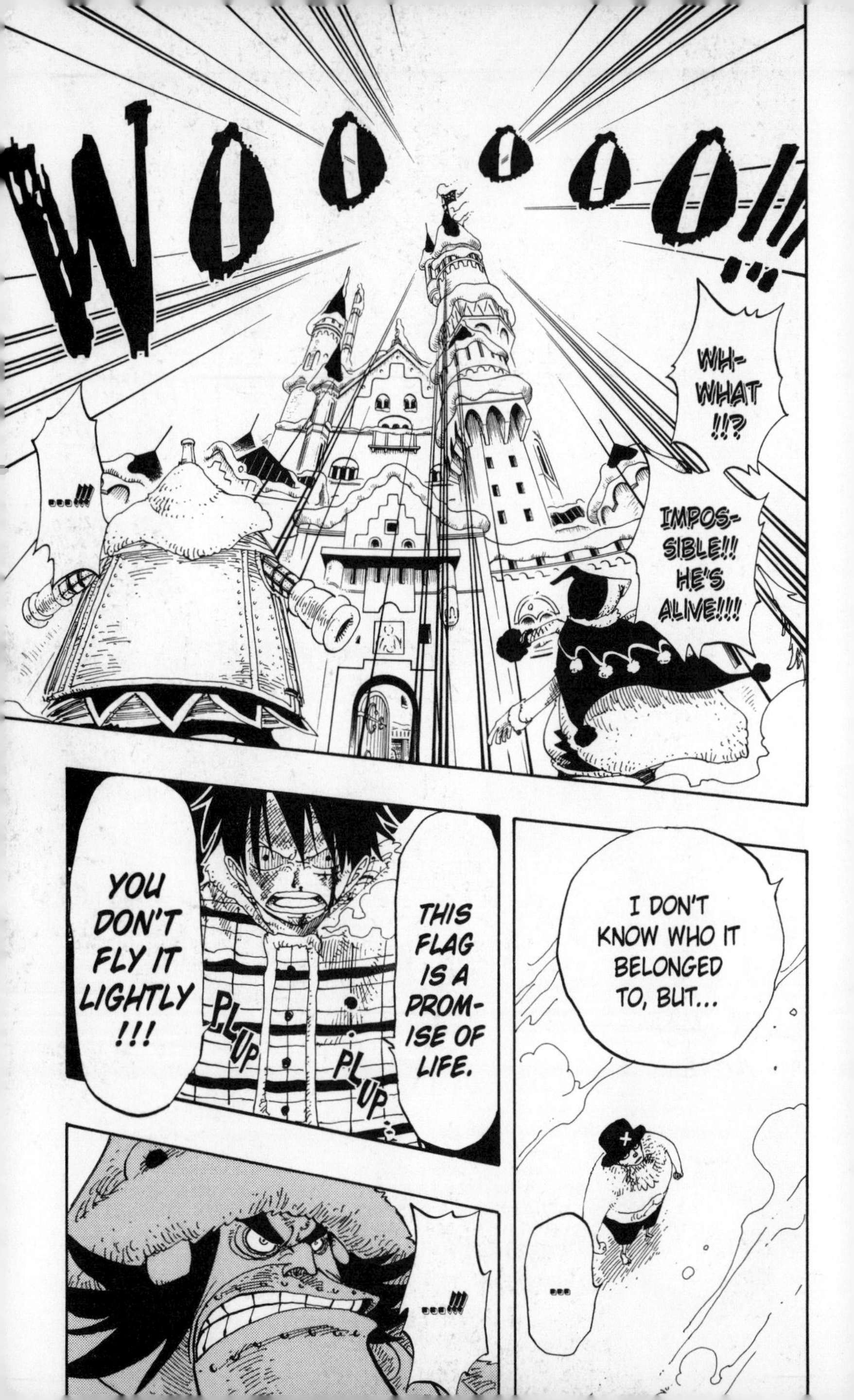
WOOOOOO!!!
WH-WHAT!!?
IMPOSSIBLE!!! HE'S ALIVE!!!!
...!!!
I DON'T KNOW WHO IT BELONGED TO, BUT...
...
THIS FLAG IS A PROMISE OF LIFE.
YOU DON'T FLY IT LIGHTLY!!!
PLUP
PLUP
...!!!

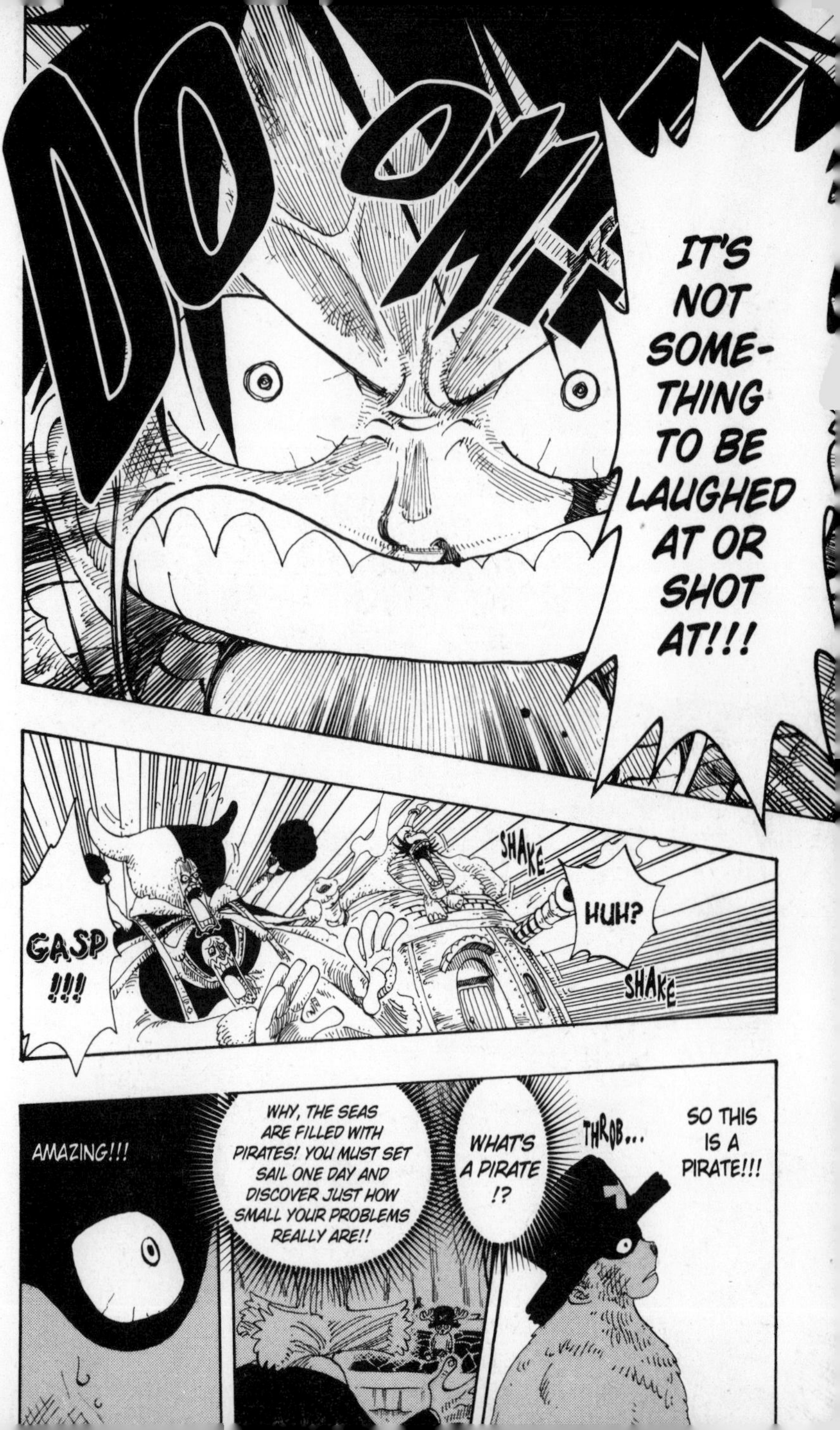
DOOM
IT'S NOT SOMETHING TO BE LAUGHED AT OR SHOT AT!!!
SHAKE
HUH?
SHAKE
GASP!!!
SO THIS IS A PIRATE!!!
THROB...
WHAT'S A PIRATE!?
WHY, THE SEAS ARE FILLED WITH PIRATES! YOU MUST SET SAIL ONE DAY AND DISCOVER JUST HOW SMALL YOUR PROBLEMS REALLY ARE!!
AMAZING!!!

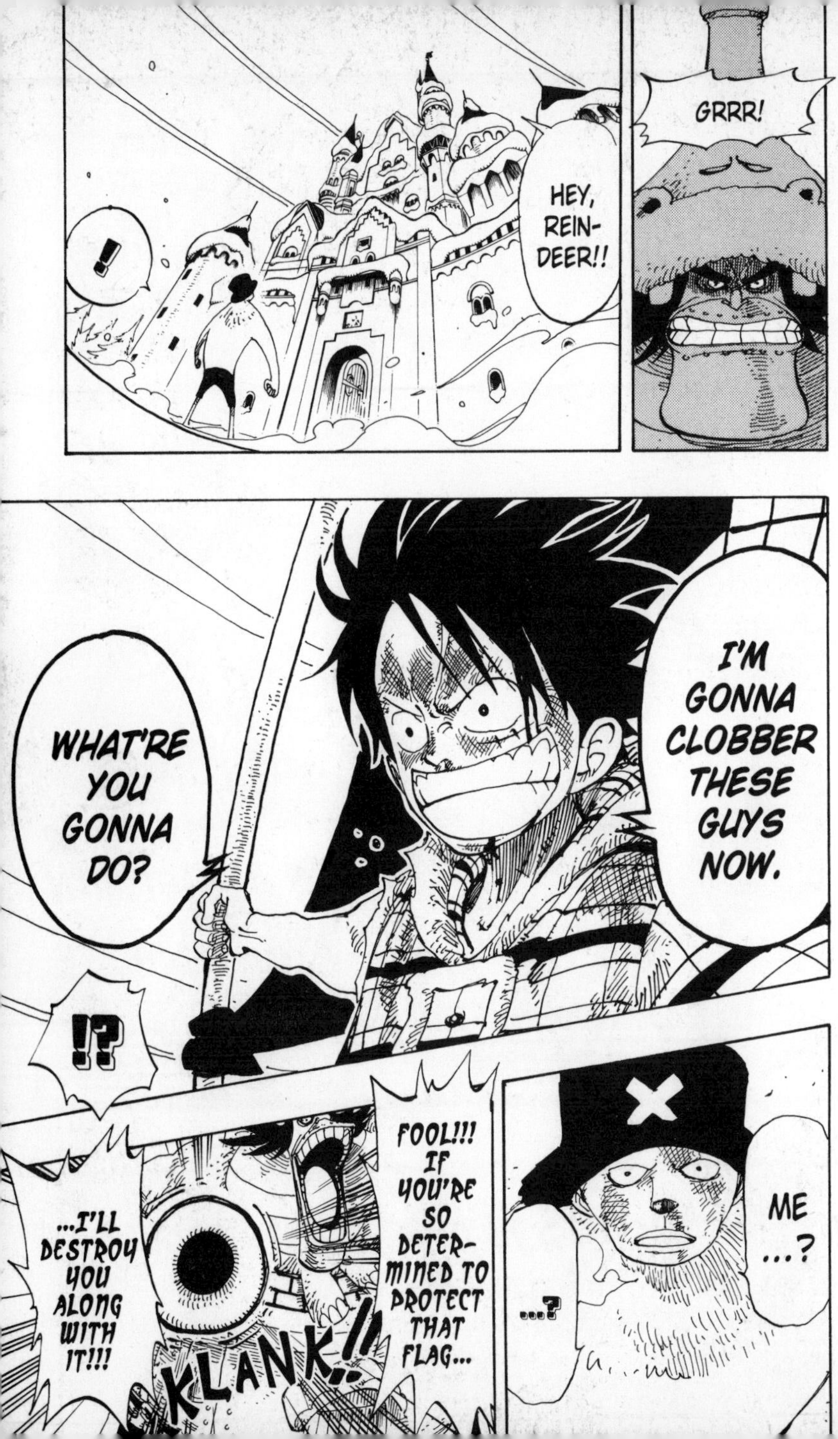
GRRR!
HEY, REINDEER!!
!
I'M GONNA CLOBBER THESE GUYS NOW.
WHAT'RE YOU GONNA DO?
!?
ME ...?
...?
FOOL!!! IF YOU'RE SO DETERMINED TO PROTECT THAT FLAG...
...I'LL DESTROY YOU ALONG WITH IT!!!
KLANK!!

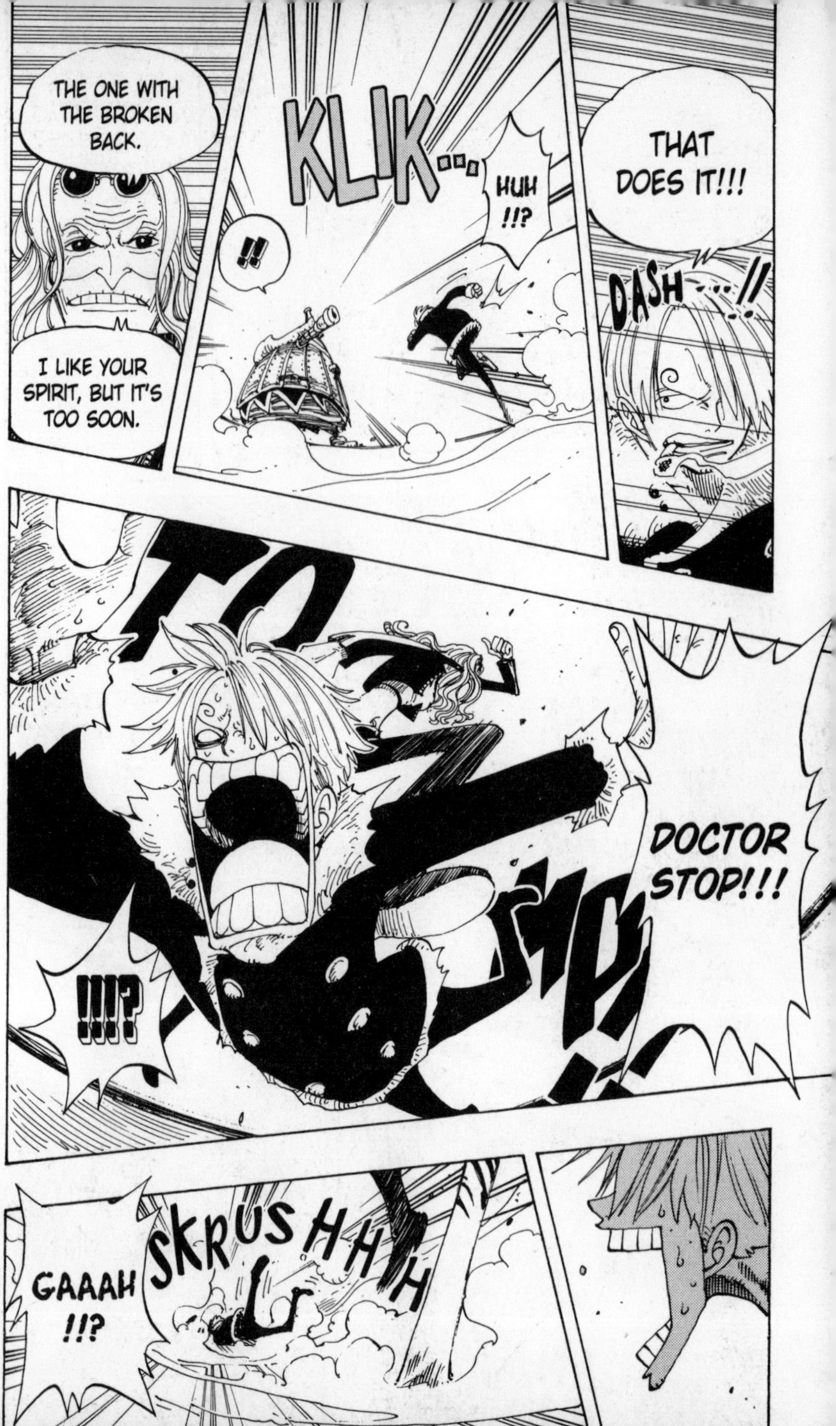
THAT DOES IT!!!
DASH...!!
KLIK...
HUH !!?
!!
THE ONE WITH THE BROKEN BACK.
I LIKE YOUR SPIRIT, BUT IT'S TOO SOON.
DOCTOR STOP!!!
!!!?
SKRUSHHHH
GAAAH !!?

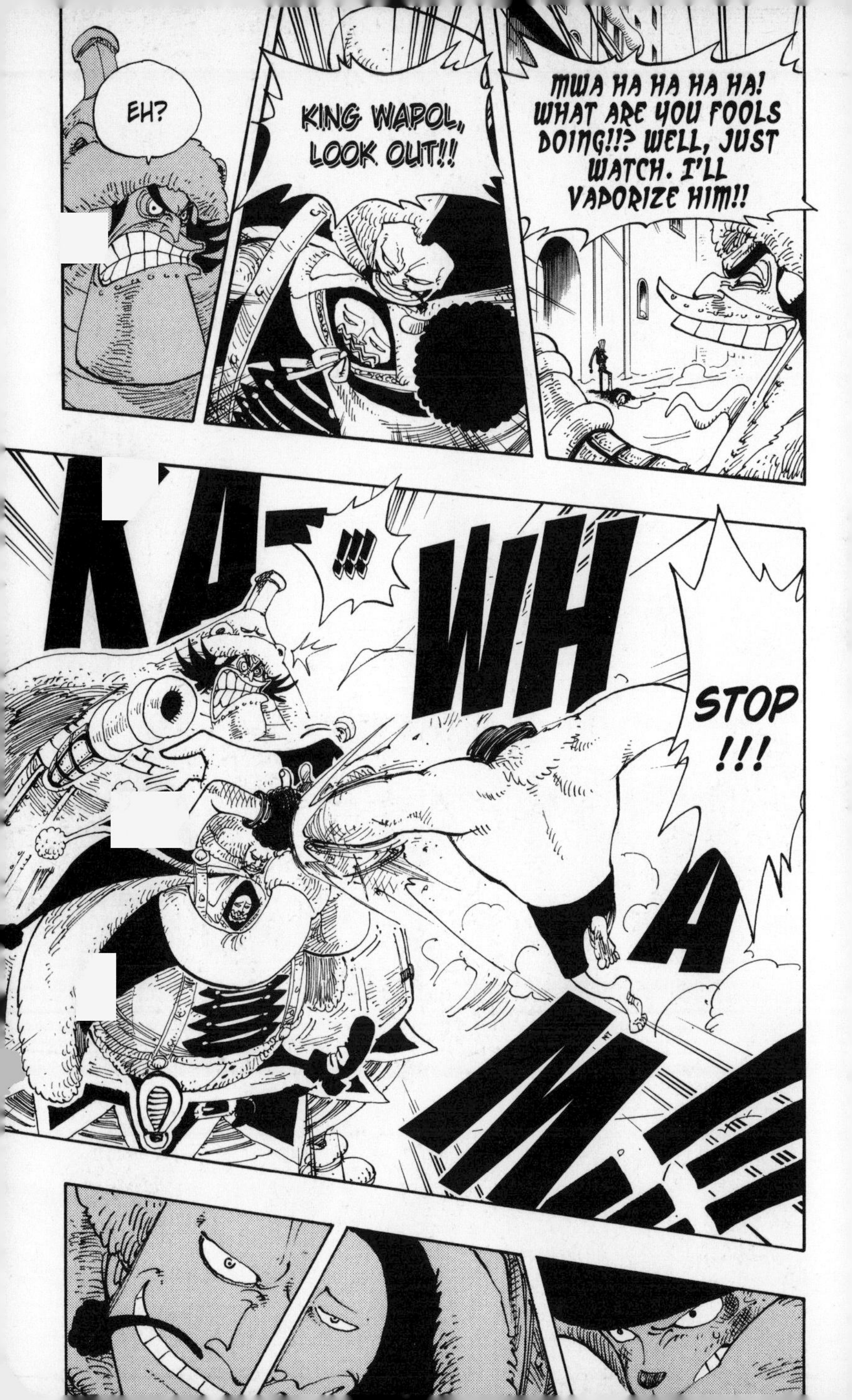
MWA HA HA HA HA! WHAT ARE YOU FOOLS DOING!!? WELL, JUST WATCH. I'LL VAPORIZE HIM!!
KING WAPOL, LOOK OUT!!
EH?
STOP!!!
!!!
KA-WHAM!!

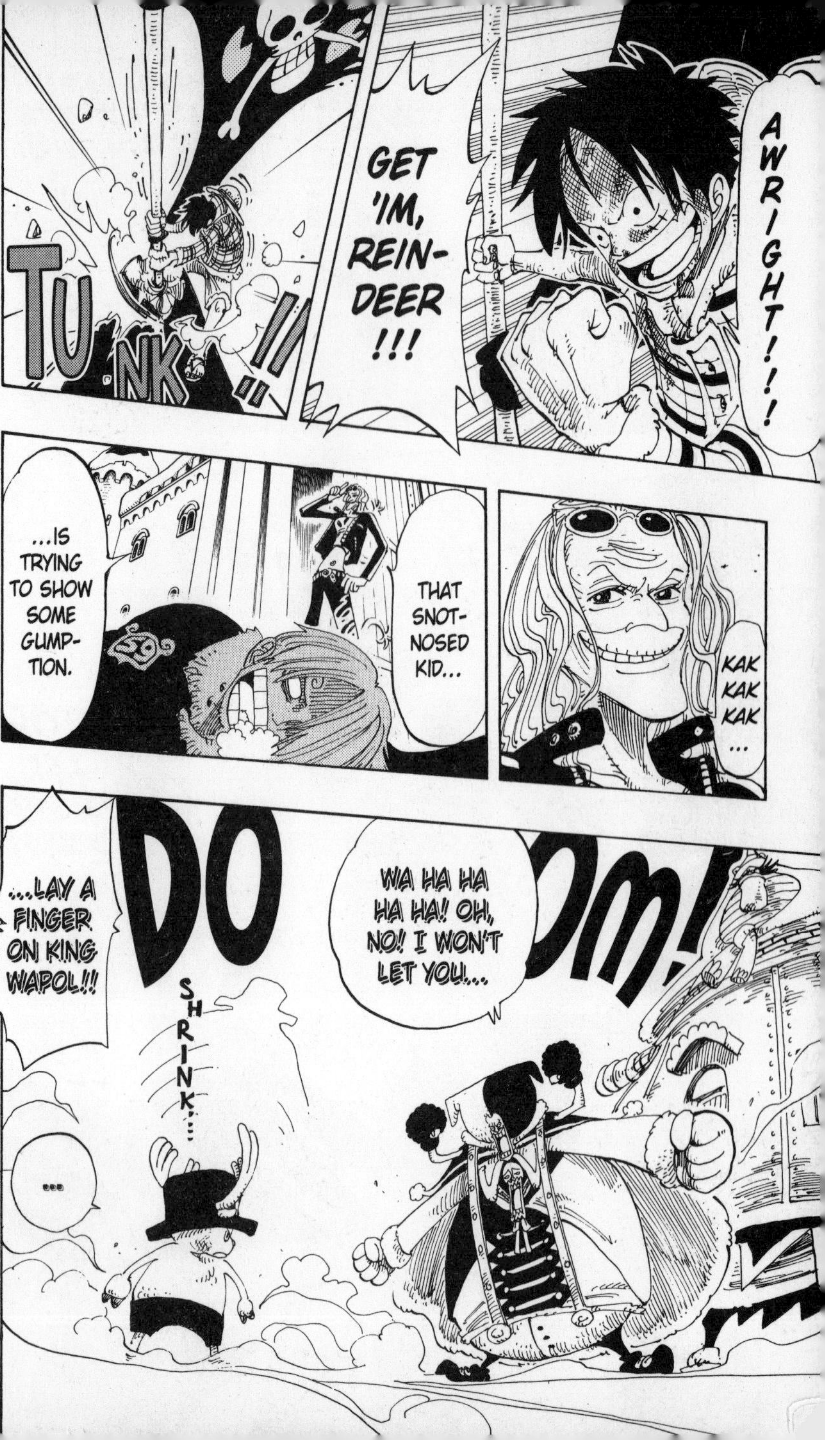
AWRIGHT!!!
GET 'IM, REIN-DEER!!!
TUNK!!
KAK KAK KAK...
THAT SNOT-NOSED KID...
...IS TRYING TO SHOW SOME GUMP-TION.
DOOM!
WA HA HA HA HA! OH, NO!! I WON'T LET YOU...
...LAY A FINGER ON KING WAPOL!!
SHRINK...
...

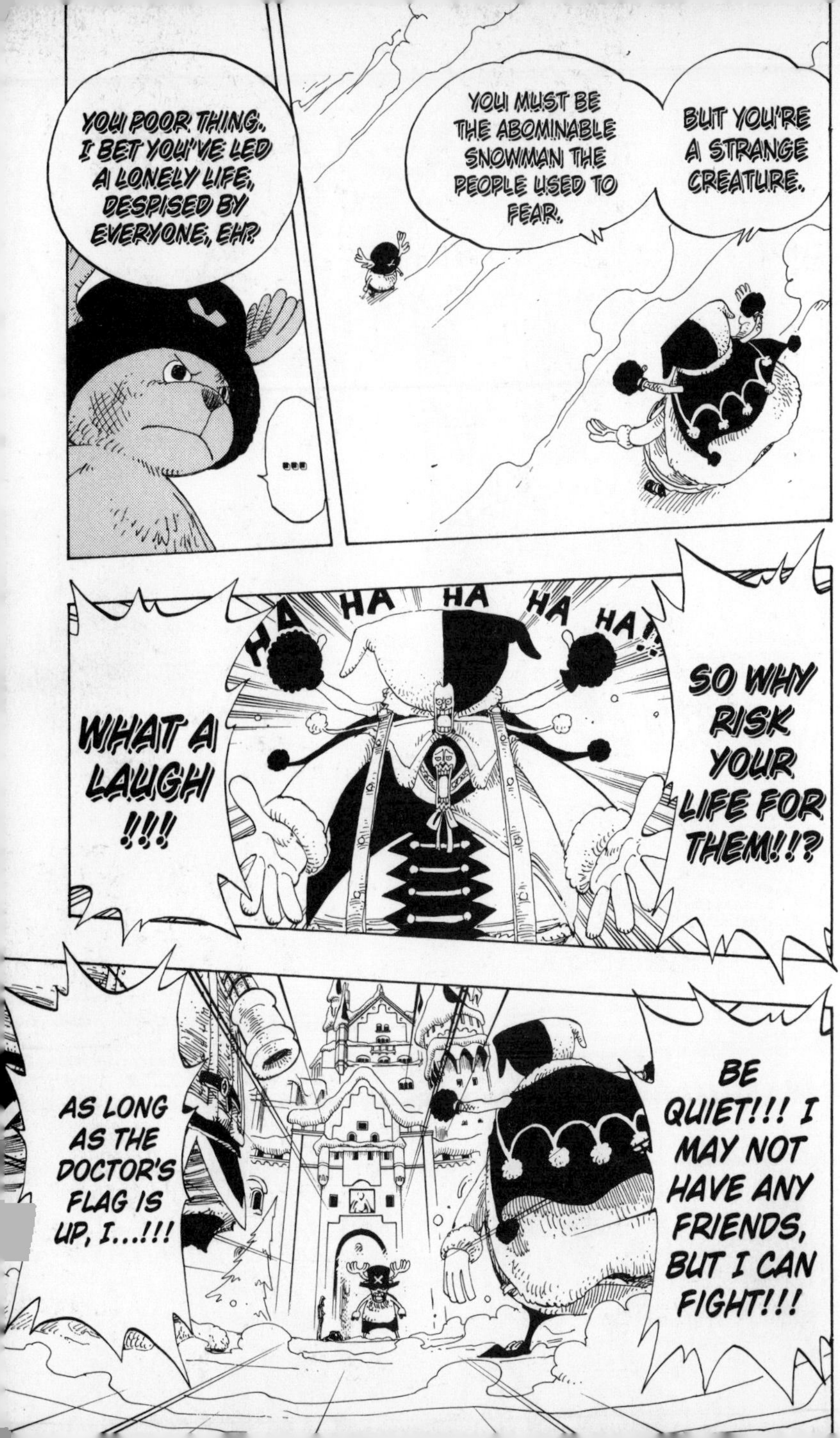
BUT YOU'RE A STRANGE CREATURE.
YOU MUST BE THE ABOMINABLE SNOWMAN THE PEOPLE USED TO FEAR.
YOU POOR THING. I BET YOU'VE LED A LONELY LIFE, DESPISED BY EVERYONE, EH?
...
HA HA HA HA!!
SO WHY RISK YOUR LIFE FOR THEM!!?
WHAT A LAUGH!!!
BE QUIET!!! I MAY NOT HAVE ANY FRIENDS, BUT I CAN FIGHT!!!
AS LONG AS THE DOCTOR'S FLAG IS UP, I...!!!

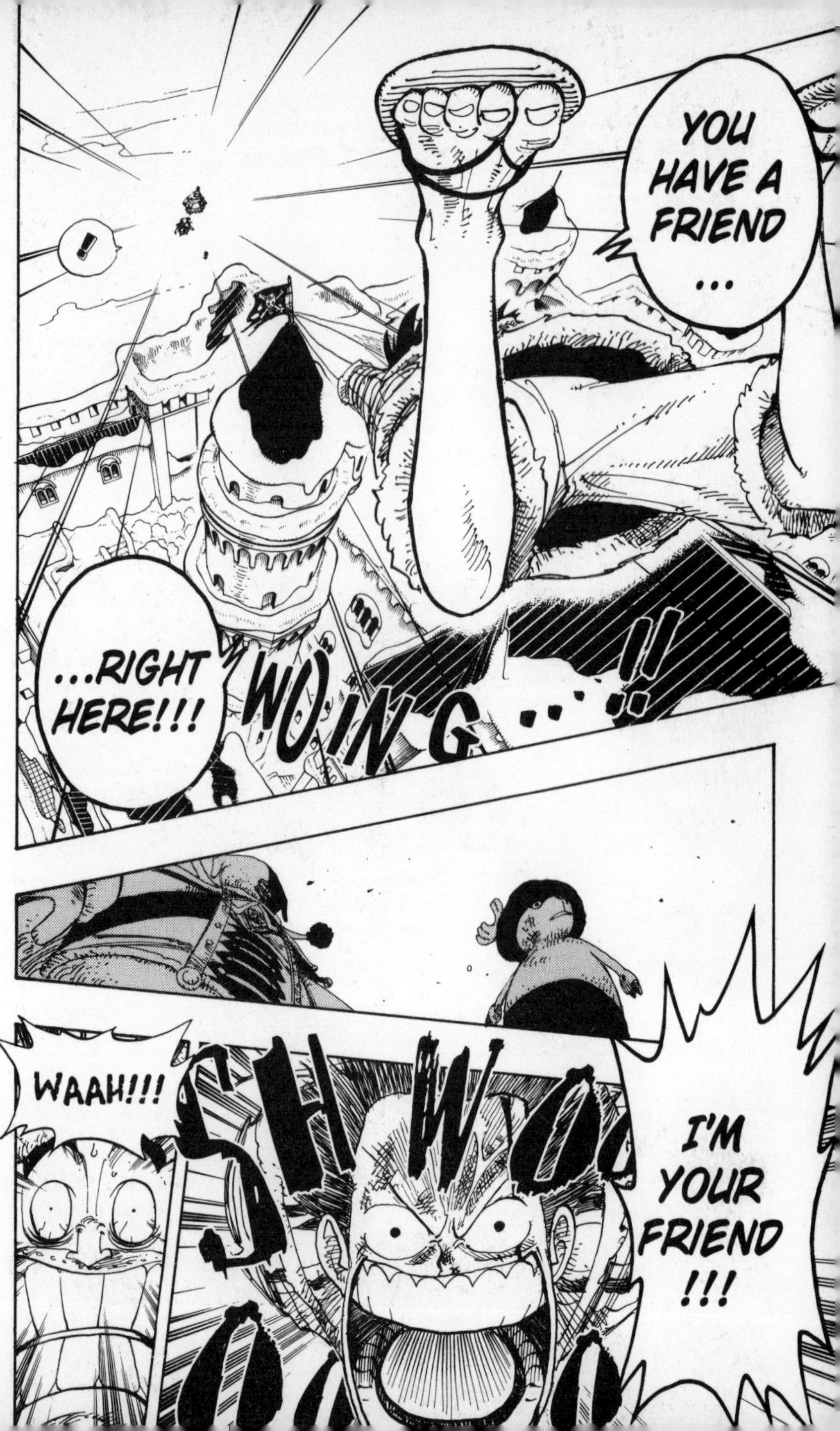
YOU HAVE A FRIEND ...
!
...RIGHT HERE!!!
WOING ..!!
I'M YOUR FRIEND !!!
SHWOO
WAAH!!!

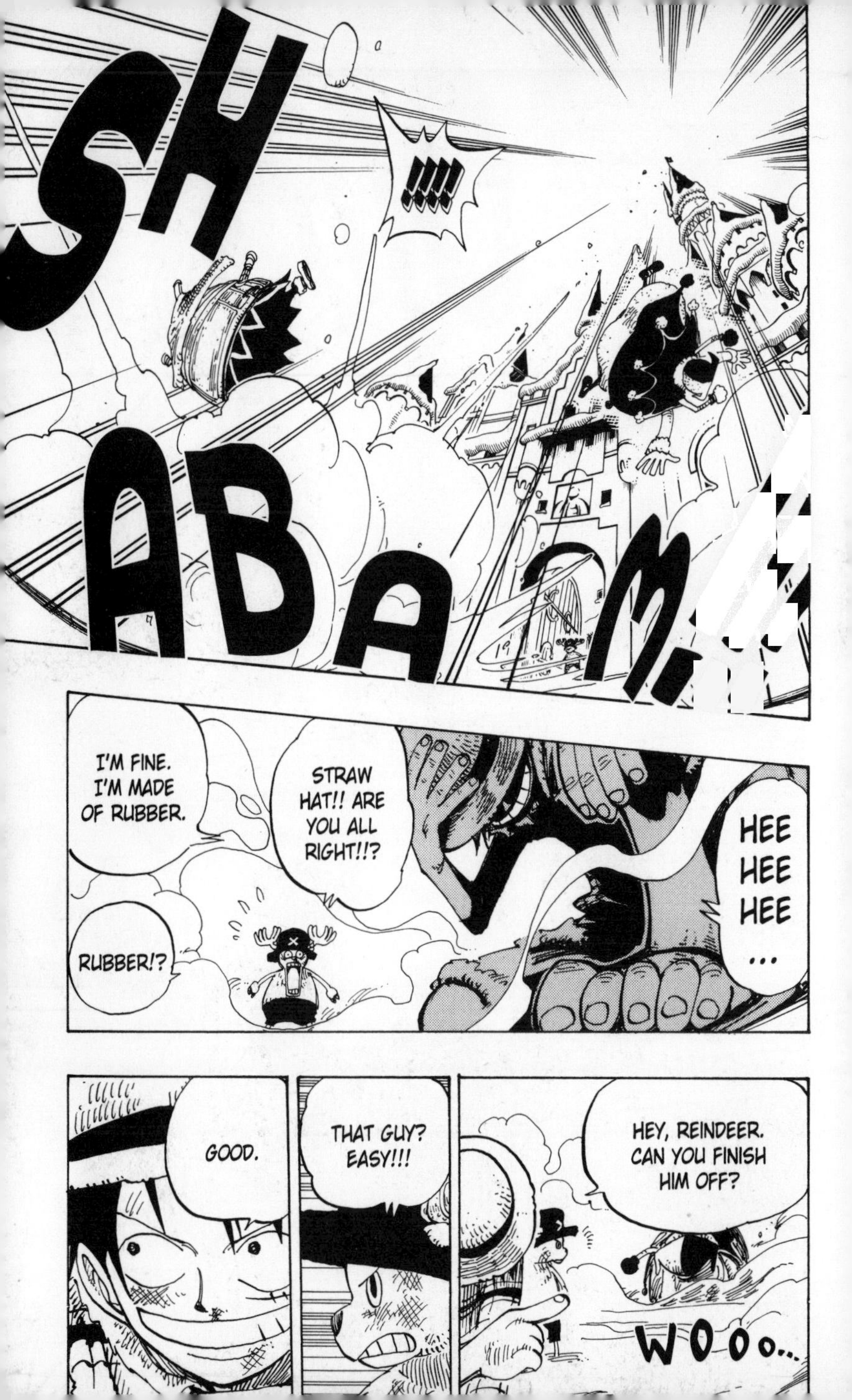
!!!!
SHABAM!!
HEE HEE HEE ...
STRAW HAT!! ARE YOU ALL RIGHT!!?
I'M FINE. I'M MADE OF RUBBER.
RUBBER!?
HEY, REINDEER. CAN YOU FINISH HIM OFF?
WOOO...
THAT GUY? EASY!!!
GOOD.

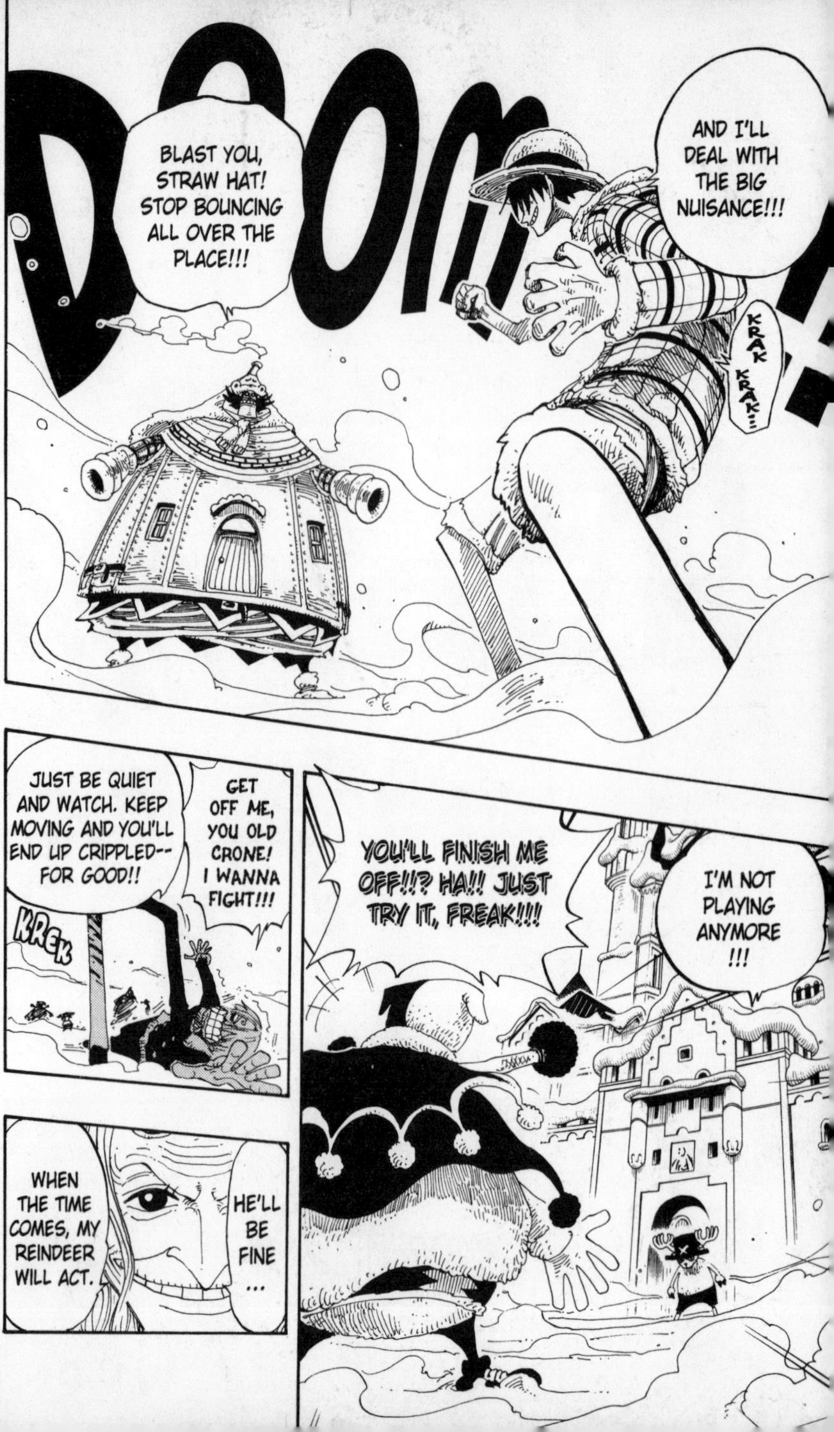
DOOM!!
AND I'LL DEAL WITH THE BIG NUISANCE!!!
BLAST YOU, STRAW HAT! STOP BOUNCING ALL OVER THE PLACE!!!
KRAK KRAK...
I'M NOT PLAYING ANYMORE!!!
YOU'LL FINISH ME OFF!!? HA!! JUST TRY IT, FREAK!!!!
GET OFF ME, YOU OLD CRONE! I WANNA FIGHT!!!
JUST BE QUIET AND WATCH. KEEP MOVING AND YOU'LL END UP CRIPPLED-- FOR GOOD!!
KREK
HE'LL BE FINE ...
WHEN THE TIME COMES, MY REINDEER WILL ACT.

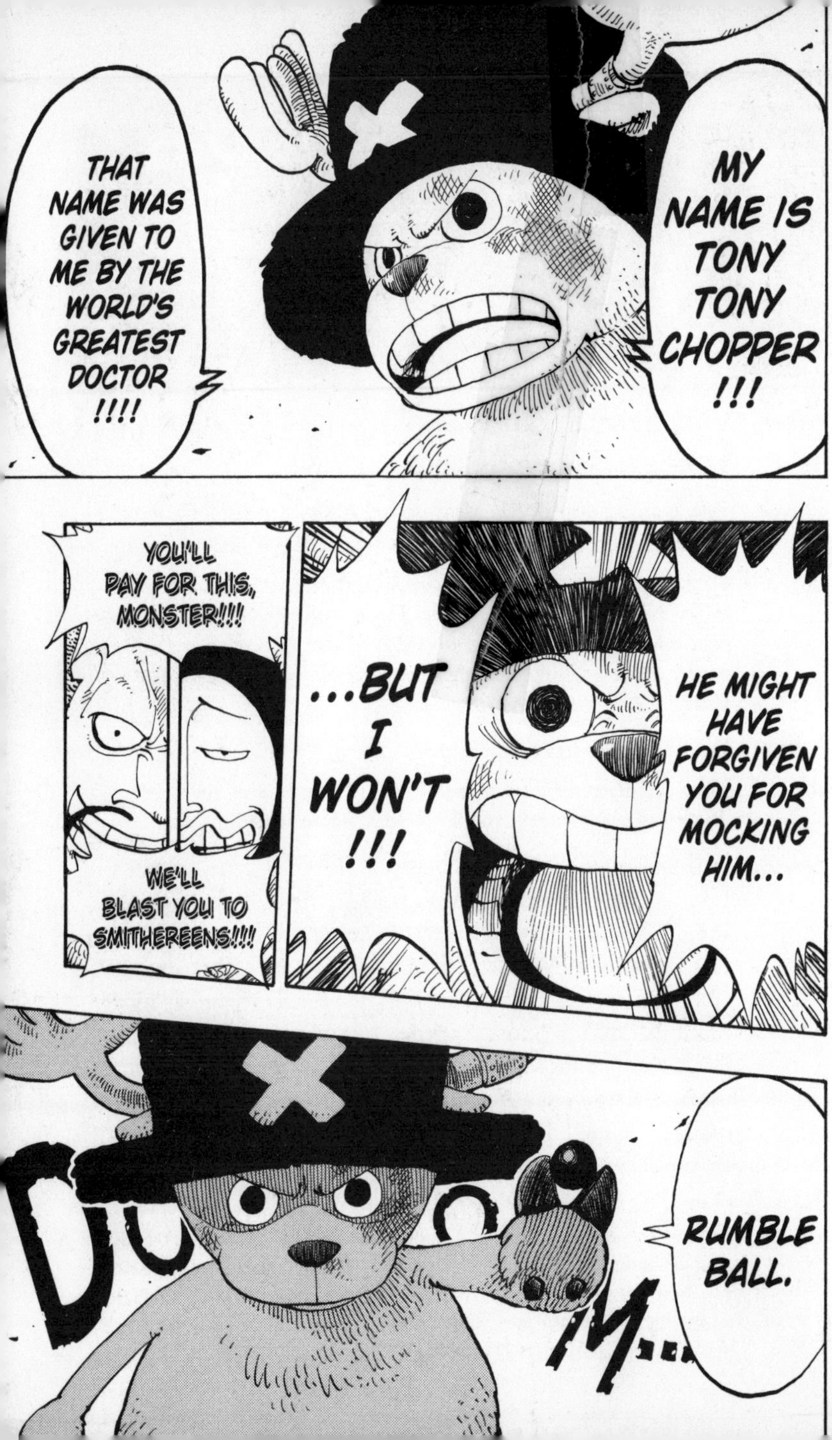
MY NAME IS TONY TONY CHOPPER !!!
THAT NAME WAS GIVEN TO ME BY THE WORLD'S GREATEST DOCTOR !!!!
HE MIGHT HAVE FORGIVEN YOU FOR MOCKING HIM...
...BUT I WON'T !!!
YOU'LL PAY FOR THIS, MONSTER!!!!
WE'LL BLAST YOU TO SMITHEREENS!!!!
RUMBLE BALL.
DOOM...

Question Corner
S
B
S
MATSU

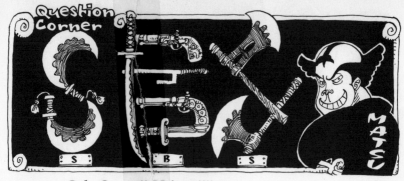

**Reader:** Oda Sensei! Yahoo!!!!

**Oda:** Yahoo!!!! (Just playing along)

**Reader:** I have a question! Does Momoo belong to the sea king family? A friend of mine said that he was something called a sea king.

**Oda:** Momoo? Actually, I have classified Momoo as a "sea monster." In our world, we have sea mammals like seals and whales and it's the same in *One Piece*. So think of a sea king as a large creature that lives in the sea that's not a sea mammal.

**Reader:** Does *One Piece* have a website?

**Oda:** Well, it does and it doesn't. *One Piece* shares the *Shonen Jump* website. Please take a look.

**Reader:** Oda Sensei, please hear me out!
I was standing in a bookstore, reading, when I thought of something. Does Vivi have any connection to ancient Egypt? Her full name is Nefeltari Vivi and her father was Nefeltari Cobra. In ancient Egypt, Nefertari had the meaning of "most beautiful one" or "most exalted one" and many queens and princesses had those hieroglyphics on their portraits. Furthermore, Alabasta seems to be a desert nation. And her father's name is Cobra. I'd like to know if I'm right. If so, please acknowledge me as Know-It-All Himeko's rival-Maimai.

**Oda:** I see... So that's what Nefertari means, huh? How nice. Actually I did model Alabasta after ancient Egypt, and I flipped through a book on Egypt and picked words that sounded interesting. It seems I managed to pick a nice name. (talking to myself.) All right! I acknowledge it! You rival Know-It-All Himeko!!

# Chapter 149: RUMBLE

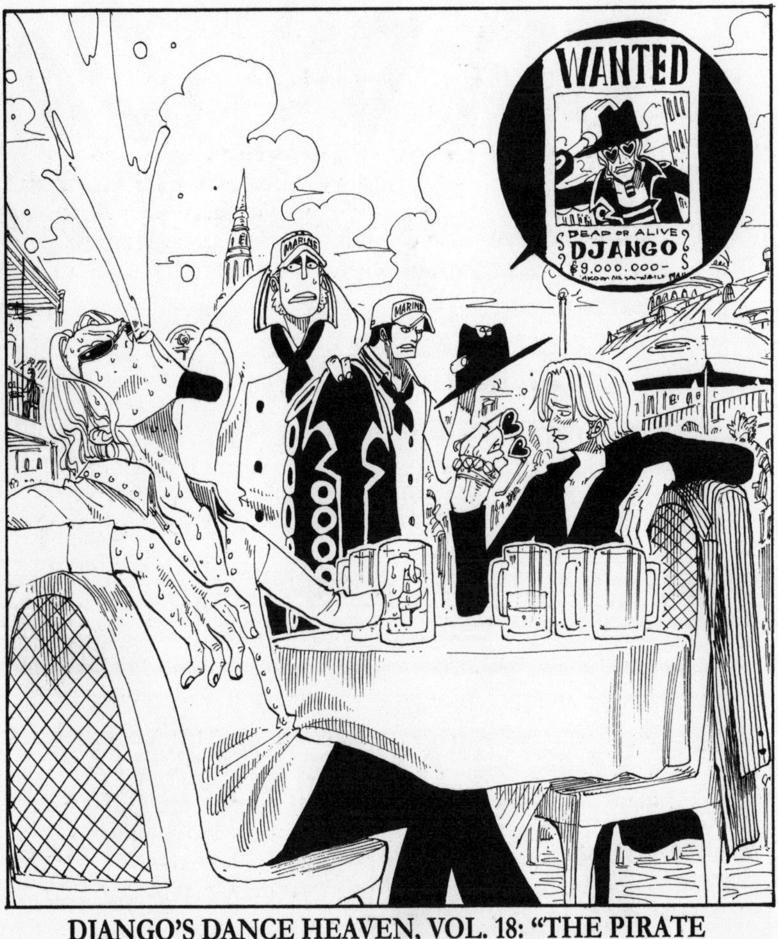
WANTED
DEAD OR ALIVE
DJANGO
$9,000,000-
MARINE
MARINE

DJANGO'S DANCE HEAVEN, VOL. 18: "THE PIRATE DJANGO'S CLOTHES ARE DISCOVERED!!"

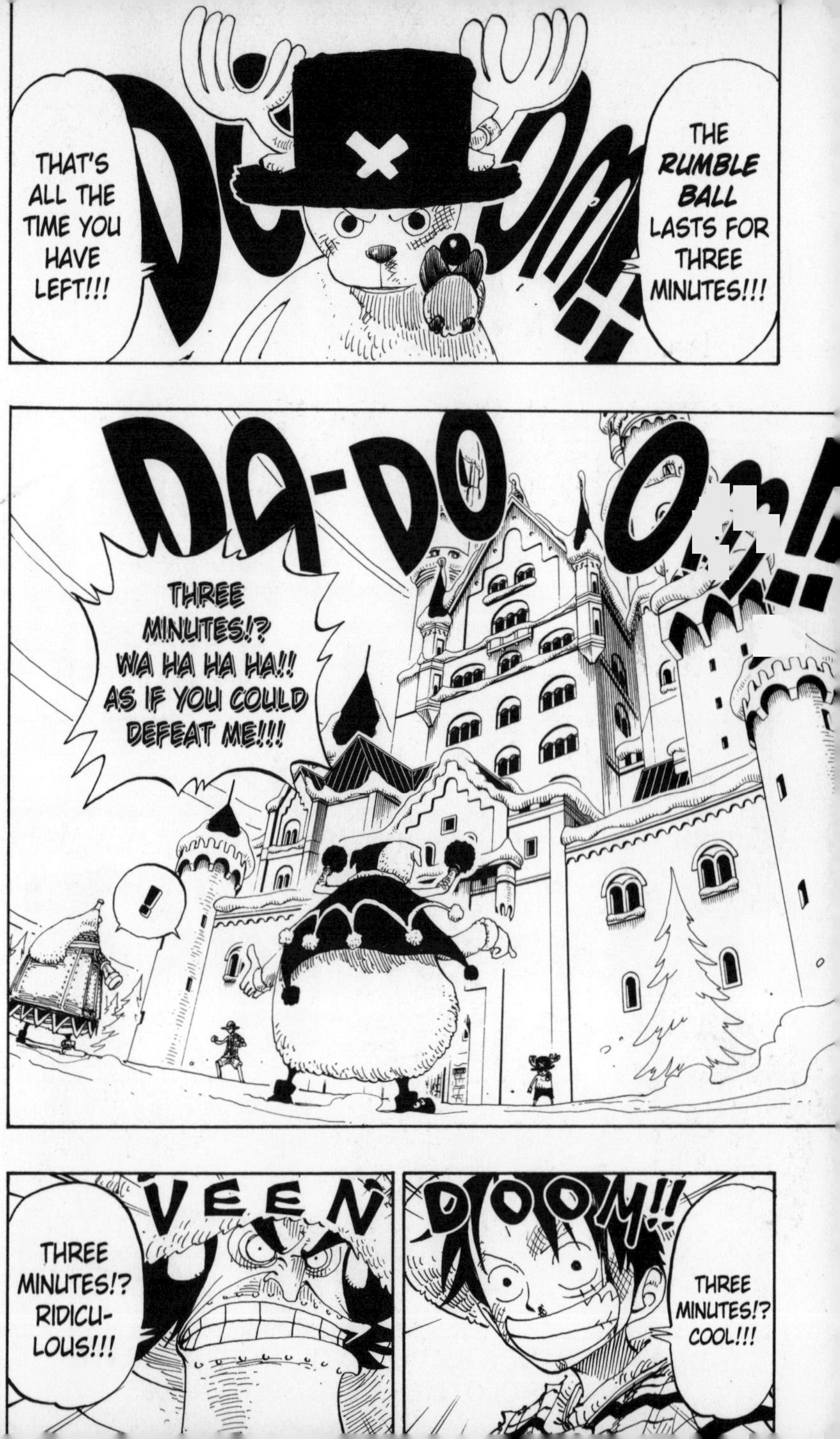
THE RUMBLE BALL LASTS FOR THREE MINUTES!!!
THAT'S ALL THE TIME YOU HAVE LEFT!!!
DA-DO
THREE MINUTES!? WA HA HA HA!! AS IF YOU COULD DEFEAT ME!!!
!
DOOM!!
THREE MINUTES!? COOL!!!
VEEN
THREE MINUTES!? RIDICU-LOUS!!!

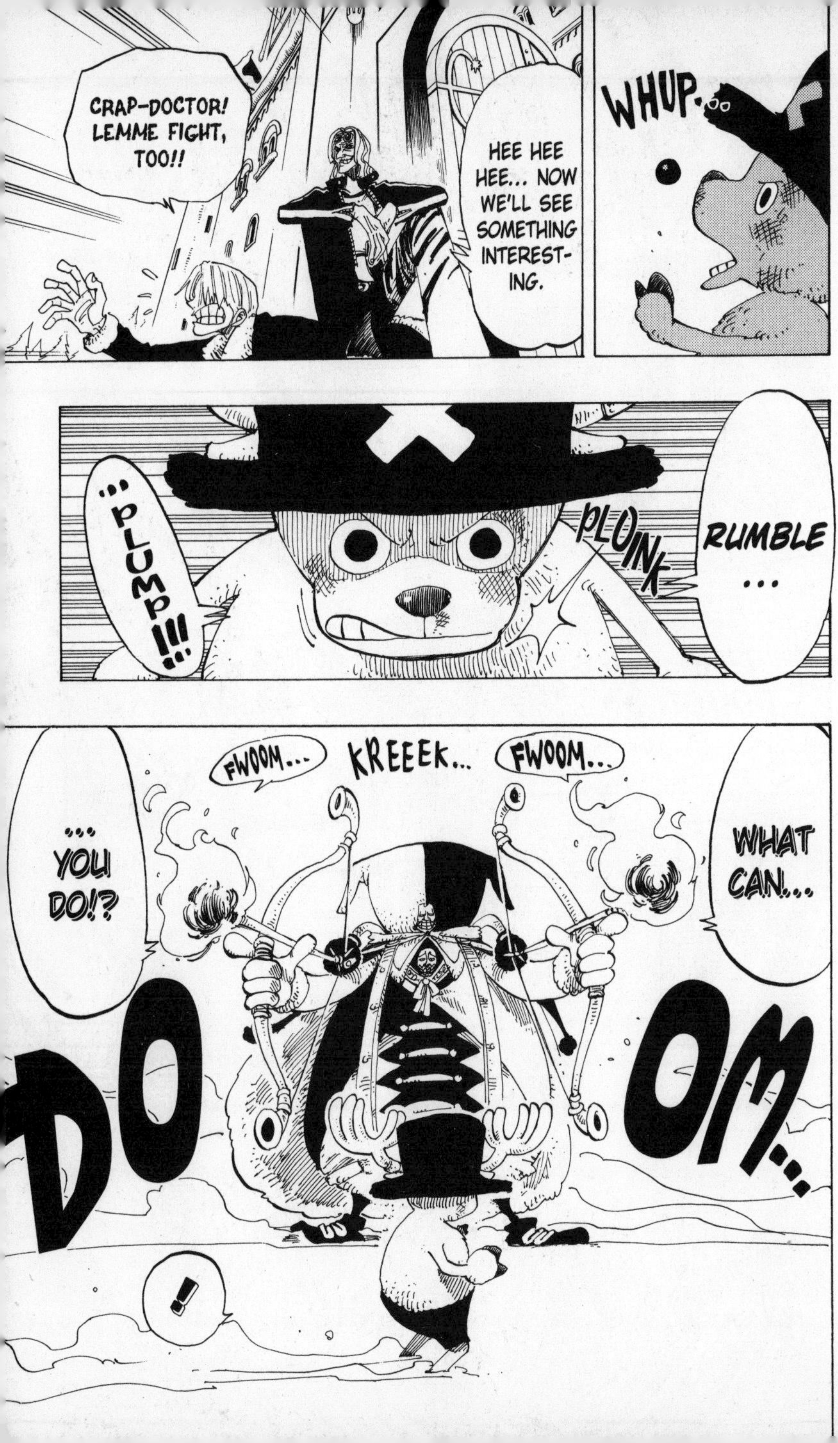
WHUP.
HEE HEE HEE... NOW WE'LL SEE SOMETHING INTEREST-ING.
CRAP-DOCTOR! LEMME FIGHT, TOO!!
RUMBLE ...
PLOINK
...PLUMP!!!
WHAT CAN...
FWOOM...
KREEEK...
FWOOM...
... YOU DO!?
DOOM...
!

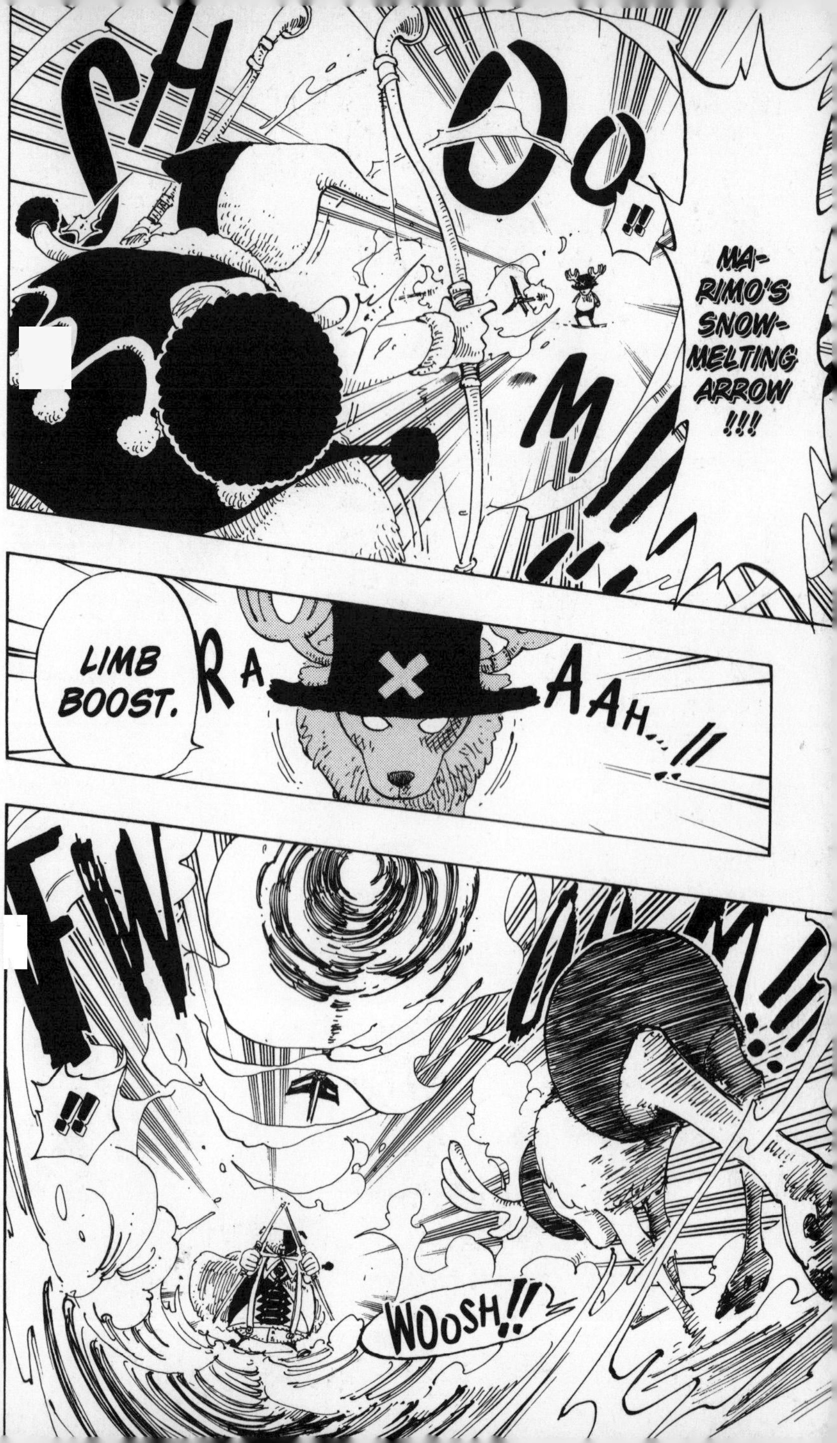
MARIMO'S SNOW-MELTING ARROW!!!
SHOOOM!!
RAAAH...!!
LIMB BOOST.
FWOOM!!
!!
WOOSH!!

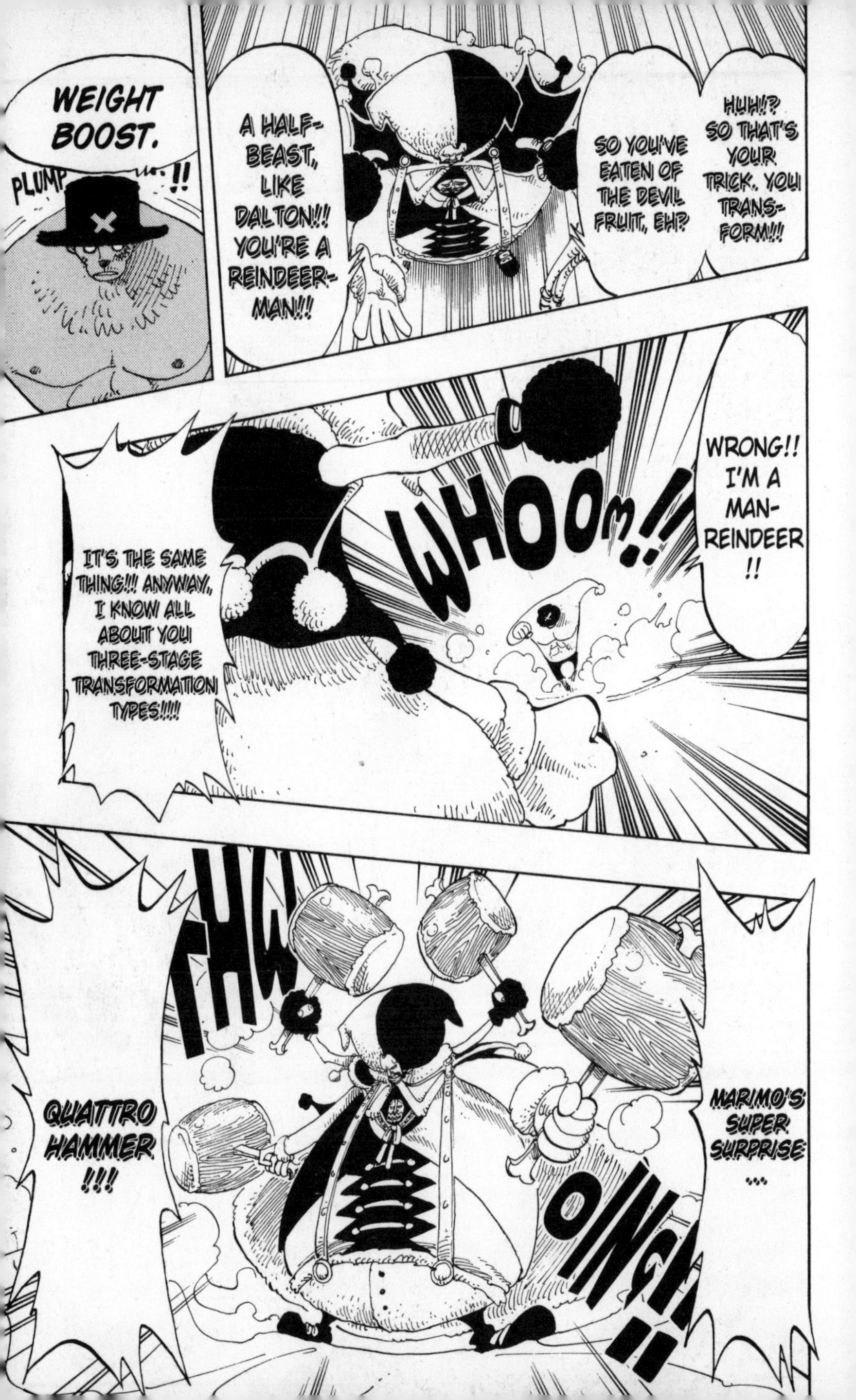
HUH!? SO THAT'S YOUR TRICK. YOU TRANS-FORM!!!
SO YOU'VE EATEN OF THE DEVIL FRUIT, EH?
A HALF-BEAST, LIKE DALTON!! YOU'RE A REINDEER-MAN!!
WEIGHT BOOST.
PLUMP
!!
WRONG!! I'M A MAN-REINDEER !!
WHOOM!!
IT'S THE SAME THING!!! ANYWAY, I KNOW ALL ABOUT YOU THREE-STAGE TRANSFORMATION TYPES!!!!
MARIMO'S SUPER SURPRISE ...
OING!!
THW
QUATTRO HAMMER !!!

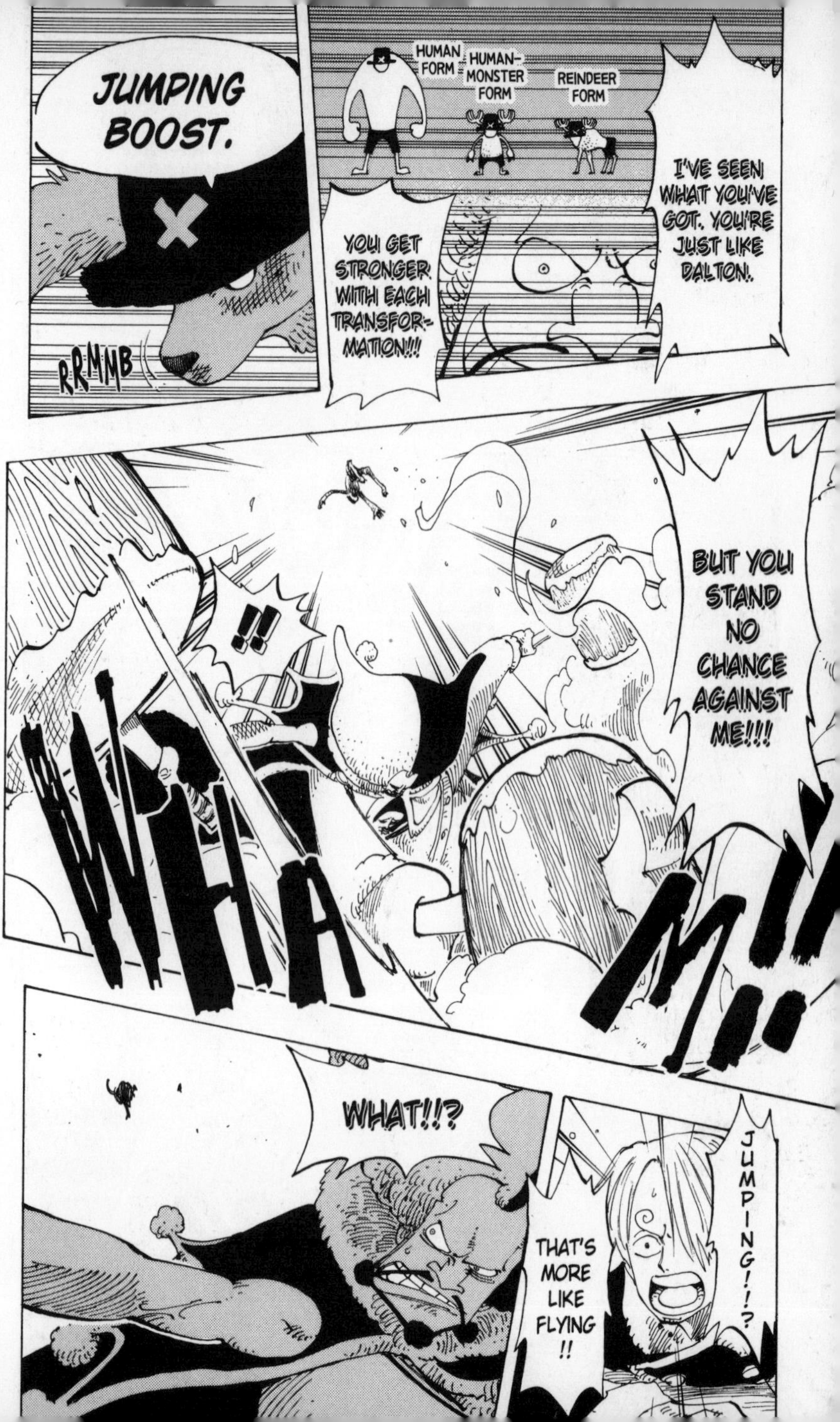
REINDEER FORM
HUMAN-MONSTER FORM
HUMAN FORM
I'VE SEEN WHAT YOU'VE GOT. YOU'RE JUST LIKE DALTON.
YOU GET STRONGER WITH EACH TRANSFORMATION!!!
JUMPING BOOST.
RRMMB
BUT YOU STAND NO CHANCE AGAINST ME!!!
!!
WHAM!!
JUMPING!!?
THAT'S MORE LIKE FLYING!!
WHAT!!?

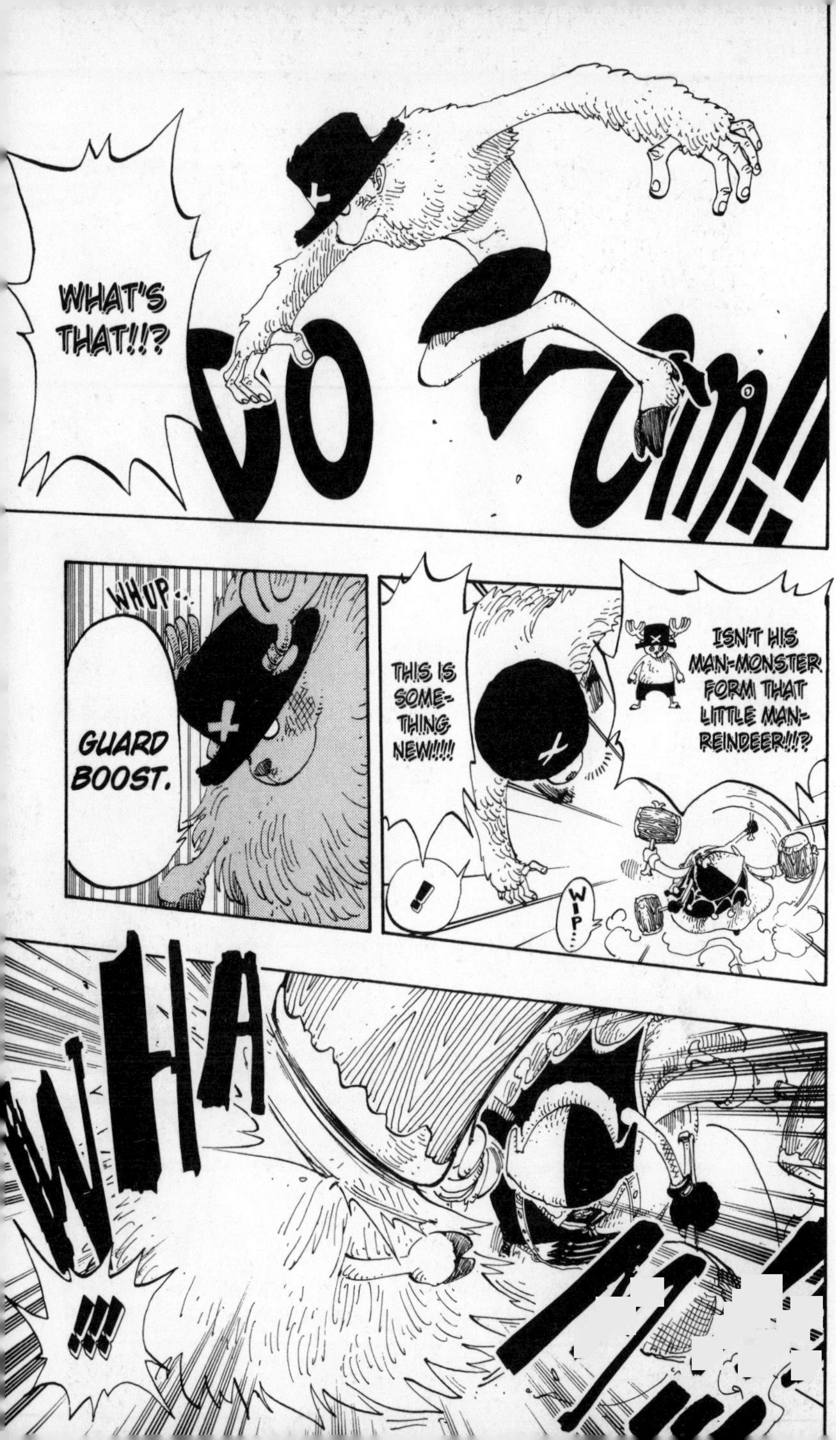
WHAT'S THAT!!?
ISN'T HIS MAN-MONSTER FORM THAT LITTLE MAN-REINDEER!!?
THIS IS SOME-THING NEW!!!!
!
WIP...
WHUP...
GUARD BOOST.
WHA
!!!

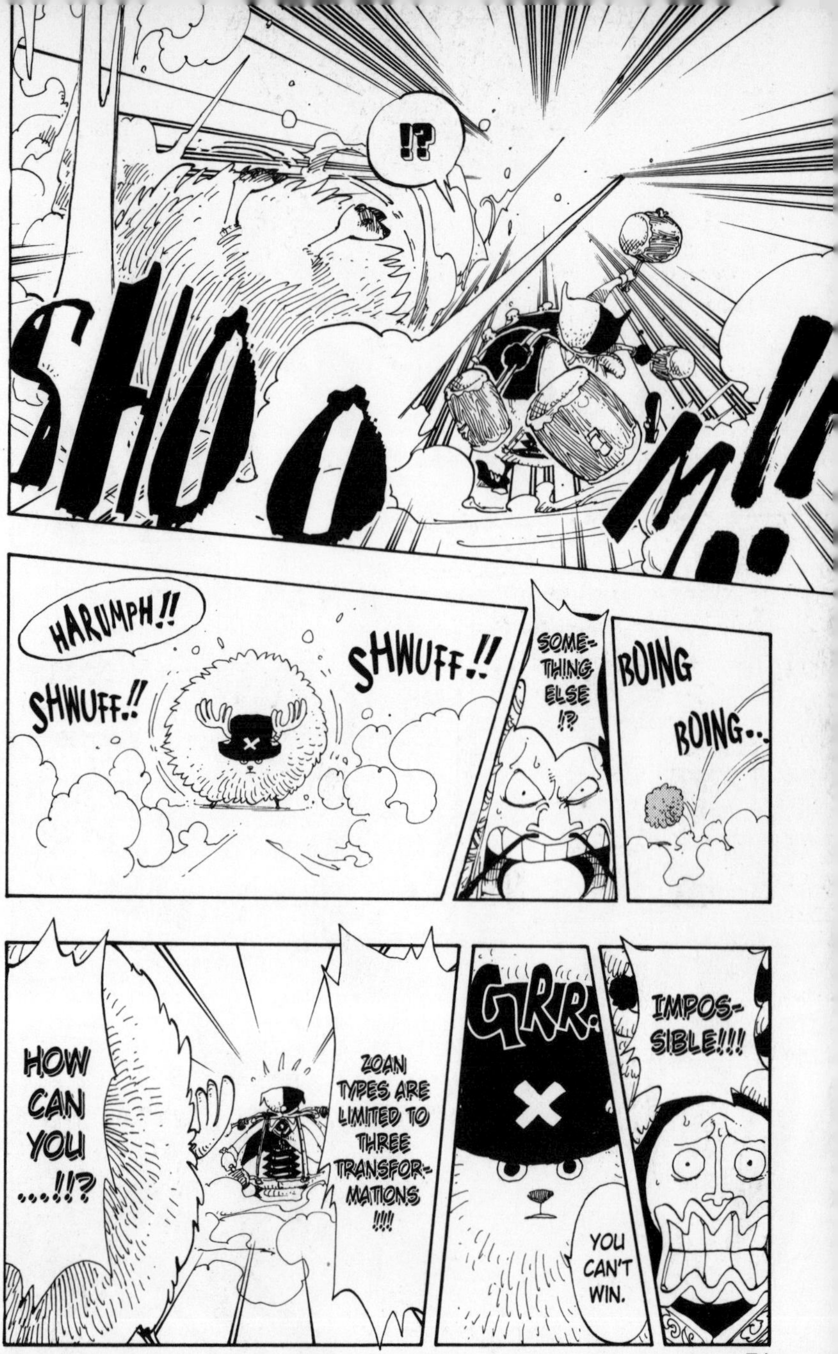
!?
SHOOON!!
BOING
BOING...
SOME-THING ELSE !?
SHWUFF!!
HARUMPH!!
SHWUFF!!
IMPOS-SIBLE!!!
GRR.
YOU CAN'T WIN.
ZOAN TYPES ARE LIMITED TO THREE TRANSFOR-MATIONS !!!!
HOW CAN YOU ...!!?

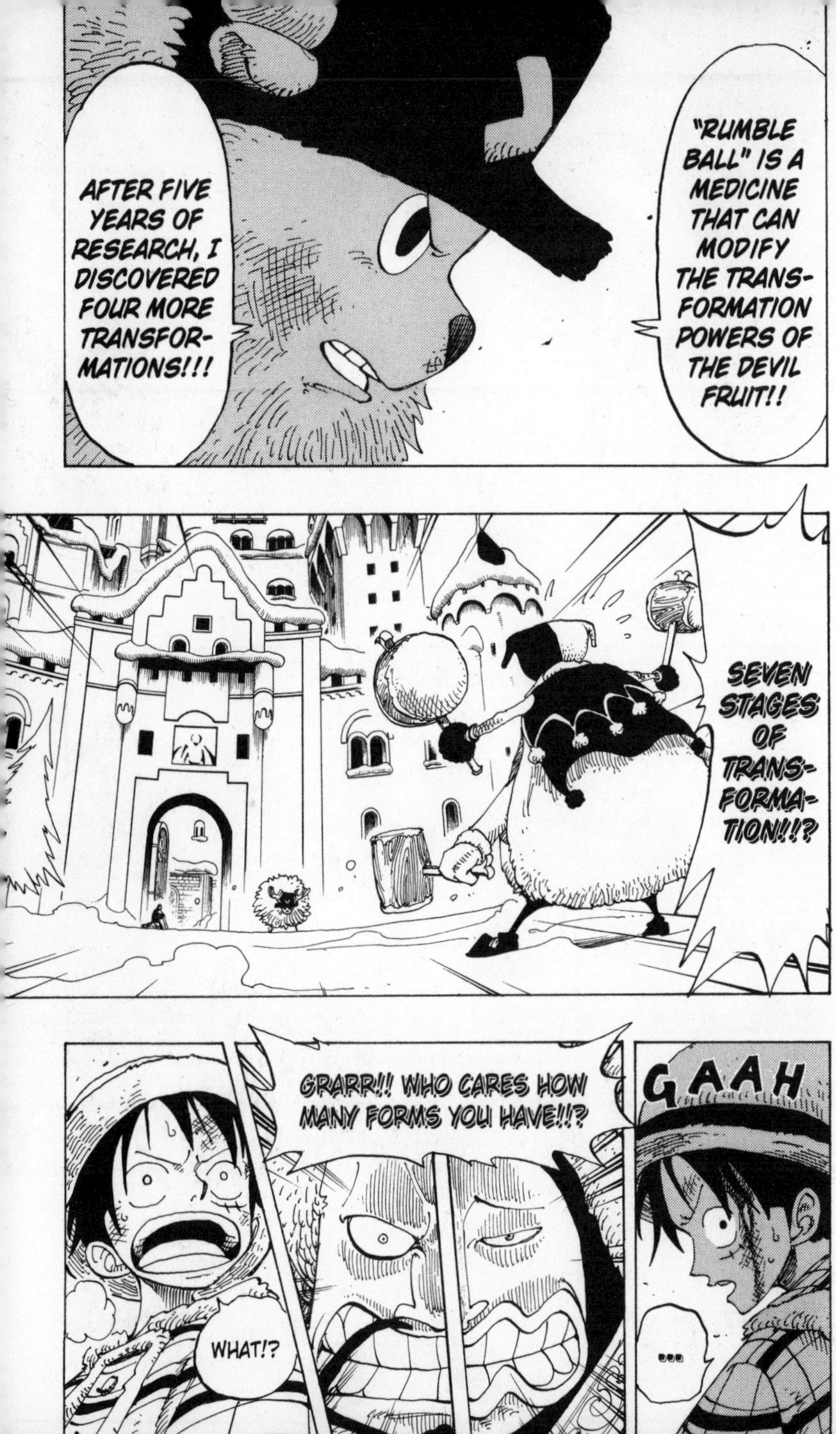
"RUMBLE BALL" IS A MEDICINE THAT CAN MODIFY THE TRANS-FORMATION POWERS OF THE DEVIL FRUIT!!
AFTER FIVE YEARS OF RESEARCH, I DISCOVERED FOUR MORE TRANSFOR-MATIONS!!!
SEVEN STAGES OF TRANS-FORMA-TION!!?
GAAH
...
GRARR!! WHO CARES HOW MANY FORMS YOU HAVE!!?
WHAT!?

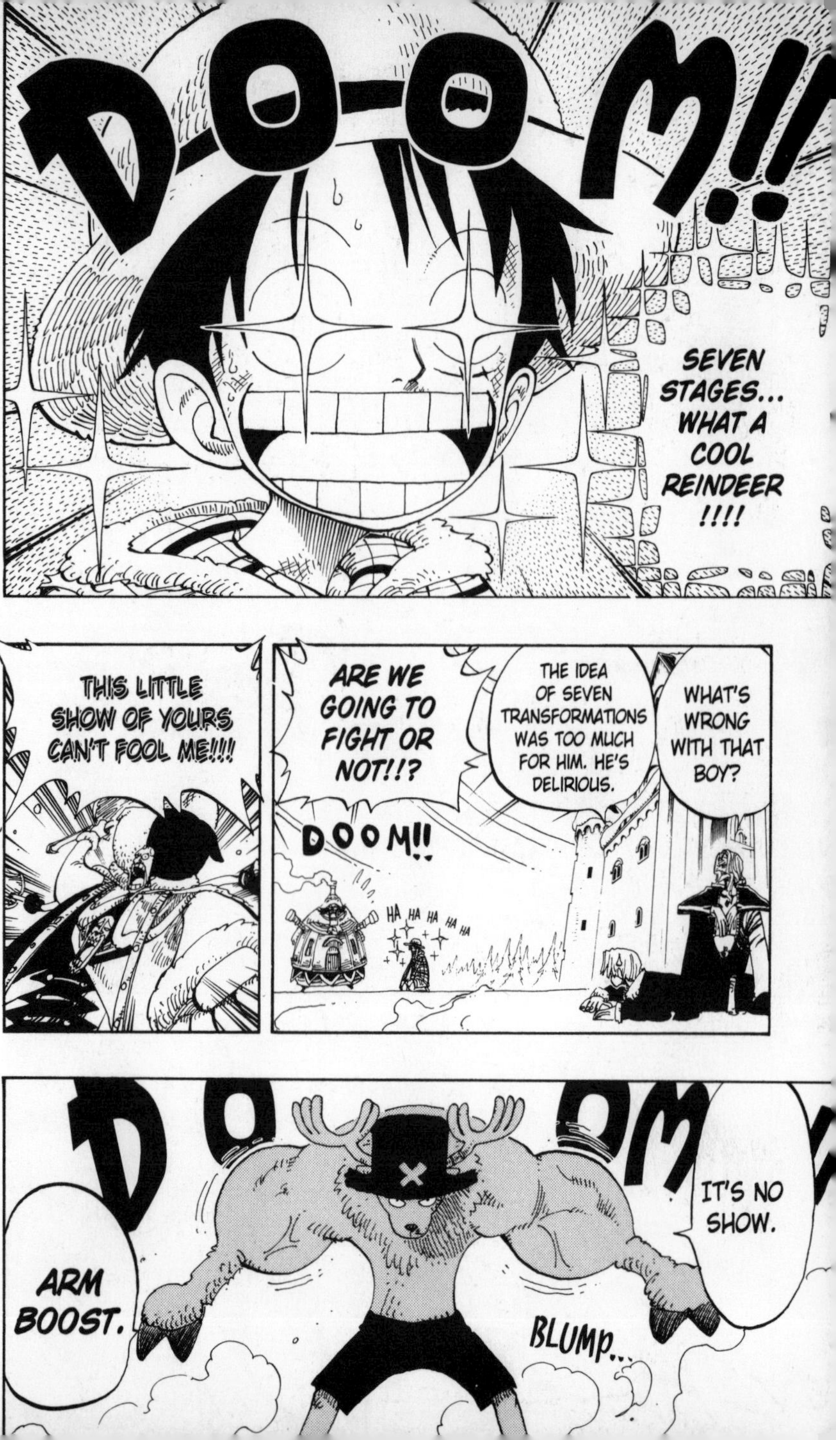
D-O-O-M!!
SEVEN STAGES... WHAT A COOL REINDEER !!!!
WHAT'S WRONG WITH THAT BOY?
THE IDEA OF SEVEN TRANSFORMATIONS WAS TOO MUCH FOR HIM. HE'S DELIRIOUS.
ARE WE GOING TO FIGHT OR NOT!!?
DOOM!!
HA HA HA HA HA
THIS LITTLE SHOW OF YOURS CAN'T FOOL ME!!!!
DOOM
IT'S NO SHOW.
ARM BOOST.
BLUMP...

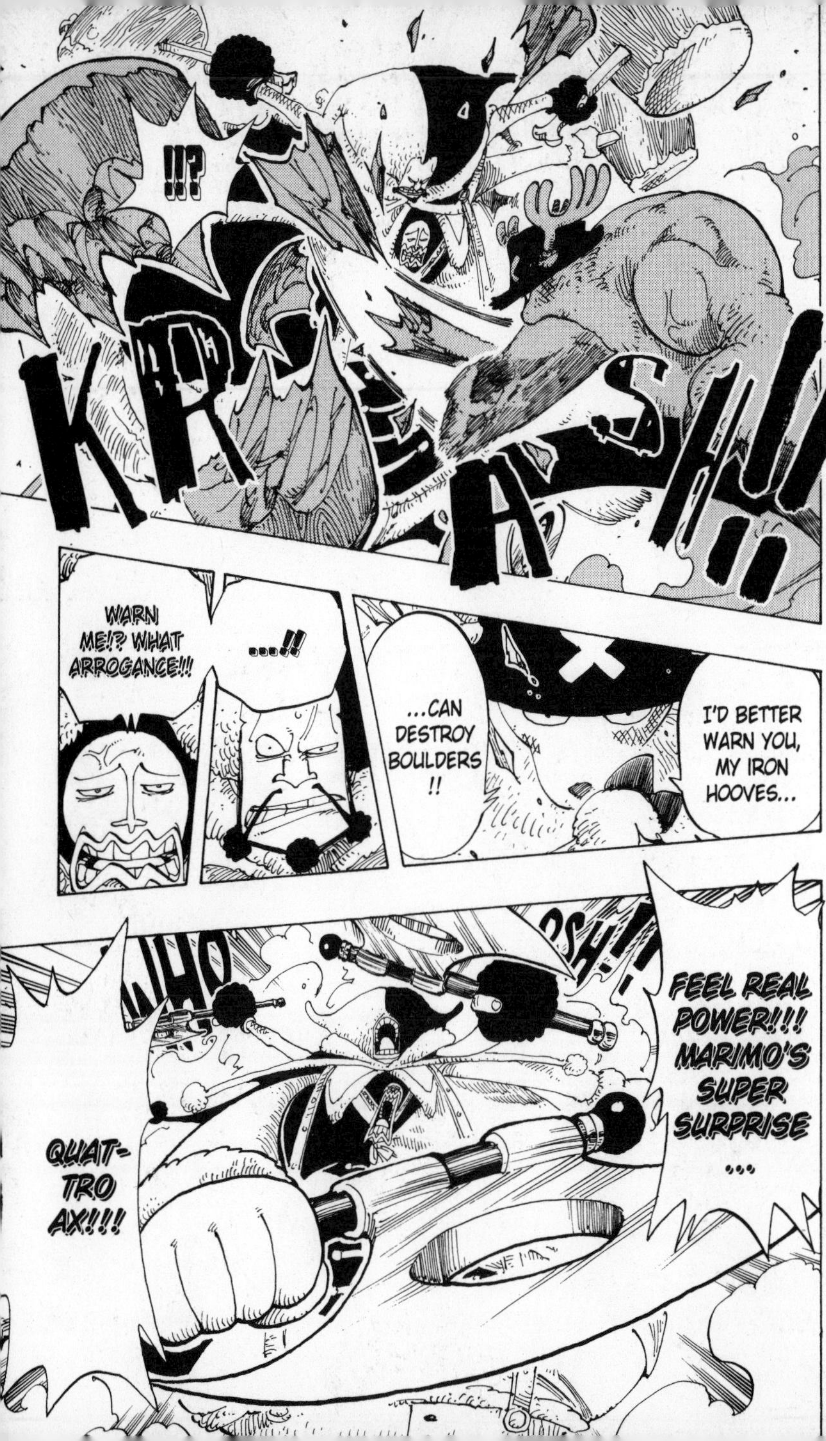
!!?
KRASH!!
I'D BETTER WARN YOU, MY IRON HOOVES...
...CAN DESTROY BOULDERS !!
...!!
WARN ME!? WHAT ARROGANCE!!!
FEEL REAL POWER!!! MARIMO'S SUPER SURPRISE...
QUAT-TRO AX!!!

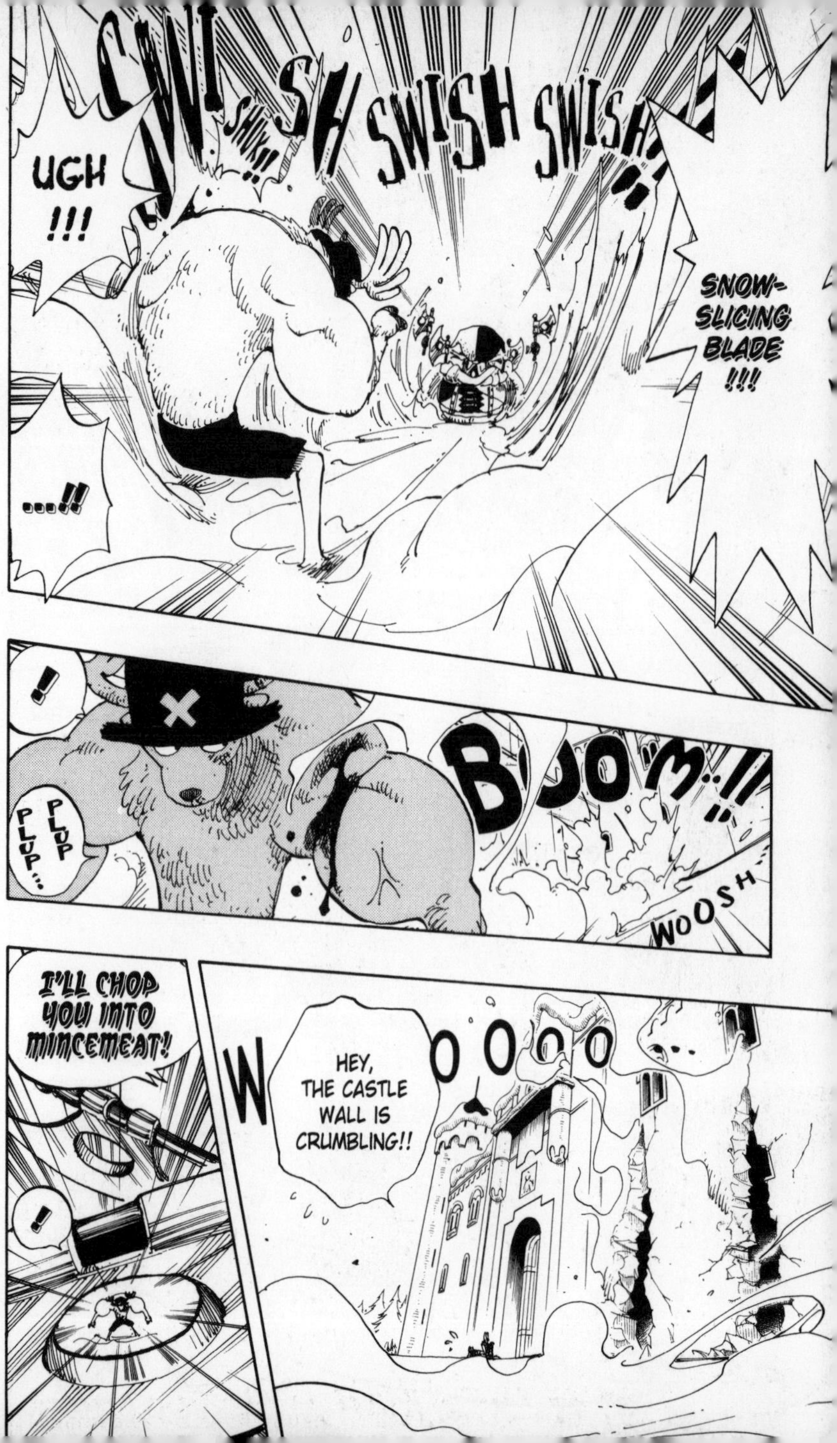
SWISH SHUK!! SWISH SWISH SWISH!!
SNOW-SLICING BLADE!!!
UGH!!!
...!!
BOOM!!
WOOSH
!
PLUP PLUP...
WOOOOO
HEY, THE CASTLE WALL IS CRUMBLING!!
I'LL CHOP YOU INTO MINCEMEAT!
!

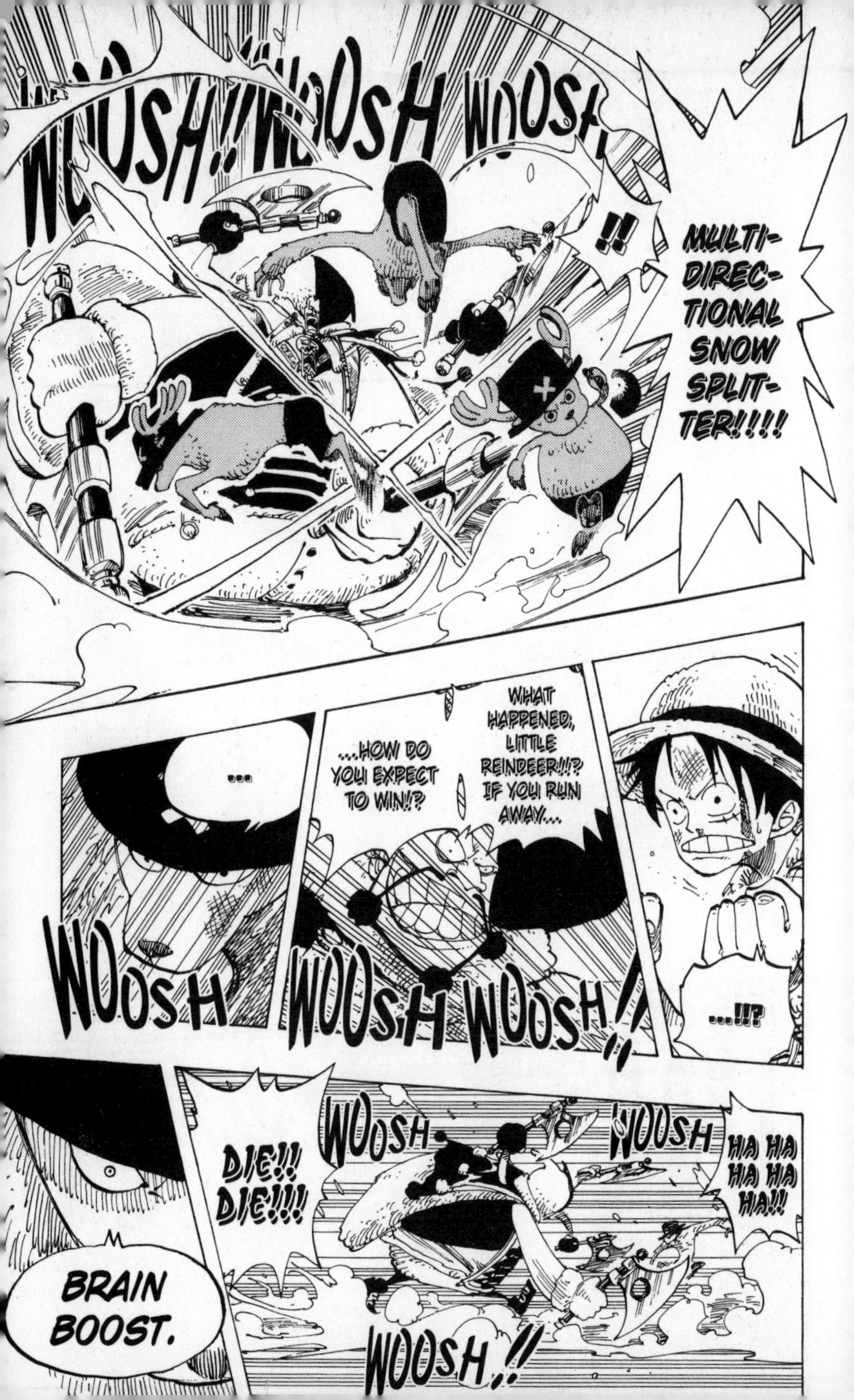

MULTI-DIRECTIONAL SNOW SPLITTER!!!!
!!
WOOSH!! WOOSH WOOSH
...!!?
WHAT HAPPENED, LITTLE REINDEER!!? IF YOU RUN AWAY...
...HOW DO YOU EXPECT TO WIN!?
WOOSH WOOSH!!
...
WOOSH
HA HA HA HA HA!!
WOOSH
DIE!! DIE!!!
WOOSH
WOOSH!!
BRAIN BOOST.

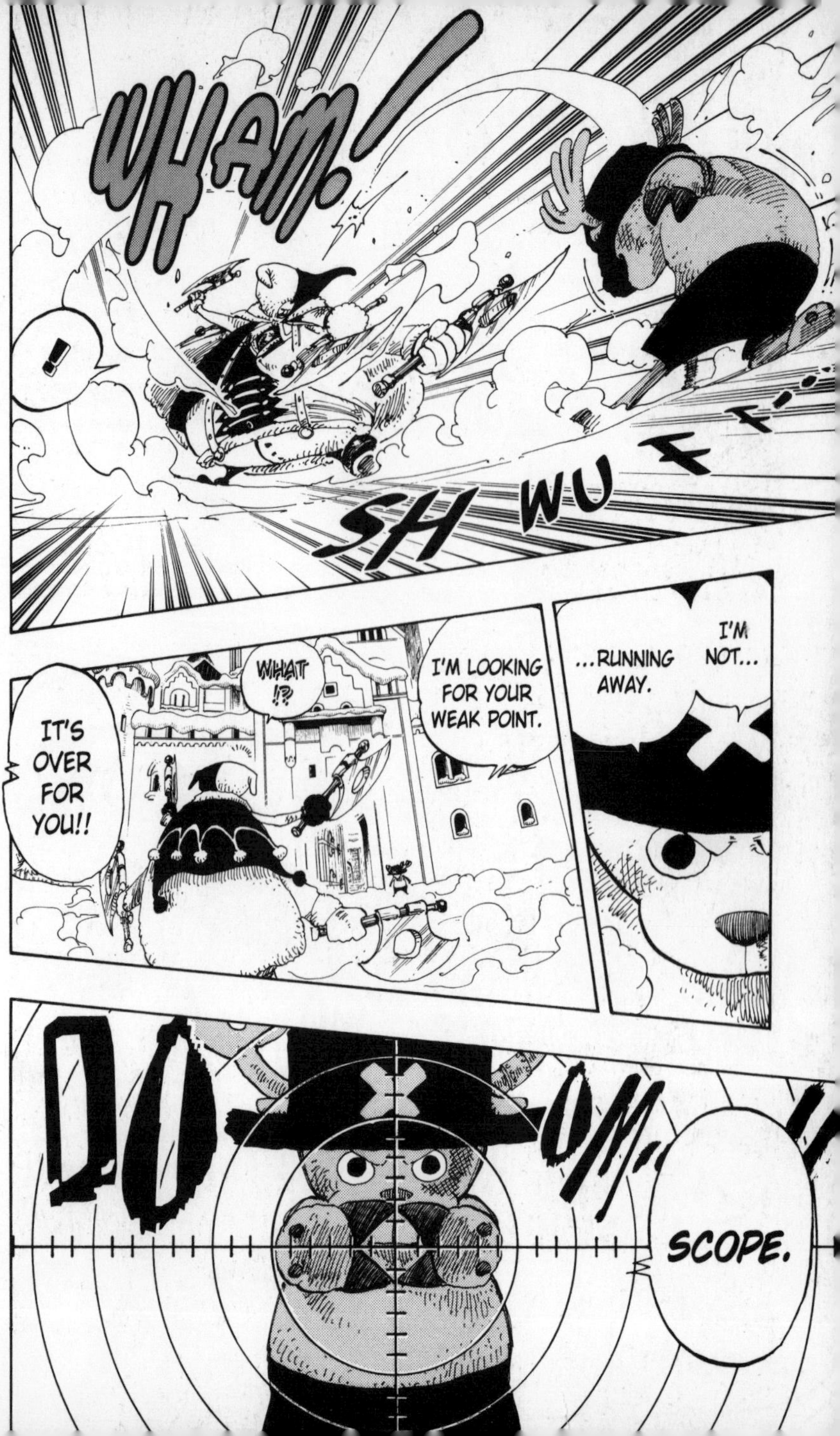
WHAM!
!
SHWUFF...
I'M NOT...
...RUNNING AWAY.
I'M LOOKING FOR YOUR WEAK POINT.
WHAT!?
IT'S OVER FOR YOU!!
DOOM..!!
SCOPE.

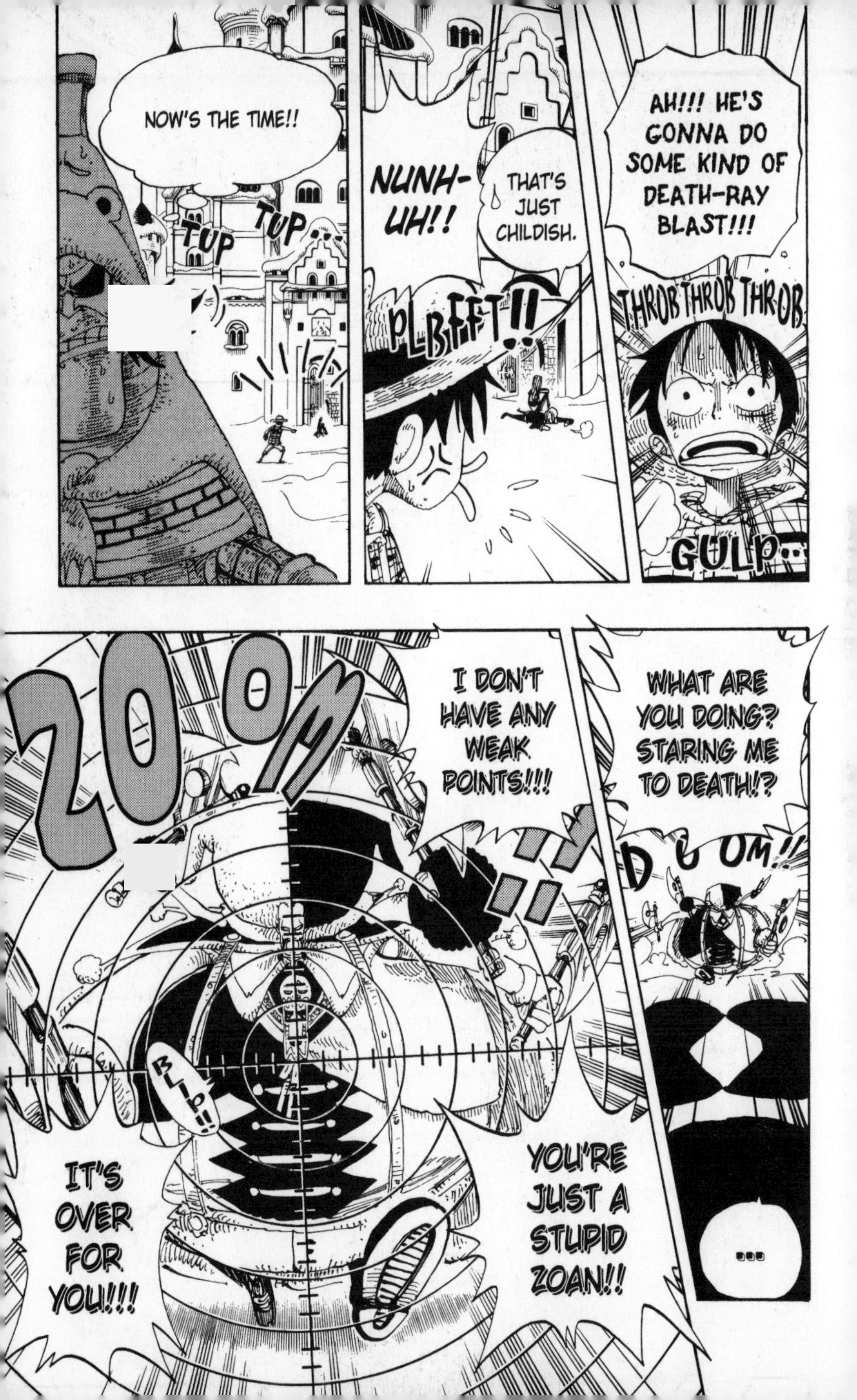
AH!!! HE'S GONNA DO SOME KIND OF DEATH-RAY BLAST!!!
THROB THROB THROB
GULP...
NUNH-UH!!
THAT'S JUST CHILDISH.
PLBFFT!!
NOW'S THE TIME!!
TUP
TUP
WHAT ARE YOU DOING? STARING ME TO DEATH!?
DOOM!!
...
ZOOM
I DON'T HAVE ANY WEAK POINTS!!!
YOU'RE JUST A STUPID ZOAN!!
BLIP!!
IT'S OVER FOR YOU!!!

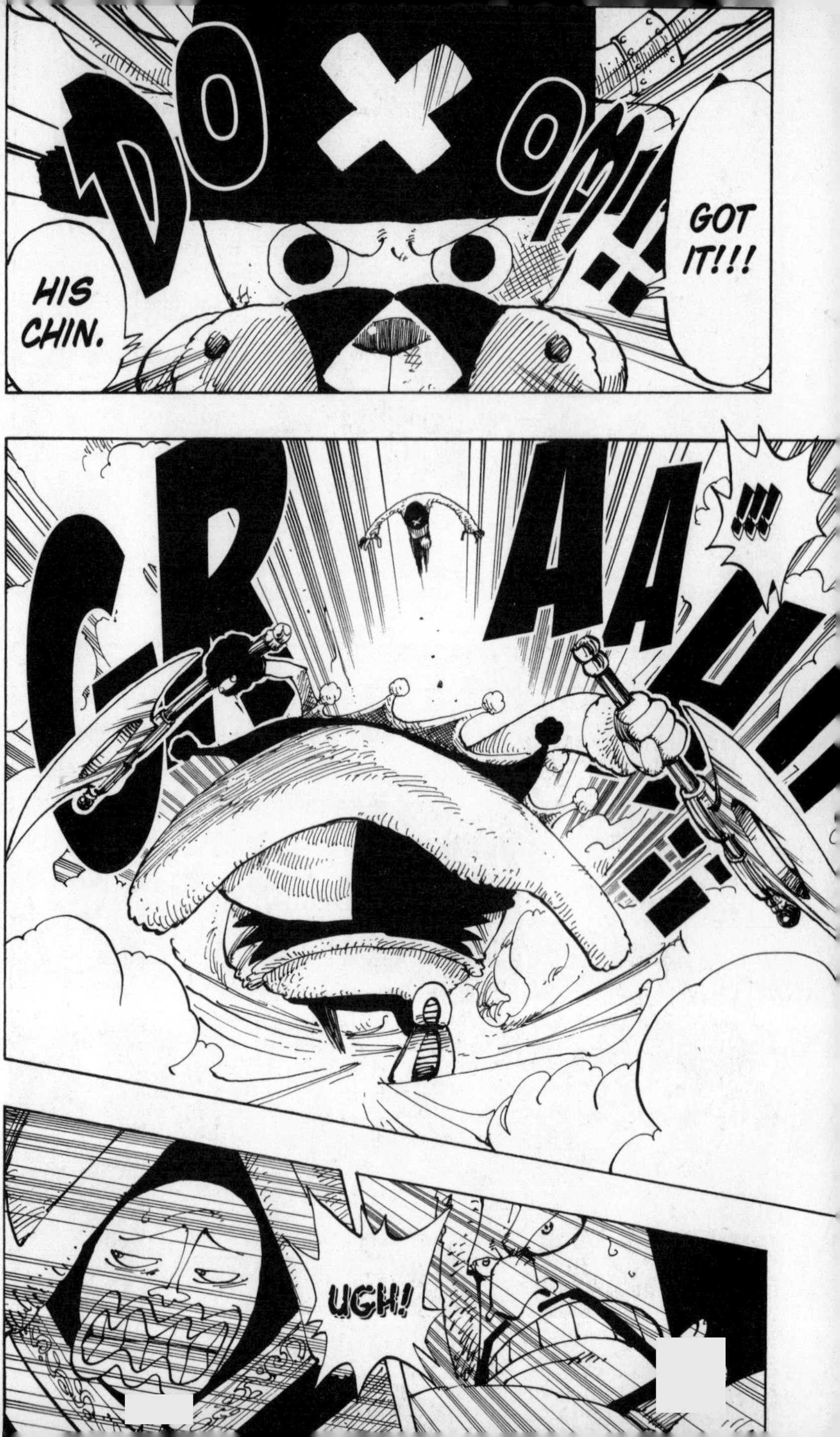
GOT IT!!!
DOOM!!
HIS CHIN.
CRAAK!!
UGH!

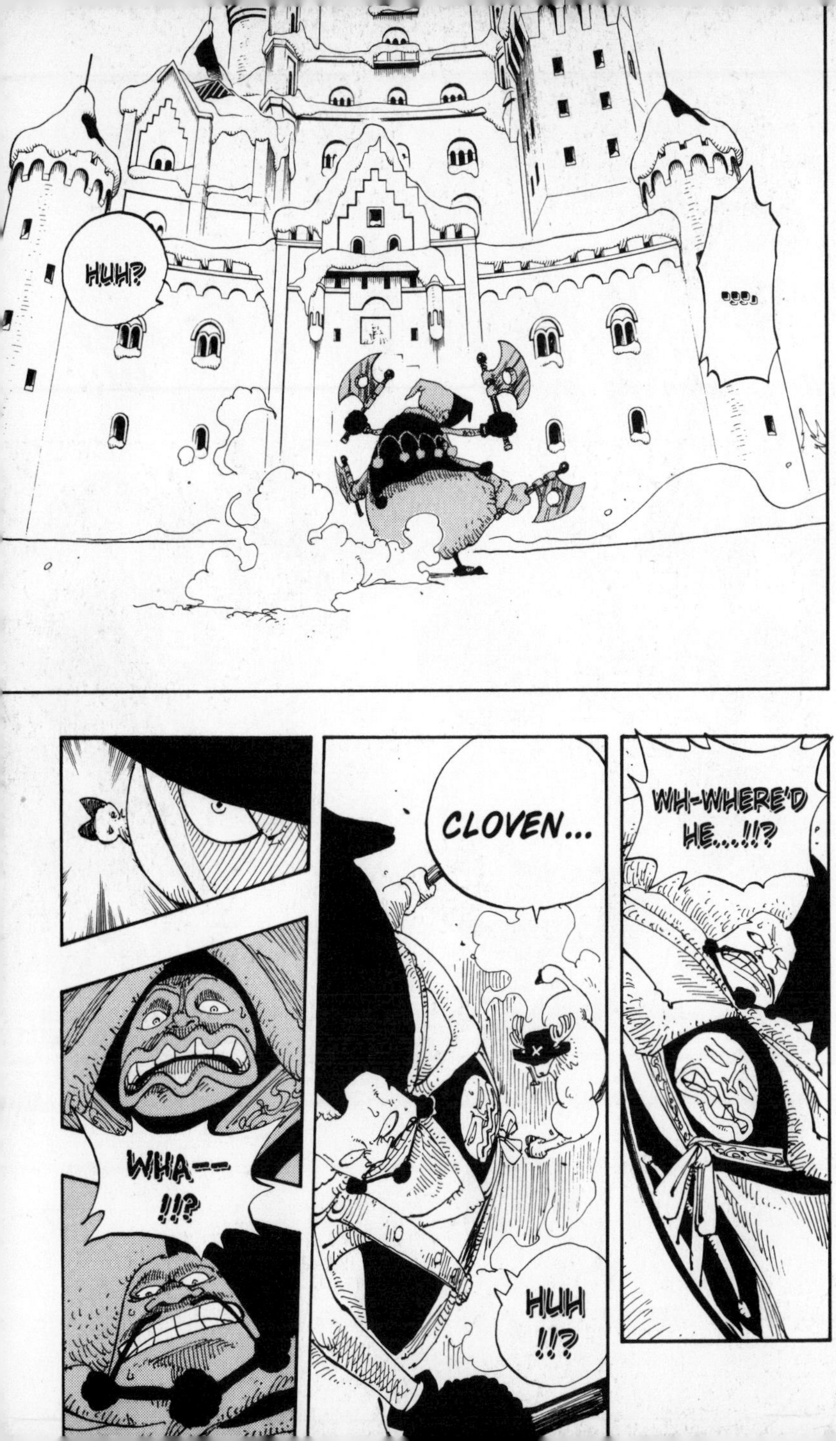
...,
HUH?
WH-WHERE'D HE...!!?
CLOVEN...
HUH !!?
WHA--- !!?

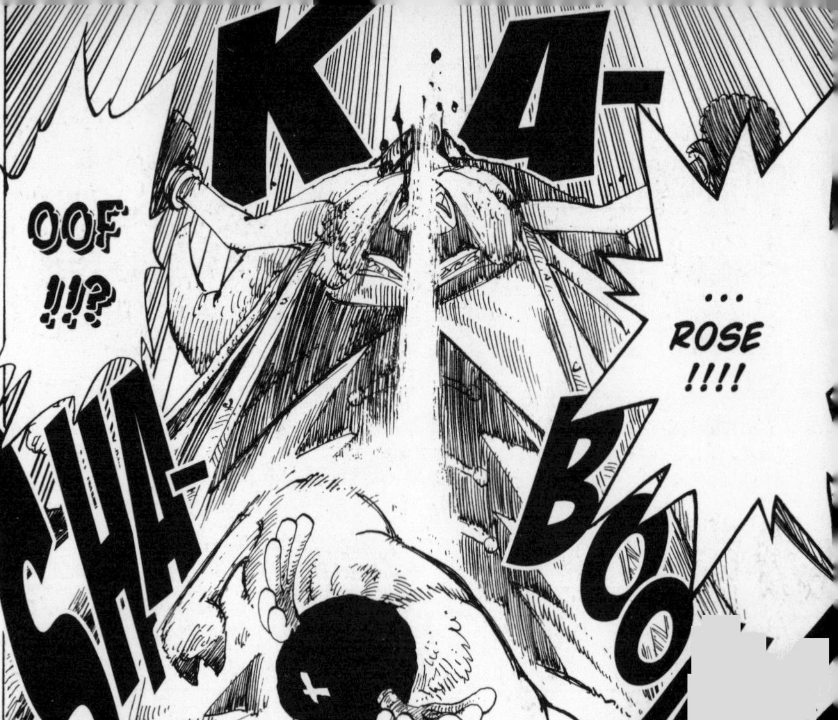
... ROSE !!!!
KA-
BOOM
OOF !!!?
SHA-
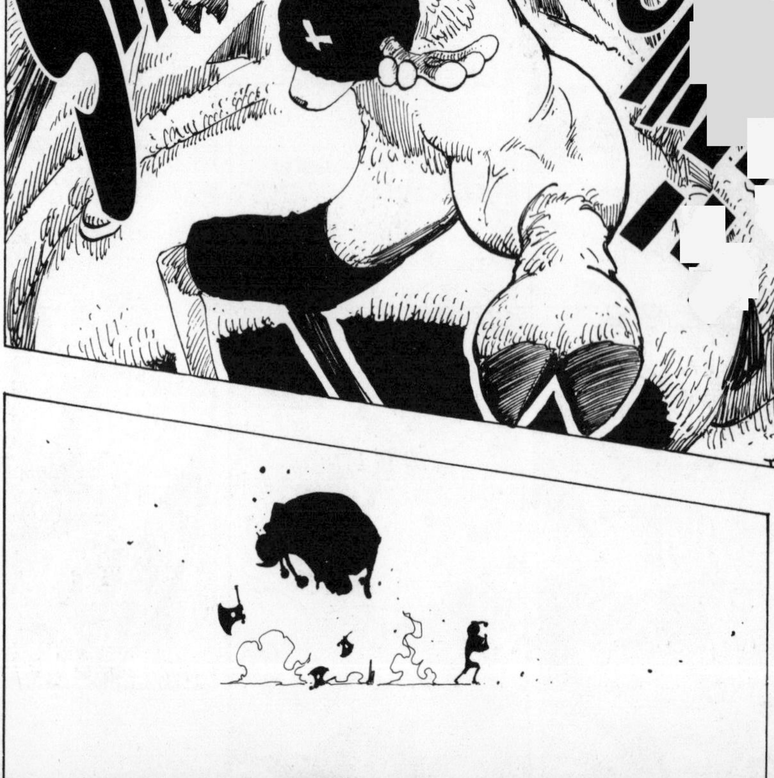

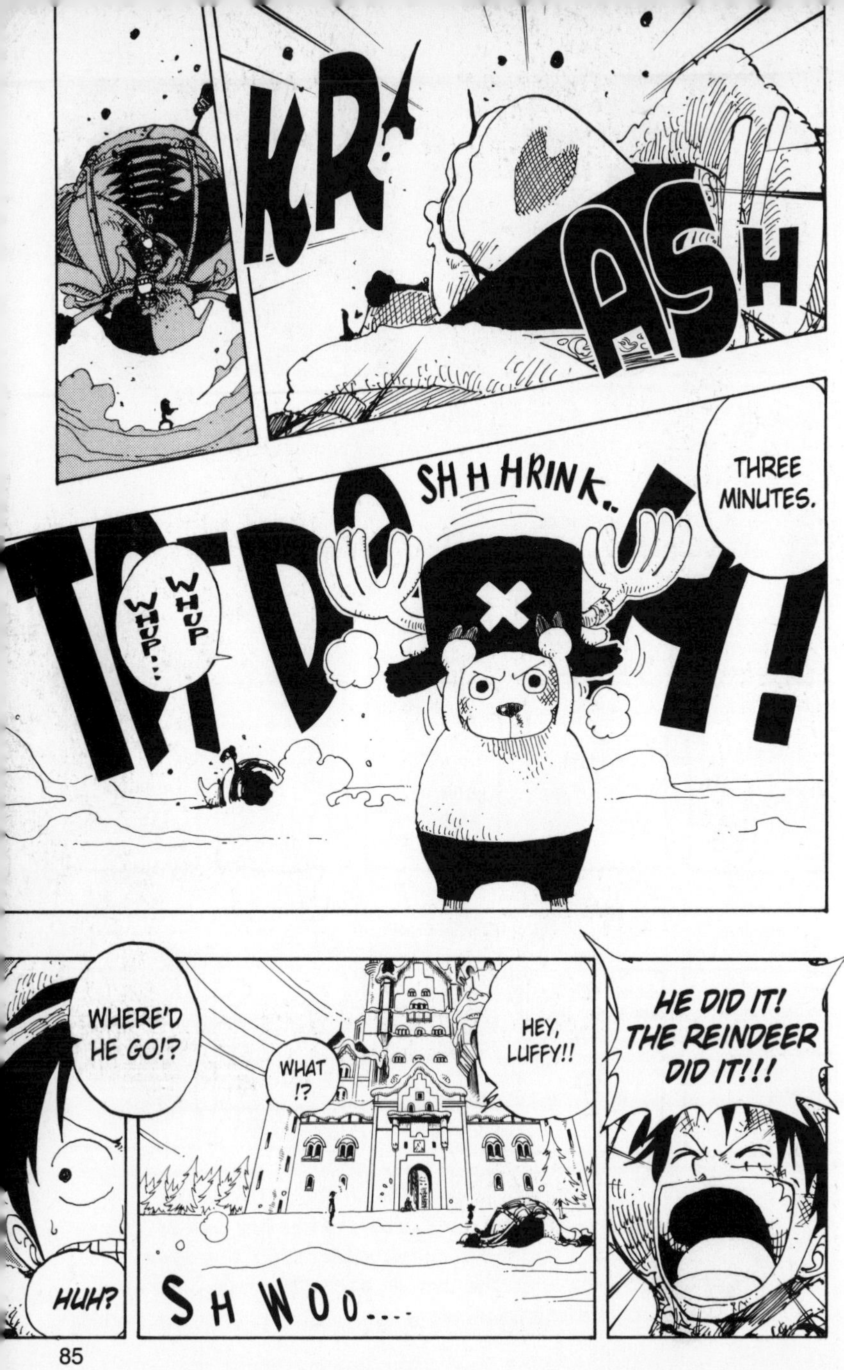
KRASH
THREE MINUTES.
SHHRINK..
WHUP WHUP...
HE DID IT! THE REINDEER DID IT!!!
HEY, LUFFY!!
WHAT !?
SHWOO....
WHERE'D HE GO!?
HUH?

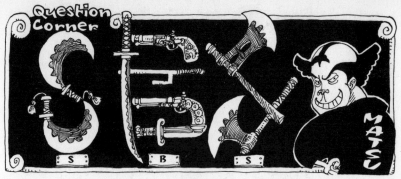

Question Corner
S
B
S
MATSU

**Reader:** What are the steps to producing a comic book? You hear the word "storyboarding" a lot, but can you tell me what this process is, and when it starts?

**Oda:** "Storyboarding," eh? Yes, we sometimes go through a big process like that. Let me explain how a graphic novel like this is produced.

**Step 1 Dazed, confused**
First, you're in a total daze.

**Step 2 Set-up meeting**
Next, you discuss your ideas with the *Jump* editor.

**Step 3 Brainstorm**
You think hard about the story.

**Step 4 Storyboarding**
On plain drawing paper, you draw the basic story.

**Step 5 Submit Storyboard**
You submit your storyboard via fax to the editor, and make any necessary revisions.

**Step 6 Fleshing out story**
My assistants come to my house and raise hell for two or three days, adding drawings to the storyboard.

**Step 7 *Jump* hits the stands**
*Jump* is sold throughout the land.

**Step 8 Set-up meeting**
Next, we discuss colors and other details with techie Mr. Y who is in charge of comics.

**Step 9 Creating bonus sections**
We add more illustrations and work on bonuses like the Question Corner.

**Step 10 The comic hits the stands**
Actually, the comic is ready about one month before it's released.

**Oda:** This is the process in a nutshell. This is my usual routine, anyway, but every author has his or her own. So the word "storyboarding" refers to the steps prior to adding all the details and drawings, when we sketch out the rough manga.

# Chapter 150: ROYAL DRUM CROWN 7-SHOT TIN TYRANT CANNON

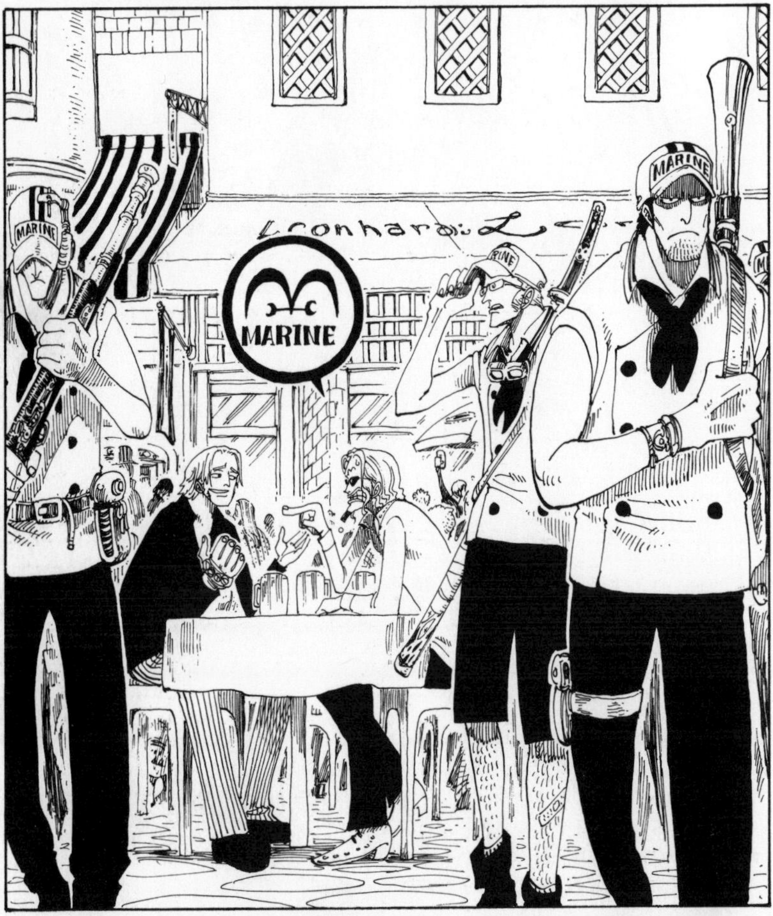
MARINE
MARINE
MARINE

DJANGO'S DANCE HEAVEN, VOL. 19: "FIND DJANGO!!"

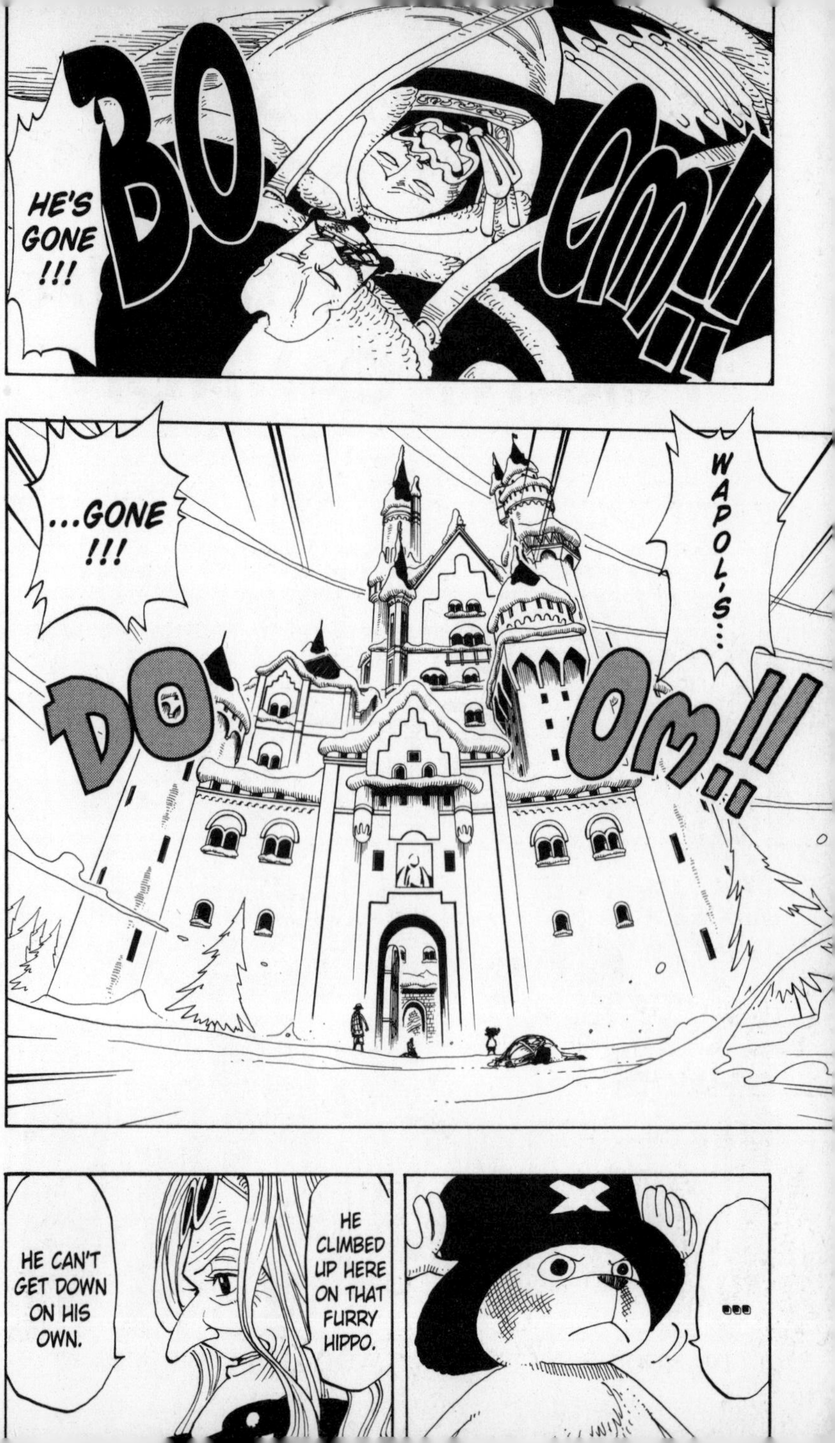
BO-OM!!!!
HE'S GONE !!!
WAPOL'S...
...GONE !!!
DO-OM!!
...
HE CLIMBED UP HERE ON THAT FURRY HIPPO.
HE CAN'T GET DOWN ON HIS OWN.

READ THIS WAY

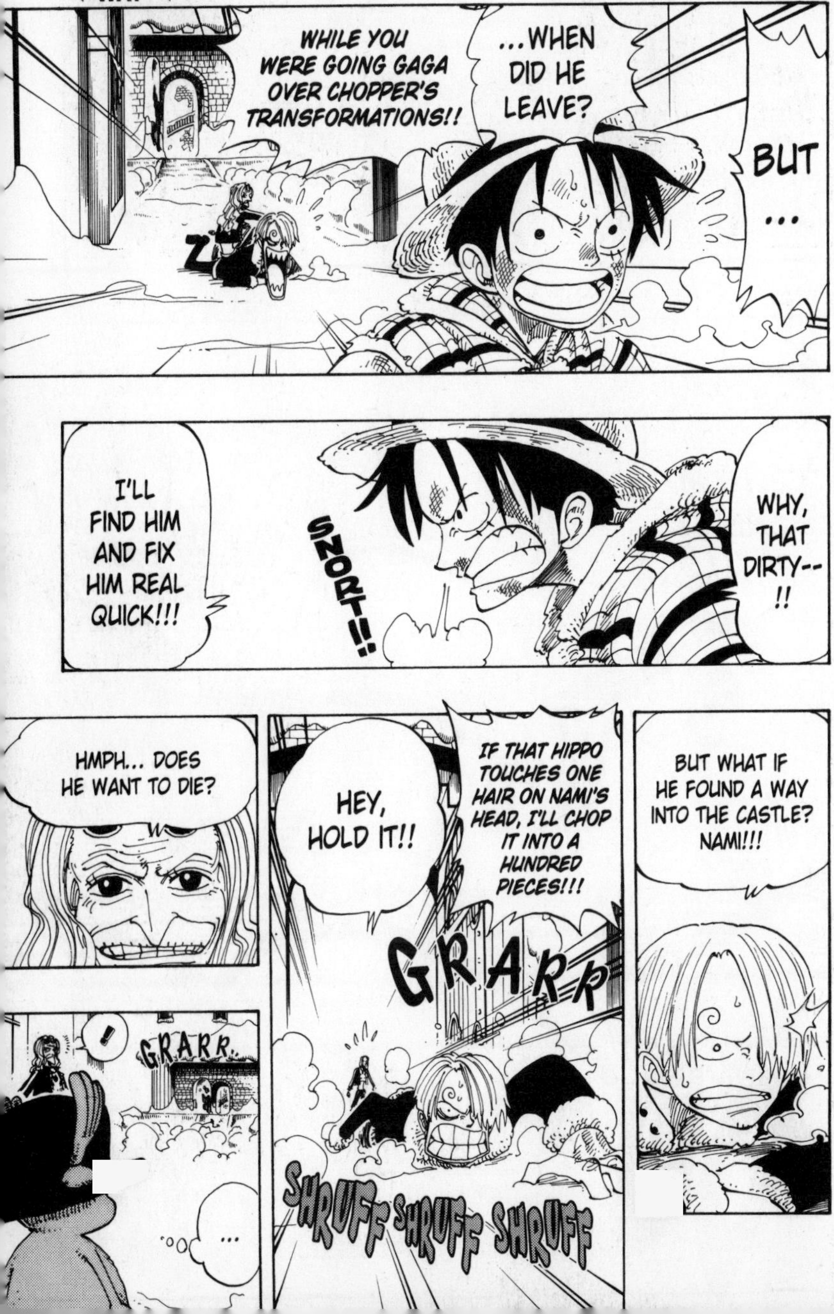
BUT ...
...WHEN DID HE LEAVE?
WHILE YOU WERE GOING GAGA OVER CHOPPER'S TRANSFORMATIONS!!
WHY, THAT DIRTY-- !!
SNORT!!
I'LL FIND HIM AND FIX HIM REAL QUICK!!!
BUT WHAT IF HE FOUND A WAY INTO THE CASTLE? NAMI!!!
IF THAT HIPPO TOUCHES ONE HAIR ON NAMI'S HEAD, I'LL CHOP IT INTO A HUNDRED PIECES!!!
HEY, HOLD IT!!
GRARR
SHRUFF SHRUFF SHRUFF
HMPH... DOES HE WANT TO DIE?
!
GRARR..
...

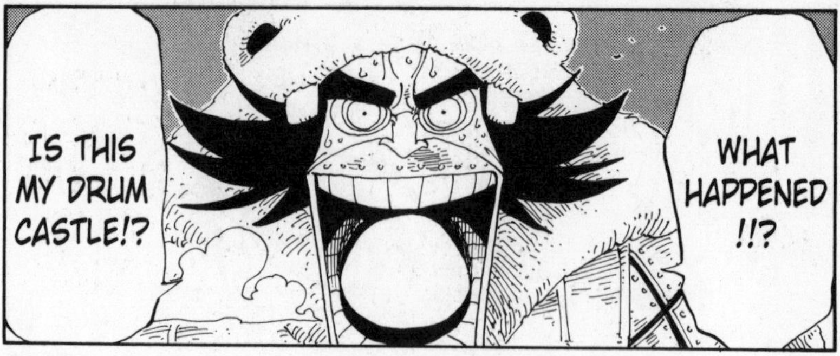
WHAT HAPPENED!!?
IS THIS MY DRUM CASTLE!?
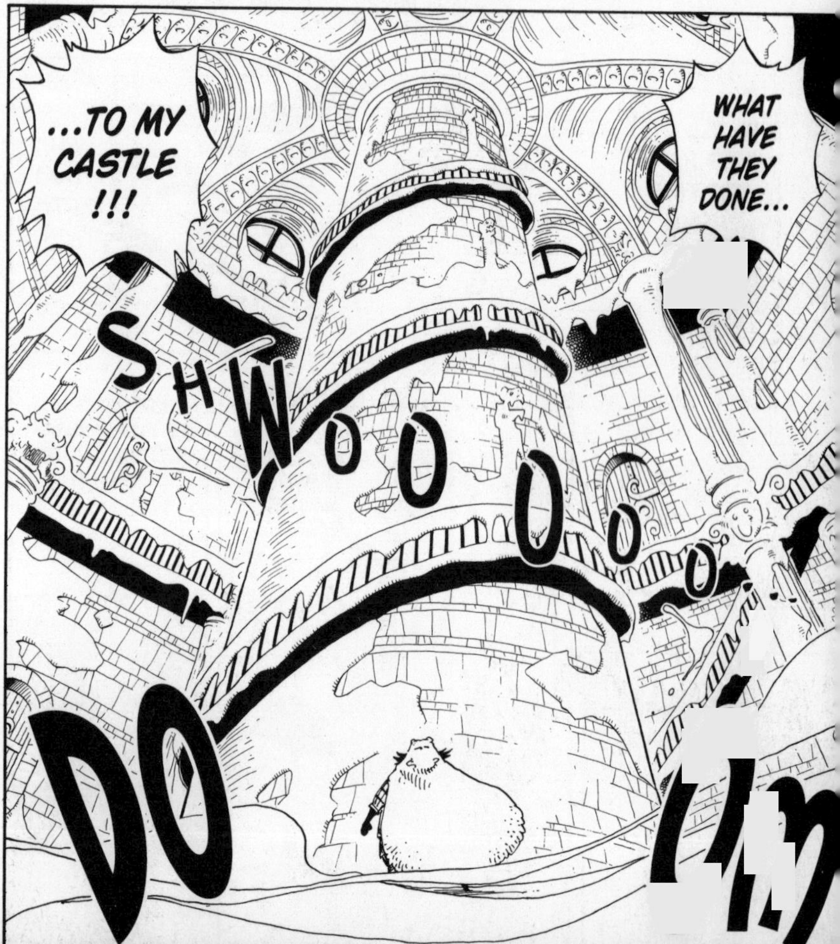
WHAT HAVE THEY DONE...
...TO MY CASTLE!!!
SHWOOOOOO
DO

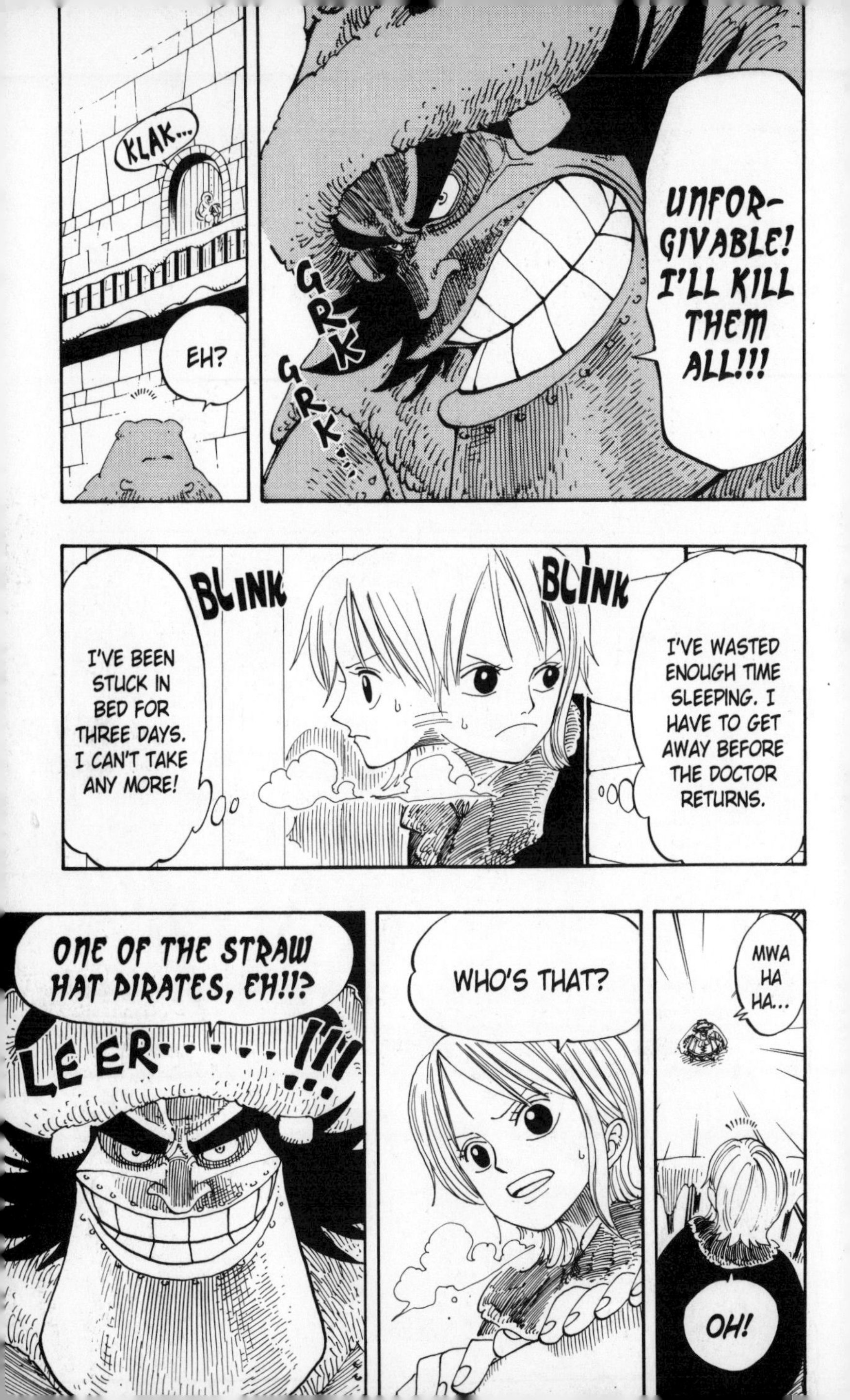
UNFOR-GIVABLE! I'LL KILL THEM ALL!!!
GRK GRK...
KLAK...
EH?
BLINK
I'VE WASTED ENOUGH TIME SLEEPING. I HAVE TO GET AWAY BEFORE THE DOCTOR RETURNS.
BLINK
I'VE BEEN STUCK IN BED FOR THREE DAYS. I CAN'T TAKE ANY MORE!
MWA HA HA...
OH!
WHO'S THAT?
ONE OF THE STRAW HAT PIRATES, EH!!?
LEER.....!!!

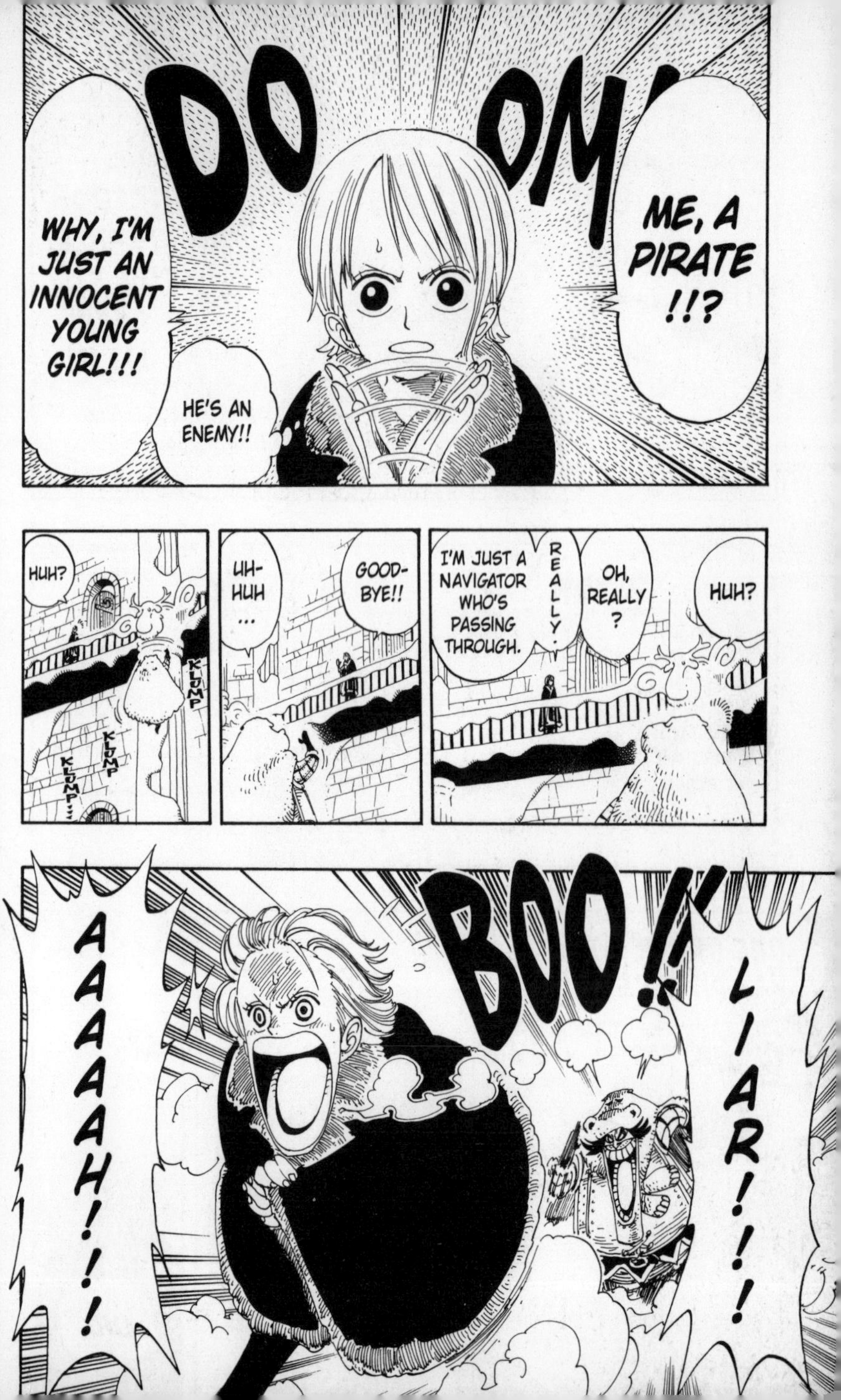
DO OM
ME, A PIRATE !!?
WHY, I'M JUST AN INNOCENT YOUNG GIRL!!!
HE'S AN ENEMY!!
HUH?
OH, REALLY?
REALLY.
I'M JUST A NAVIGATOR WHO'S PASSING THROUGH.
GOOD-BYE!!
UH-HUH ...
HUH?
KLUMP
KLUMP
KLUMP...
LIAR!!!
BOO K!!
AAAAAH!!!!

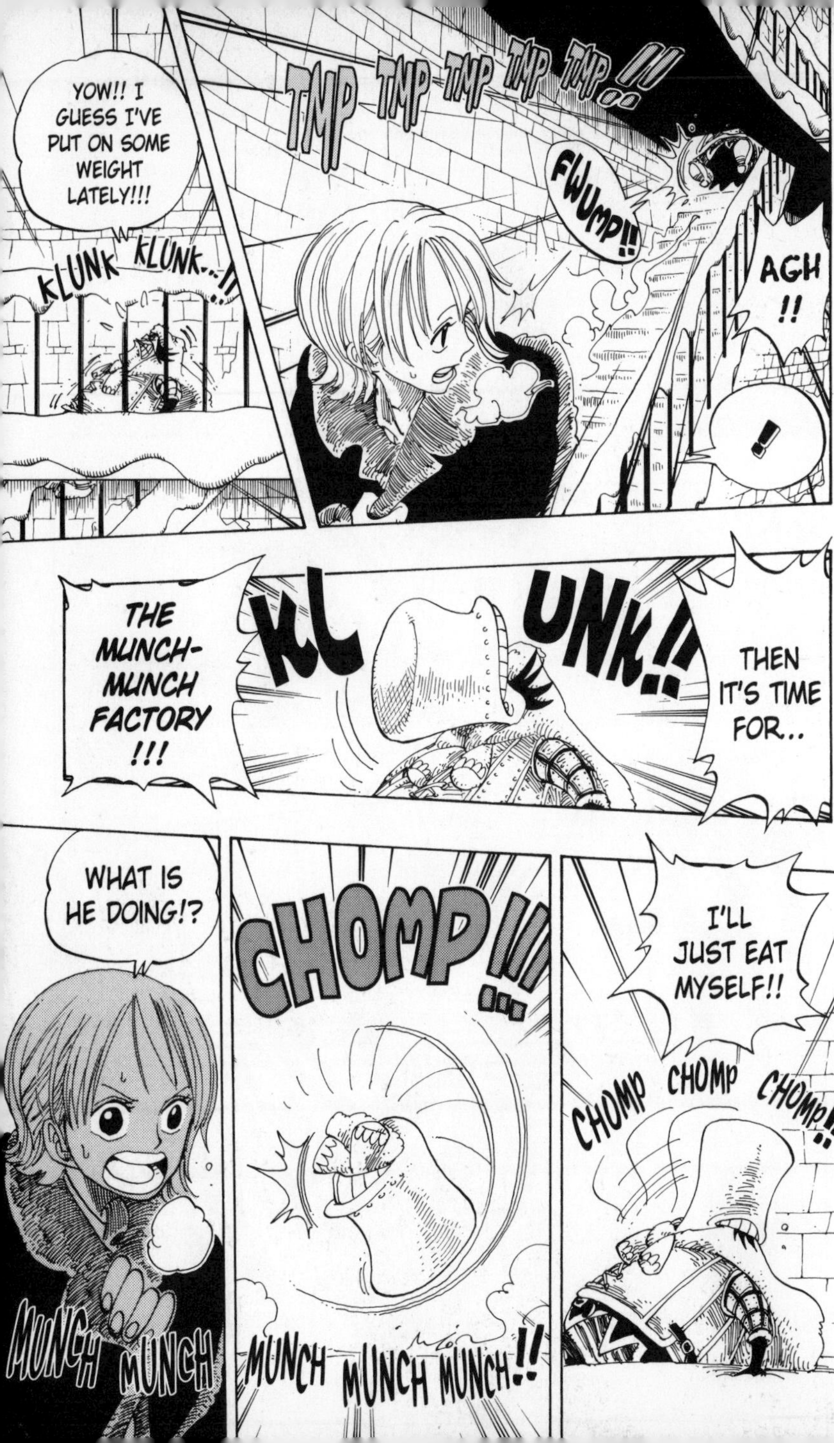
TMP TMP TMP TMP TMP..!!
FWUMP!!
AGH!!
!
YOW!! I GUESS I'VE PUT ON SOME WEIGHT LATELY!!!
KLUNK KLUNK...!!
THEN IT'S TIME FOR..
KLUNK..!!
THE MUNCH-MUNCH FACTORY!!!
I'LL JUST EAT MYSELF!!
CHOMP CHOMP CHOMP!!
CHOMP!!!...
MUNCH MUNCH MUNCH!!
WHAT IS HE DOING!?
MUNCH MUNCH

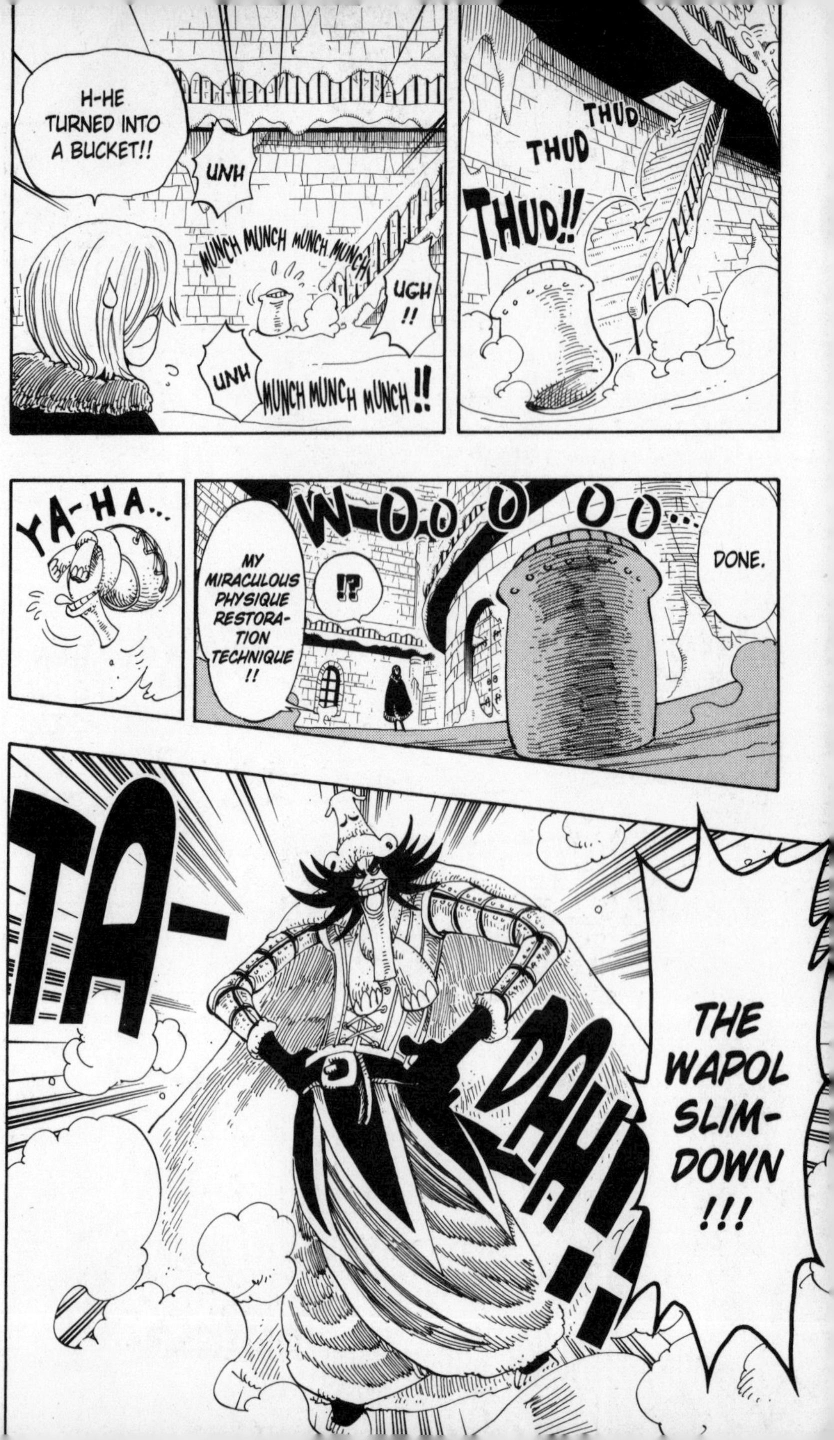
THUD
THUD
THUD!!
H-HE TURNED INTO A BUCKET!!
UNH
MUNCH MUNCH MUNCH MUNCH
UGH!!
UNH
MUNCH MUNCH MUNCH!!
W-O-O-U-O-O...
DONE.
!?
MY MIRACULOUS PHYSIQUE RESTORATION TECHNIQUE!!
YA-HA...
THE WAPOL SLIM-DOWN!!!
TA-DAH!!

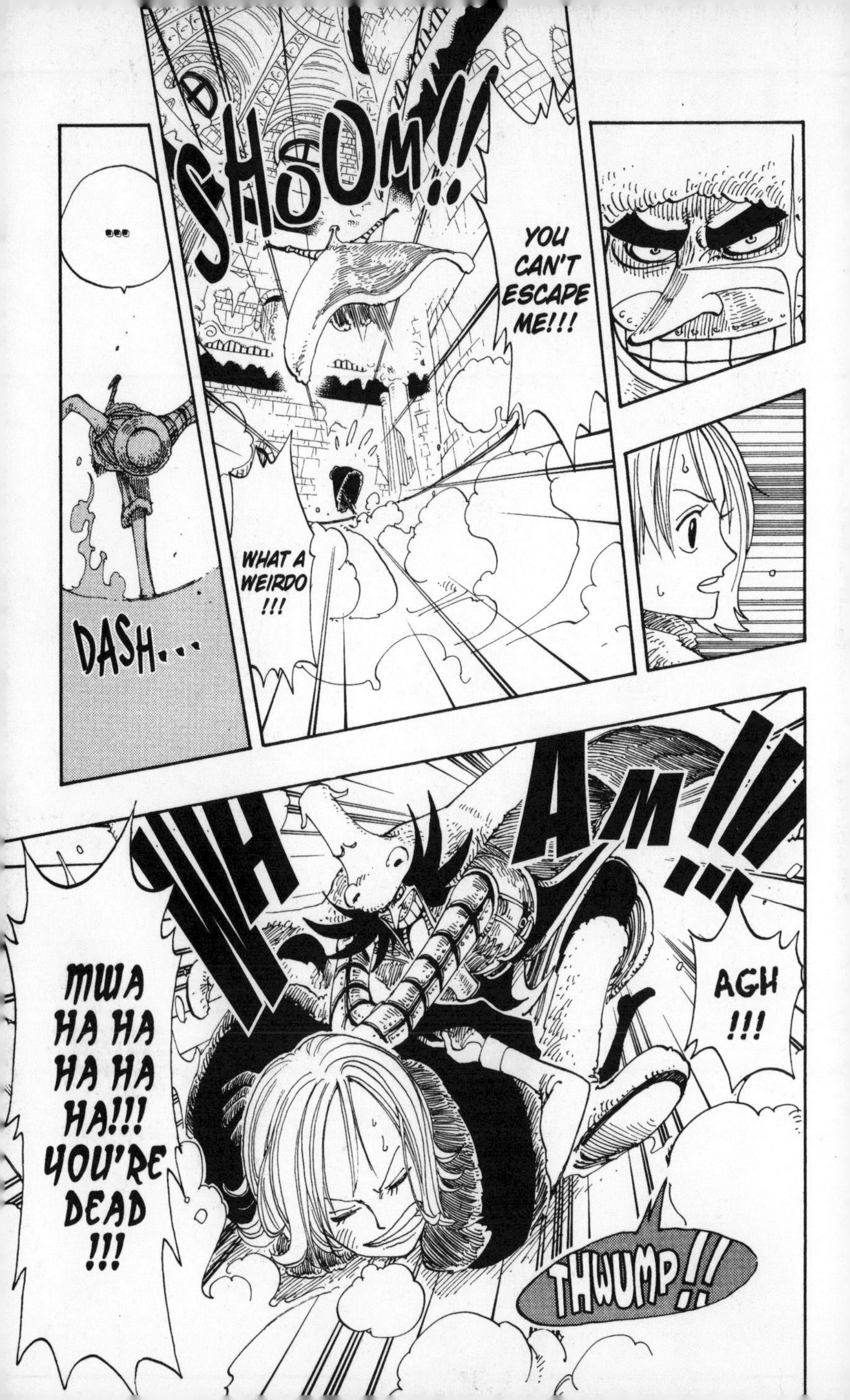
SHOOM!!
YOU CAN'T ESCAPE ME!!!
WHAT A WEIRDO!!!
...
DASH...
WHAM!!
AGH!!!
MWA HA HA HA HA HA HA!!! YOU'RE DEAD!!!
THWUMP!!

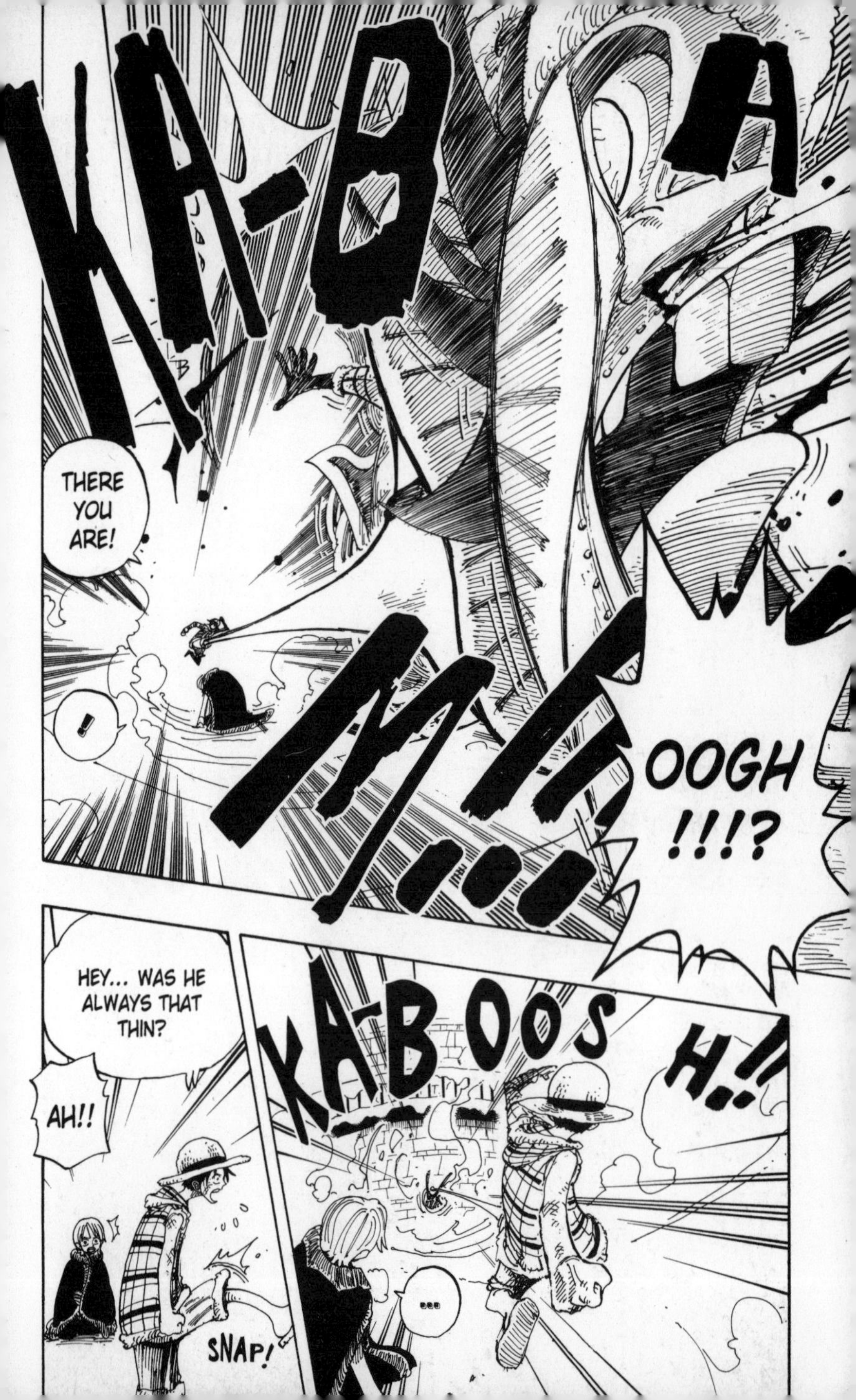
KA-BA
OOGH!!!?
THERE YOU ARE!
!
KA-BOOSH!!
...
HEY... WAS HE ALWAYS THAT THIN?
AH!!
SNAP!

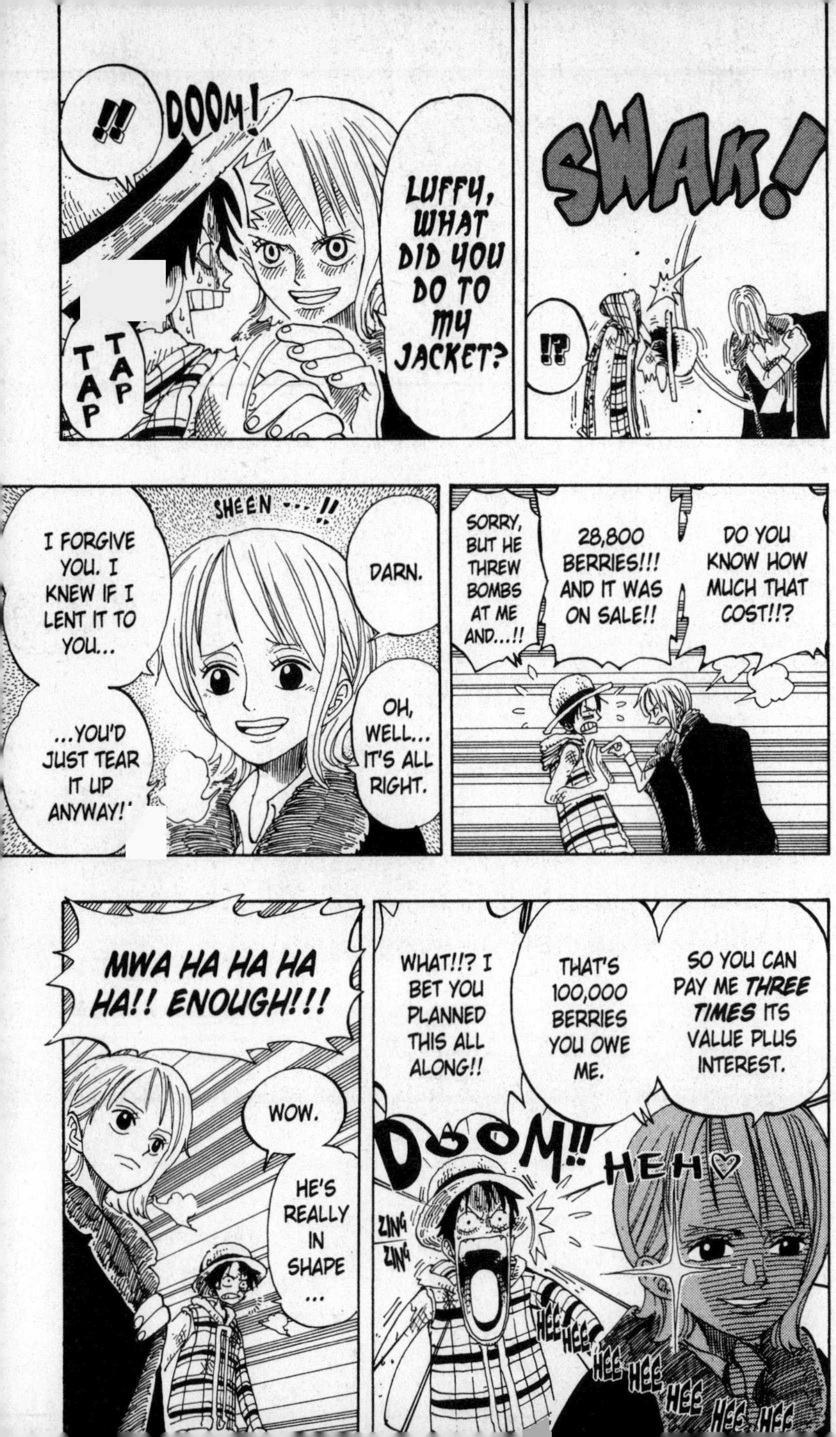
SHAK!
!?
LUFFY, WHAT DID YOU DO TO MY JACKET?
!!
DOOM!
TAP TAP
DO YOU KNOW HOW MUCH THAT COST!!?
28,800 BERRIES!!! AND IT WAS ON SALE!!
SORRY, BUT HE THREW BOMBS AT ME AND...!!
SHEEN...!!
DARN.
OH, WELL... IT'S ALL RIGHT.
I FORGIVE YOU. I KNEW IF I LENT IT TO YOU...
...YOU'D JUST TEAR IT UP ANYWAY!!
SO YOU CAN PAY ME THREE TIMES ITS VALUE PLUS INTEREST.
THAT'S 100,000 BERRIES YOU OWE ME.
WHAT!!? I BET YOU PLANNED THIS ALL ALONG!!
DOOM!!
HEH♡
ZING ZING
HEE HEE HEE HEE HEE HEE HEE
MWA HA HA HA HA!! ENOUGH!!!
WOW.
HE'S REALLY IN SHAPE ...

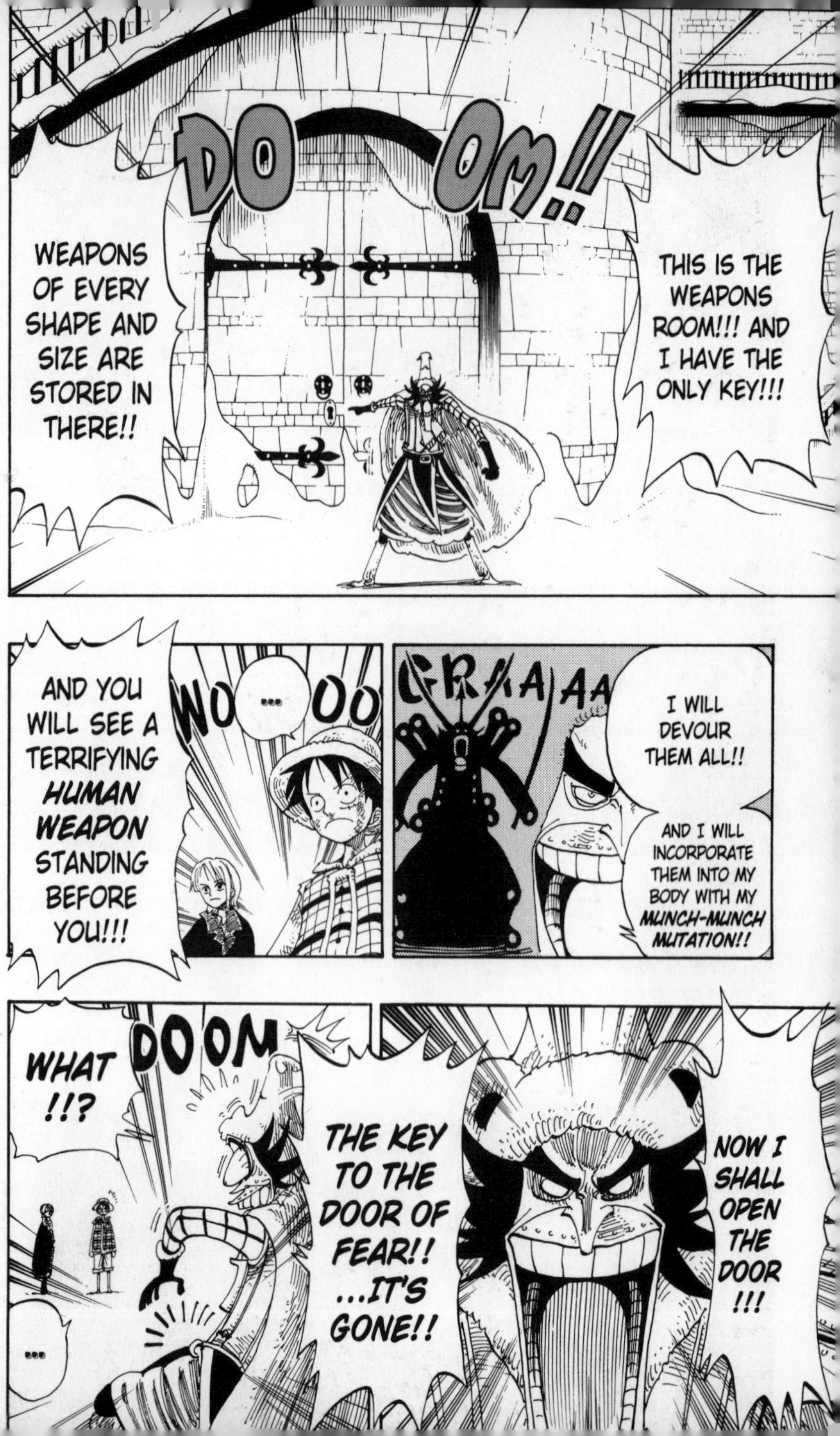
DO—OM!!
THIS IS THE WEAPONS ROOM!!! AND I HAVE THE ONLY KEY!!!
WEAPONS OF EVERY SHAPE AND SIZE ARE STORED IN THERE!!
GRAAAA
I WILL DEVOUR THEM ALL!!
AND I WILL INCORPORATE THEM INTO MY BODY WITH MY *MUNCH-MUNCH MUTATION!!*
WOOO
...
AND YOU WILL SEE A TERRIFYING *HUMAN WEAPON* STANDING BEFORE YOU!!!
NOW I SHALL OPEN THE DOOR!!!
THE KEY TO THE DOOR OF FEAR!! ...IT'S GONE!!
DOOM
WHAT!!?
...

READ THIS WAY

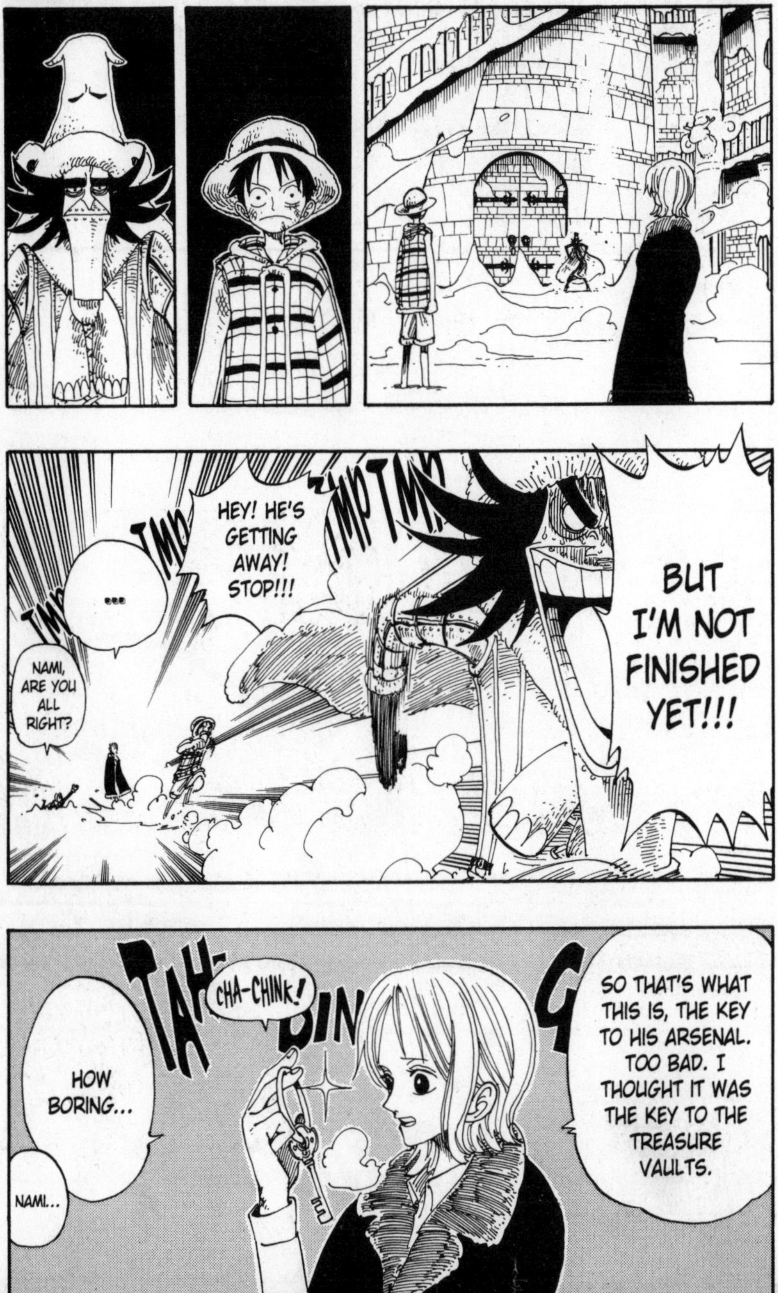
BUT I'M NOT FINISHED YET!!!
TMP TMP TMP
HEY! HE'S GETTING AWAY! STOP!!!
...
NAMI, ARE YOU ALL RIGHT?
SO THAT'S WHAT THIS IS, THE KEY TO HIS ARSENAL. TOO BAD. I THOUGHT IT WAS THE KEY TO THE TREASURE VAULTS.
TAH-BING
CHA-CHINK!
HOW BORING...
NAMI...

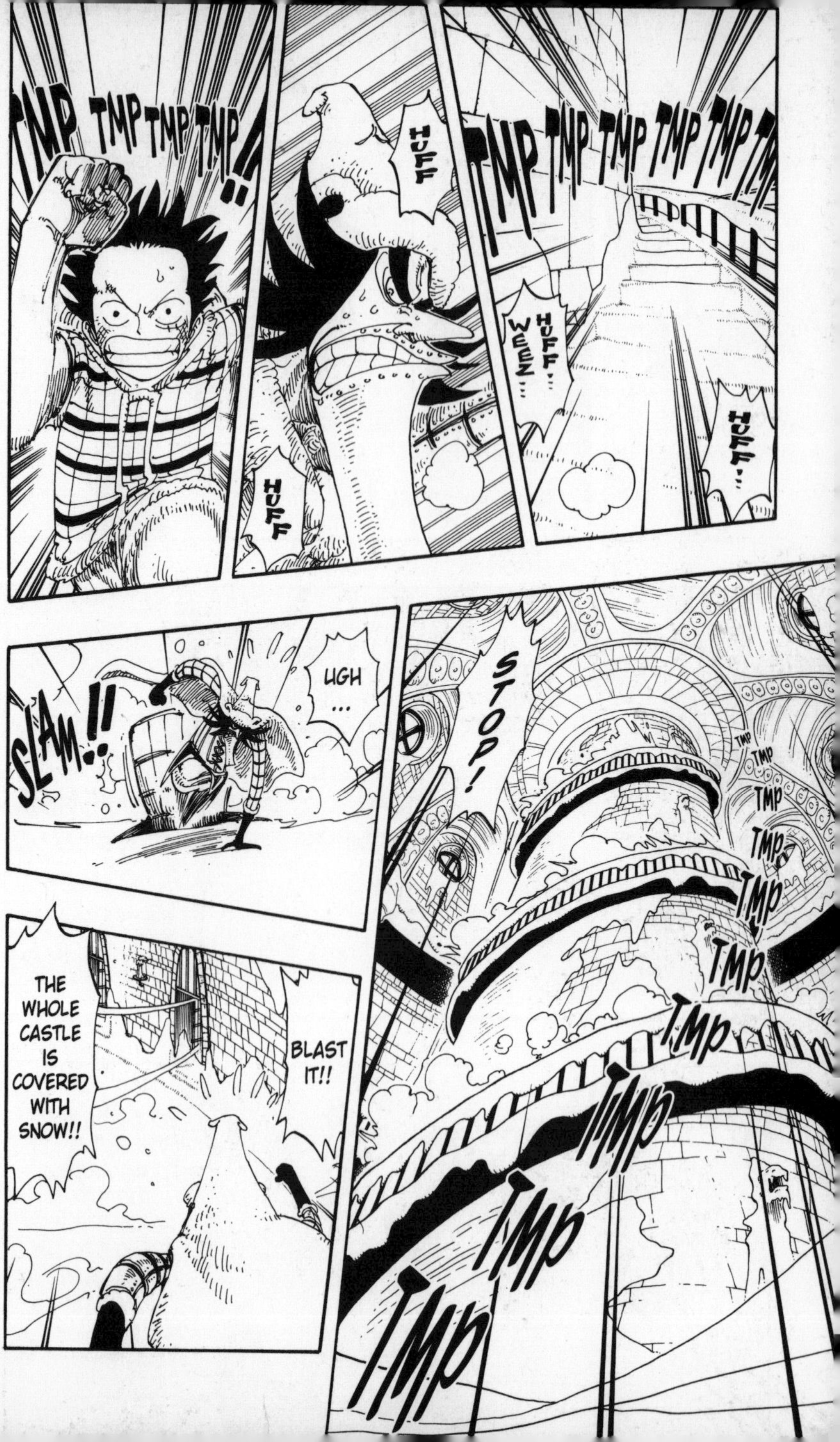
TMP TMP TMP TMP TMP TM
HUFF...
WEEZ...
HUFF...
HUFF
HUFF
TMP TMP TMP TMP!!
STOP!
TMP TMP TMP TMP TMP TMP TMP TMP TMP TMP
UGH ...
SLAM!!
BLAST IT!!
THE WHOLE CASTLE IS COVERED WITH SNOW!!

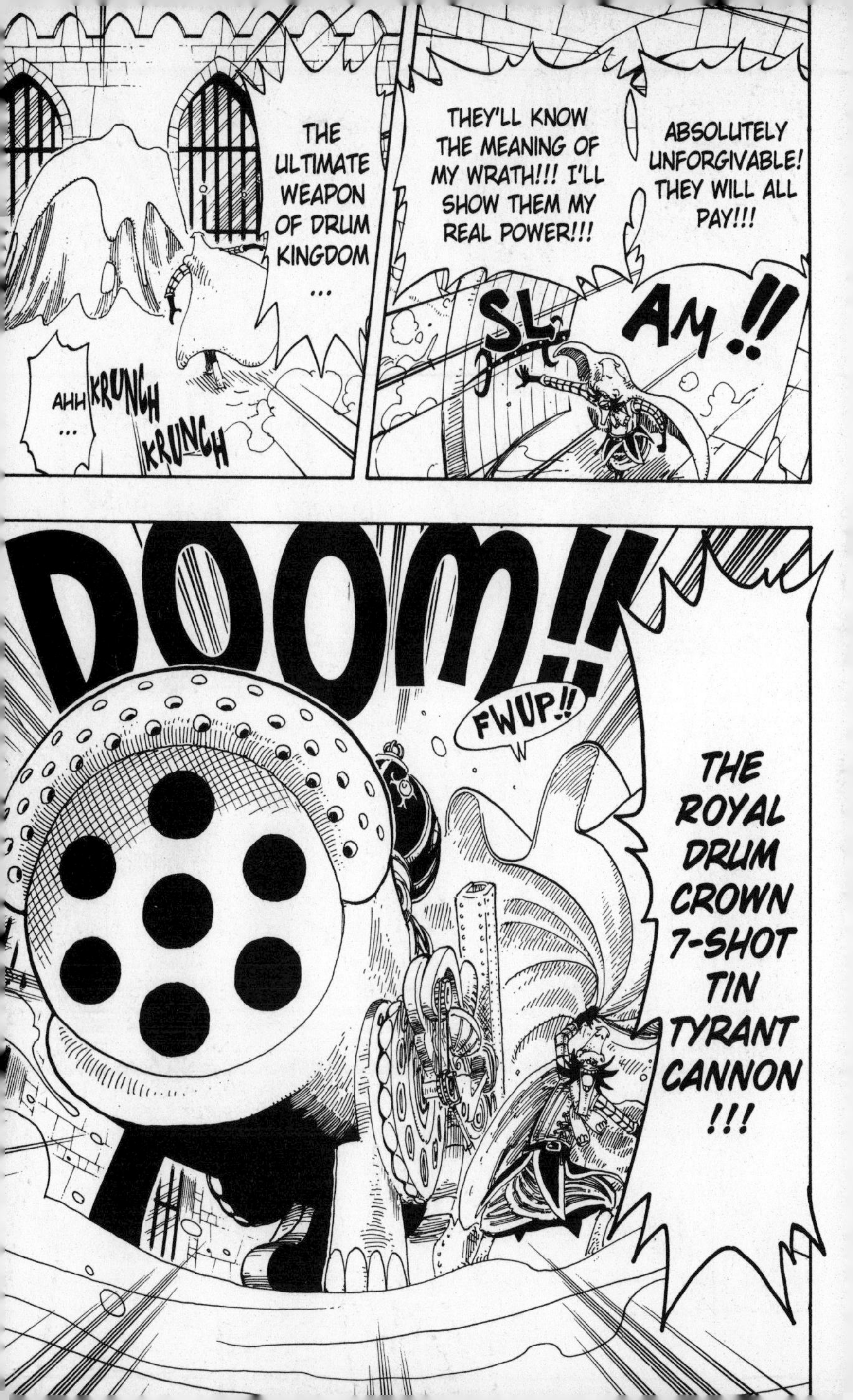
ABSOLUTELY UNFORGIVABLE! THEY WILL ALL PAY!!!
THEY'LL KNOW THE MEANING OF MY WRATH!!! I'LL SHOW THEM MY REAL POWER!!!
SLAM!!
THE ULTIMATE WEAPON OF DRUM KINGDOM ...
AHH ...
KRUNCH
KRUNCH
DOOM!!
FWUP!!
THE ROYAL DRUM CROWN 7-SHOT TIN TYRANT CANNON !!!

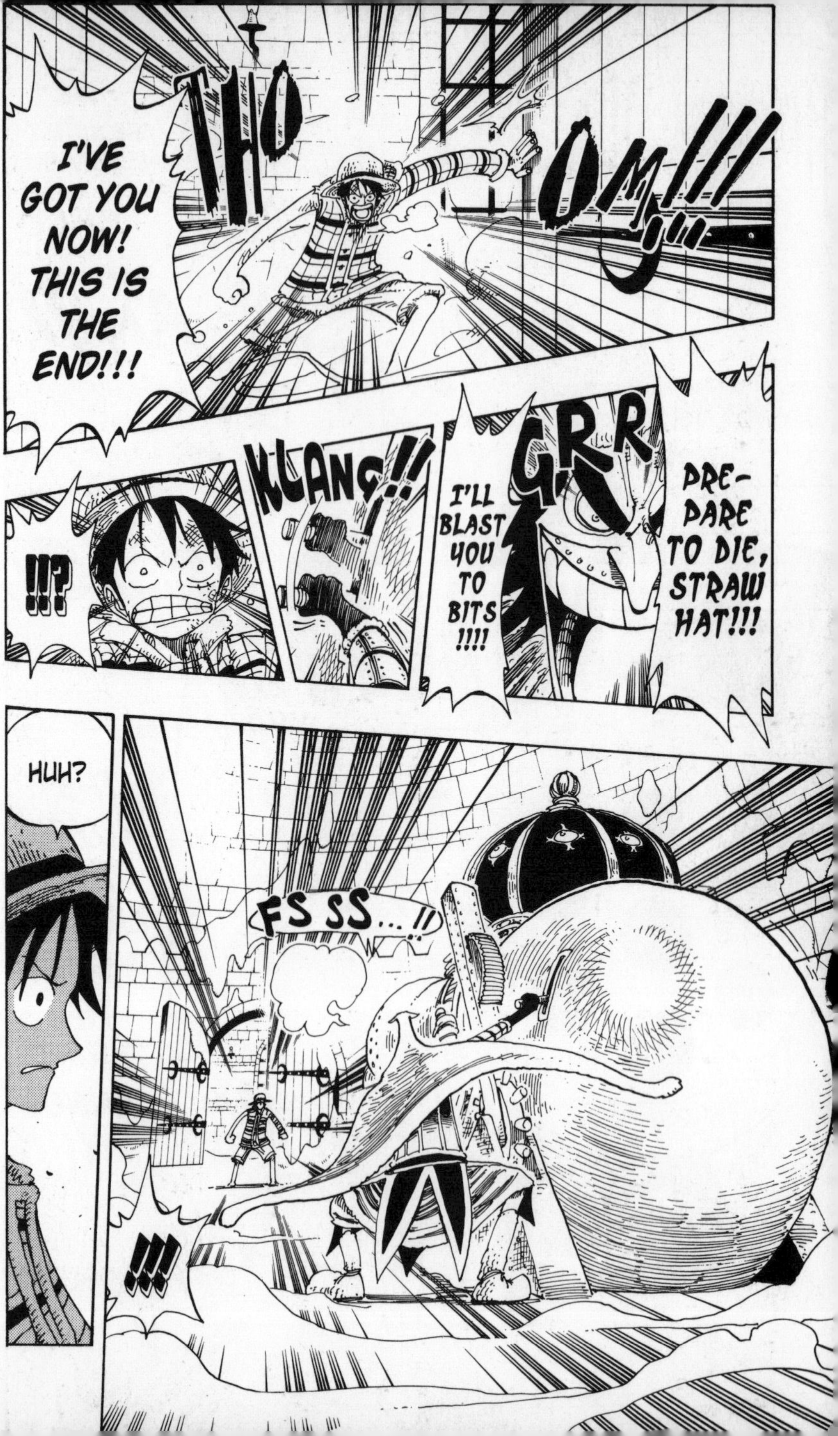
THOOM!!!
I'VE GOT YOU NOW! THIS IS THE END!!!
GRR
PRE-PARE TO DIE, STRAW HAT!!!
I'LL BLAST YOU TO BITS!!!!
KLANG!!
!!?
FS SS...!!
!!!
HUH?

...!?

...

FSS FSS

FSS

FSS

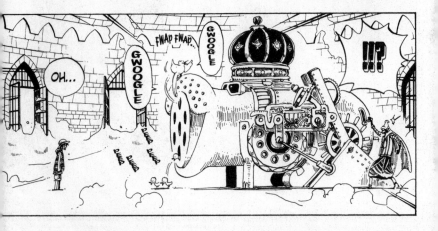

OH...

GWOOGLE

FWAP FWAP...

GWOOGLE

!!!?

SNOWBIRDS!

GWOOGLE!

GWOOGLE!

A NEST!?

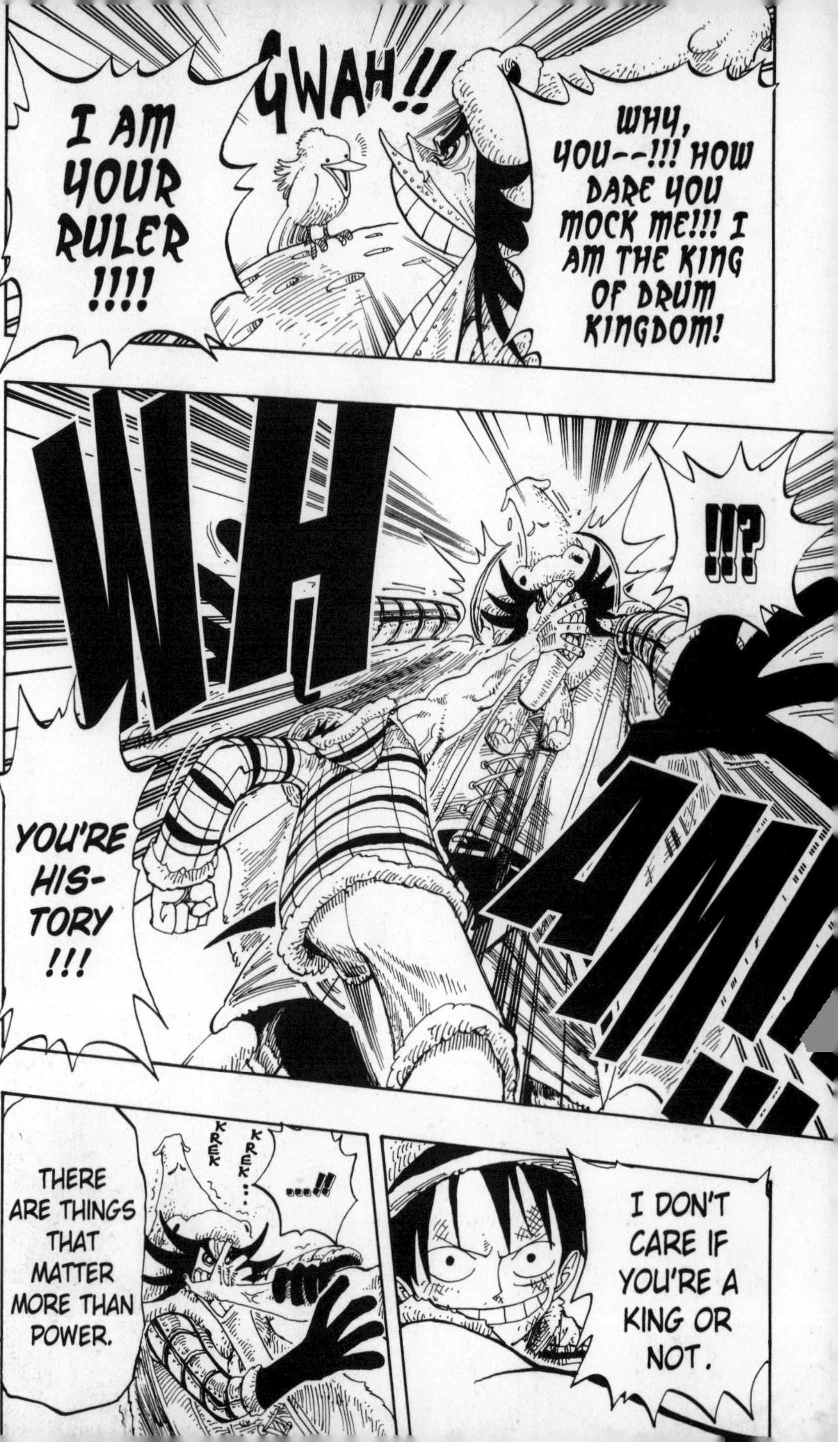
WHY, YOU--!!! HOW DARE YOU MOCK ME!!! I AM THE KING OF DRUM KINGDOM!
GWAH!!
I AM YOUR RULER !!!!
!!?
WHAM!!
YOU'RE HIS- TORY !!!
I DON'T CARE IF YOU'RE A KING OR NOT.
KREK KREK...
...!!
THERE ARE THINGS THAT MATTER MORE THAN POWER.

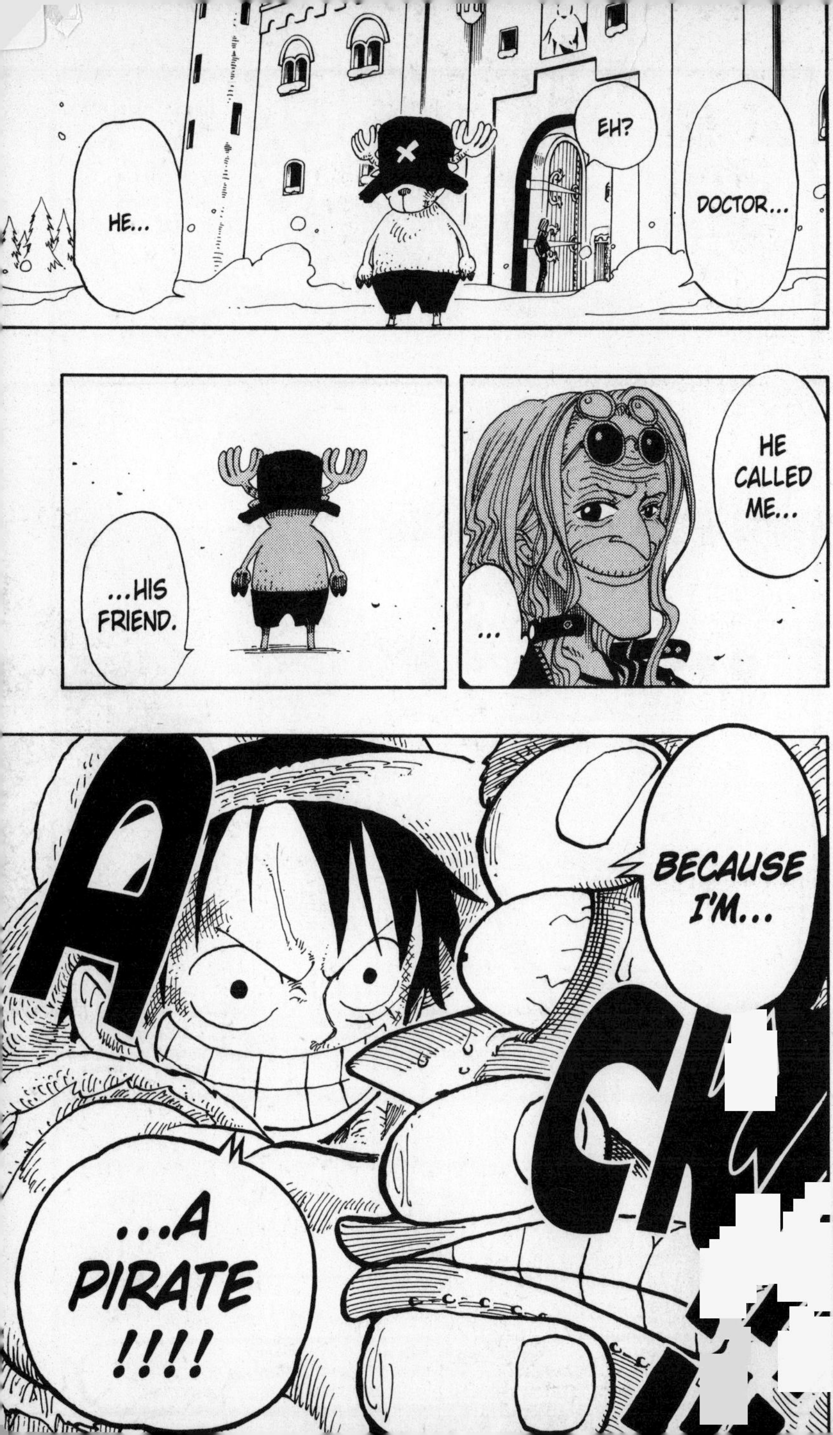
DOCTOR...
EH?
HE...
HE CALLED ME...
...
...HIS FRIEND.
BECAUSE I'M...
...A PIRATE !!!!

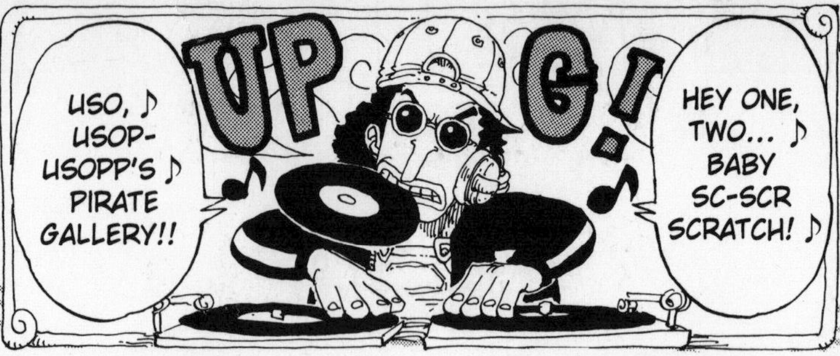
UP G!
HEY ONE, TWO... ♪ BABY SC-SCR SCRATCH! ♪
USO, ♪ USOP-USOPP'S ♪ PIRATE GALLERY!!

YOU CRACK ME UP!

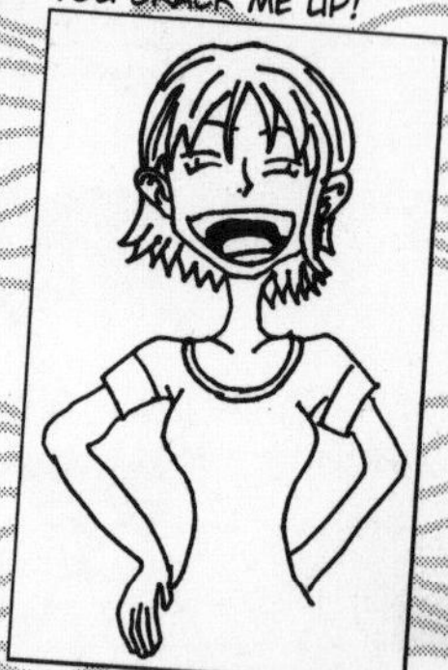

MARIO, 12

THE GANG'S ALL HERE!!

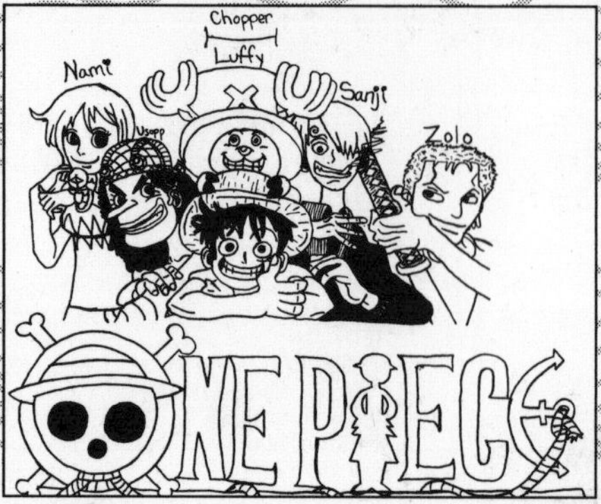
Chopper
Luffy
Nami
Sanji
Usopp
Zolo
ONE PIECE

ALYSSA

I *WILL* BECOME KING OF THE PIRATES!!

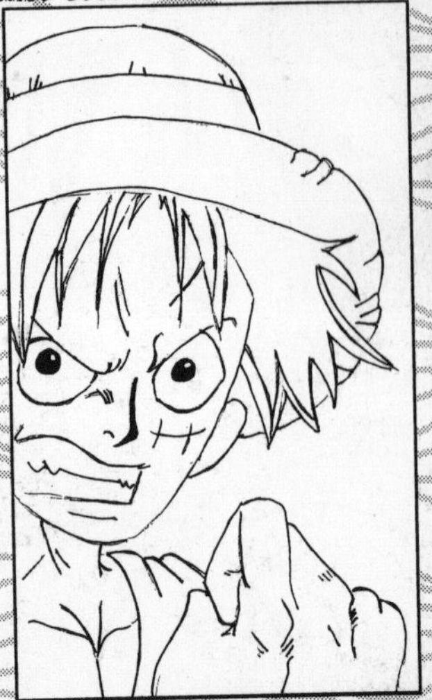

LUIS

NO FLESH-EATING SNOW BUNNY IS GONNA CATCH ME!

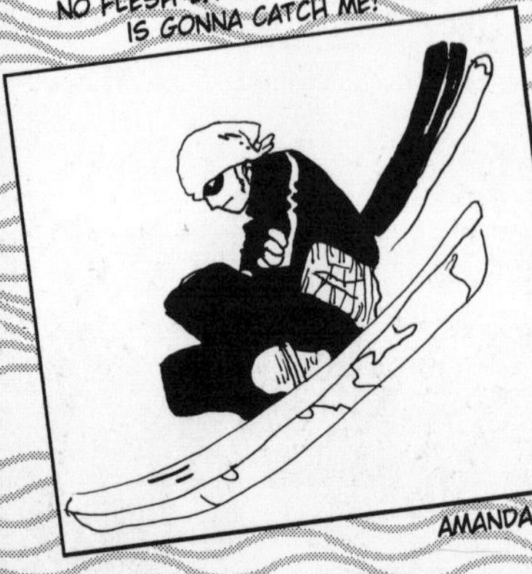

AMANDA, 14

SUBMIT YOUR FAN ART TO:
SHONEN JUMP C/O VIZ MEDIA, LLC P.O. BOX 77010 SAN FRANCISCO, CA 94107
*REMEMBER TO INCLUDE YOUR NAME, AGE AND PARENT RELEASE FORM!!

USOPP'S COMMENTS WERE TRANSMITTED THROUGH THE U.S. SHONEN JUMP TEAM -*EDITOR*

# Chapter 151:
# THE SKIES OF DRUM

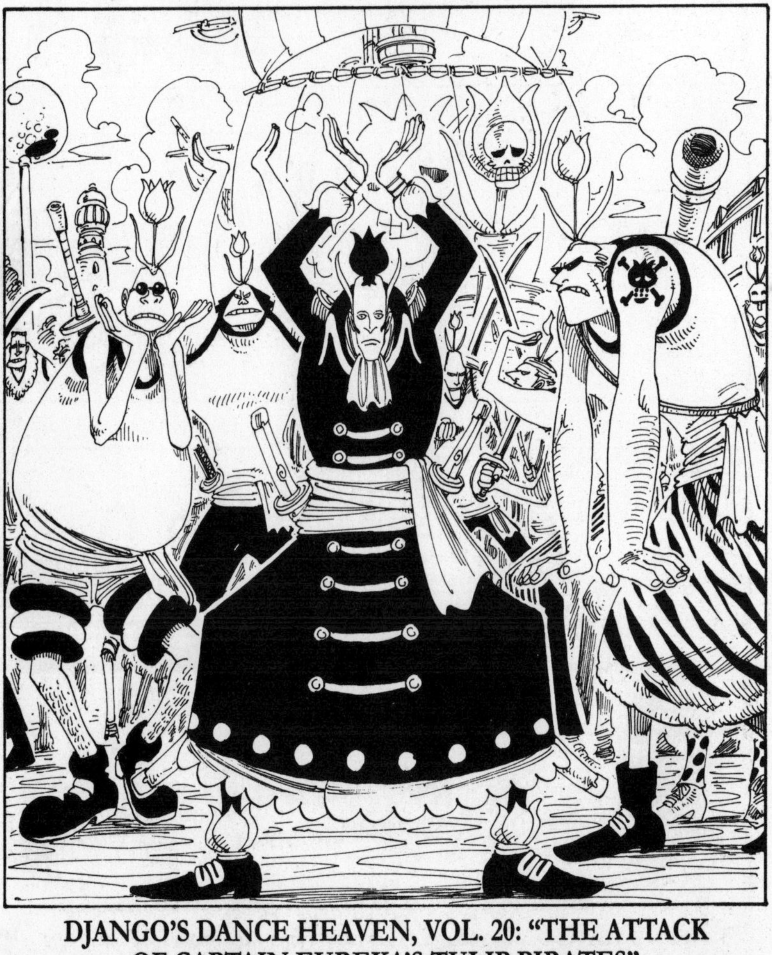

DJANGO'S DANCE HEAVEN, VOL. 20: "THE ATTACK OF CAPTAIN EUREKA'S TULIP PIRATES"

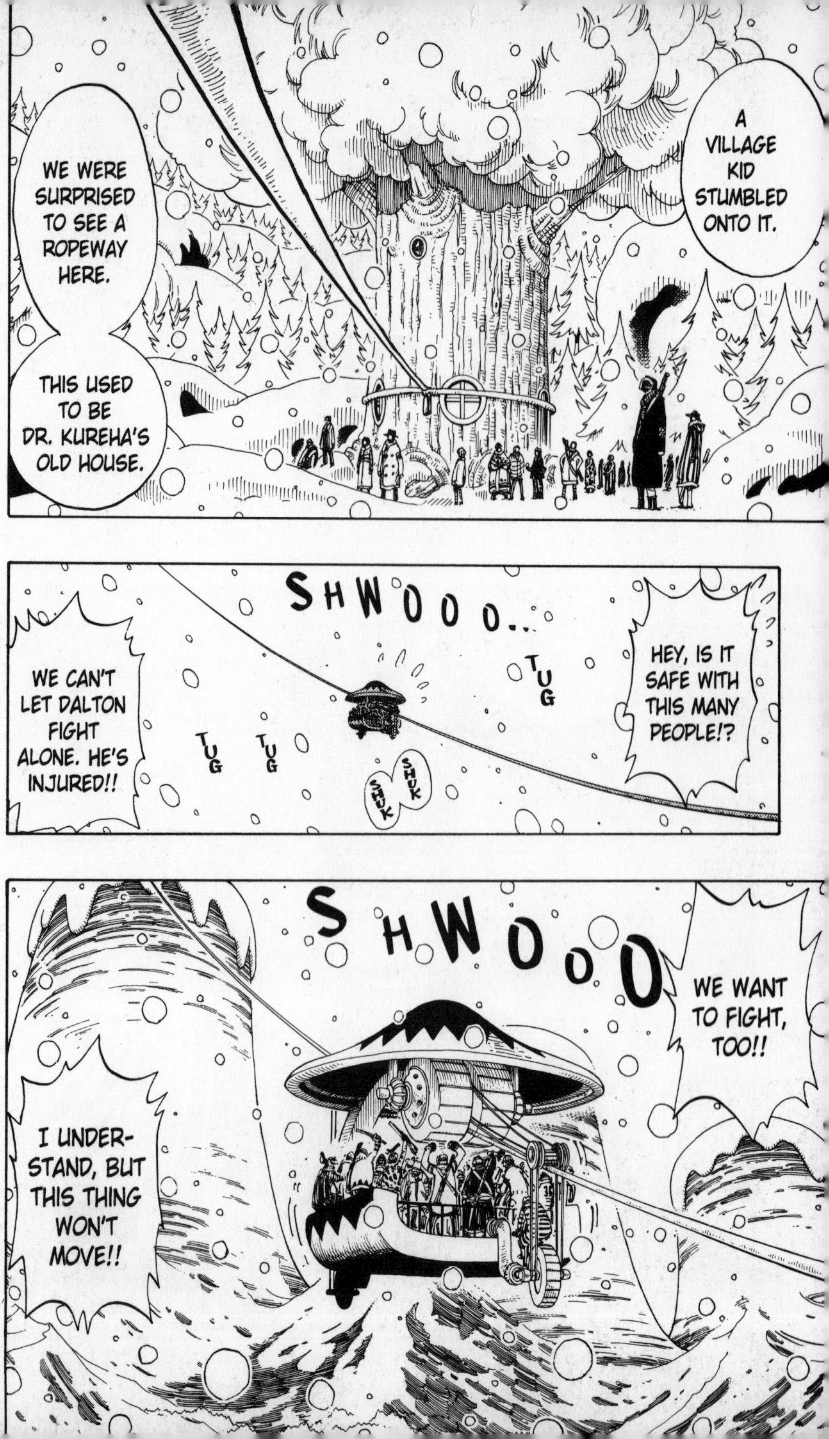
A VILLAGE KID STUMBLED ONTO IT.
WE WERE SURPRISED TO SEE A ROPEWAY HERE.
THIS USED TO BE DR. KUREHA'S OLD HOUSE.
SHWOOO...
HEY, IS IT SAFE WITH THIS MANY PEOPLE!?
TUG
WE CAN'T LET DALTON FIGHT ALONE. HE'S INJURED!!
TUG
TUG
SHUK
SHUK
SHWOOO
WE WANT TO FIGHT, TOO!!
I UNDER-STAND, BUT THIS THING WON'T MOVE!!

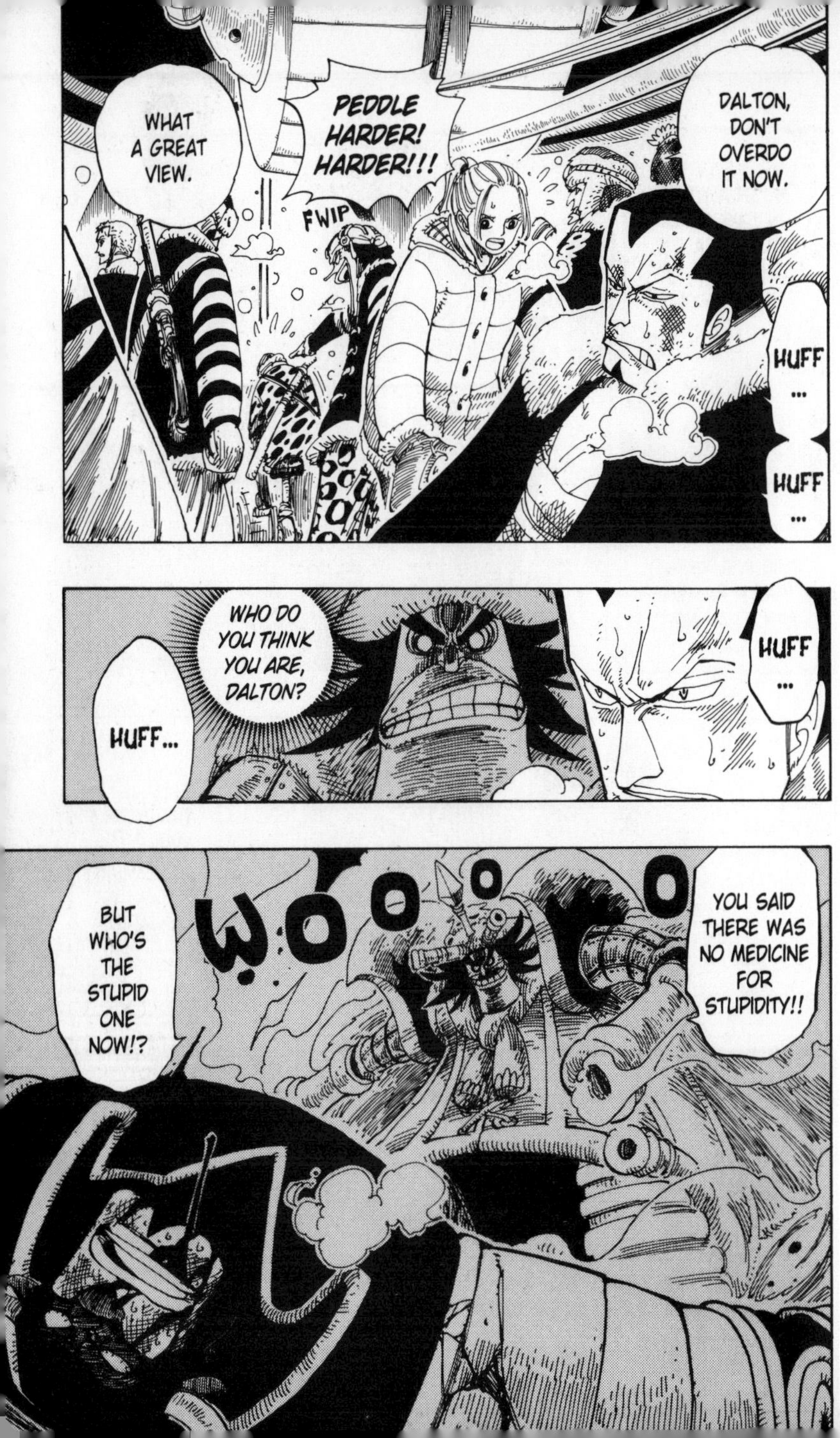
DALTON, DON'T OVERDO IT NOW.
HUFF ... HUFF ...
PEDDLE HARDER! HARDER!!!
FWIP
WHAT A GREAT VIEW.
HUFF ...
WHO DO YOU THINK YOU ARE, DALTON?
HUFF...
YOU SAID THERE WAS NO MEDICINE FOR STUPIDITY!!
WOOOO
BUT WHO'S THE STUPID ONE NOW!?

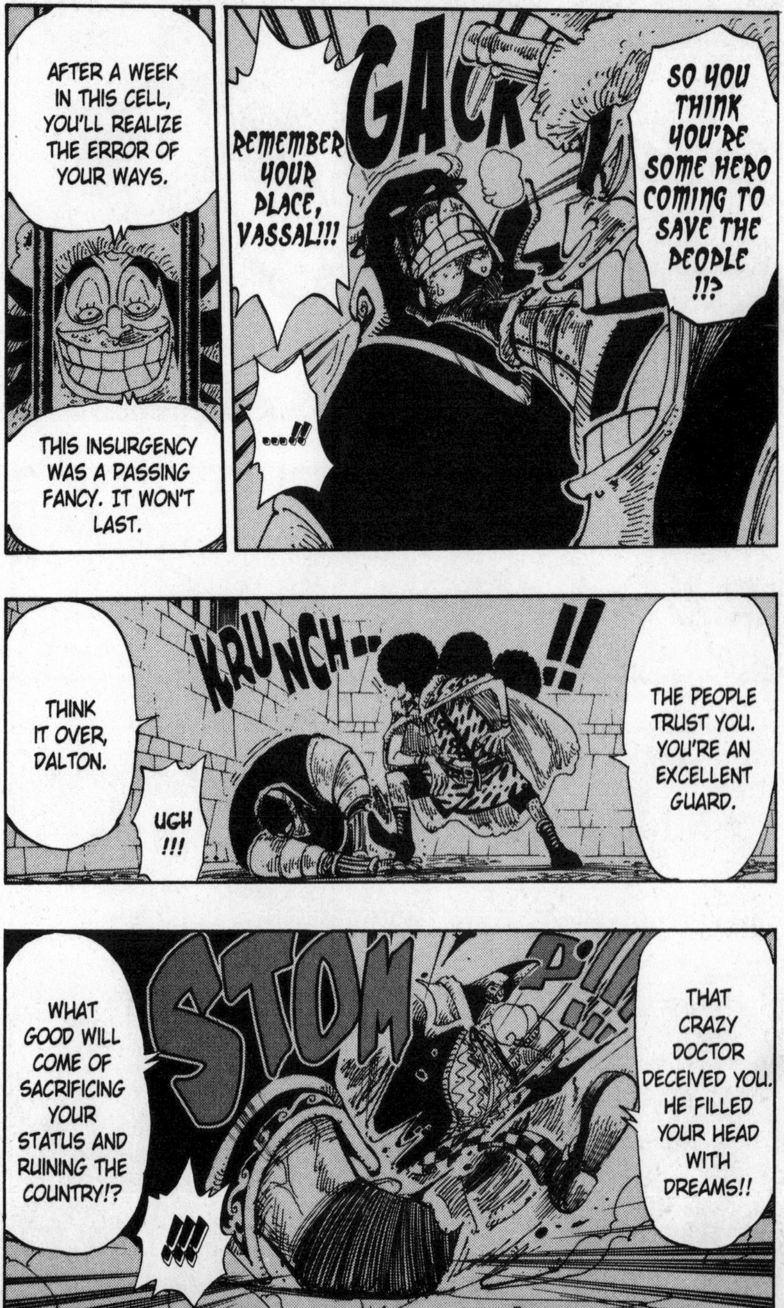
SO YOU THINK YOU'RE SOME HERO COMING TO SAVE THE PEOPLE !!?
GACK
REMEMBER YOUR PLACE, VASSAL!!!
...!!
AFTER A WEEK IN THIS CELL, YOU'LL REALIZE THE ERROR OF YOUR WAYS.
THIS INSURGENCY WAS A PASSING FANCY. IT WON'T LAST.
THE PEOPLE TRUST YOU. YOU'RE AN EXCELLENT GUARD.
KRUNCH..!!
UGH !!!
THINK IT OVER, DALTON.
THAT CRAZY DOCTOR DECEIVED YOU. HE FILLED YOUR HEAD WITH DREAMS!!
STOMP!!
!!!
WHAT GOOD WILL COME OF SACRIFICING YOUR STATUS AND RUINING THE COUNTRY!?

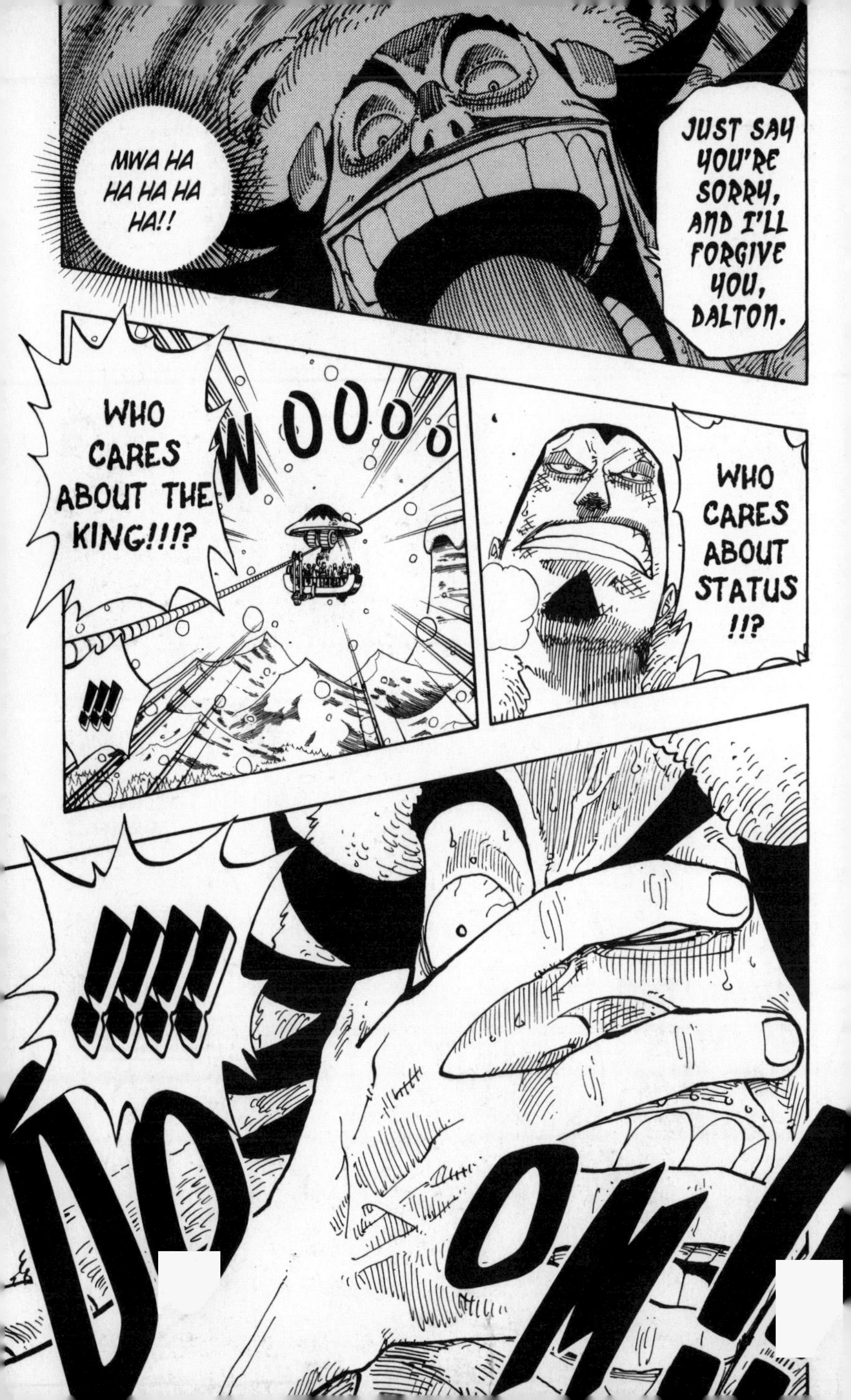
JUST SAY YOU'RE SORRY, AND I'LL FORGIVE YOU, DALTON.
MWA HA HA HA HA HA!!
WHO CARES ABOUT STATUS !!?
WHO CARES ABOUT THE KING!!!?
WOOOO
!!!
!!!!
DOOM!!

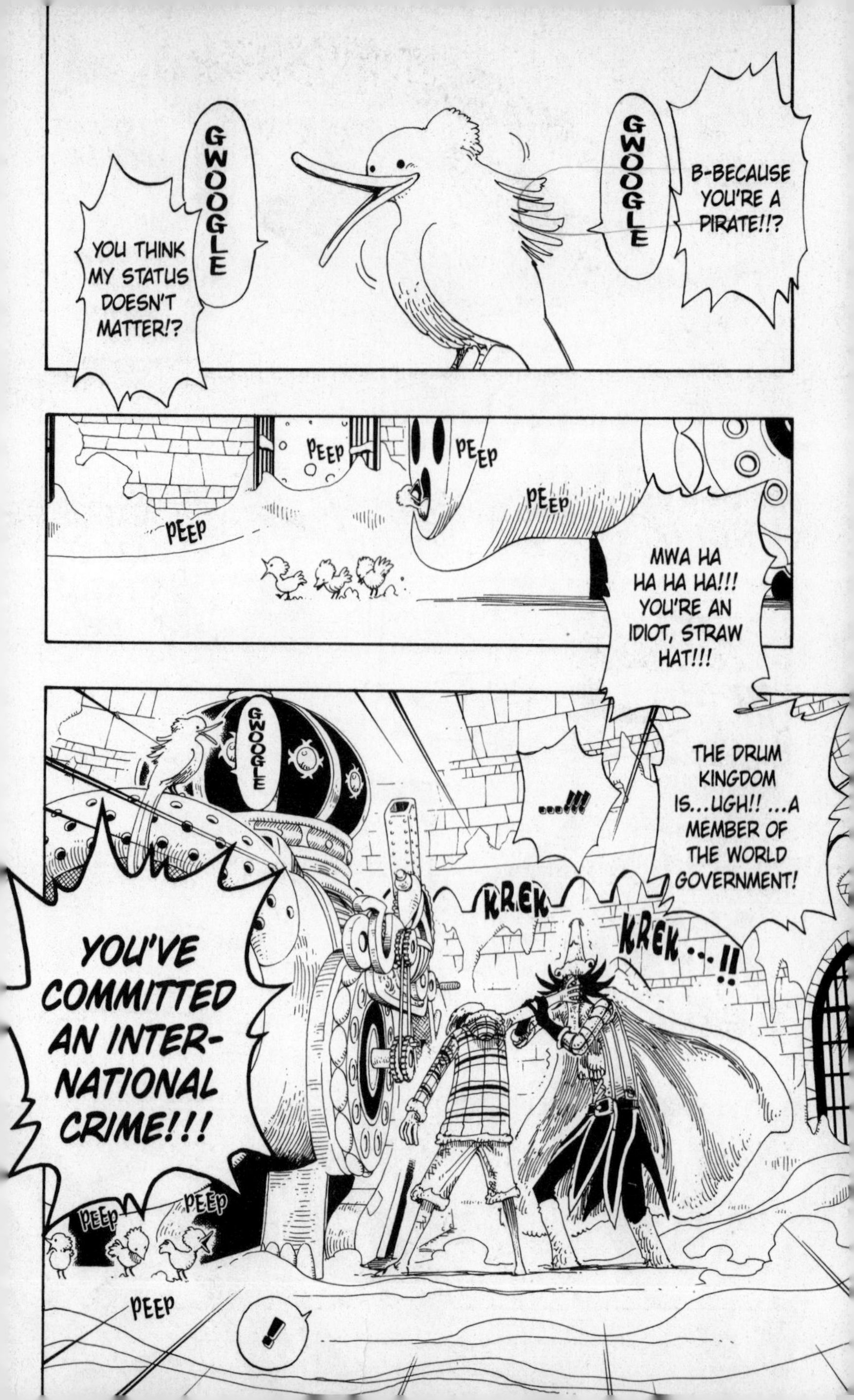
B-BECAUSE YOU'RE A PIRATE!!?
GWOOGLE
GWOOGLE
YOU THINK MY STATUS DOESN'T MATTER!?
PEEP
PEEP
PEEP
PEEP
MWA HA HA HA HA!!! YOU'RE AN IDIOT, STRAW HAT!!!
THE DRUM KINGDOM IS...UGH!! ...A MEMBER OF THE WORLD GOVERNMENT!
...!!!
GWOOGLE
KREK
KREK...!!
YOU'VE COMMITTED AN INTER-NATIONAL CRIME!!!
PEEP
PEEP
PEEP
!

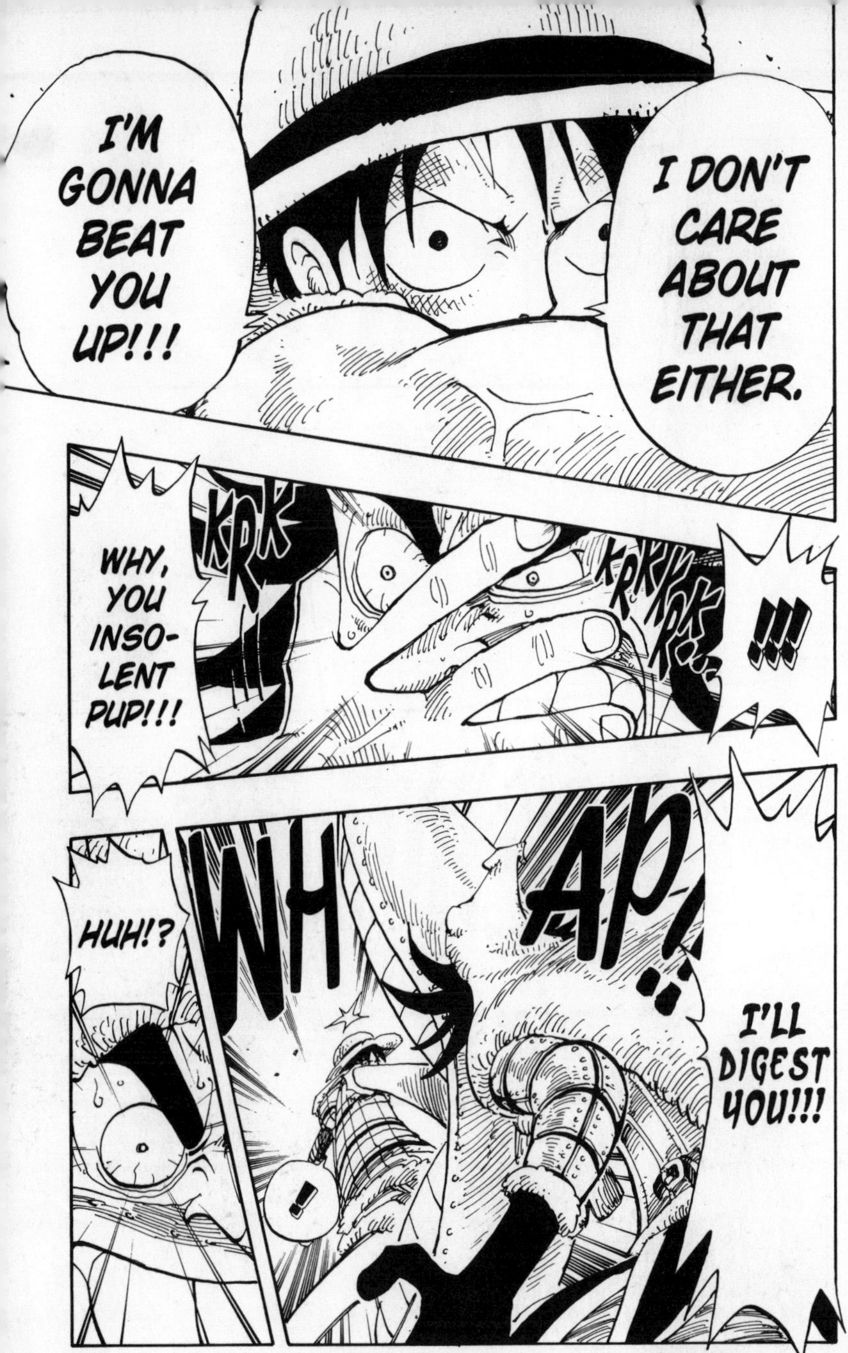
I DON'T CARE ABOUT THAT EITHER.
I'M GONNA BEAT YOU UP!!!
!!!
KRK
WHY, YOU INSO-LENT PUP!!!
I'LL DIGEST YOU!!!
WHAP!!
HUH!?
!

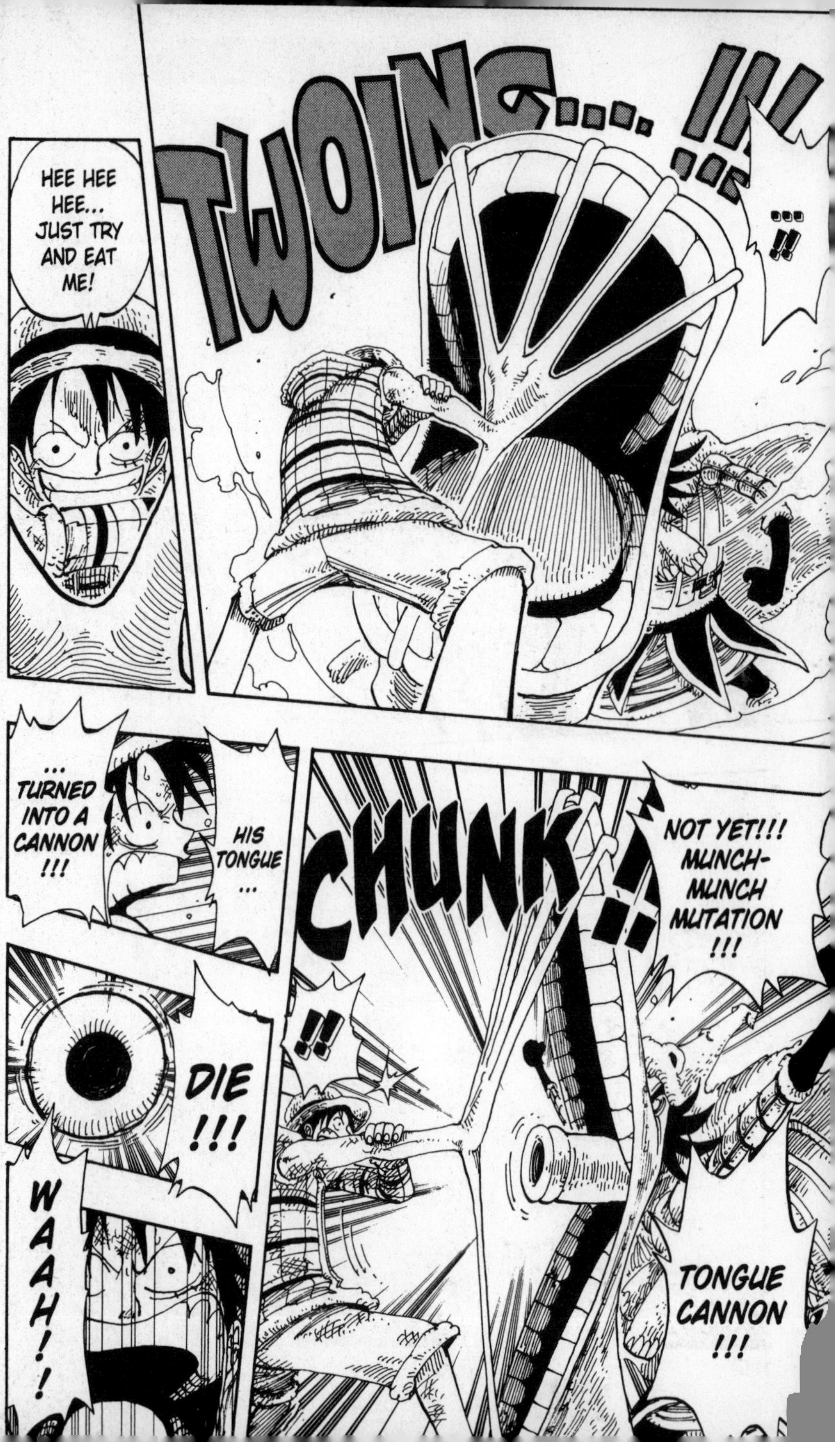
TWOING....!!!
...!!
HEE HEE HEE... JUST TRY AND EAT ME!
CHUNK!!
NOT YET!!! MUNCH-MUNCH MUTATION!!!
!!
TONGUE CANNON!!!
HIS TONGUE...
...TURNED INTO A CANNON!!!
DIE!!!
WAAAH!!

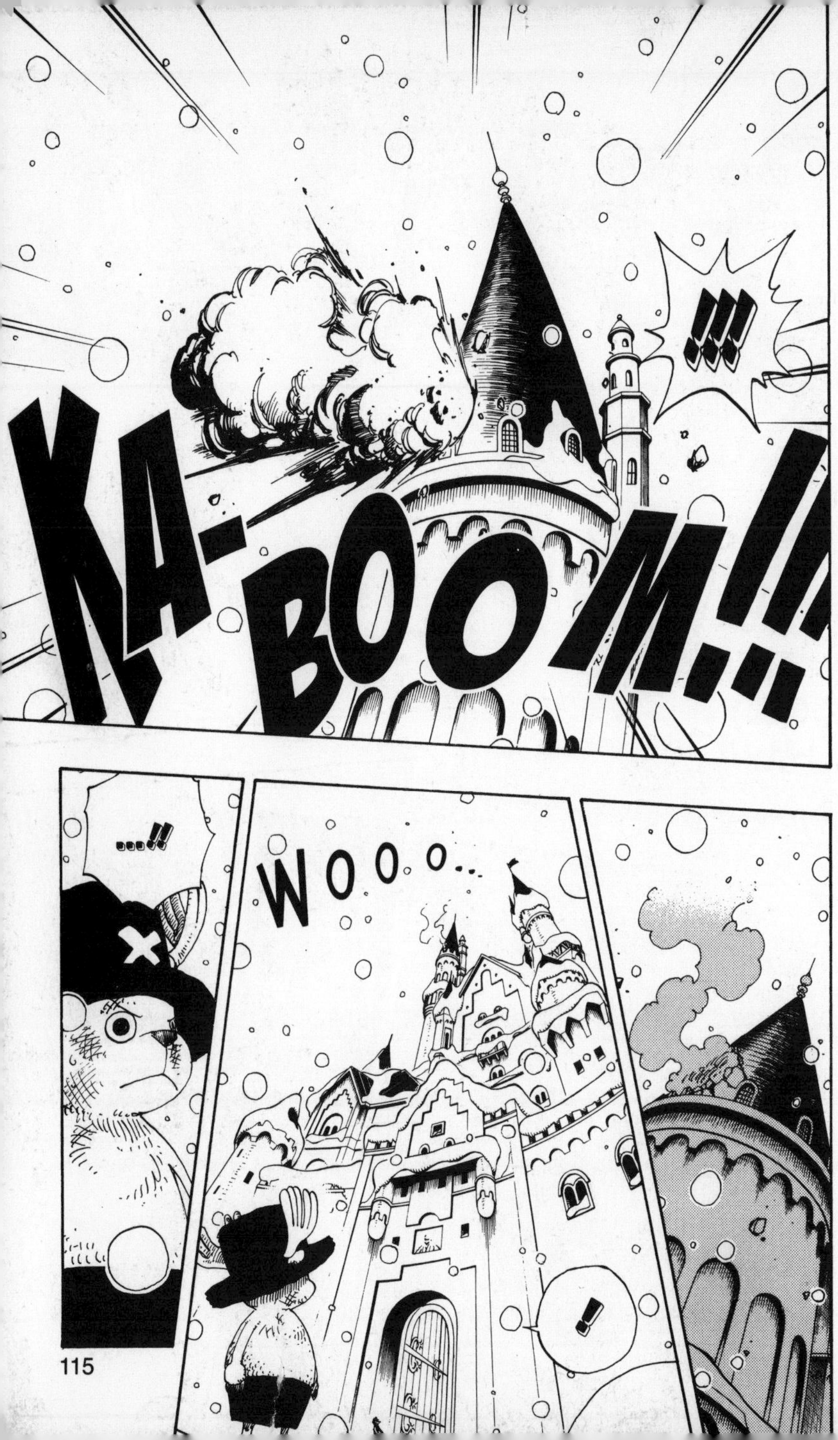
!!!!
KA-BOOM!!!
WOOO...
!
...!!

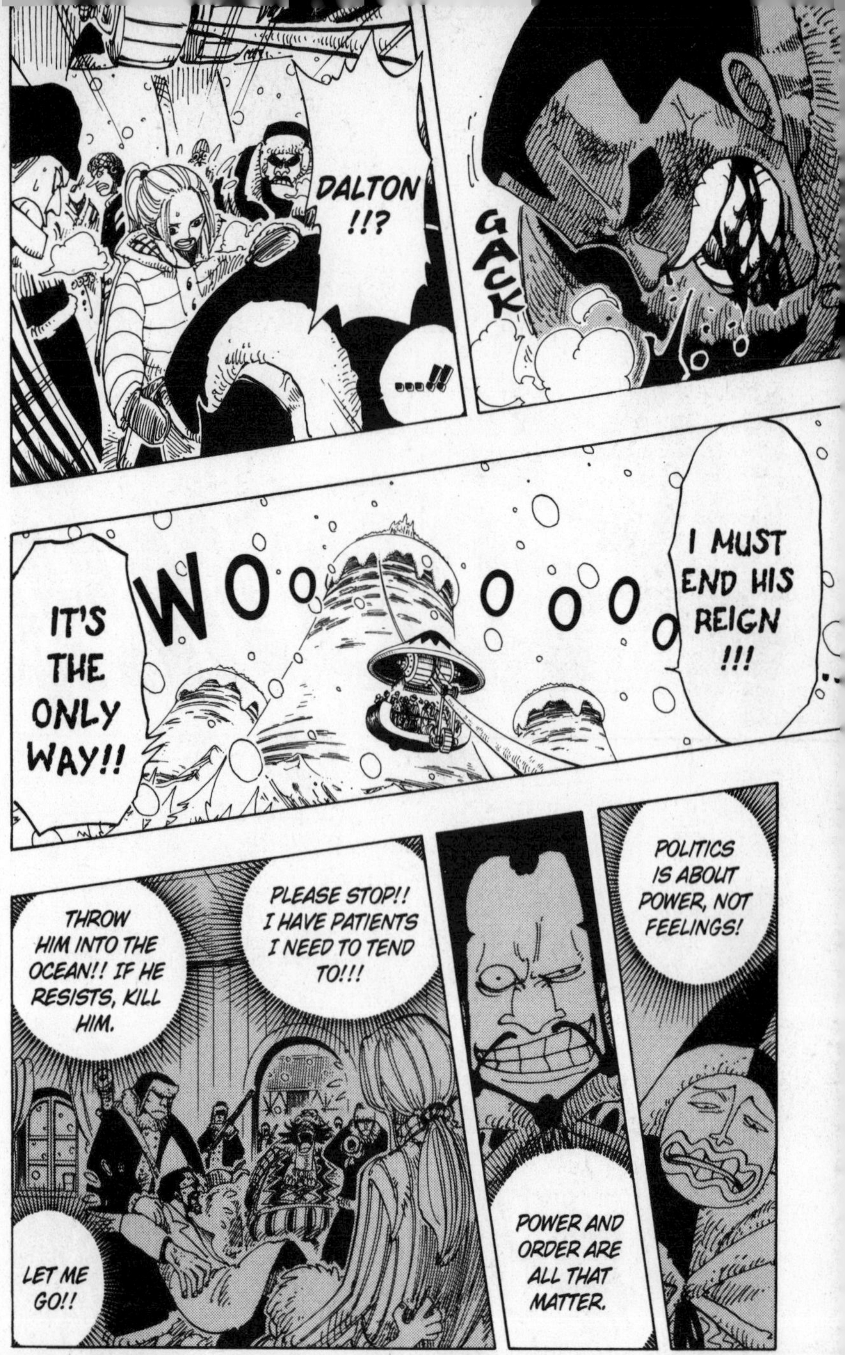
GACK
DALTON !!?
...!!
I MUST END HIS REIGN !!!
WOOOOOOO
IT'S THE ONLY WAY!!
POLITICS IS ABOUT POWER, NOT FEELINGS!
POWER AND ORDER ARE ALL THAT MATTER.
PLEASE STOP!! I HAVE PATIENTS I NEED TO TEND TO!!!
THROW HIM INTO THE OCEAN!! IF HE RESISTS, KILL HIM.
LET ME GO!!

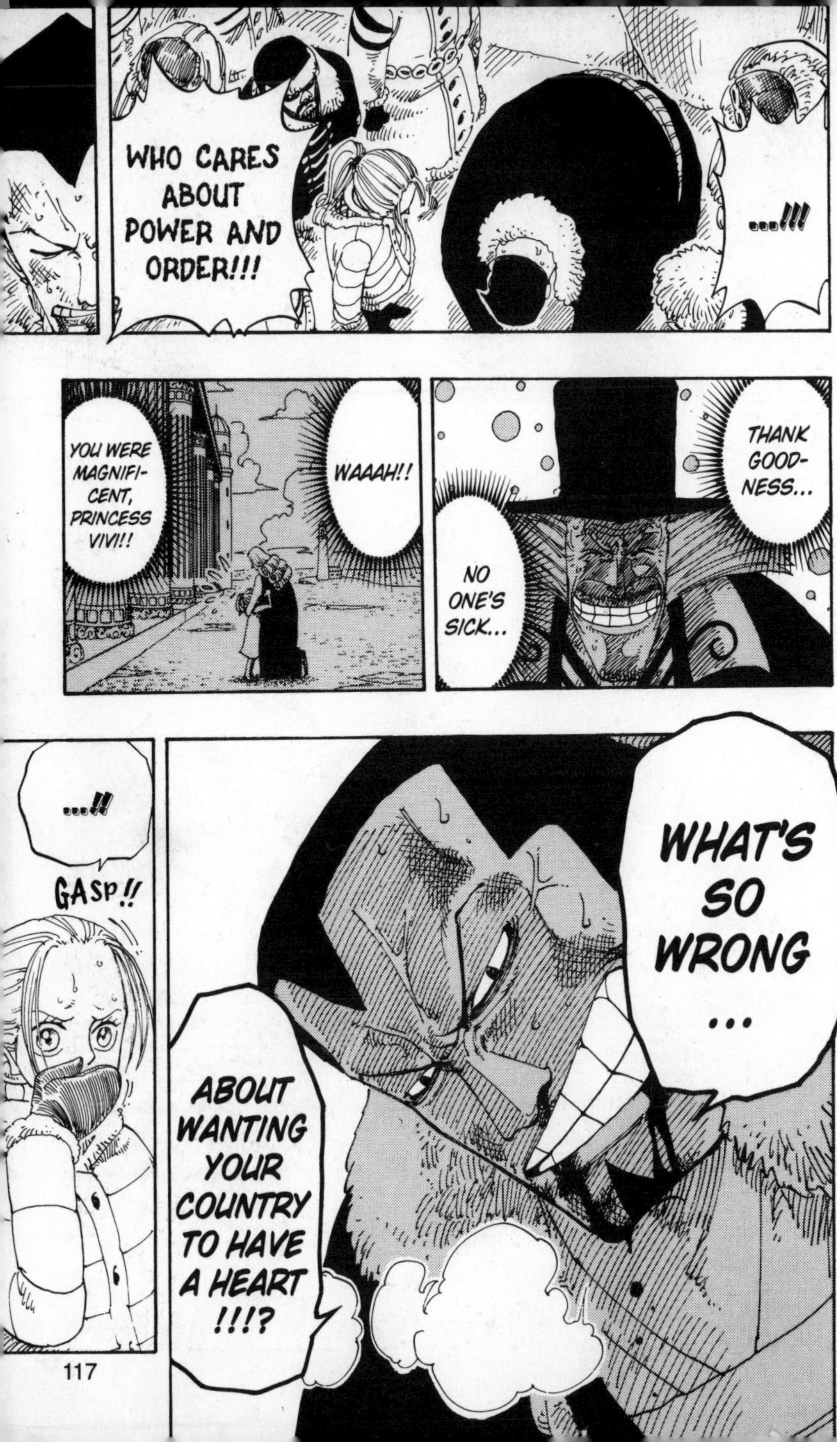
...!!!
WHO CARES ABOUT POWER AND ORDER!!!
THANK GOODNESS...
NO ONE'S SICK...
WAAAH!!
YOU WERE MAGNIFICENT, PRINCESS VIVI!!
WHAT'S SO WRONG ...
ABOUT WANTING YOUR COUNTRY TO HAVE A HEART!!!?
...!!
GASP!!

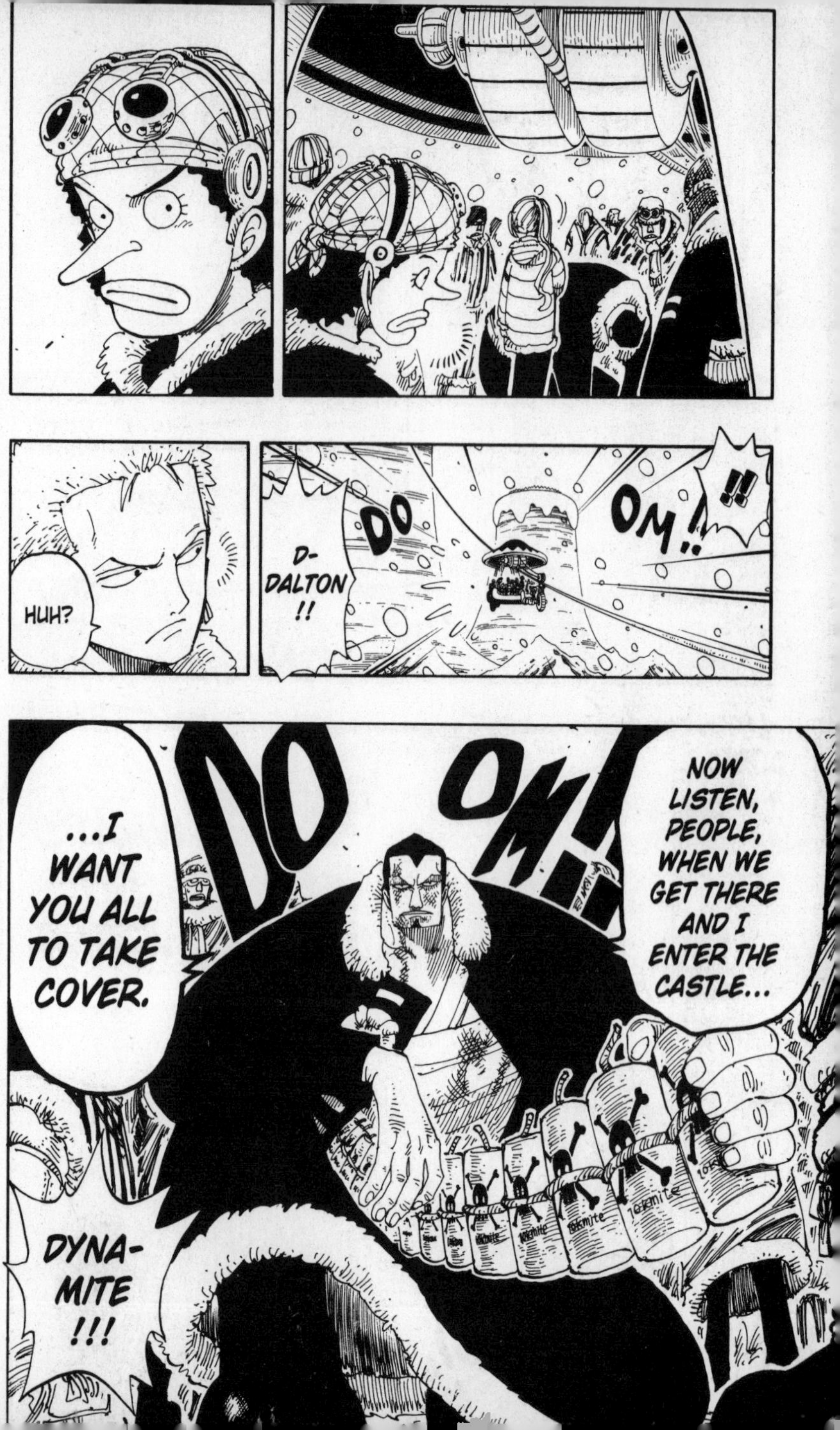
DO
OM!! !!
D-DALTON!!
HUH?
NOW LISTEN, PEOPLE, WHEN WE GET THERE AND I ENTER THE CASTLE...
DO OM!!
...I WANT YOU ALL TO TAKE COVER.
DYNA-MITE!!!

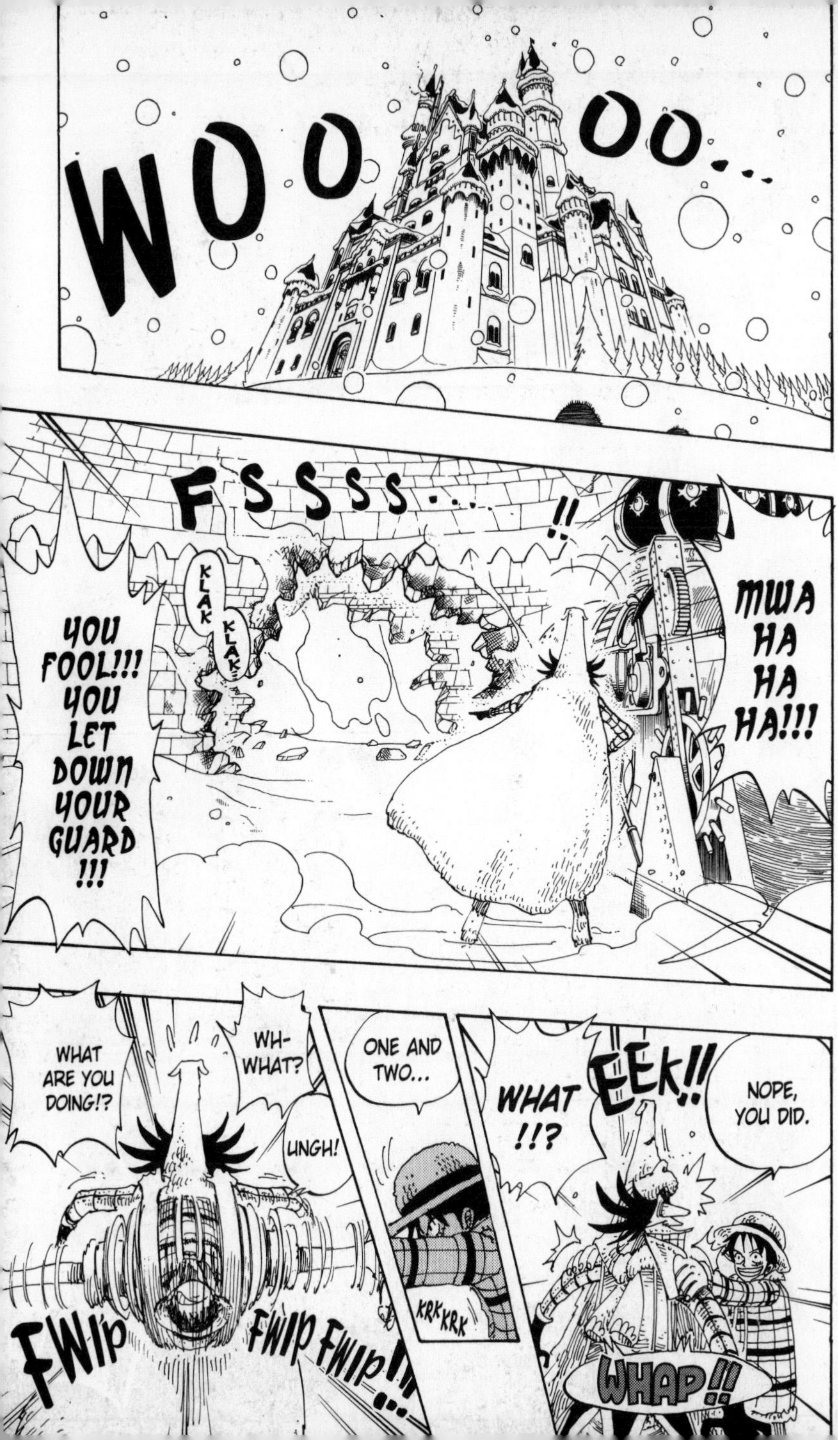
WOO OO...
FSSSS...!!
MWA HA HA HA!!!
KLAK KLAK
YOU FOOL!!! YOU LET DOWN YOUR GUARD!!!
NOPE, YOU DID.
EEK!!
WHAT!!?
WHAP!!
ONE AND TWO...
UNGH!
KRK KRK
WH-WHAT?
WHAT ARE YOU DOING!?
FWIP FWIP FWIP!!

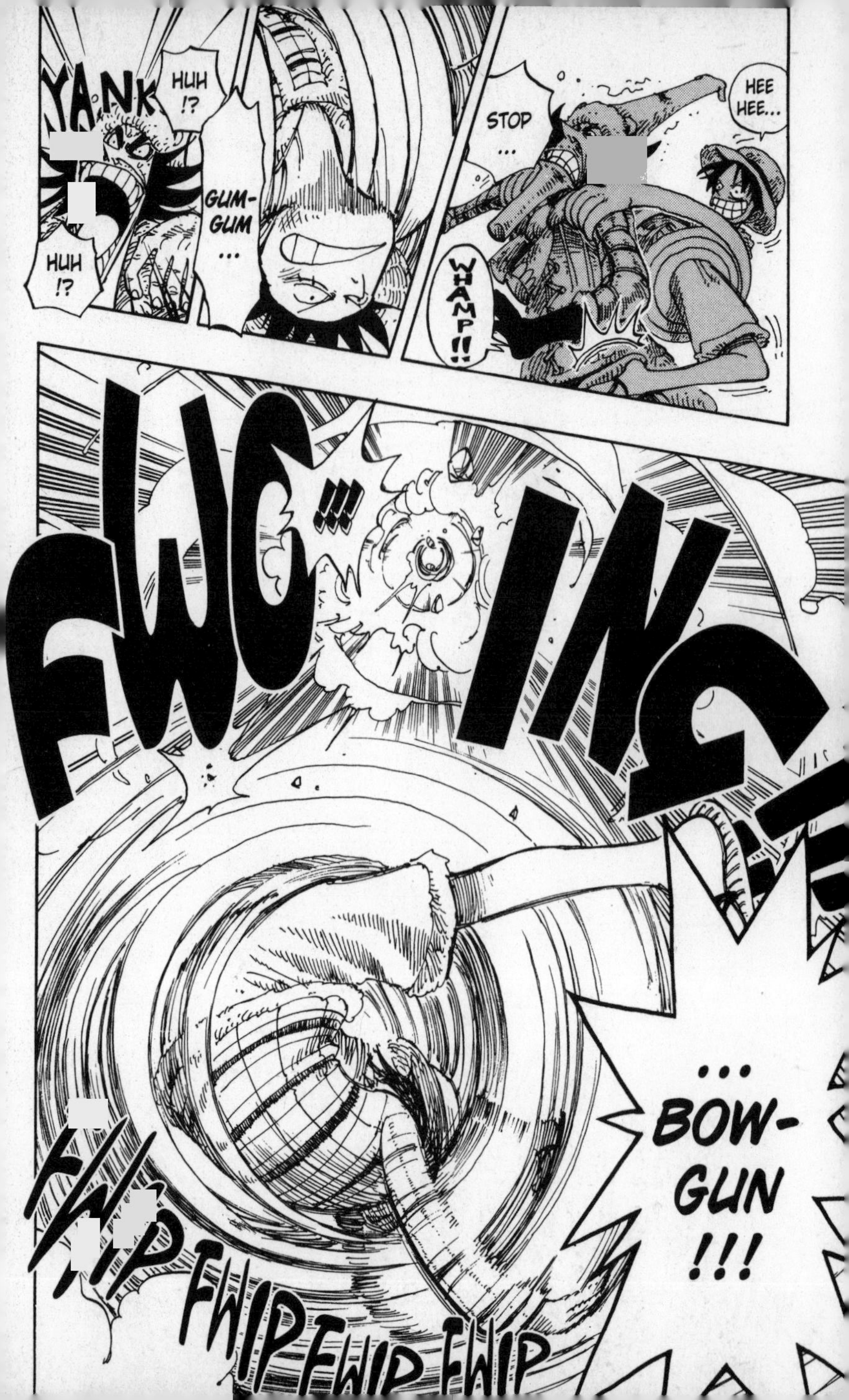
HEE HEE...
STOP ...
WHAMP!!
HUH !?
YANK
GUM-GUM ...
HUH !?
FWOING!!!
... BOW-GUN !!!
FWIP
FWIP
FWIP
FWIP
FWIP

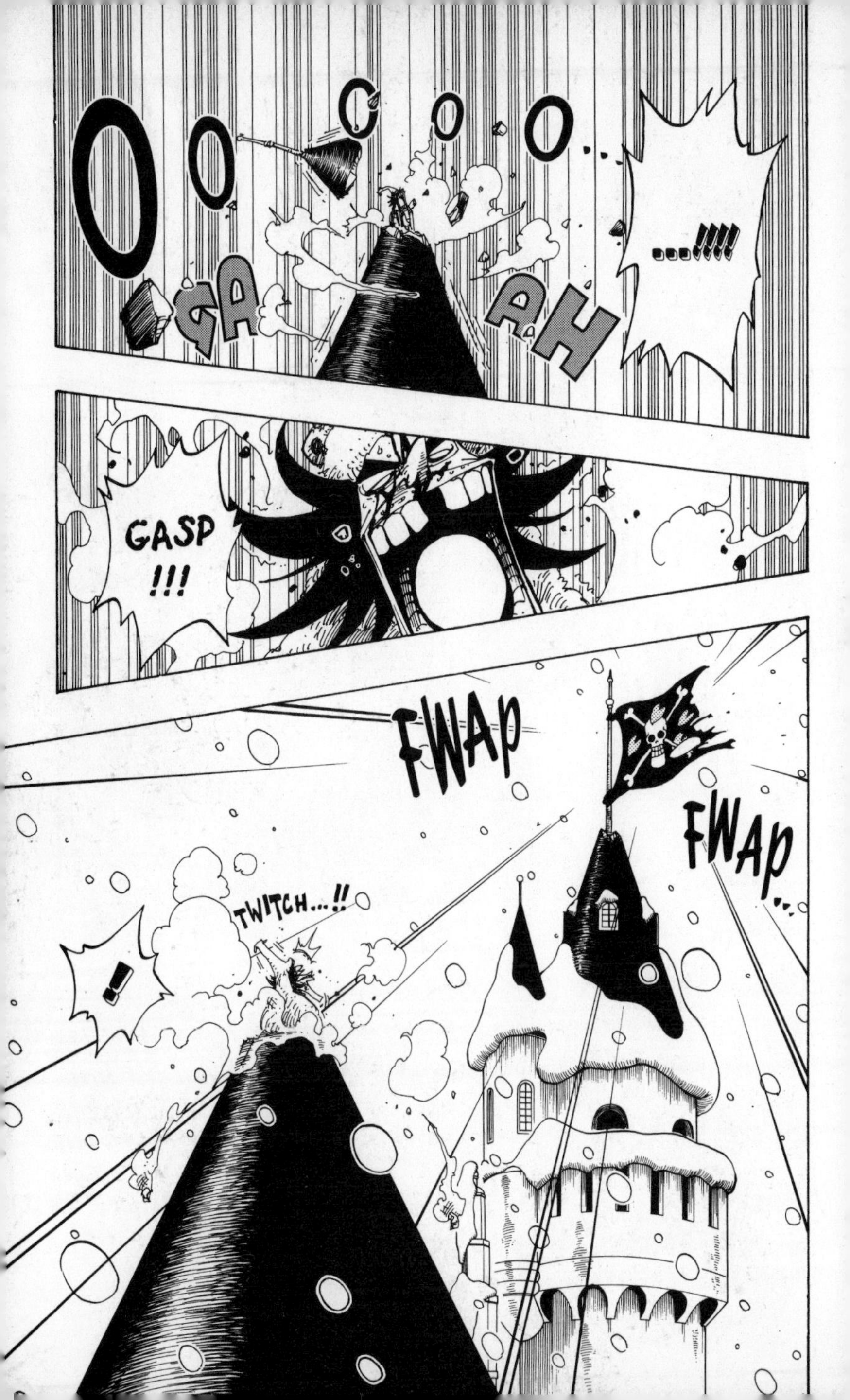
...!!!!
OOOOO...
GAAH
GASP!!!
FWAP...
FWAP
TWITCH...!!
!

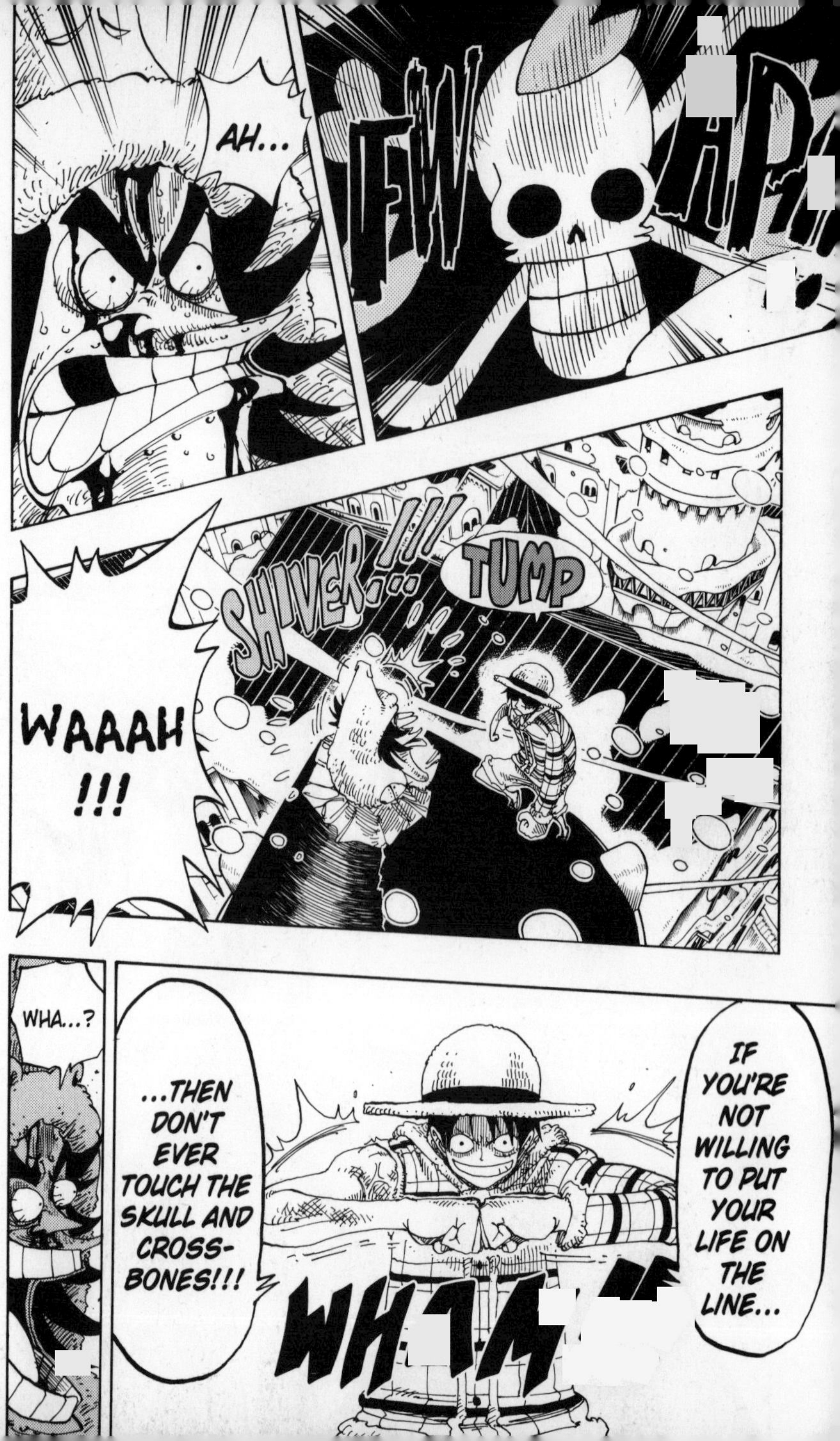
FWAP
AH...
TUMP
SHIVER...!!!
WAAAH !!!
IF YOU'RE NOT WILLING TO PUT YOUR LIFE ON THE LINE...
...THEN DON'T EVER TOUCH THE SKULL AND CROSS-BONES!!!
WHAM
WHA...?

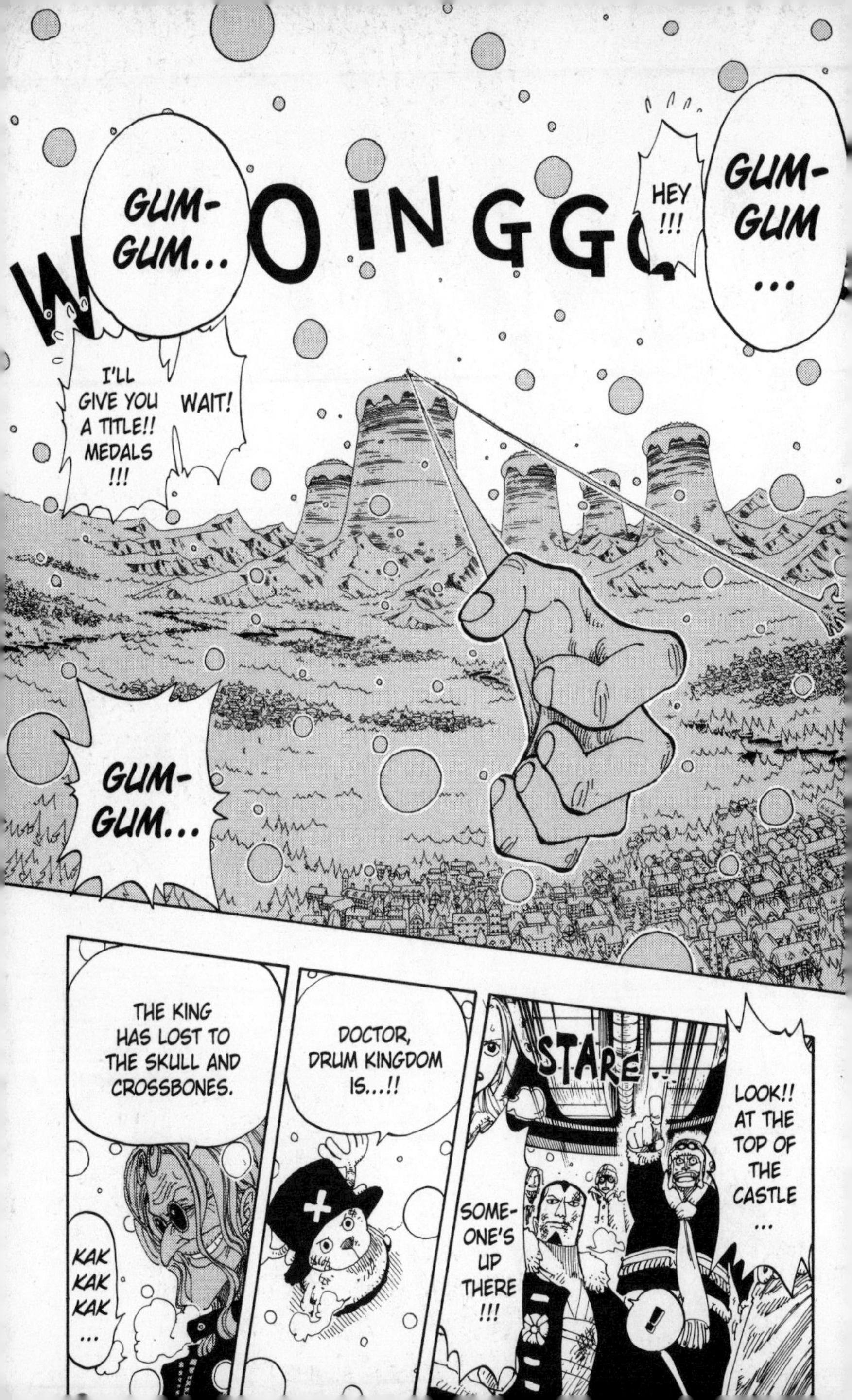
GUM-GUM ...
HEY !!!
W OINGG
GUM-GUM...
WAIT!
I'LL GIVE YOU A TITLE!! MEDALS !!!
GUM-GUM...
LOOK!! AT THE TOP OF THE CASTLE ...
STARE
SOME-ONE'S UP THERE !!!
!
DOCTOR, DRUM KINGDOM IS...!!
THE KING HAS LOST TO THE SKULL AND CROSSBONES.
KAK KAK KAK ...

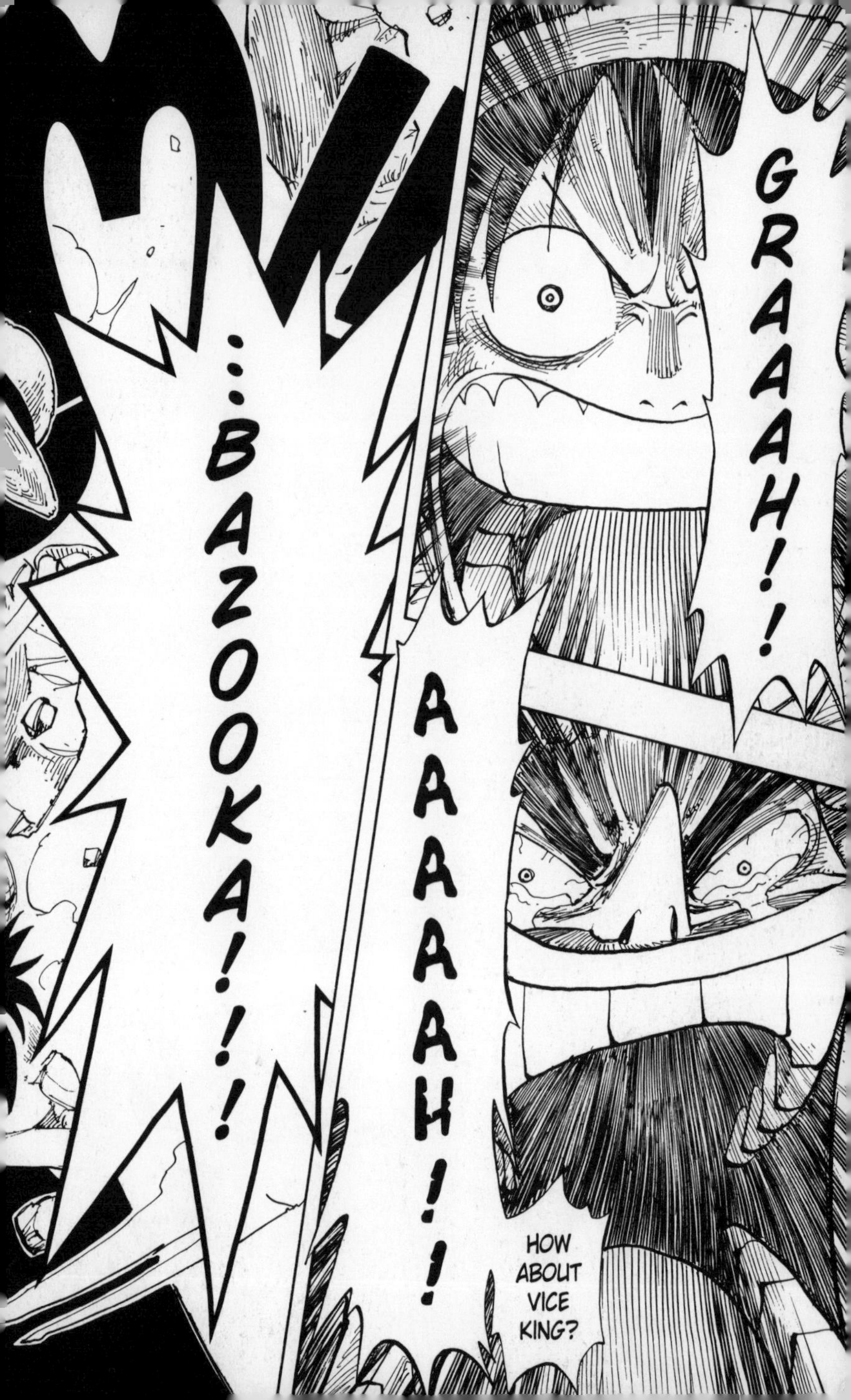
GRAAAH!!
AAAAAH!!!
HOW ABOUT VICE KING?
...BAZOOKA!!!

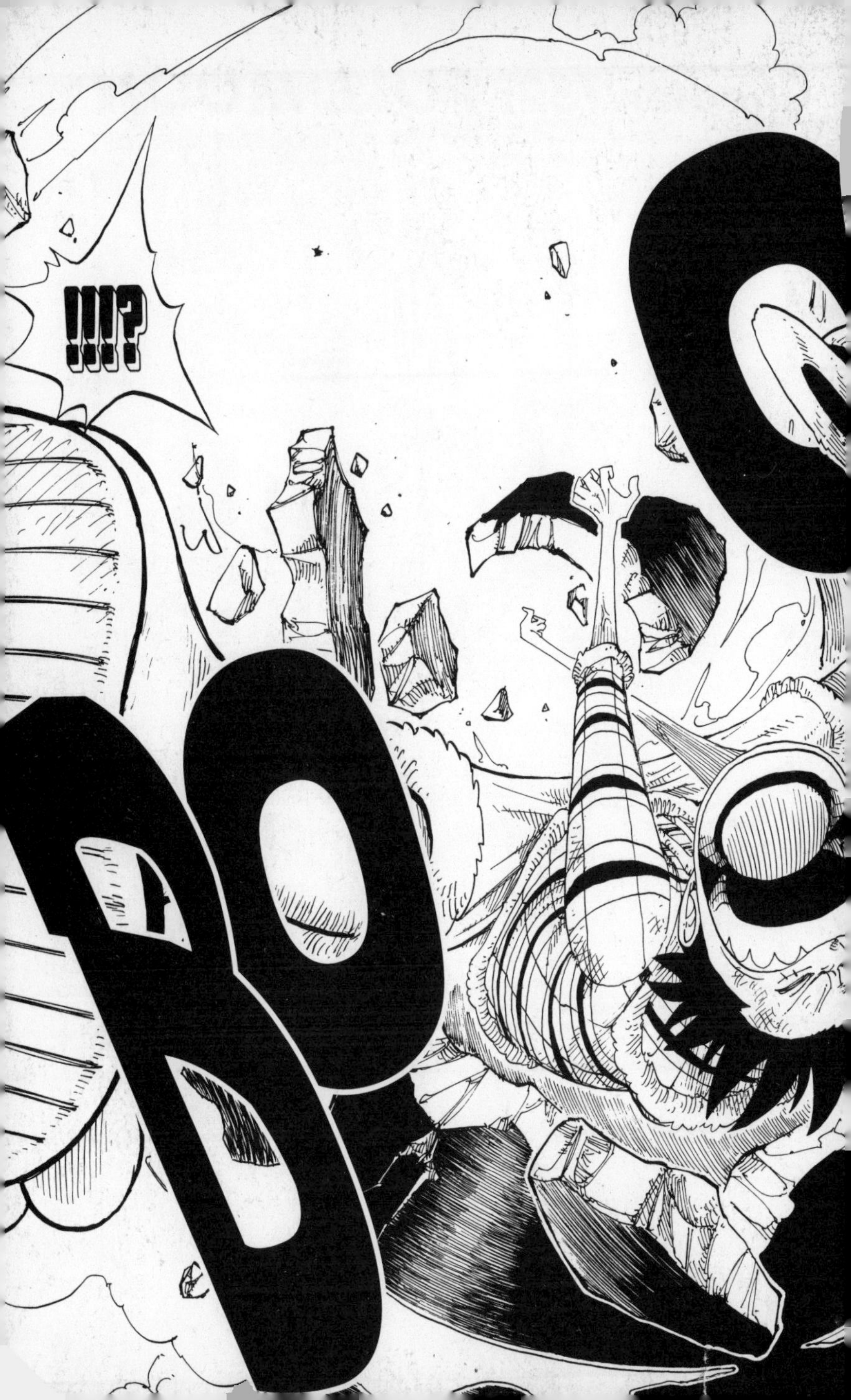
!!!?
BO

# Chapter 152: FULL MOON

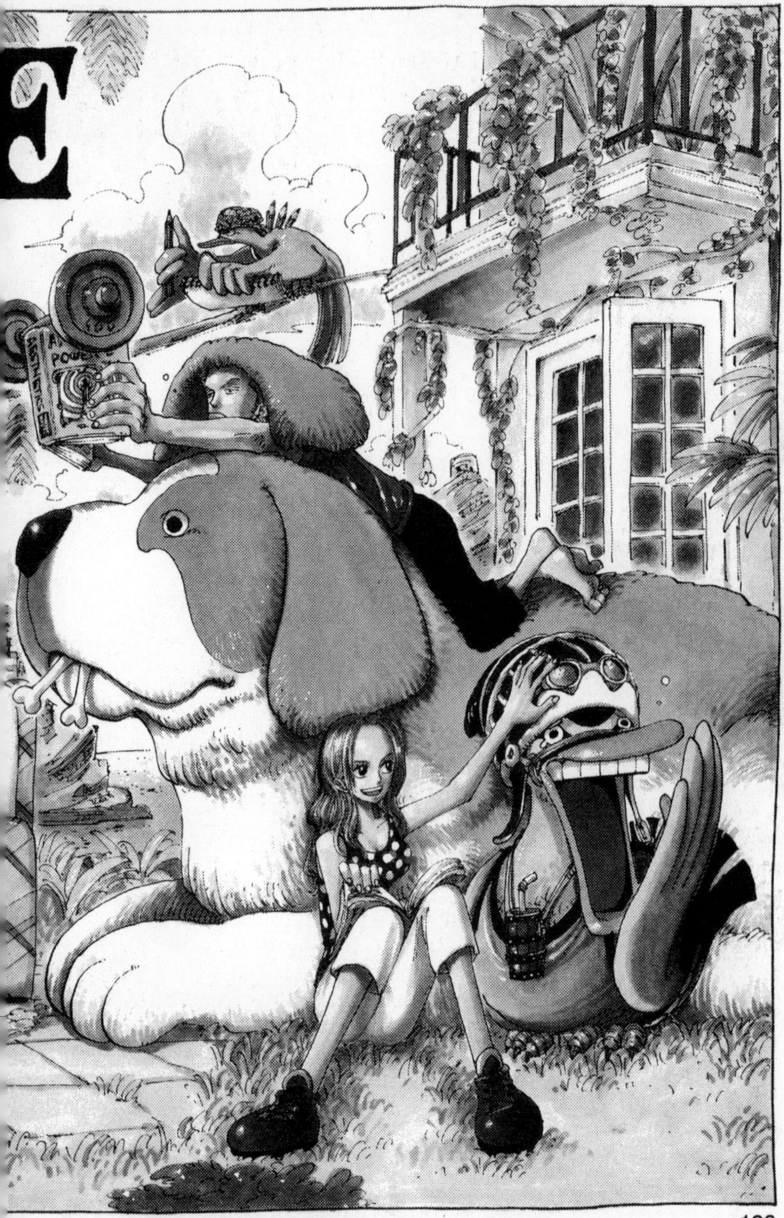

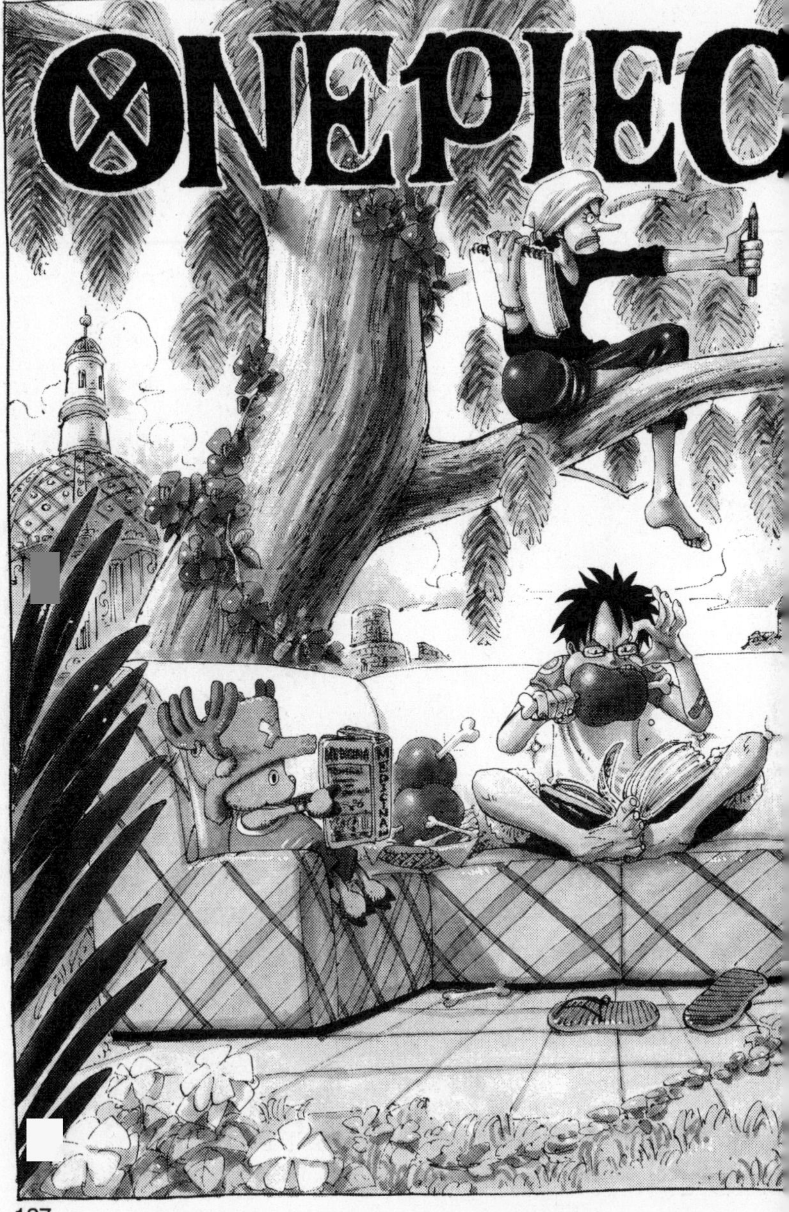
ONE PIEC
MEDICINA

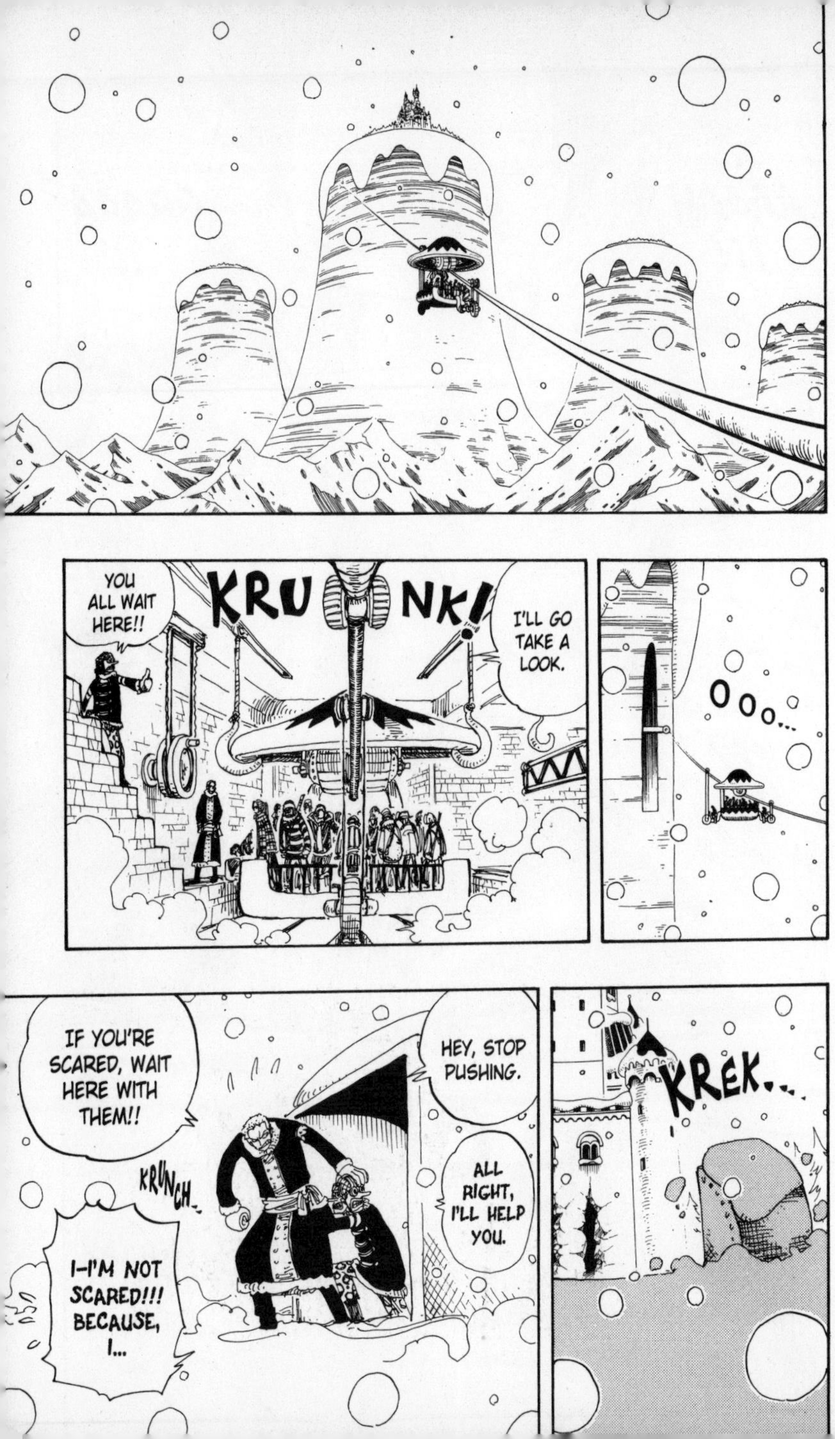
OOO...
YOU ALL WAIT HERE!!
KRUNK!
I'LL GO TAKE A LOOK.
KREK...
HEY, STOP PUSHING.
ALL RIGHT, I'LL HELP YOU.
IF YOU'RE SCARED, WAIT HERE WITH THEM!!
KRUNCH
I-I'M NOT SCARED!!! BECAUSE, I...

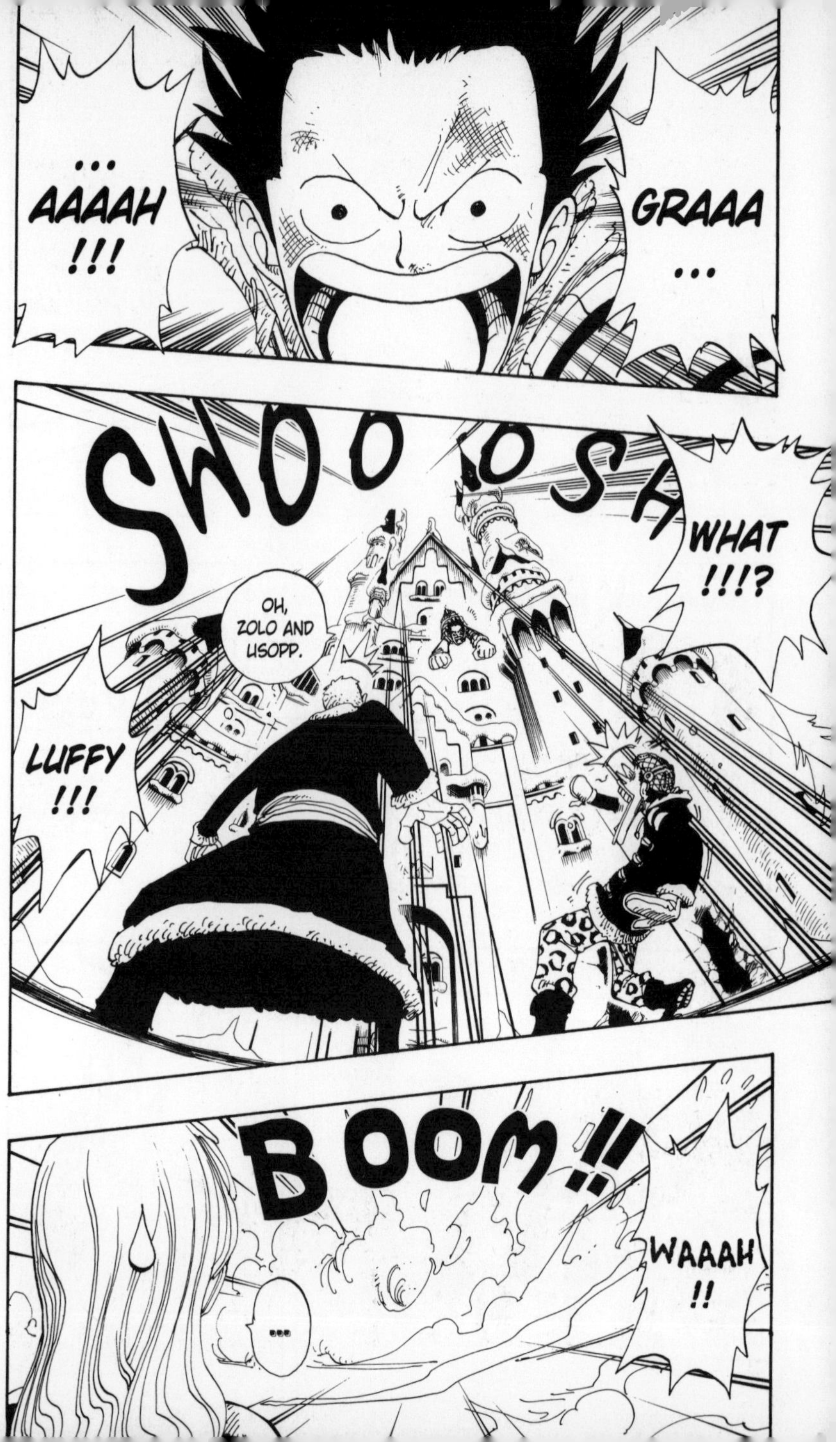
GRAAA ...
... AAAAH !!!
SHOOOSH
WHAT !!!?
OH, ZOLO AND USOPP.
LUFFY !!!
BOOM!!
WAAAH !!
...

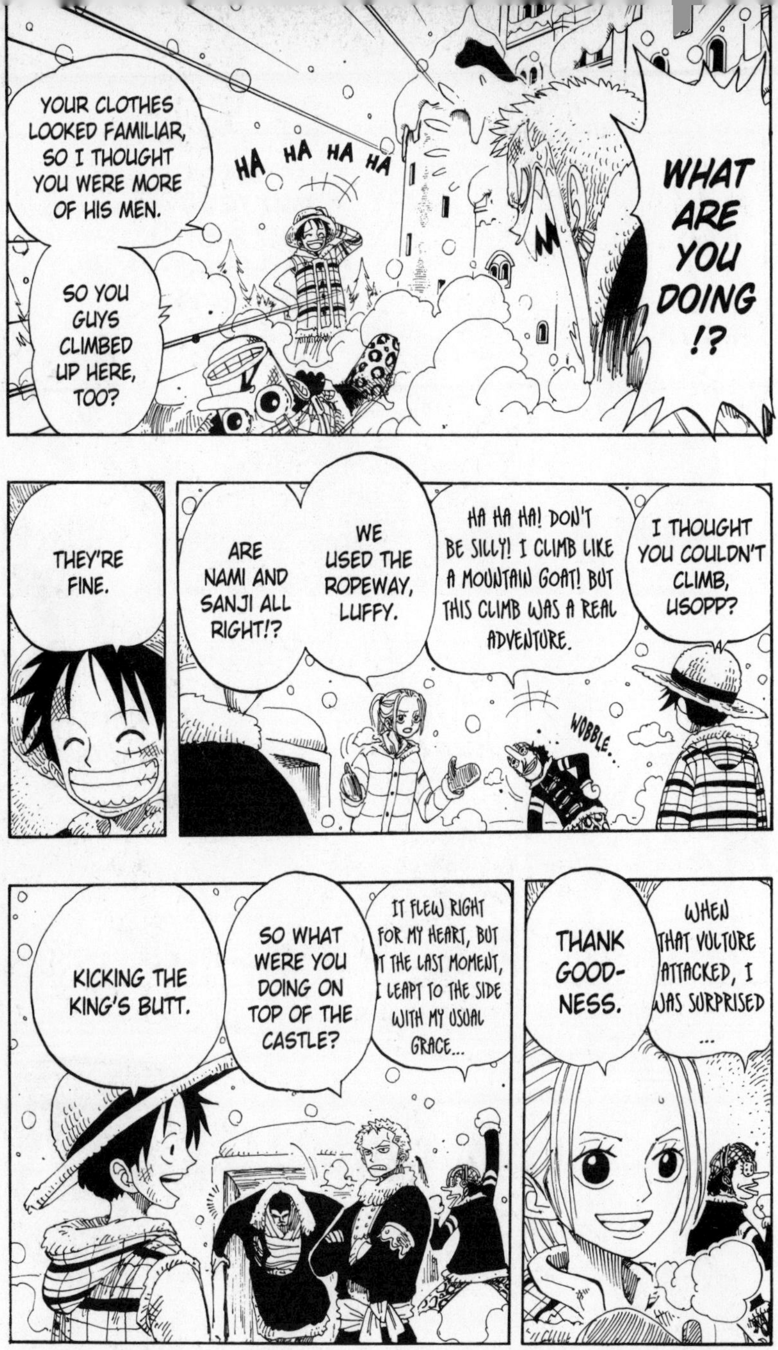
WHAT ARE YOU DOING!?
HA HA HA HA
YOUR CLOTHES LOOKED FAMILIAR, SO I THOUGHT YOU WERE MORE OF HIS MEN.
SO YOU GUYS CLIMBED UP HERE, TOO?
I THOUGHT YOU COULDN'T CLIMB, USOPP?
HA HA HA! DON'T BE SILLY! I CLIMB LIKE A MOUNTAIN GOAT! BUT THIS CLIMB WAS A REAL ADVENTURE.
WE USED THE ROPEWAY, LUFFY.
ARE NAMI AND SANJI ALL RIGHT!?
WOBBLE...
THEY'RE FINE.
WHEN THAT VULTURE ATTACKED, I WAS SURPRISED ...
THANK GOODNESS.
IT FLEW RIGHT FOR MY HEART, BUT T THE LAST MOMENT, LEAPT TO THE SIDE WITH MY USUAL GRACE...
SO WHAT WERE YOU DOING ON TOP OF THE CASTLE?
KICKING THE KING'S BUTT.

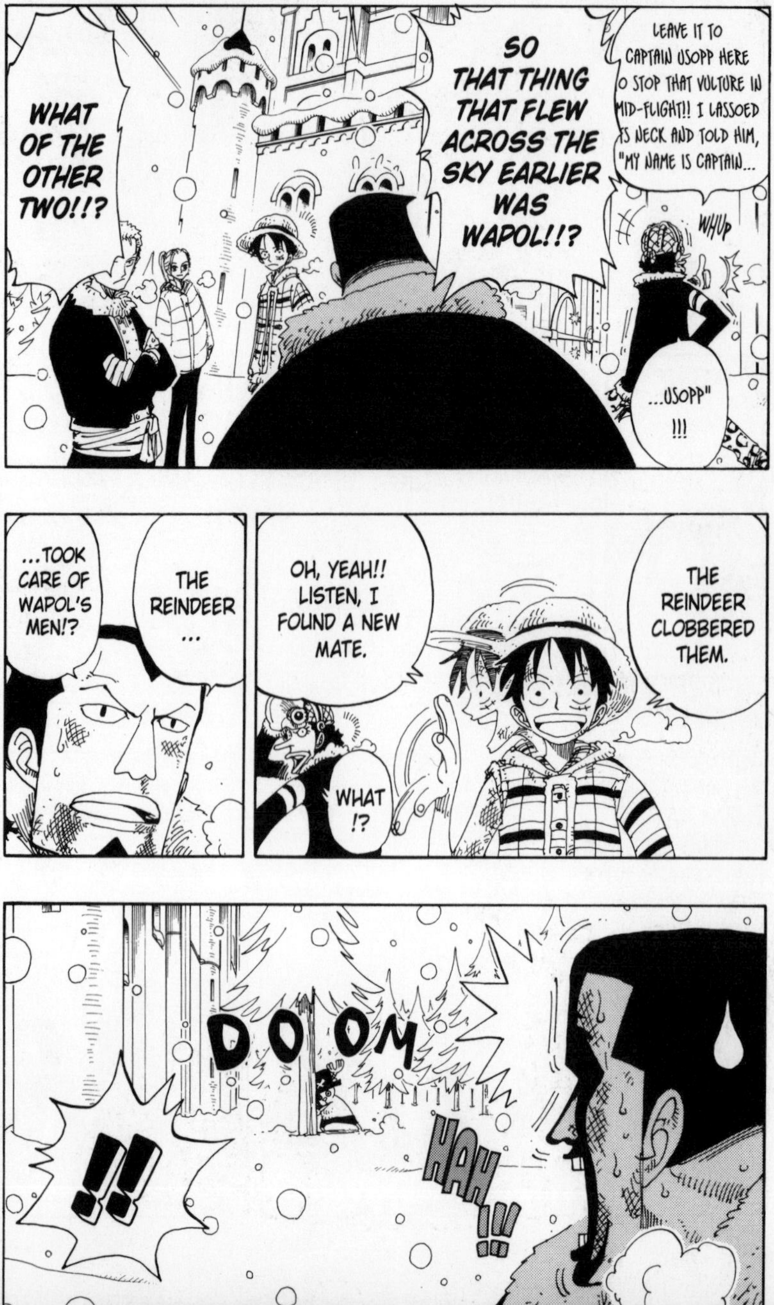

LEAVE IT TO CAPTAIN USOPP HERE O STOP THAT VULTURE IN MID-FLIGHT!! I LASSOED TS NECK AND TOLD HIM, "MY NAME IS CAPTAIN...
WHUP
...USOPP" !!!
SO THAT THING THAT FLEW ACROSS THE SKY EARLIER WAS WAPOL!!?
WHAT OF THE OTHER TWO!!?
THE REINDEER CLOBBERED THEM.
OH, YEAH!! LISTEN, I FOUND A NEW MATE.
WHAT !?
THE REINDEER ...
...TOOK CARE OF WAPOL'S MEN!?
HAH!!
DOOM
!!

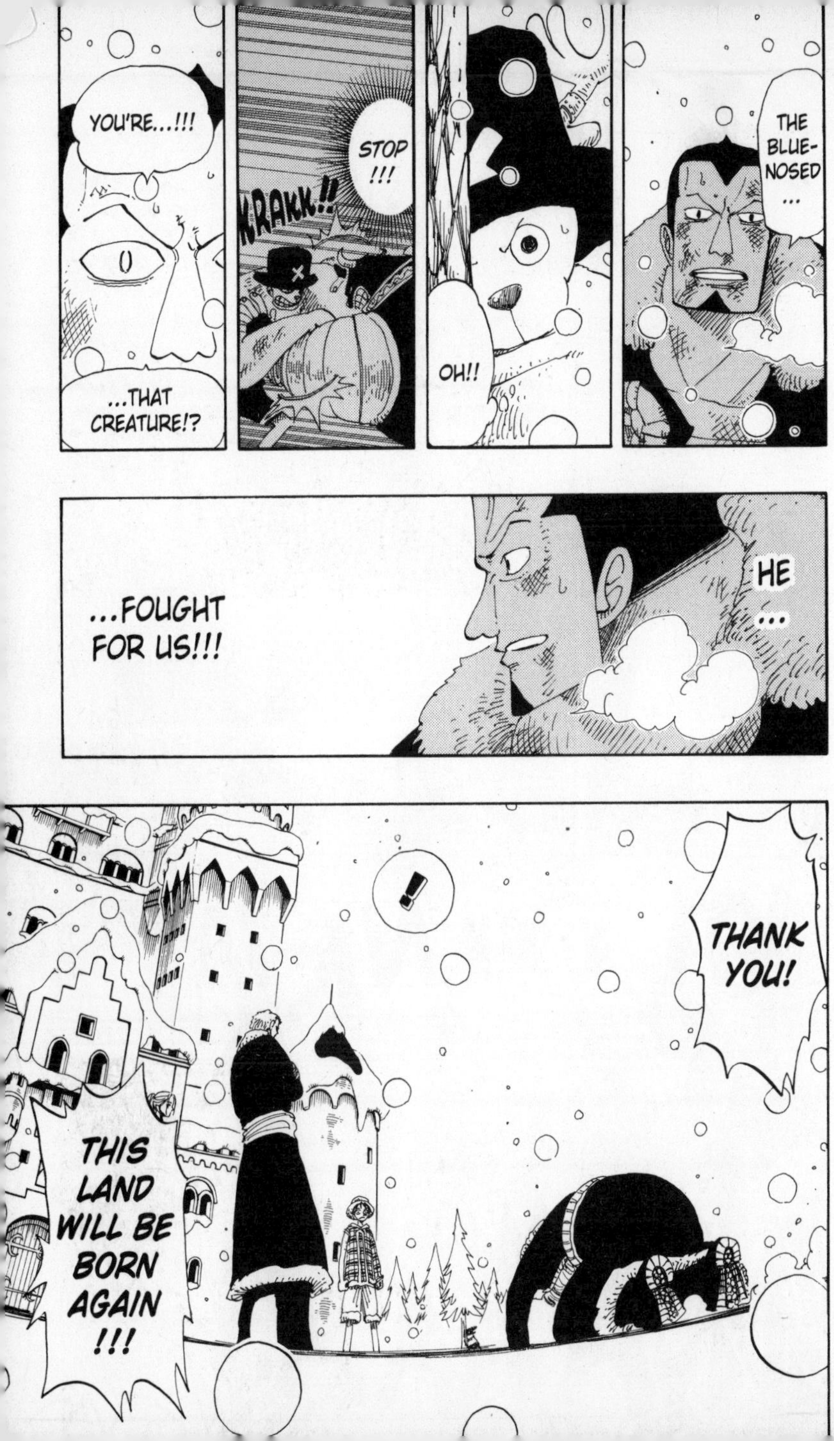
THE BLUE-NOSED ...
OH!!
STOP !!!
KRAKK!!
YOU'RE...!!!
...THAT CREATURE!?
HE ...
...FOUGHT FOR US!!!
THANK YOU!
!
THIS LAND WILL BE BORN AGAIN !!!

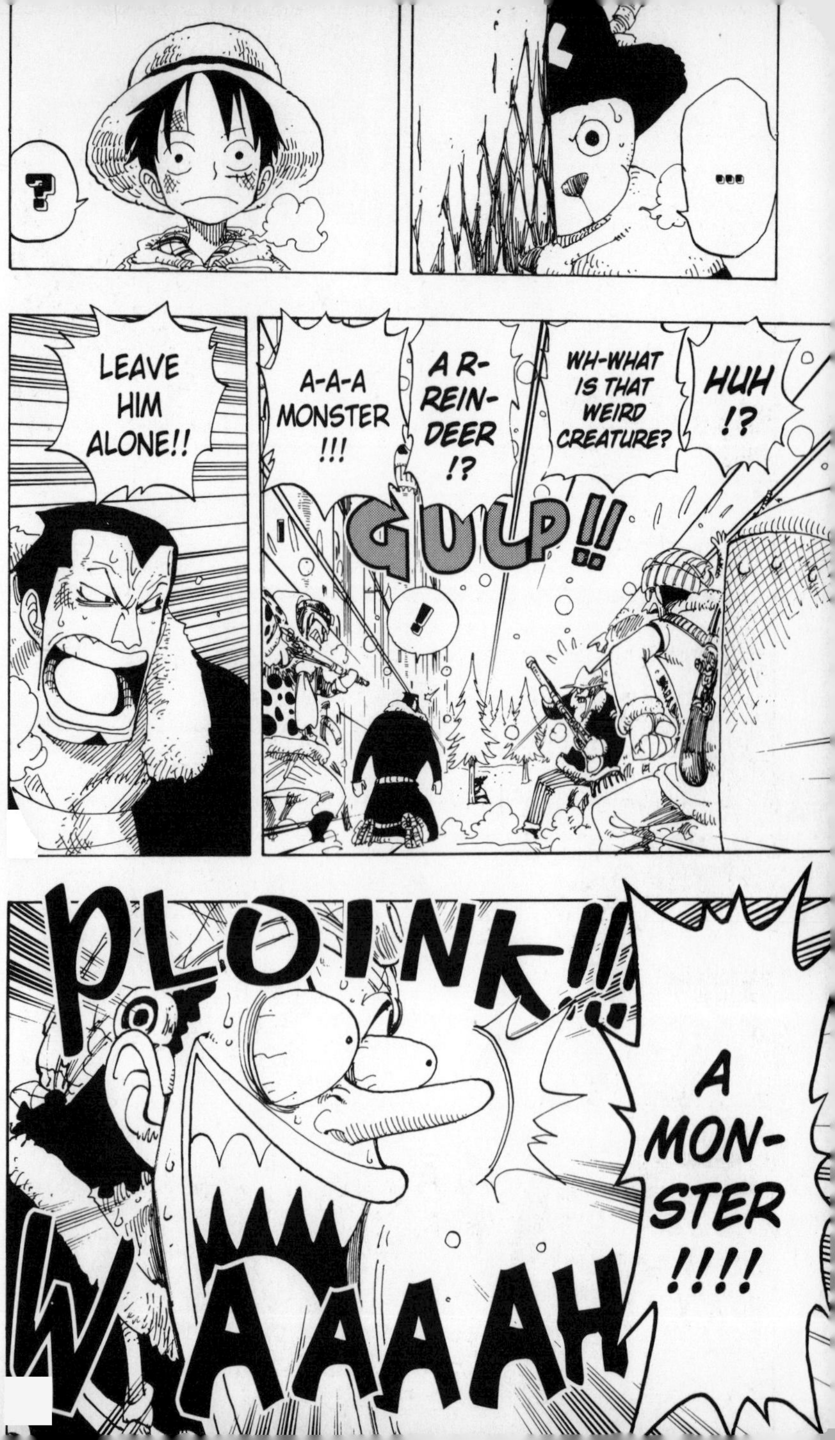
...
?
HUH !?
WH-WHAT IS THAT WEIRD CREATURE?
A R-REIN-DEER !?
A-A-A MONSTER !!!
GULP!!
!
LEAVE HIM ALONE!!
PLOINK!!
A MON-STER !!!!
WAAAAH

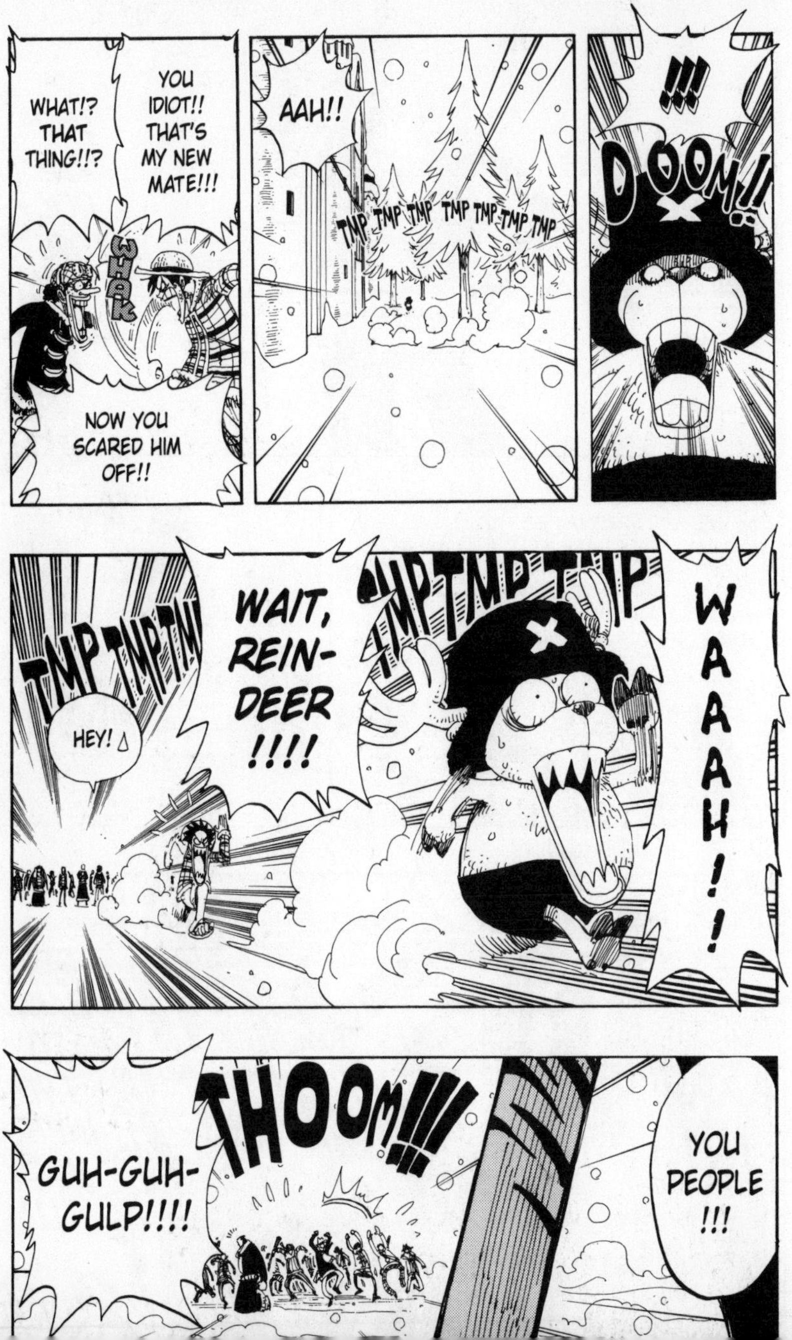
!!!
DOOM!!
AAH!!
TMP TMP TMP TMP TMP TMP TMP
YOU IDIOT!! THAT'S MY NEW MATE!!!
WHAT!? THAT THING!!?
WHAK
NOW YOU SCARED HIM OFF!!
WAAAH!!
TMP TMP TMP
WAIT, REIN-DEER!!!!
TMP TMP TM
HEY!
YOU PEOPLE!!!
THOOM!!!
GUH-GUH-GULP!!!!

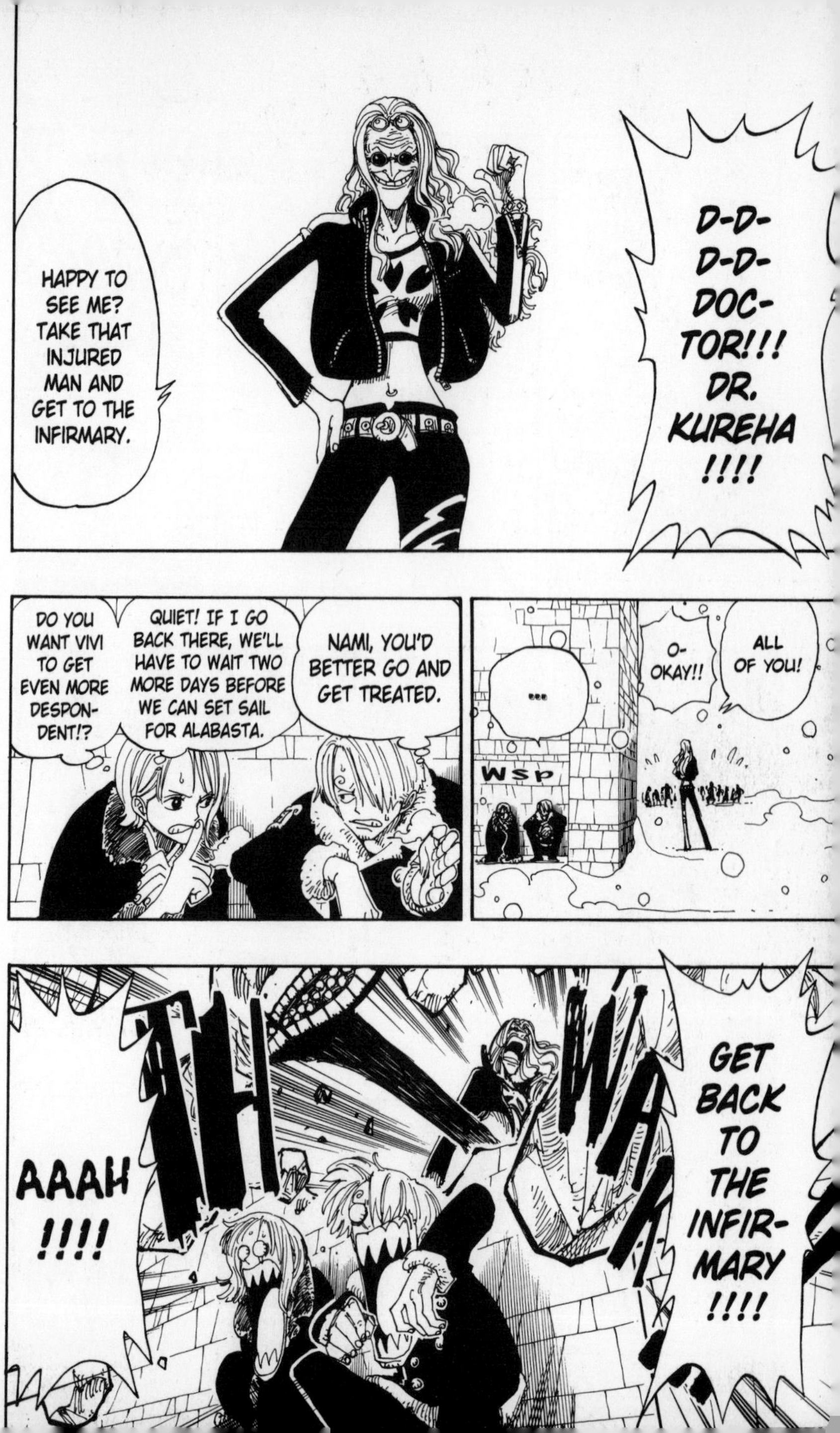

D-D-D-D-DOC-TOR!!! DR. KUREHA!!!!
HAPPY TO SEE ME? TAKE THAT INJURED MAN AND GET TO THE INFIRMARY.
ALL OF YOU!
O-OKAY!!
...
WSP
NAMI, YOU'D BETTER GO AND GET TREATED.
QUIET! IF I GO BACK THERE, WE'LL HAVE TO WAIT TWO MORE DAYS BEFORE WE CAN SET SAIL FOR ALABASTA.
DO YOU WANT VIVI TO GET EVEN MORE DESPON-DENT!?
GET BACK TO THE INFIR-MARY!!!!
AAAH!!!!

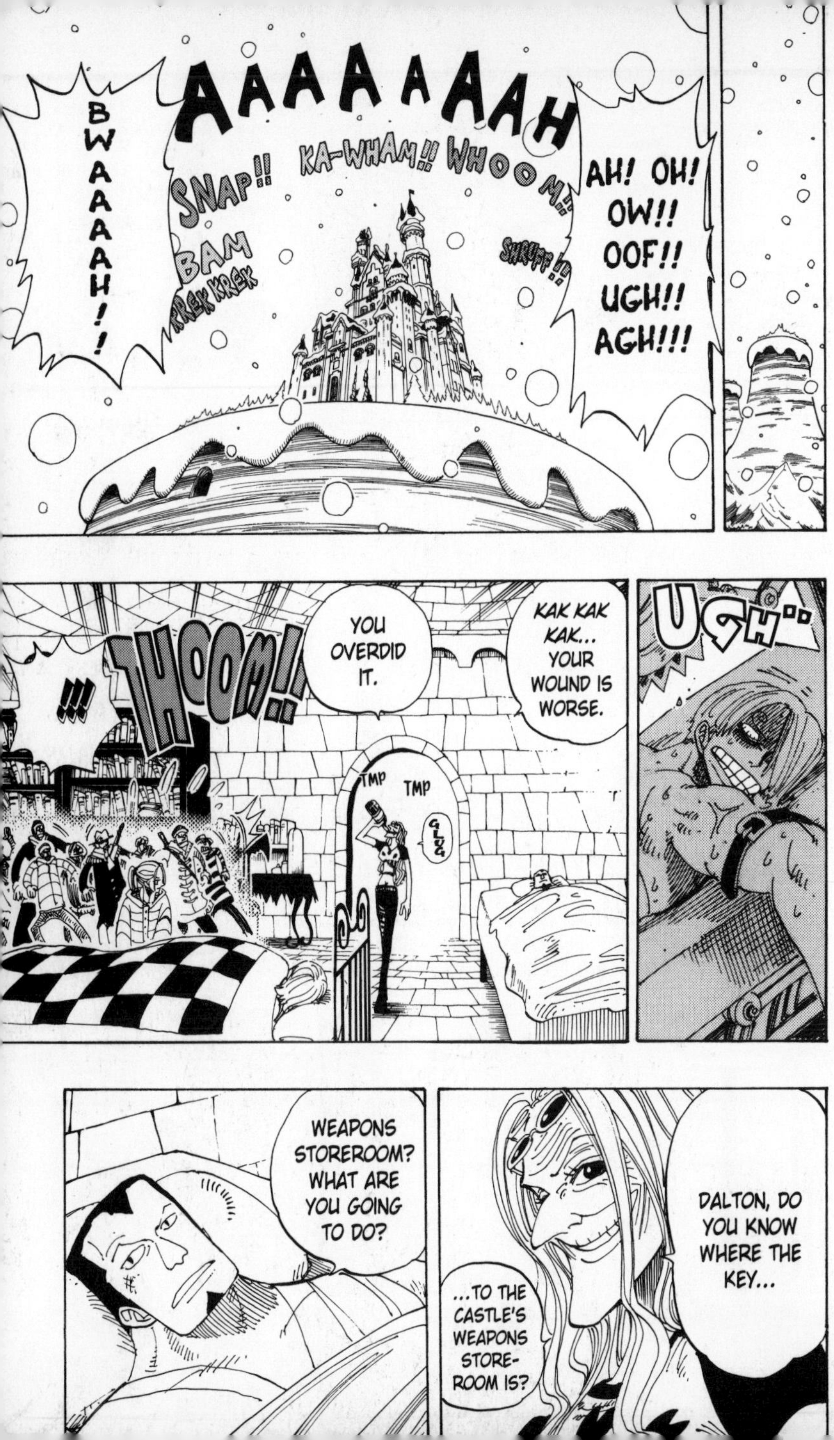
AH! OH! OW!! OOF!! UGH!! AGH!!!
AAAAAAAH
WHOOOM!!
KA-WHAM!!
SNAP!!
BWAAAAAAH!!
SHRUFF!!
BAM
KREK KREK
UGH
KAK KAK KAK... YOUR WOUND IS WORSE.
YOU OVERDID IT.
THOOM!!
!!!
TMP
TMP
GLUG
DALTON, DO YOU KNOW WHERE THE KEY...
...TO THE CASTLE'S WEAPONS STORE-ROOM IS?
WEAPONS STOREROOM? WHAT ARE YOU GOING TO DO?

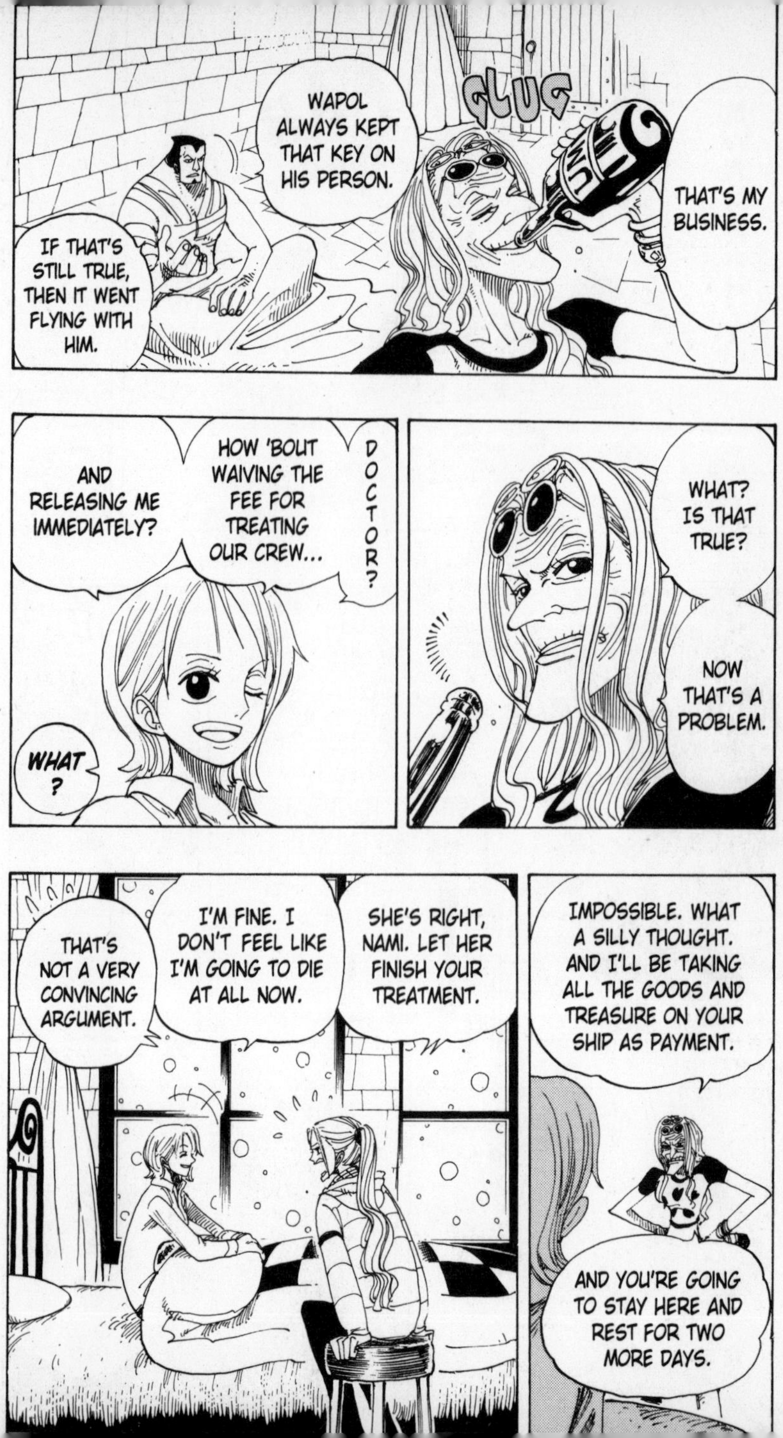
GLUG
THAT'S MY BUSINESS.
WAPOL ALWAYS KEPT THAT KEY ON HIS PERSON.
IF THAT'S STILL TRUE, THEN IT WENT FLYING WITH HIM.
WHAT? IS THAT TRUE?
NOW THAT'S A PROBLEM.
DOCTOR?
HOW 'BOUT WAIVING THE FEE FOR TREATING OUR CREW...
AND RELEASING ME IMMEDIATELY?
WHAT?
IMPOSSIBLE. WHAT A SILLY THOUGHT. AND I'LL BE TAKING ALL THE GOODS AND TREASURE ON YOUR SHIP AS PAYMENT.
AND YOU'RE GOING TO STAY HERE AND REST FOR TWO MORE DAYS.
SHE'S RIGHT, NAMI. LET HER FINISH YOUR TREATMENT.
I'M FINE. I DON'T FEEL LIKE I'M GOING TO DIE AT ALL NOW.
THAT'S NOT A VERY CONVINCING ARGUMENT.

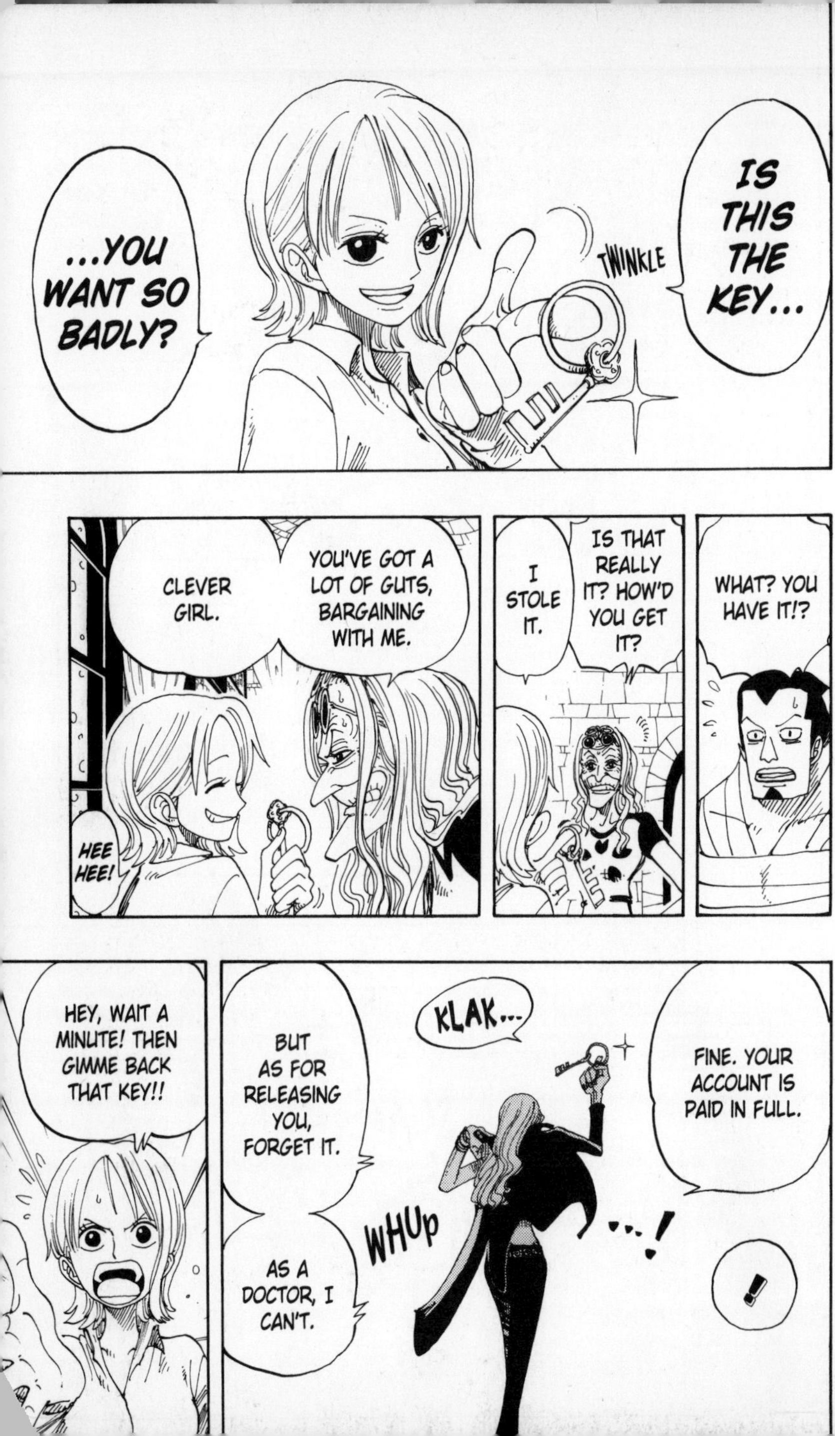
IS THIS THE KEY...
TWINKLE
...YOU WANT SO BADLY?
WHAT? YOU HAVE IT!?
IS THAT REALLY IT? HOW'D YOU GET IT?
I STOLE IT.
YOU'VE GOT A LOT OF GUTS, BARGAINING WITH ME.
CLEVER GIRL.
HEE HEE!
FINE. YOUR ACCOUNT IS PAID IN FULL.
KLAK...
...!
!
WHUP
BUT AS FOR RELEASING YOU, FORGET IT.
AS A DOCTOR, I CAN'T.
HEY, WAIT A MINUTE! THEN GIMME BACK THAT KEY!!

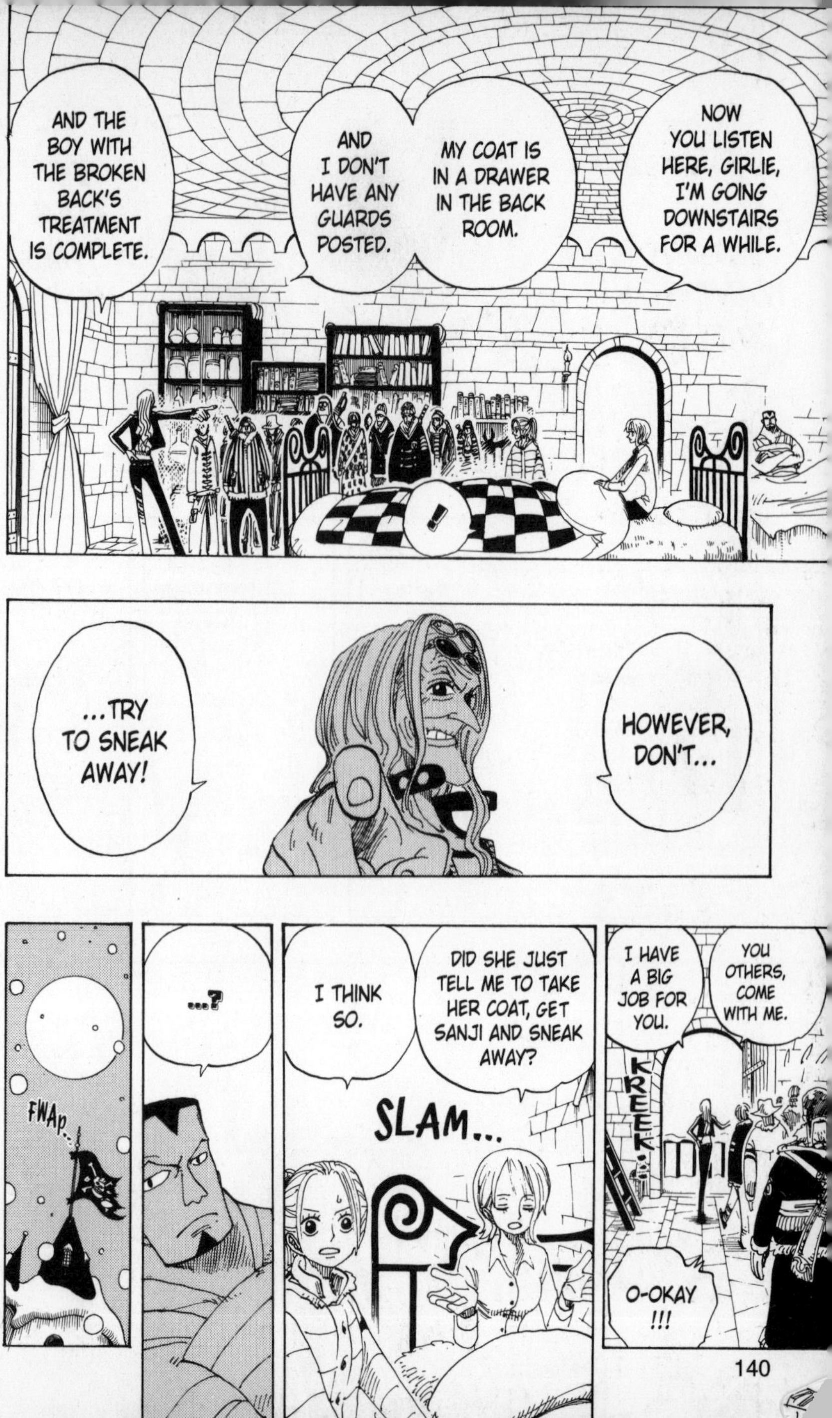
NOW YOU LISTEN HERE, GIRLIE, I'M GOING DOWNSTAIRS FOR A WHILE.
MY COAT IS IN A DRAWER IN THE BACK ROOM.
AND I DON'T HAVE ANY GUARDS POSTED.
AND THE BOY WITH THE BROKEN BACK'S TREATMENT IS COMPLETE.
!
HOWEVER, DON'T...
...TRY TO SNEAK AWAY!
YOU OTHERS, COME WITH ME.
I HAVE A BIG JOB FOR YOU.
KREEK...
O-OKAY !!!
DID SHE JUST TELL ME TO TAKE HER COAT, GET SANJI AND SNEAK AWAY?
I THINK SO.
SLAM...
...?
FWAp...

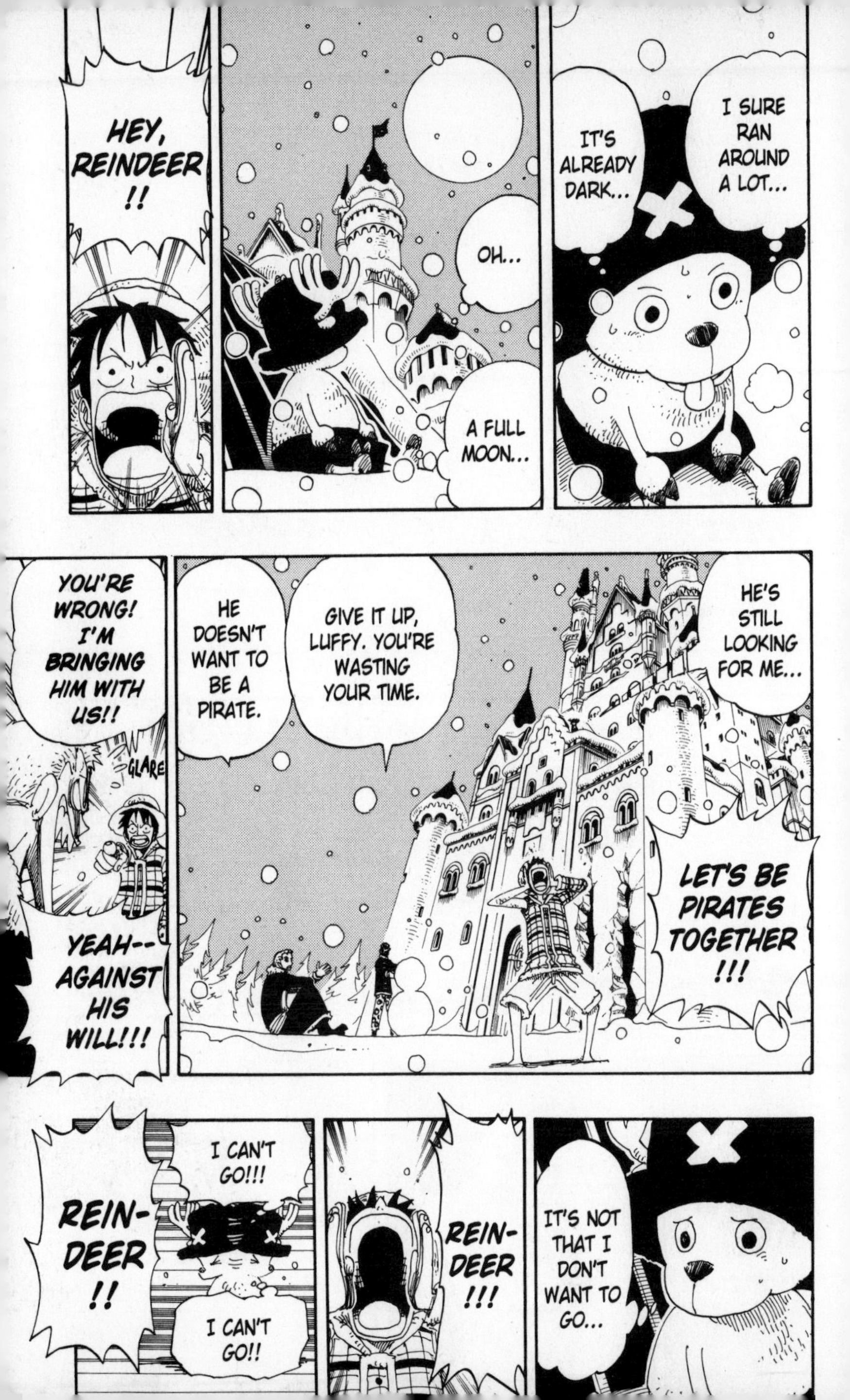
I SURE RAN AROUND A LOT...
IT'S ALREADY DARK...
OH...
A FULL MOON...
HEY, REINDEER!!
HE'S STILL LOOKING FOR ME...
LET'S BE PIRATES TOGETHER!!!
GIVE IT UP, LUFFY. YOU'RE WASTING YOUR TIME.
HE DOESN'T WANT TO BE A PIRATE.
YOU'RE WRONG! I'M BRINGING HIM WITH US!!
GLARE
YEAH--AGAINST HIS WILL!!!
IT'S NOT THAT I DON'T WANT TO GO...
REIN-DEER!!!
I CAN'T GO!!!
REIN-DEER!!
I CAN'T GO!!

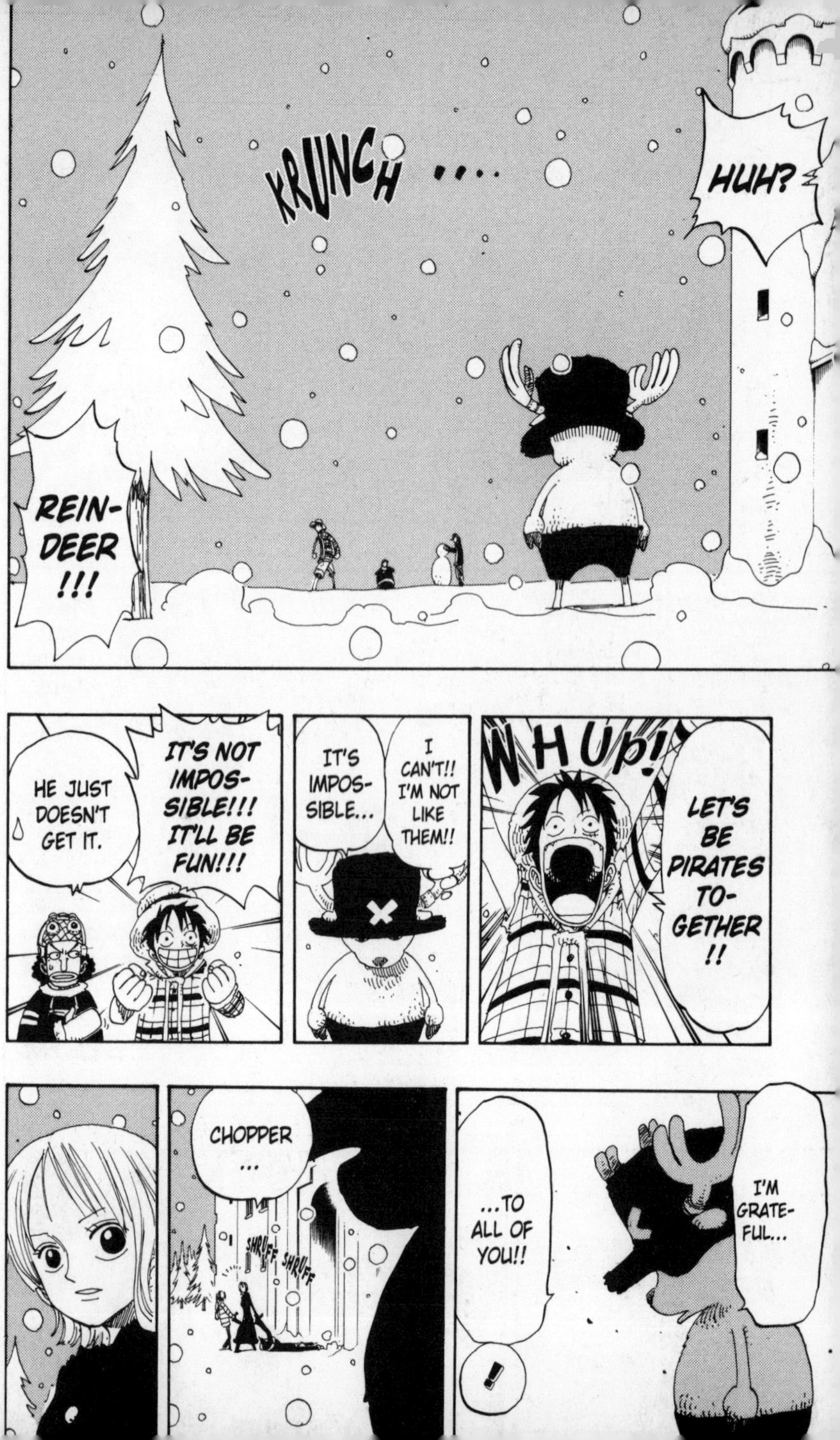
HUH?
KRUNCH ...
REIN-DEER !!!
WHUP!
LET'S BE PIRATES TO-GETHER !!
I CAN'T!! I'M NOT LIKE THEM!!
IT'S IMPOS-SIBLE...
IT'S NOT IMPOS-SIBLE!!! IT'LL BE FUN!!!
HE JUST DOESN'T GET IT.
I'M GRATE-FUL...
...TO ALL OF YOU!!
!
CHOPPER ...
SHRUFF
SHRUFF

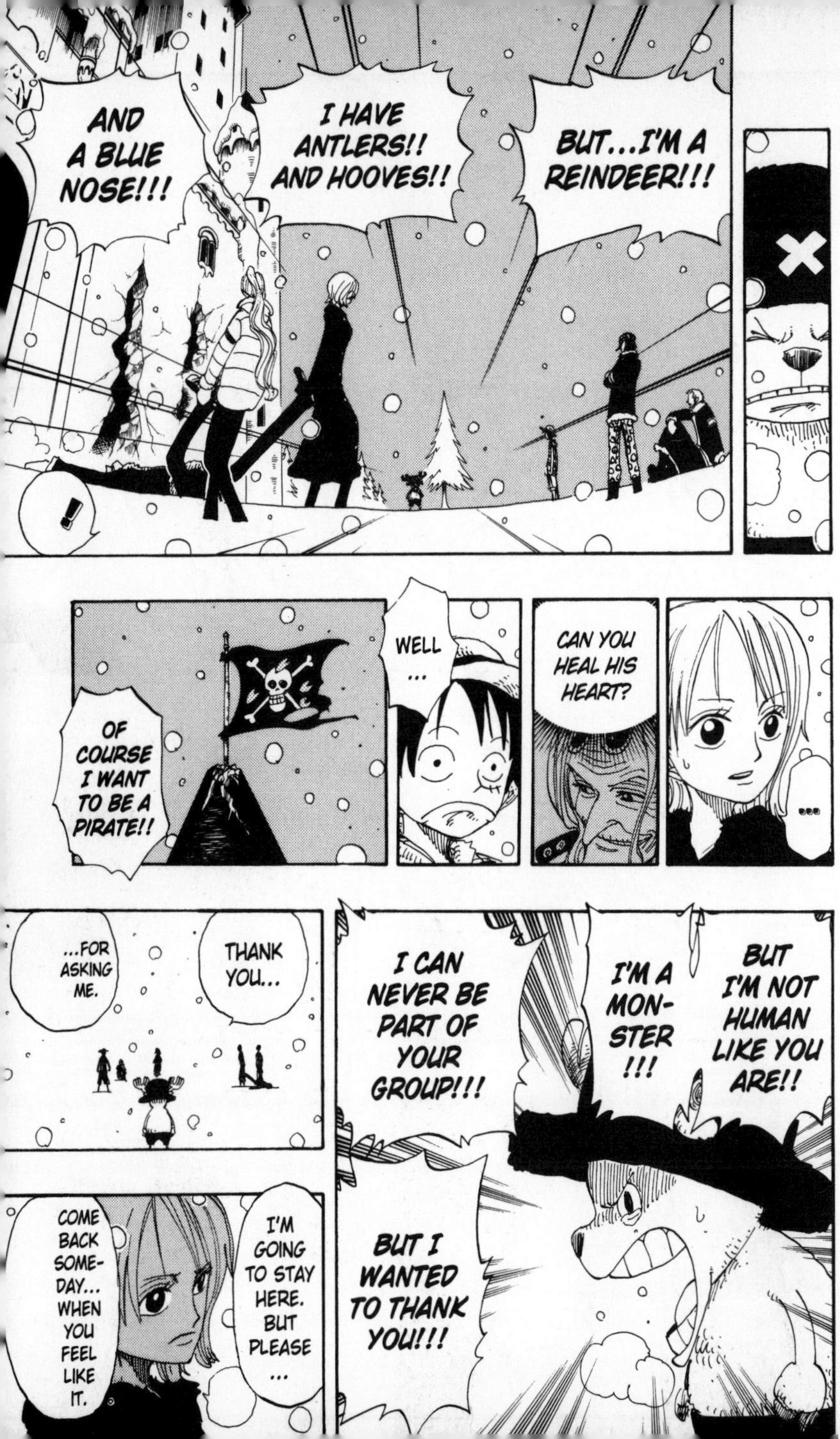
BUT...I'M A REINDEER!!!
I HAVE ANTLERS!! AND HOOVES!!
AND A BLUE NOSE!!!
!
...
CAN YOU HEAL HIS HEART?
WELL ...
OF COURSE I WANT TO BE A PIRATE!!
BUT I'M NOT HUMAN LIKE YOU ARE!!
I'M A MON-STER!!!
I CAN NEVER BE PART OF YOUR GROUP!!!
BUT I WANTED TO THANK YOU!!!
THANK YOU...
...FOR ASKING ME.
I'M GOING TO STAY HERE. BUT PLEASE ...
COME BACK SOME-DAY... WHEN YOU FEEL LIKE IT.

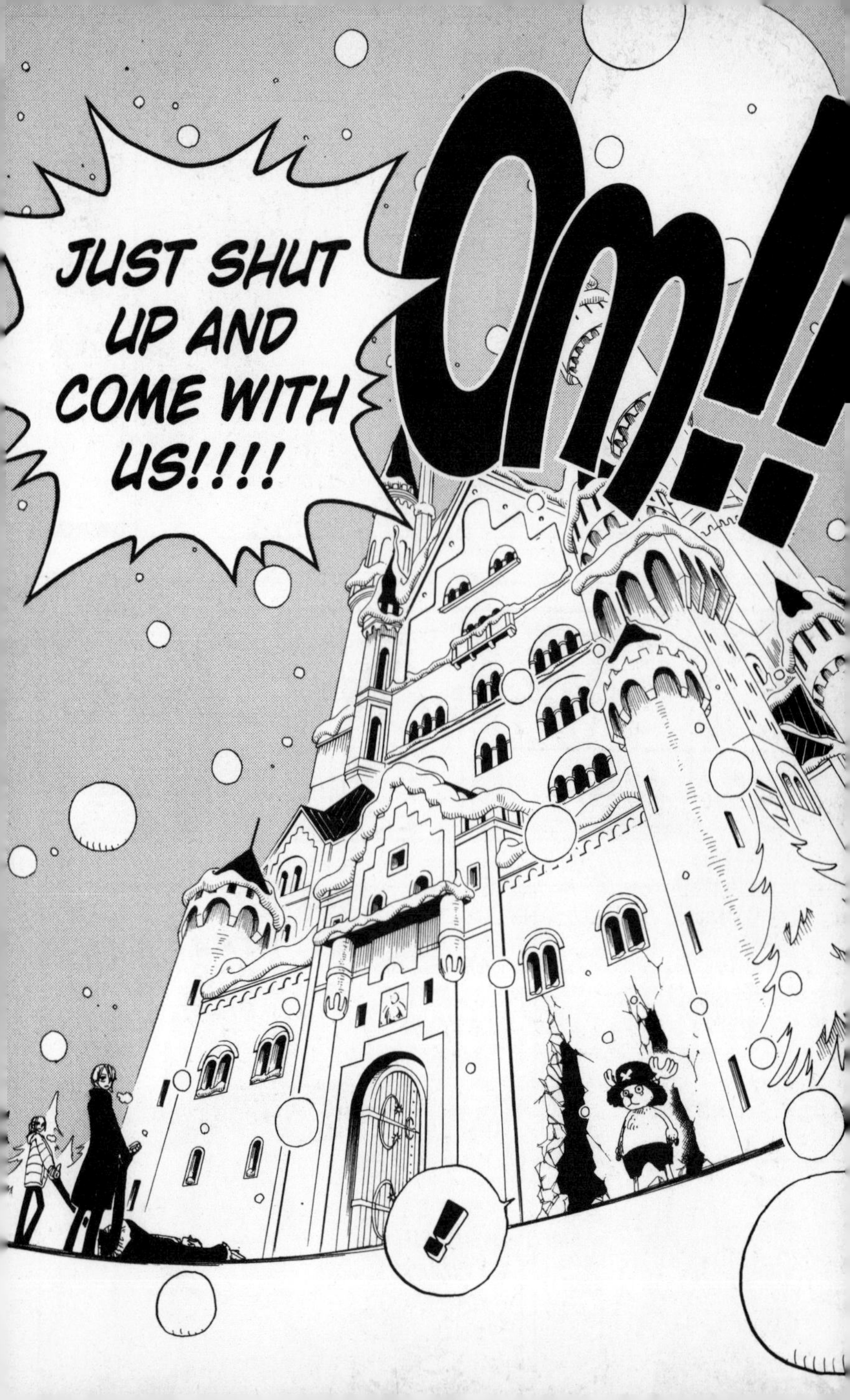
JUST SHUT UP AND COME WITH US!!!!
OM!!
!

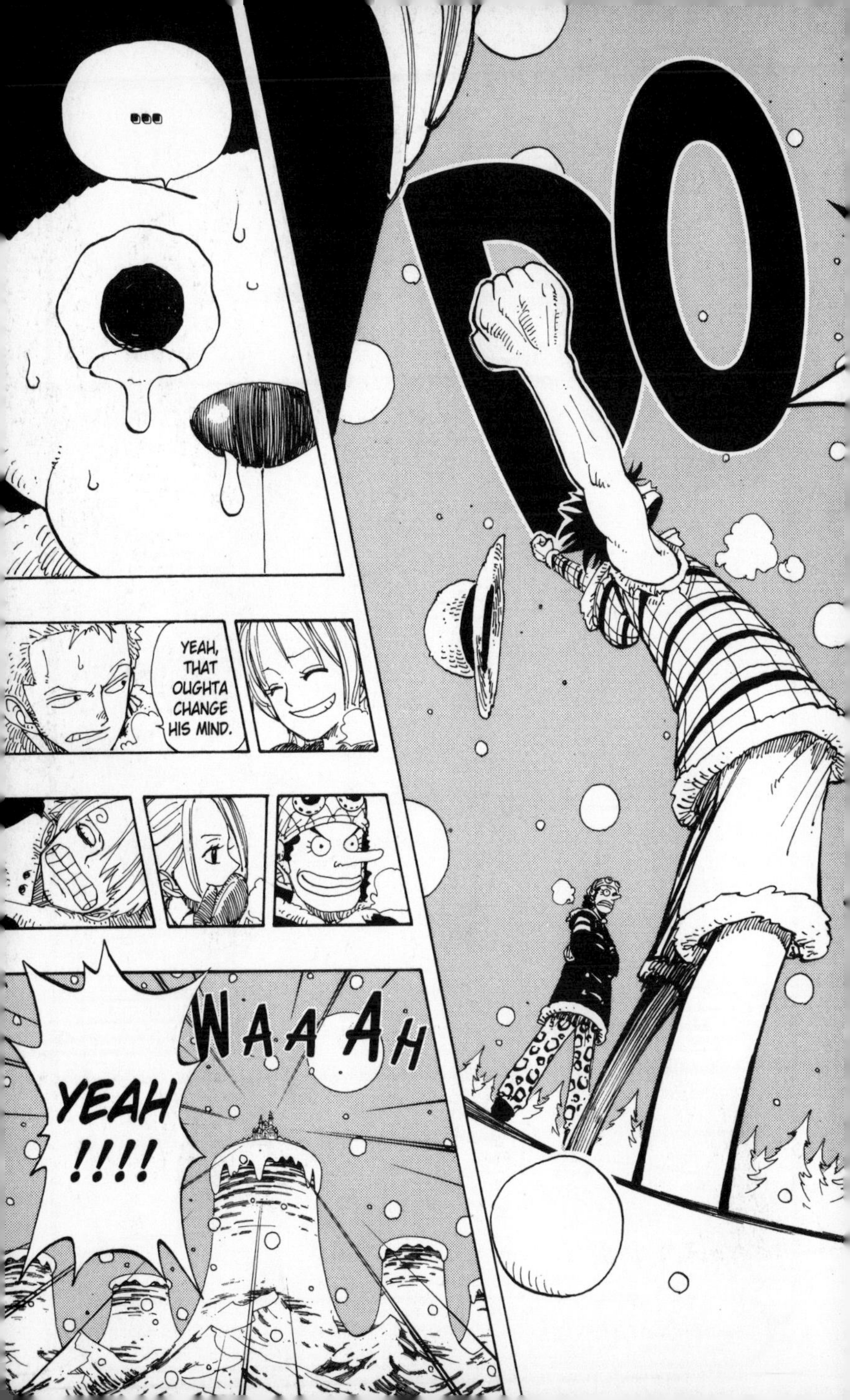
DO
...
YEAH, THAT OUGHTA CHANGE HIS MIND.
WAAAAH
YEAH!!!!

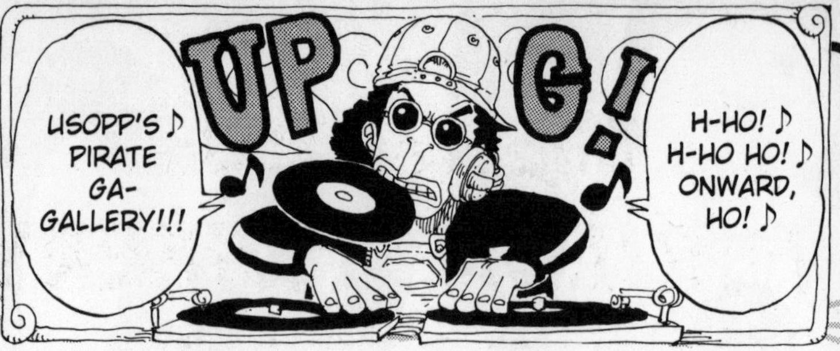
H-HO! ♪
H-HO HO! ♪
ONWARD,
HO! ♪
USOPP'S ♪
PIRATE
GA-
GALLERY!!!

NO ONE'S GONNA STOP ME!

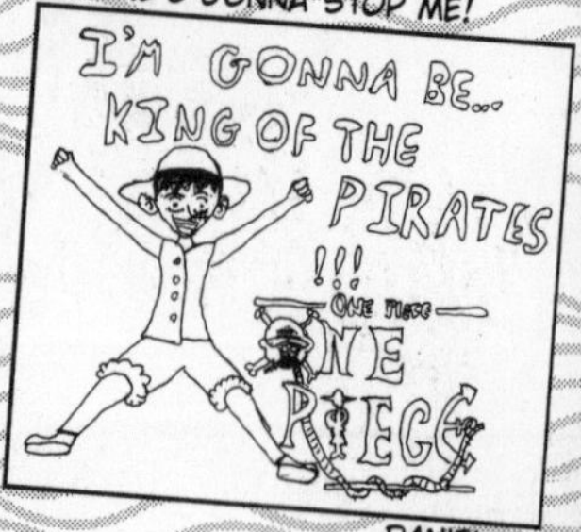
I'M GONNA BE...
KING OF THE
PIRATES
!!!
ONE PIECE
ONE
PIECE

DANIEL, 12

JUST KICKIN' IT OLD SKOOL...

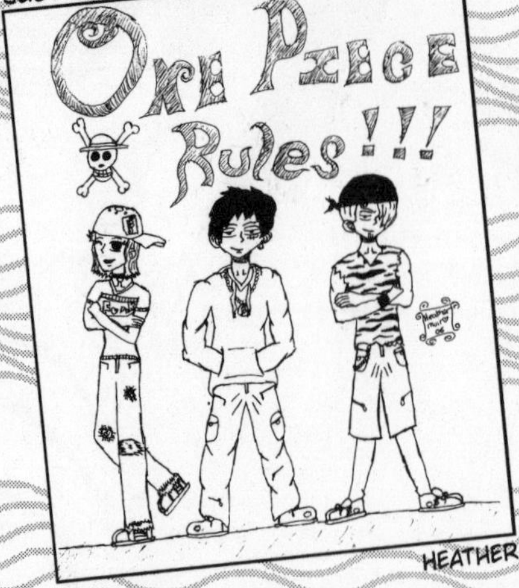
ONE PIECE
Rules!!!

HEATHER

GOT SWORD?

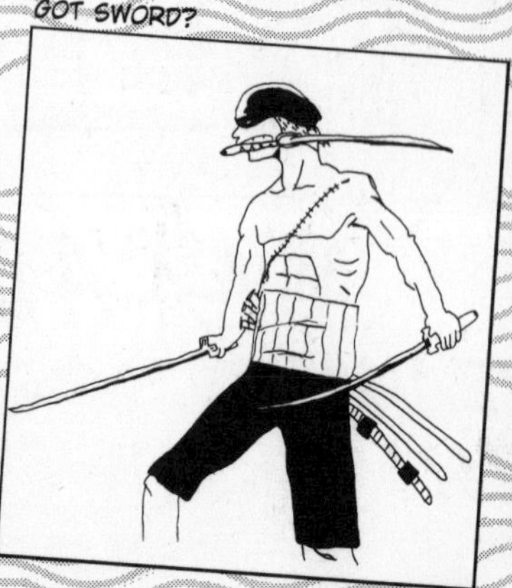

DENNIS

EAT YOUR VEGETABLES!!

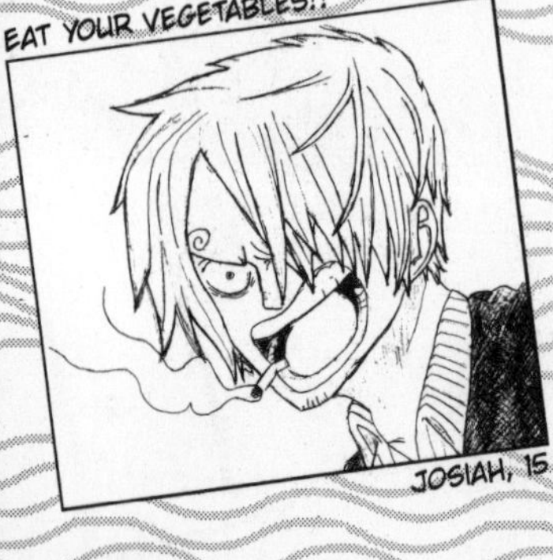

JOSIAH, 15

SUBMIT YOUR FAN ART TO:
SHONEN JUMP C/O VIZ MEDIA, LLC P.O. BOX 77010 SAN FRANCISCO, CA 94107
*REMEMBER TO INCLUDE YOUR NAME, AGE AND PARENT RELEASE FORM!!

USOPP'S COMMENTS WERE TRANSMITTED THROUGH THE U.S. SHONEN JUMP TEAM -EDITOR

# Chapter 153:
# HIRILUK'S CHERRY BLOSSOMS

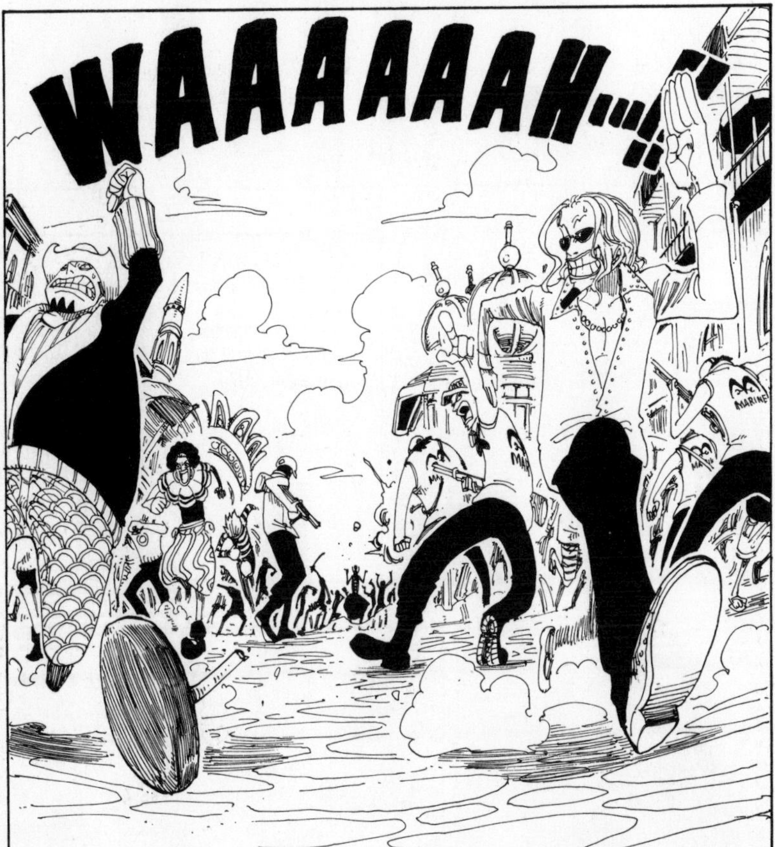
WAAAAAAAH...!!

DJANGO'S DANCE HEAVEN, VOL. 21:
"WHAT LUCK – DJANGO ON THE RUN"

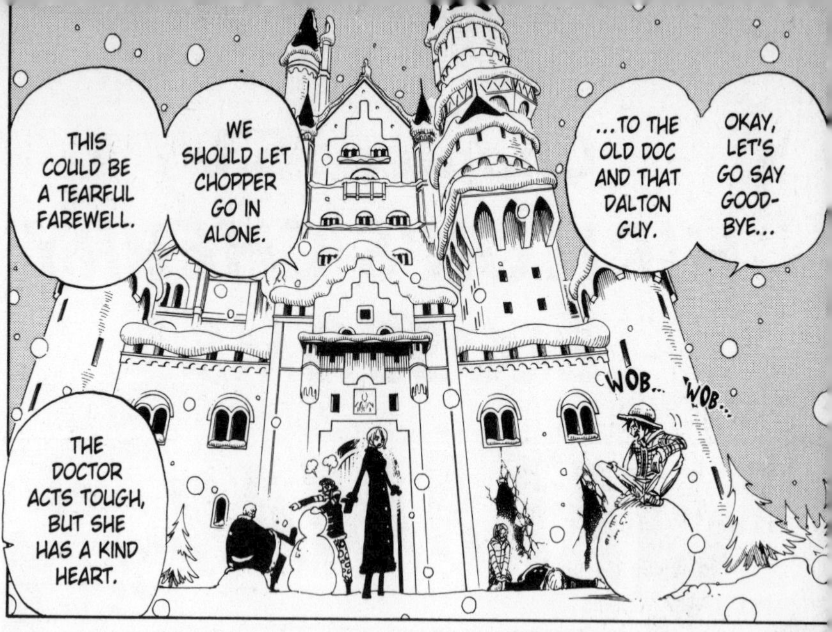
OKAY, LET'S GO SAY GOOD-BYE...
...TO THE OLD DOC AND THAT DALTON GUY.
WE SHOULD LET CHOPPER GO IN ALONE.
THIS COULD BE A TEARFUL FAREWELL.
WOB... WOB...
THE DOCTOR ACTS TOUGH, BUT SHE HAS A KIND HEART.

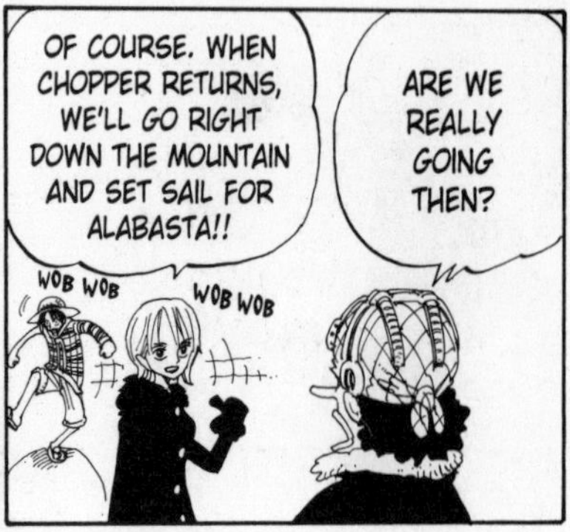
ARE WE REALLY GOING THEN?
OF COURSE. WHEN CHOPPER RETURNS, WE'LL GO RIGHT DOWN THE MOUNTAIN AND SET SAIL FOR ALABASTA!!
WOB WOB
WOB WOB

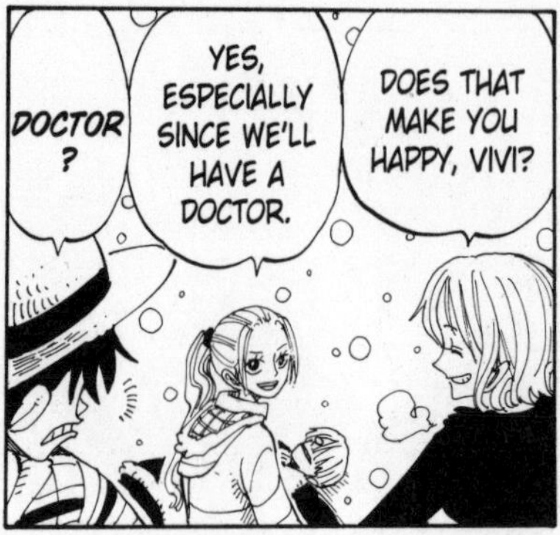
DOES THAT MAKE YOU HAPPY, VIVI?
YES, ESPECIALLY SINCE WE'LL HAVE A DOCTOR.
DOCTOR?

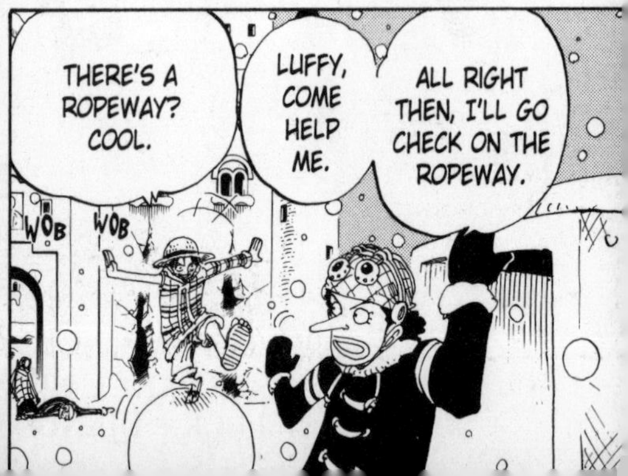
ALL RIGHT THEN, I'LL GO CHECK ON THE ROPEWAY.
LUFFY, COME HELP ME.
THERE'S A ROPEWAY? COOL.
WOB
WOB

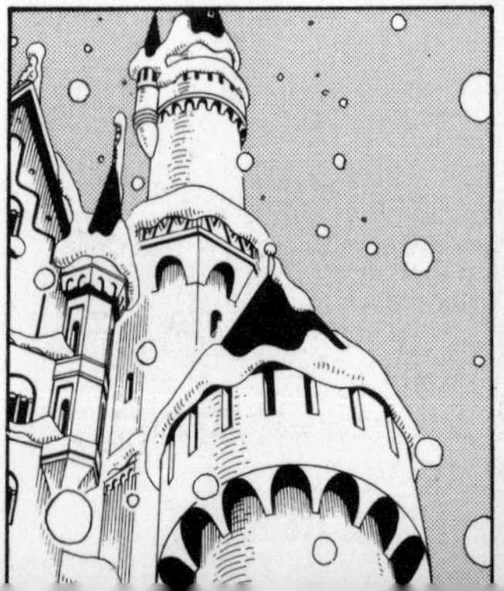

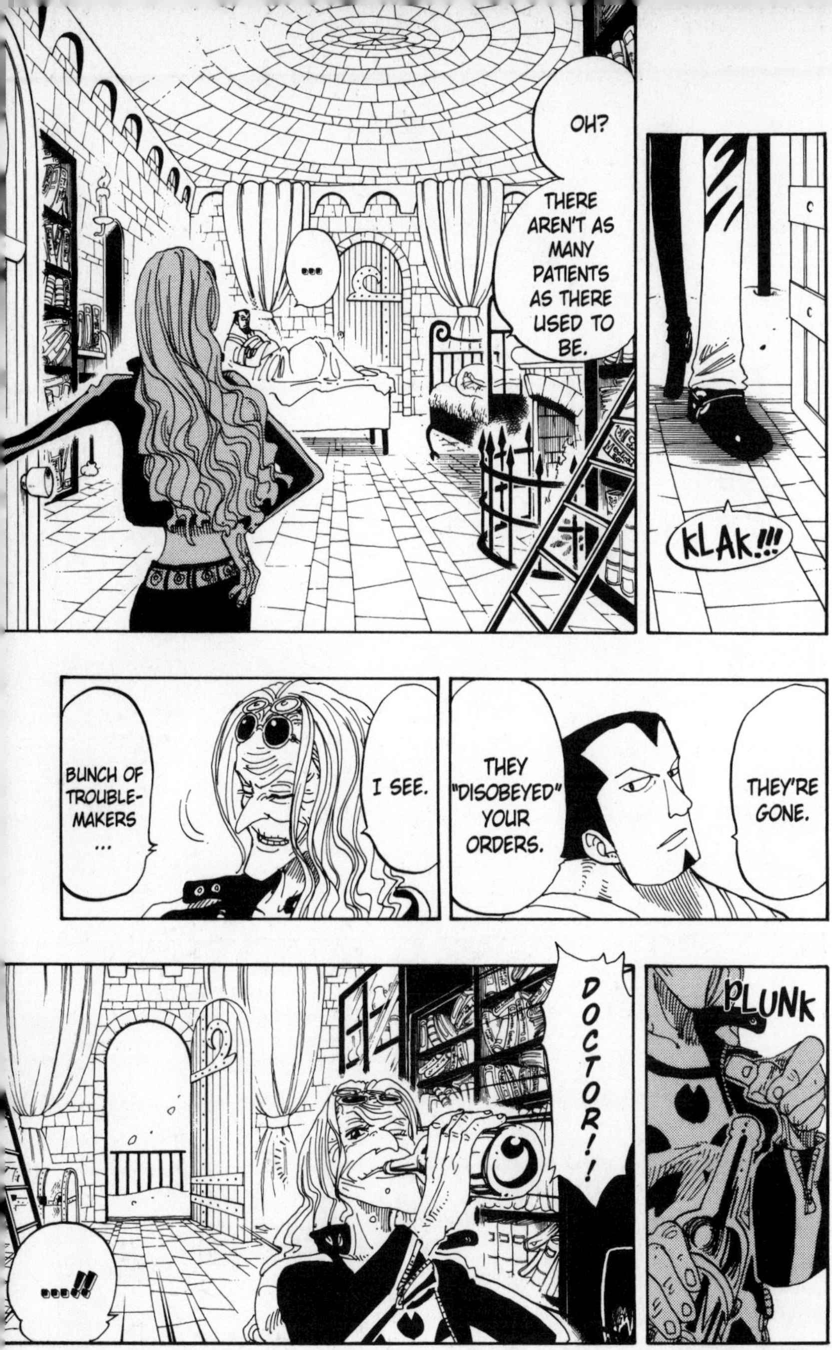

KLAK!!!
OH?
THERE AREN'T AS MANY PATIENTS AS THERE USED TO BE.
...
THEY'RE GONE.
THEY "DISOBEYED" YOUR ORDERS.
I SEE.
BUNCH OF TROUBLE-MAKERS ...
PLUNK
DOCTOR!!
...!!

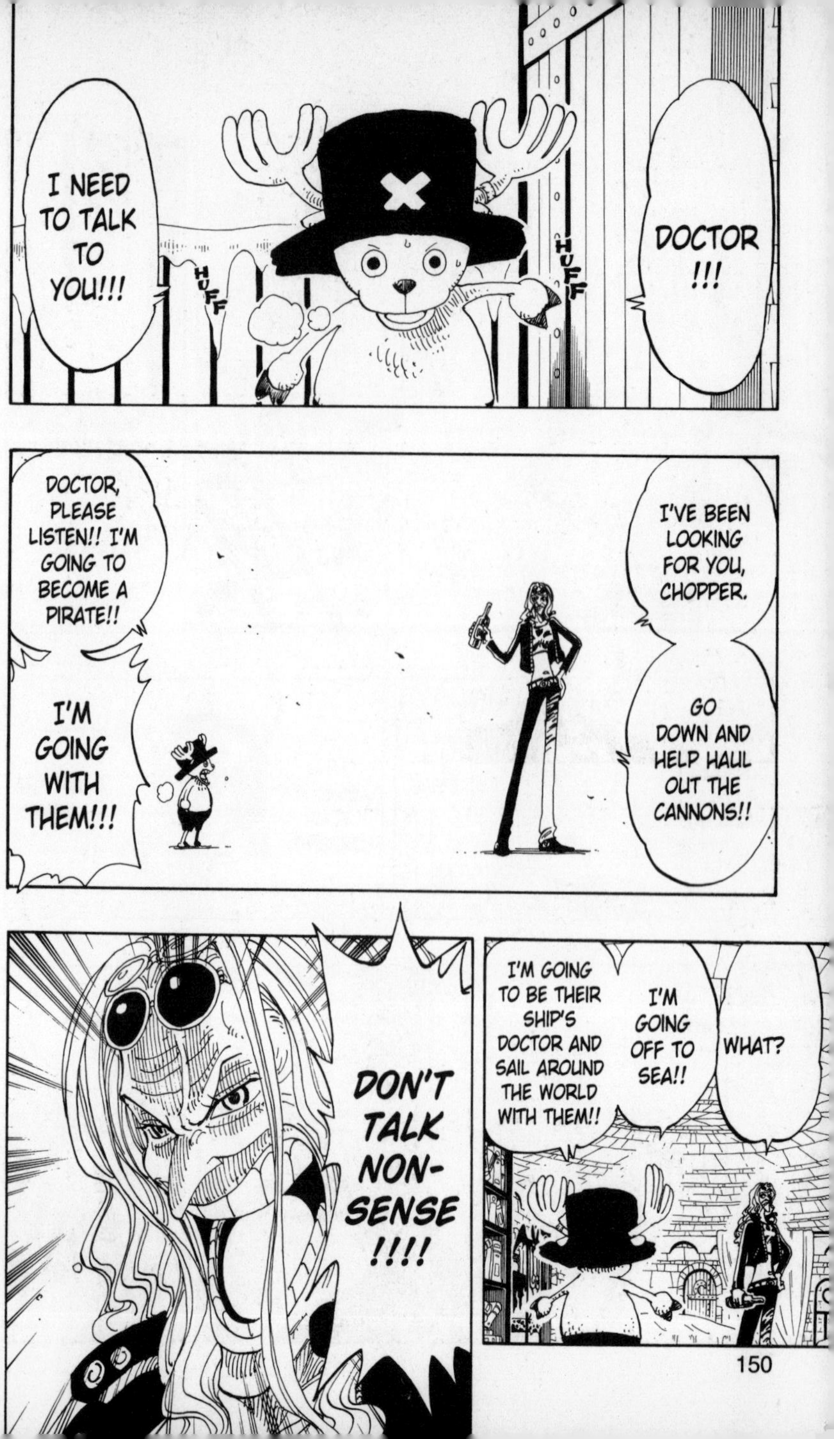
DOCTOR !!!
HUFF
HUFF
I NEED TO TALK TO YOU!!!
I'VE BEEN LOOKING FOR YOU, CHOPPER.
GO DOWN AND HELP HAUL OUT THE CANNONS!!
DOCTOR, PLEASE LISTEN!! I'M GOING TO BECOME A PIRATE!!
I'M GOING WITH THEM!!!
WHAT?
I'M GOING OFF TO SEA!!
I'M GOING TO BE THEIR SHIP'S DOCTOR AND SAIL AROUND THE WORLD WITH THEM!!
DON'T TALK NON-SENSE!!!!

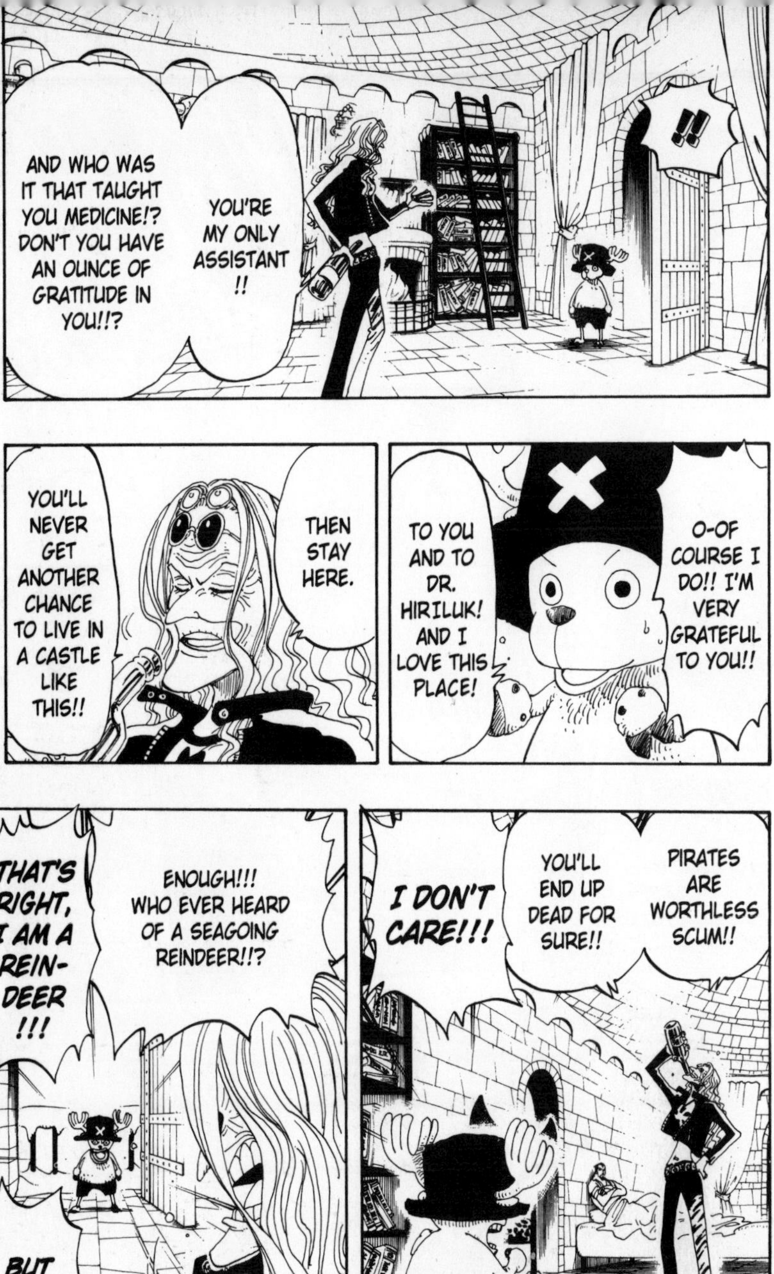
!!
YOU'RE MY ONLY ASSISTANT!!
AND WHO WAS IT THAT TAUGHT YOU MEDICINE!? DON'T YOU HAVE AN OUNCE OF GRATITUDE IN YOU!!?
O-OF COURSE I DO!! I'M VERY GRATEFUL TO YOU!!
TO YOU AND TO DR. HIRILUK! AND I LOVE THIS PLACE!
THEN STAY HERE.
YOU'LL NEVER GET ANOTHER CHANCE TO LIVE IN A CASTLE LIKE THIS!!
PIRATES ARE WORTHLESS SCUM!!
YOU'LL END UP DEAD FOR SURE!!
I DON'T CARE!!!
ENOUGH!!! WHO EVER HEARD OF A SEAGOING REINDEER!!?
THAT'S RIGHT, I AM A REINDEER!!!
BUT ...!!!

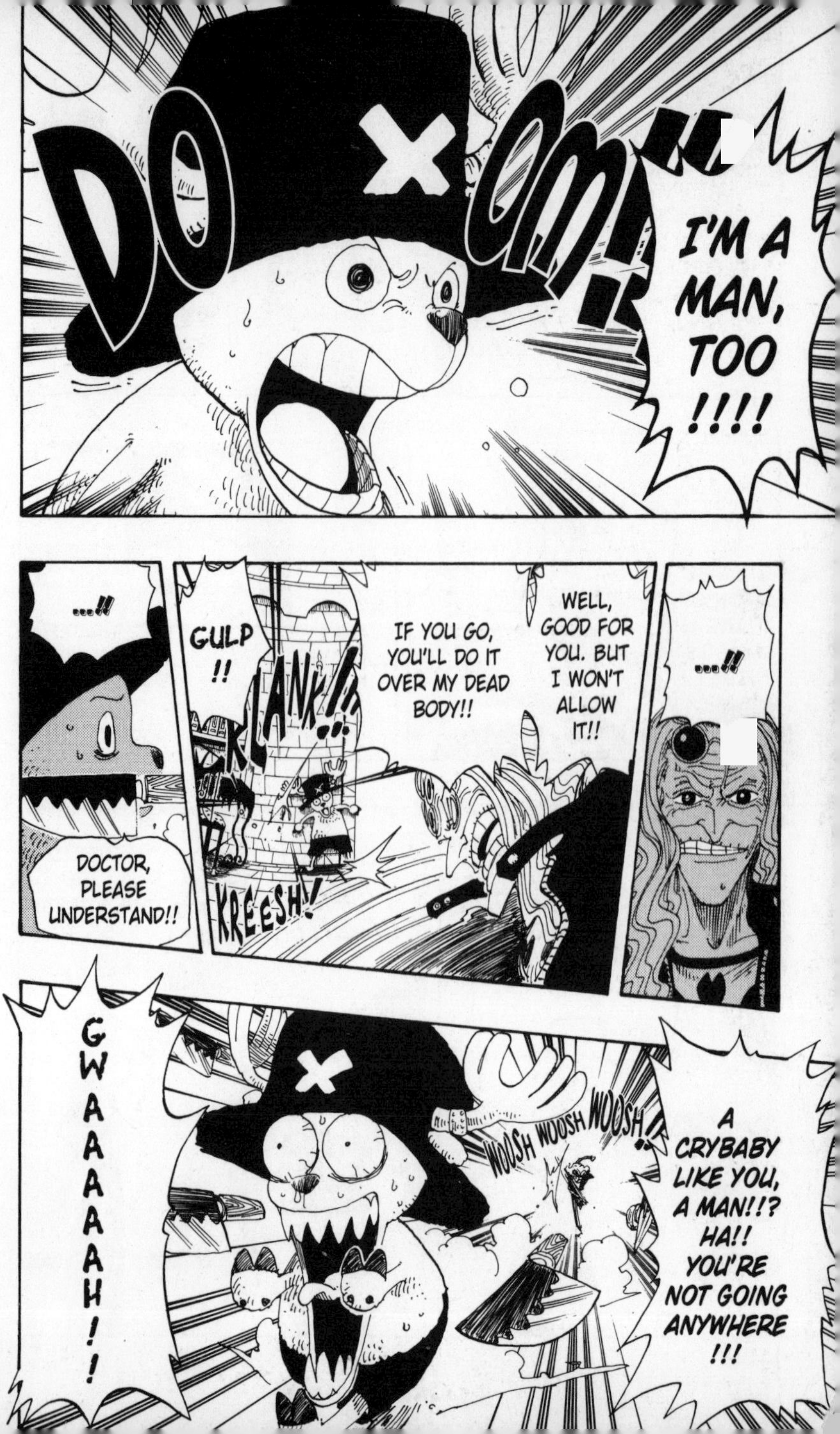
DOOM!!
I'M A MAN, TOO!!!!
...!!
WELL, GOOD FOR YOU. BUT I WON'T ALLOW IT!!
IF YOU GO, YOU'LL DO IT OVER MY DEAD BODY!!
KLANK!!
GULP!!
KREESH!
...!!
DOCTOR, PLEASE UNDERSTAND!!
A CRYBABY LIKE YOU, A MAN!!? HA!! YOU'RE NOT GOING ANYWHERE!!!
WOOSH WOOSH WOOSH!!
GWAAAAAAH!!!

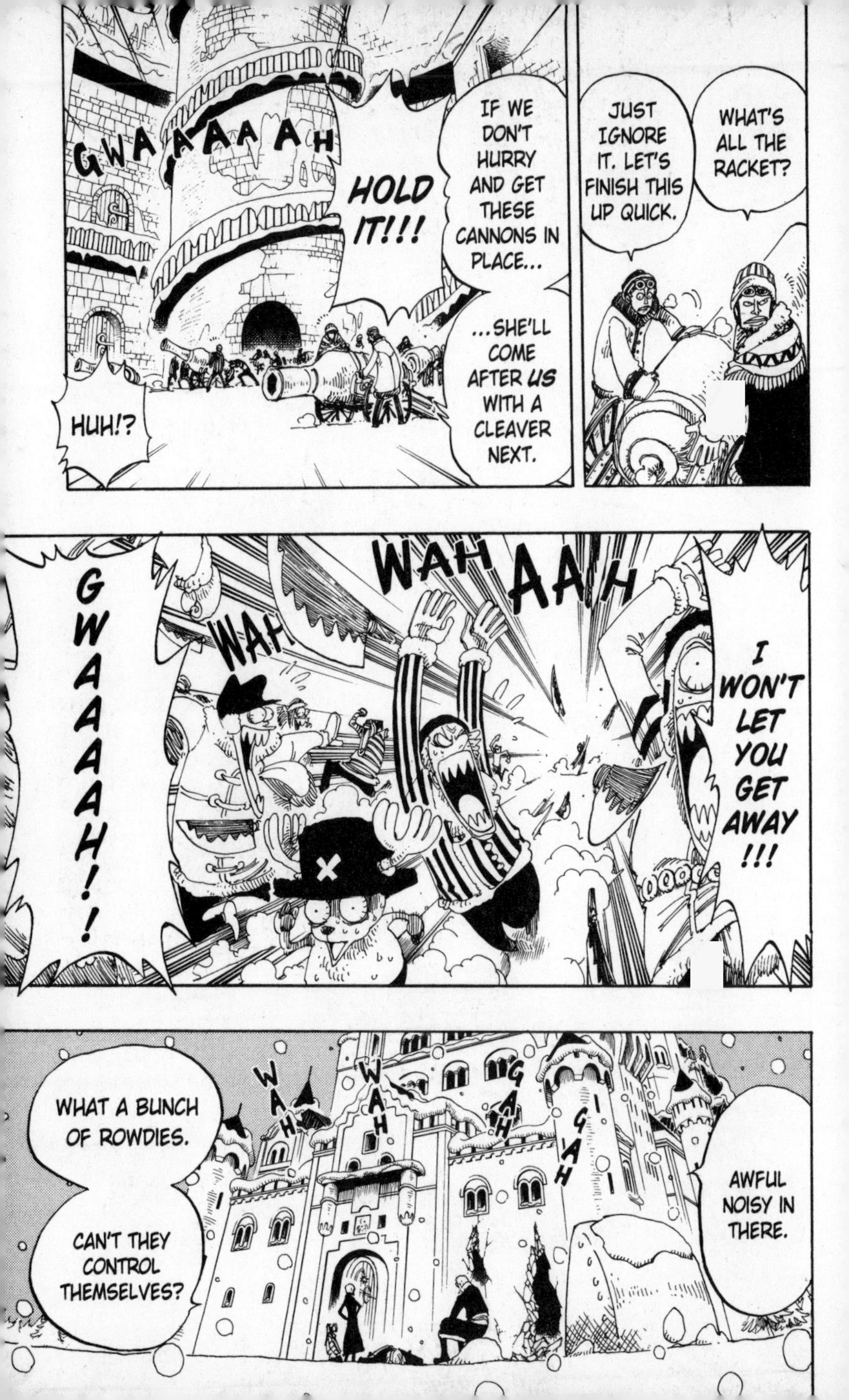
WHAT'S ALL THE RACKET?
JUST IGNORE IT. LET'S FINISH THIS UP QUICK.
IF WE DON'T HURRY AND GET THESE CANNONS IN PLACE...
...SHE'LL COME AFTER US WITH A CLEAVER NEXT.
HOLD IT!!!
GWAAAAAH
HUH!?
I WON'T LET YOU GET AWAY!!!
WAHAAAH
WAH
GWAAAAAAH!!
AWFUL NOISY IN THERE.
GAH
GAH
WAH
WAH
WHAT A BUNCH OF ROWDIES.
CAN'T THEY CONTROL THEMSELVES?

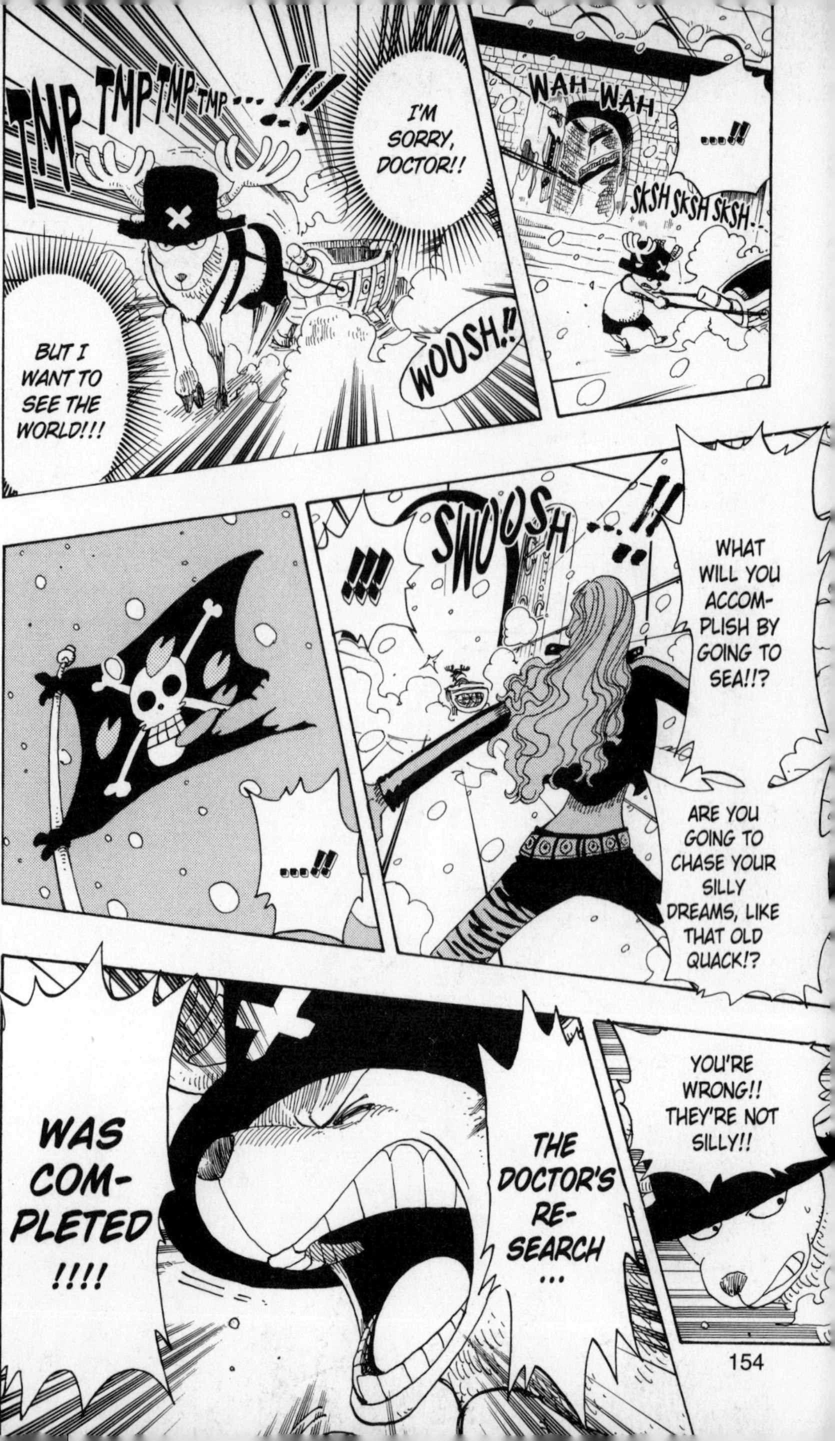
WAH WAH
...!!
SKSH SKSH SKSH..
I'M SORRY, DOCTOR!!
TMP TMP TMP TMP...!!!
WOOSH!!
BUT I WANT TO SEE THE WORLD!!!
WHAT WILL YOU ACCOM-PLISH BY GOING TO SEA!!?
SWOOSH...!!
!!!
ARE YOU GOING TO CHASE YOUR SILLY DREAMS, LIKE THAT OLD QUACK!?
...!!
YOU'RE WRONG!! THEY'RE NOT SILLY!!
THE DOCTOR'S RE-SEARCH...
WAS COM-PLETED!!!!

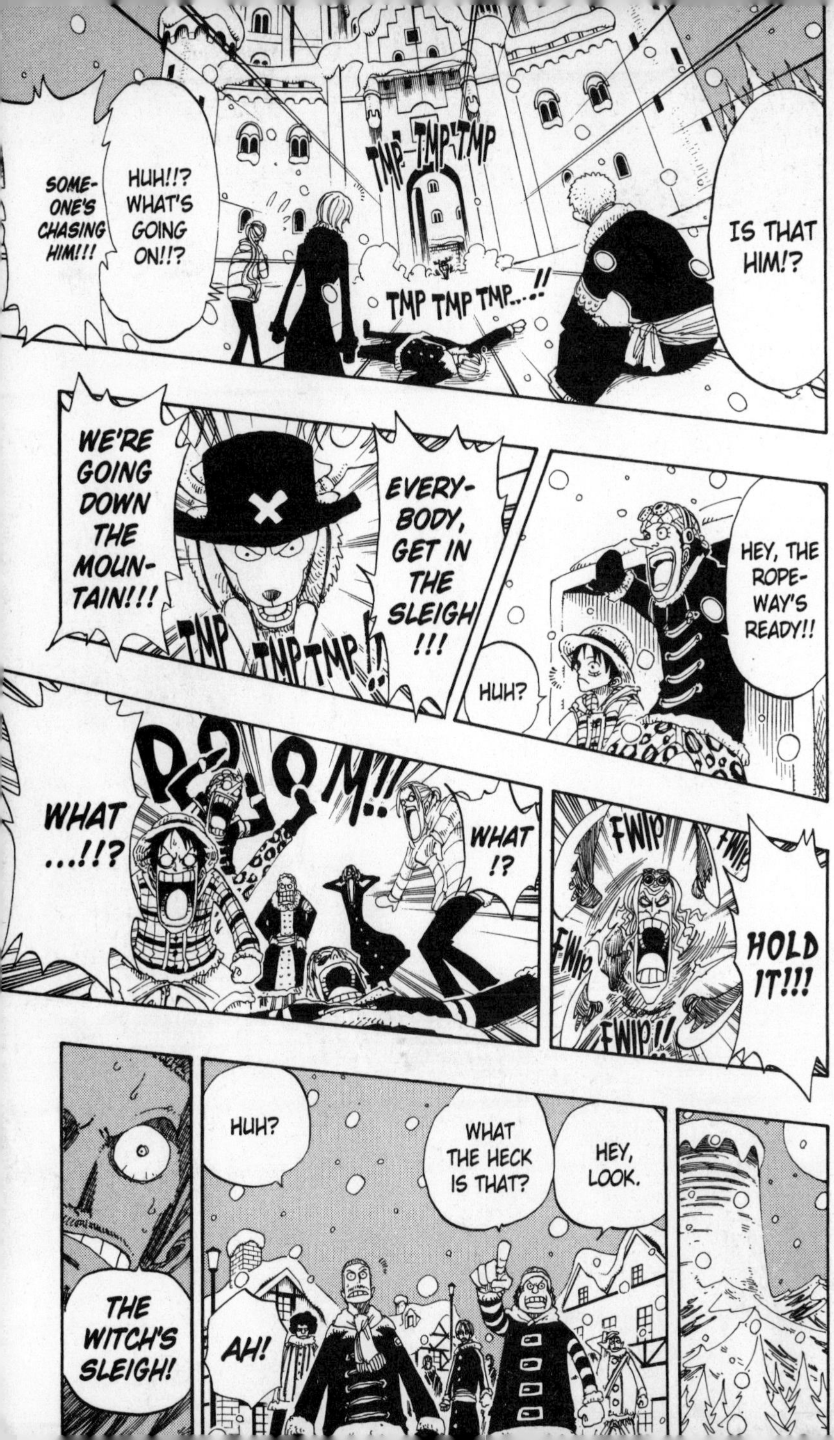
IS THAT HIM!?
TMP TMP TMP
HUH!!? WHAT'S GOING ON!!?
SOME-ONE'S CHASING HIM!!!
TMP TMP TMP...!!
HEY, THE ROPE-WAY'S READY!!
HUH?
EVERY-BODY, GET IN THE SLEIGH!!!
WE'RE GOING DOWN THE MOUN-TAIN!!!
TMP TMP TMP!!
FWIP
FWIP
HOLD IT!!!
FWIP
FWIP!!
WHAT !?
BOOM!!
WHAT ...!!?
HEY, LOOK.
WHAT THE HECK IS THAT?
HUH?
AH!
THE WITCH'S SLEIGH!

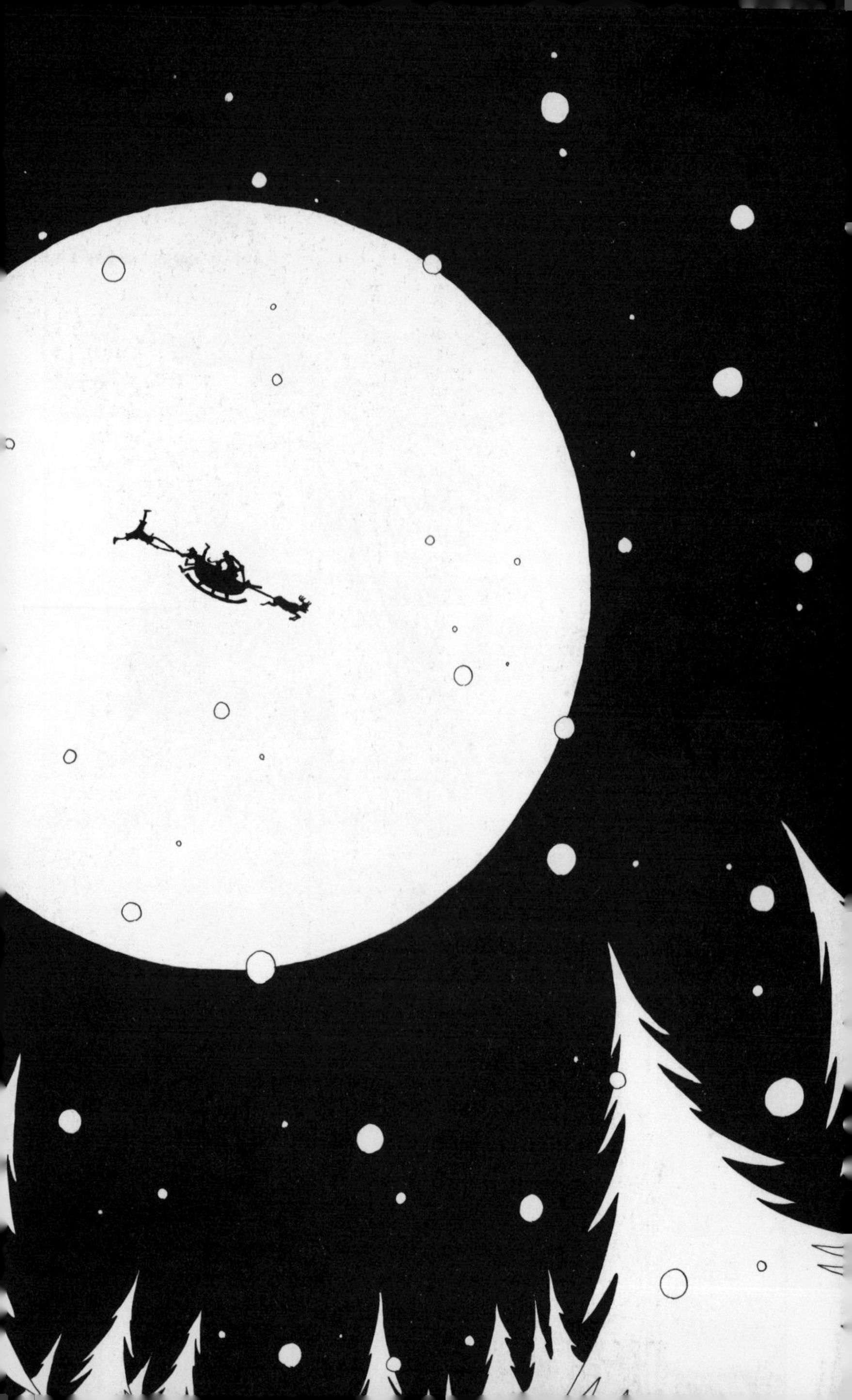

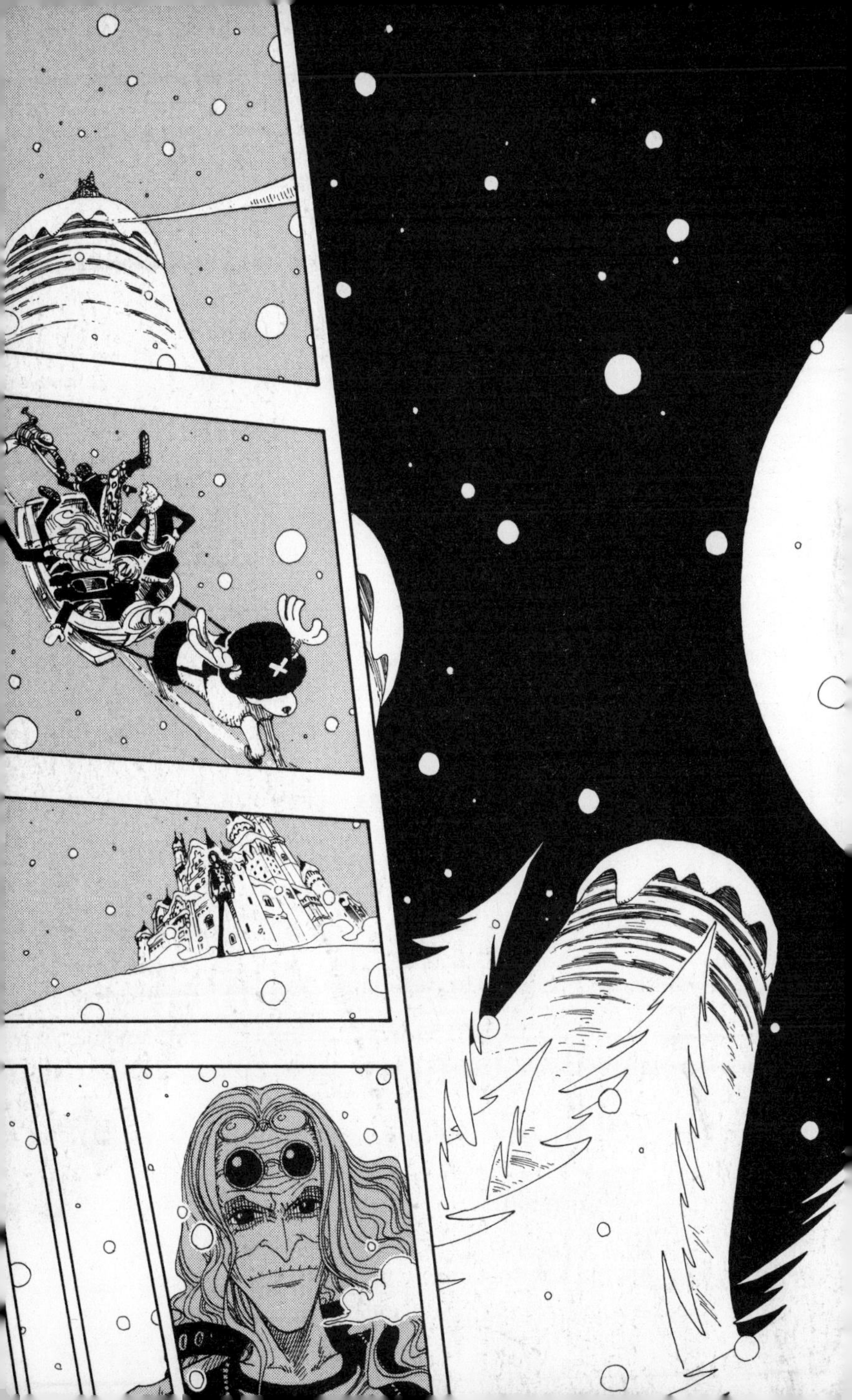

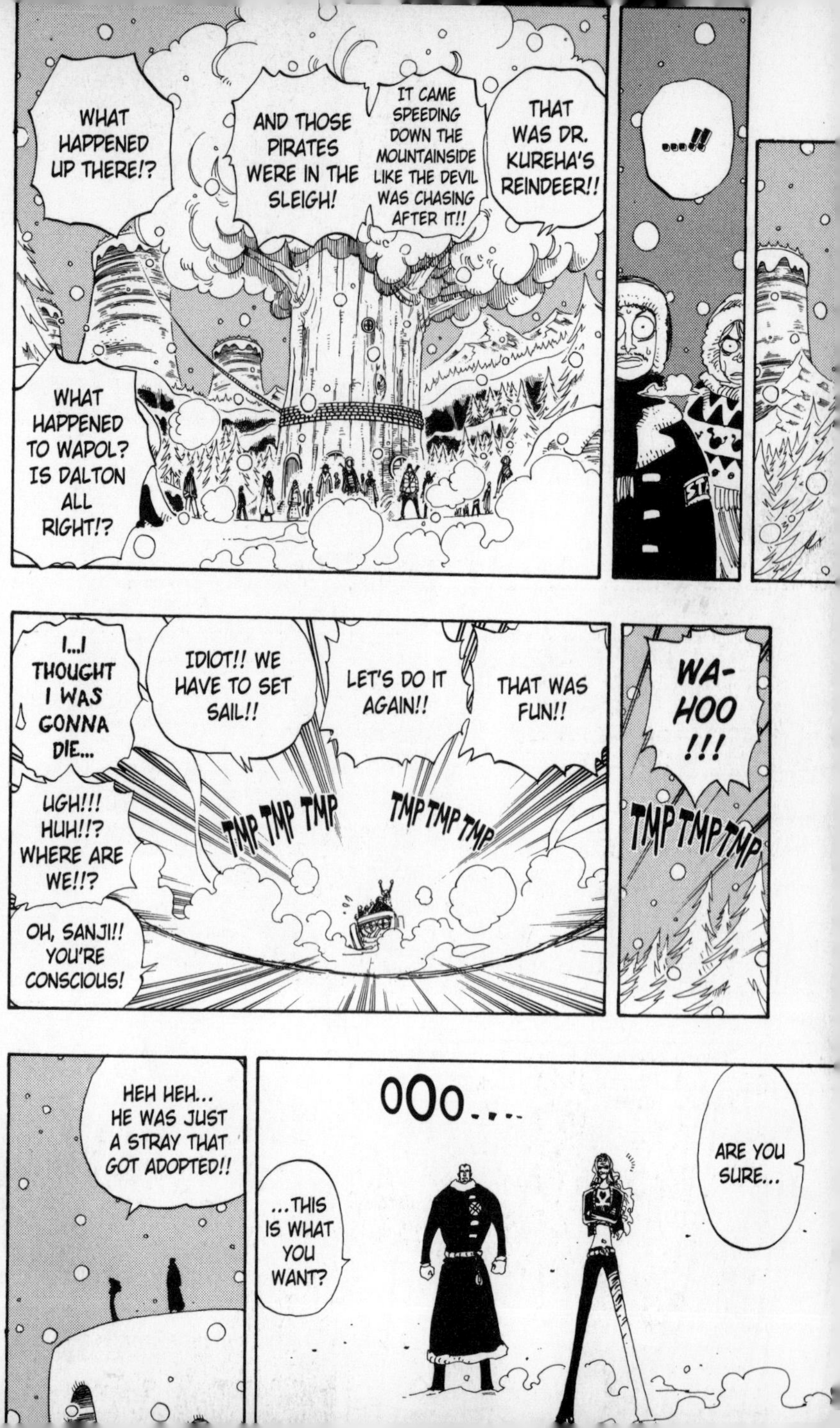
...!!
THAT WAS DR. KUREHA'S REINDEER!!
IT CAME SPEEDING DOWN THE MOUNTAINSIDE LIKE THE DEVIL WAS CHASING AFTER IT!!
AND THOSE PIRATES WERE IN THE SLEIGH!
WHAT HAPPENED UP THERE!?
WHAT HAPPENED TO WAPOL? IS DALTON ALL RIGHT!?
WA-HOO!!!
TMP TMP TMP TMP
THAT WAS FUN!!
LET'S DO IT AGAIN!!
TMP TMP TMP
IDIOT!! WE HAVE TO SET SAIL!!
I...I THOUGHT I WAS GONNA DIE...
TMP TMP TMP
UGH!!! HUH!!? WHERE ARE WE!!?
OH, SANJI!! YOU'RE CONSCIOUS!
OOo...
ARE YOU SURE...
...THIS IS WHAT YOU WANT?
HEH HEH... HE WAS JUST A STRAY THAT GOT ADOPTED!!

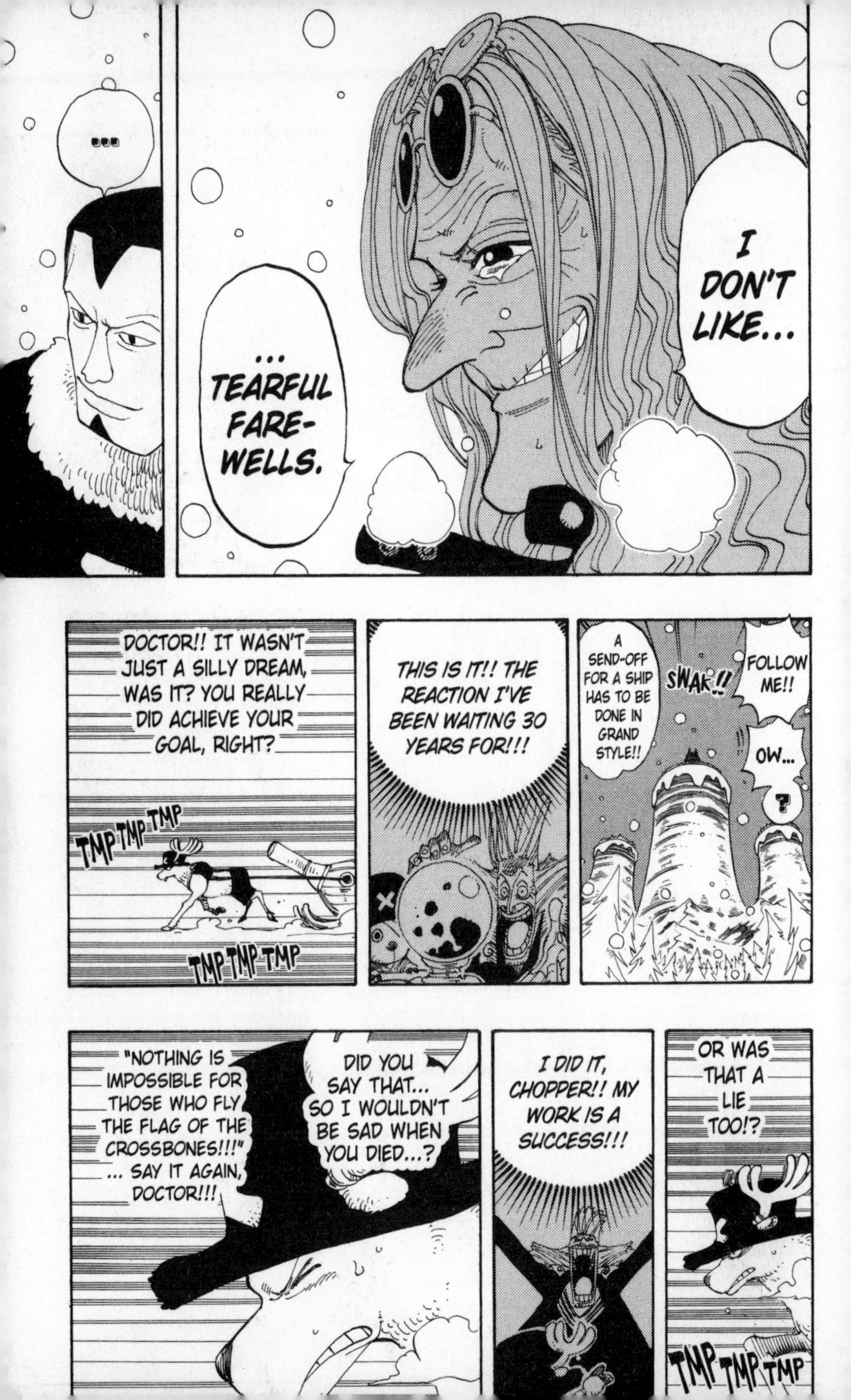
I DON'T LIKE...
... TEARFUL FARE-WELLS.
...
FOLLOW ME!!
A SEND-OFF FOR A SHIP HAS TO BE DONE IN GRAND STYLE!!
SWAK!!
OW...
?
THIS IS IT!! THE REACTION I'VE BEEN WAITING 30 YEARS FOR!!!
DOCTOR!! IT WASN'T JUST A SILLY DREAM, WAS IT? YOU REALLY DID ACHIEVE YOUR GOAL, RIGHT?
TMP TMP TMP
TMP TMP TMP
OR WAS THAT A LIE TOO!?
TMP TMP TMP
I DID IT, CHOPPER!! MY WORK IS A SUCCESS!!!
DID YOU SAY THAT... SO I WOULDN'T BE SAD WHEN YOU DIED...?
"NOTHING IS IMPOSSIBLE FOR THOSE WHO FLY THE FLAG OF THE CROSSBONES!!!" ... SAY IT AGAIN, DOCTOR!!!

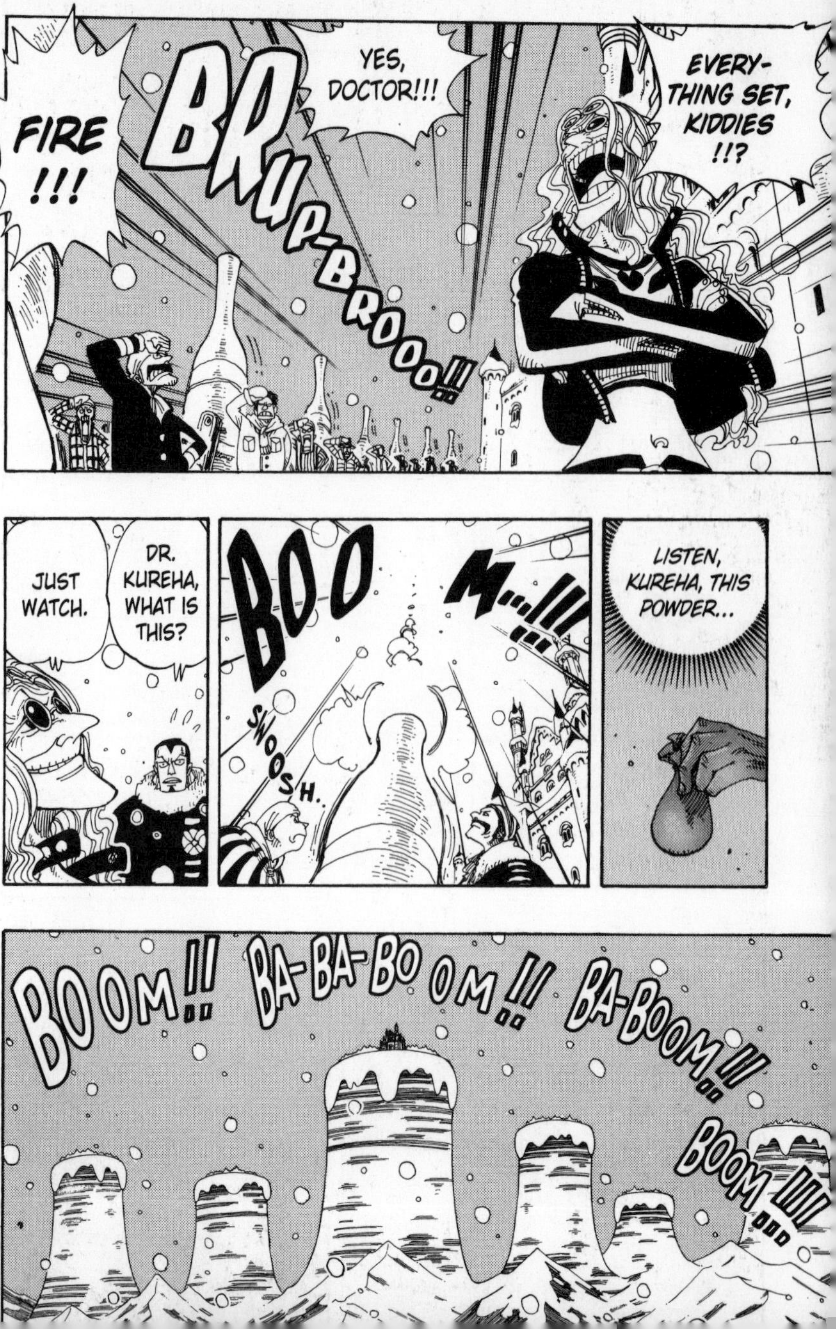
EVERY-THING SET, KIDDIES!!?
YES, DOCTOR!!!
BRRUP-BROOOO!!!
FIRE!!!
LISTEN, KUREHA, THIS POWDER...
BOOOM...!!!
SWOOSH.
DR. KUREHA, WHAT IS THIS?
JUST WATCH.
BA-BOOM!!
BOOM!!!
BA-BA-BOOM!!
BOOM!!

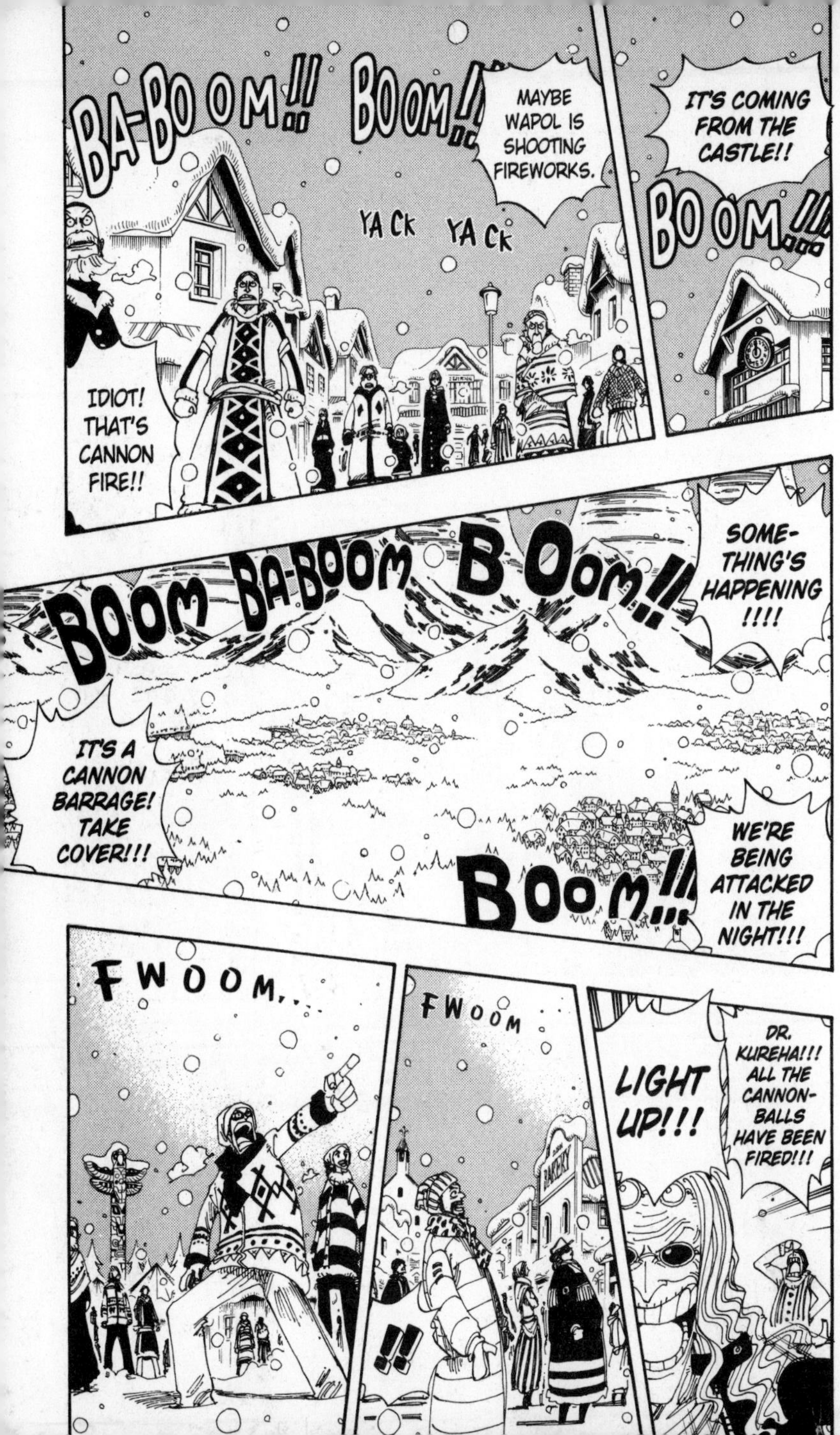
IT'S COMING FROM THE CASTLE!!
BOOM!!
MAYBE WAPOL IS SHOOTING FIREWORKS.
BOOM!!
BA-BOOM!!
YACK YACK
IDIOT! THAT'S CANNON FIRE!!
SOME-THING'S HAPPENING!!!!
BOOM BA-BOOM BOOM!!
IT'S A CANNON BARRAGE! TAKE COVER!!!
WE'RE BEING ATTACKED IN THE NIGHT!!!
BOOM!!
DR. KUREHA!!! ALL THE CANNON-BALLS HAVE BEEN FIRED!!!
LIGHT UP!!!
FWOOM
!!
FWOOM...

IT'S SO PRETTY...

WOW...

YEAH.

WAAAAAH!!!!

WAAAAAH!!!!

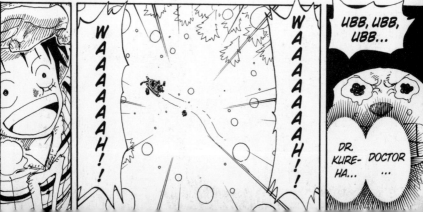

WAAAAAAAH!!

WAAAAAAAH!!

UBB, UBB, UBB...

DR. KURE-HA...

DOCTOR...

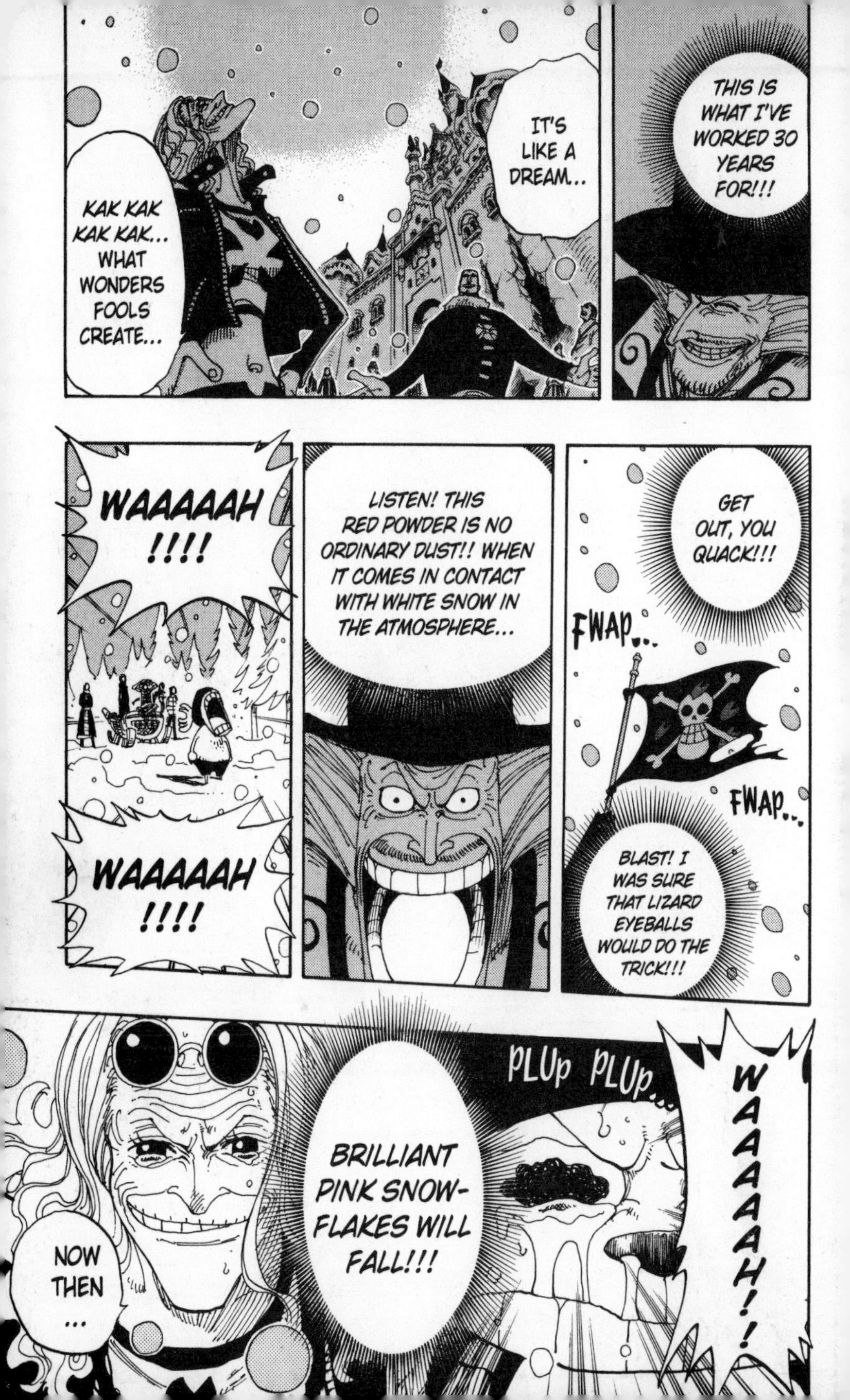
THIS IS WHAT I'VE WORKED 30 YEARS FOR!!!
IT'S LIKE A DREAM...
KAK KAK KAK KAK... WHAT WONDERS FOOLS CREATE...
GET OUT, YOU QUACK!!!
FWAP...
FWAP...
BLAST! I WAS SURE THAT LIZARD EYEBALLS WOULD DO THE TRICK!!!
LISTEN! THIS RED POWDER IS NO ORDINARY DUST!! WHEN IT COMES IN CONTACT WITH WHITE SNOW IN THE ATMOSPHERE...
WAAAAAH !!!!
WAAAAAH !!!!
WAAAAAAH!!!
PLUp PLUp...
BRILLIANT PINK SNOW-FLAKES WILL FALL!!!
NOW THEN ...

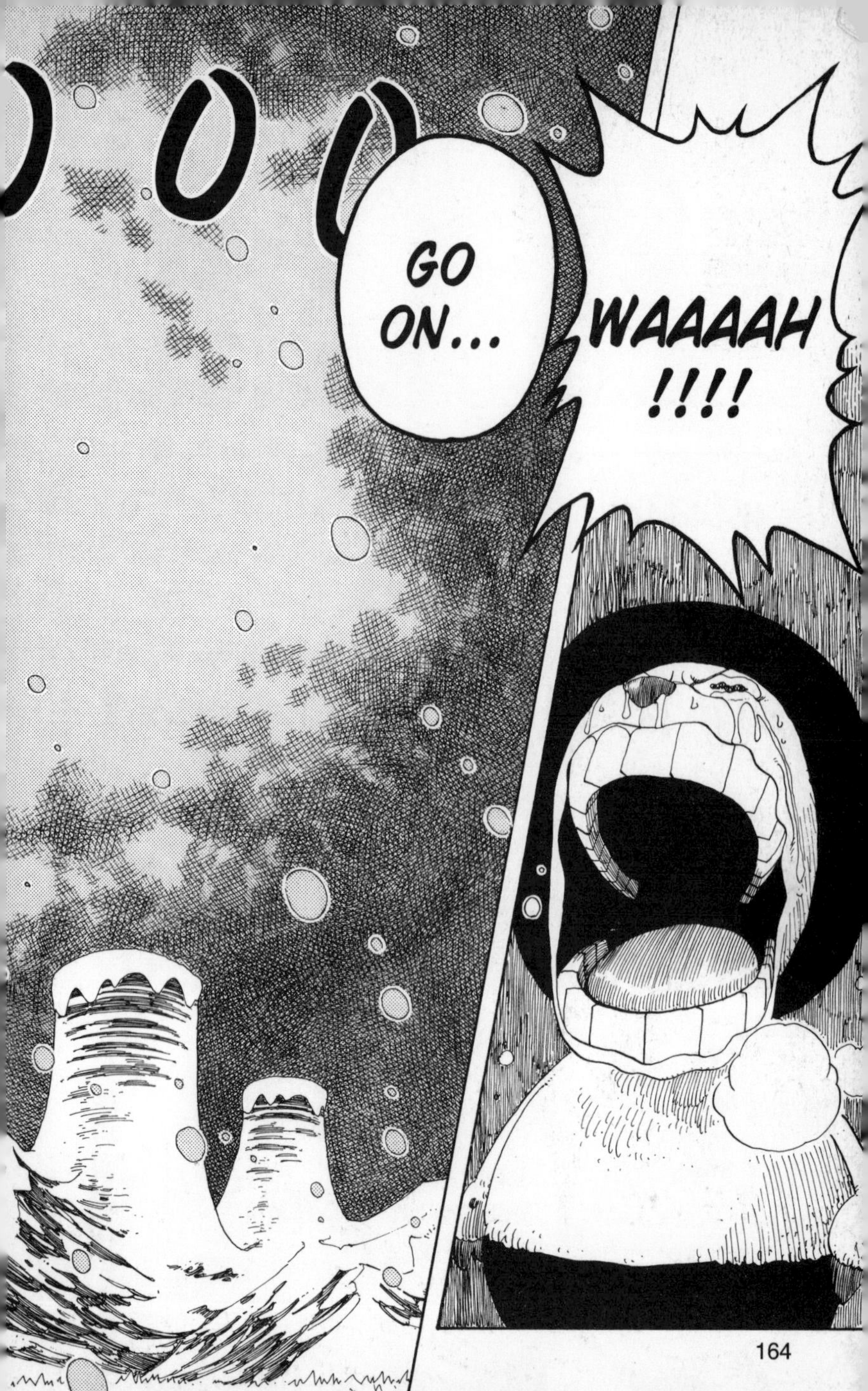
WAAAAH!!!!
GO ON...

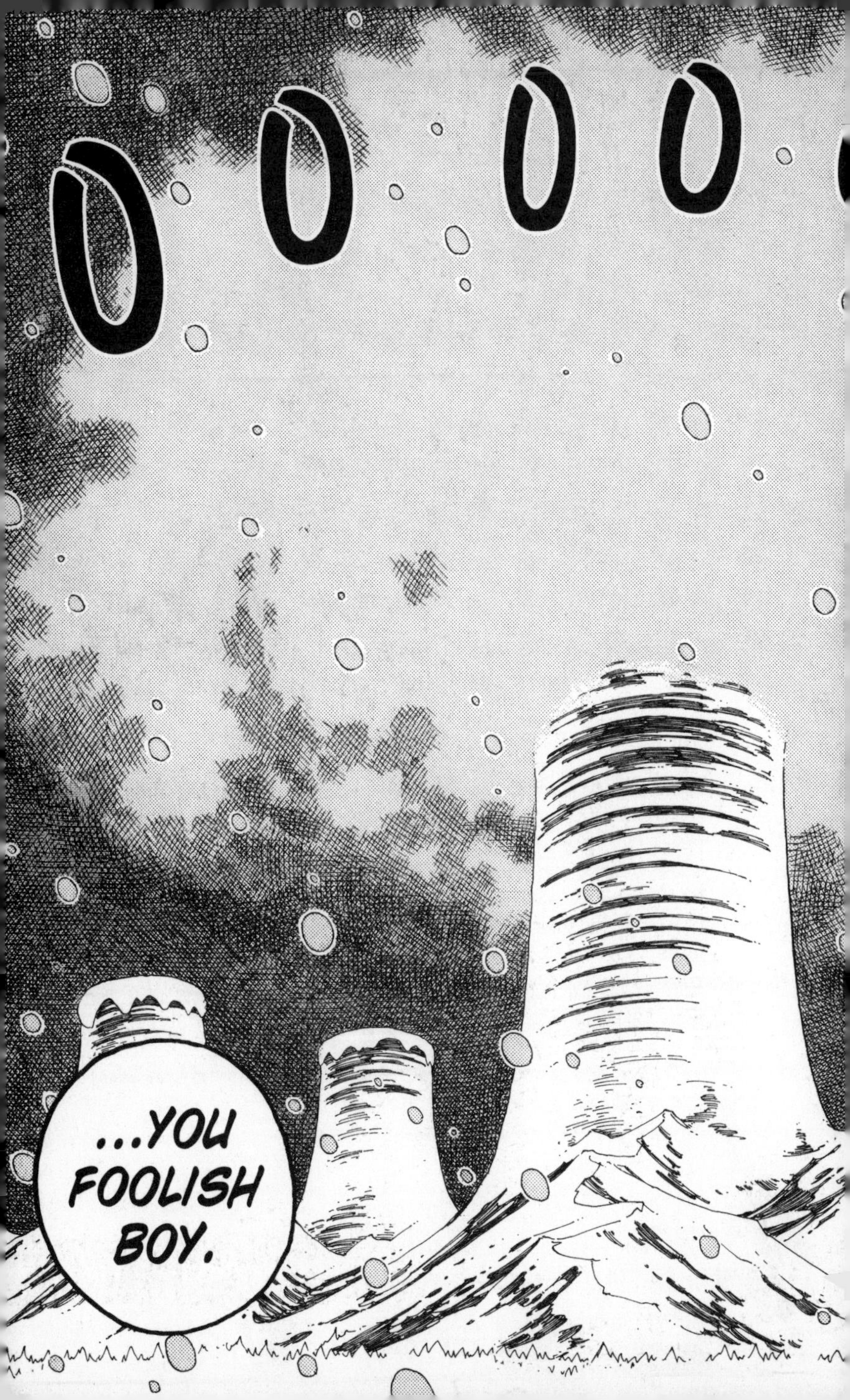
OOOOO
...YOU FOOLISH BOY.

Question Corner
SBS
MATSU

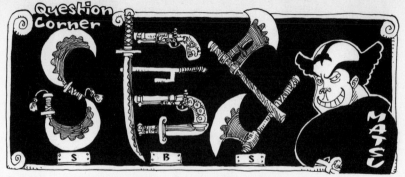

Reader: Hello, Oda Sensei. It's me, "Always Serious Aiko"!! In Vol. 15, you mentioned writing a fan letter to Toei Animation. I want to write to them, but I don't have the address. Would you give it to me? Thank you very much.

Oda: Sure. I received quite a few postcards like this, so I got permission from Toei Animation to give out this address.

| |
|---|
| 〒178-8567<br>10-5 2 Chome Higashi Oizumi Nerima Ward Tokyo<br>Toei Animation Planning Department<br>"One Piece" |

Oda: Please send all letters for One Piece animators to the above address. Even one postcard from a viewer (or reader, in my case), even one sentence, can give us a huge boost of energy. Once in a while, I get letters addressed to me personally complimenting the animators. It would be nice if you would send those comments directly to them.

Reader: Dalton, leader of the Drum Island Civilian Guard, always answers questions with bits of unnecessary information. Is that just because he's a nice person?

Oda: He does add unnecessary comments, doesn't he? I guess it's because he's a nice person, yes.
Oh, by the way, he loves chestnut rice.

IT'S A LAKESIDE TOWN JUST NORTH OF HERE.
THEY LIKE TO ICE SKATE THERE.

HER SKILLS AS A DOCTOR ARE INDISPUTABLE. BUT SHE'S...
...RATHER ECCENTRIC. SHE'S NEARLY 140 YEARS OLD.
WHAT? 140!? AND SHE'S STILL KICKING!?
AND... LET'S SEE... SHE LIKES PICKLED PLUMS.

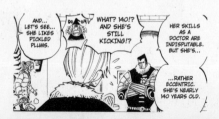

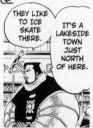

# Chapter 154:
# ON TO ALABASTA

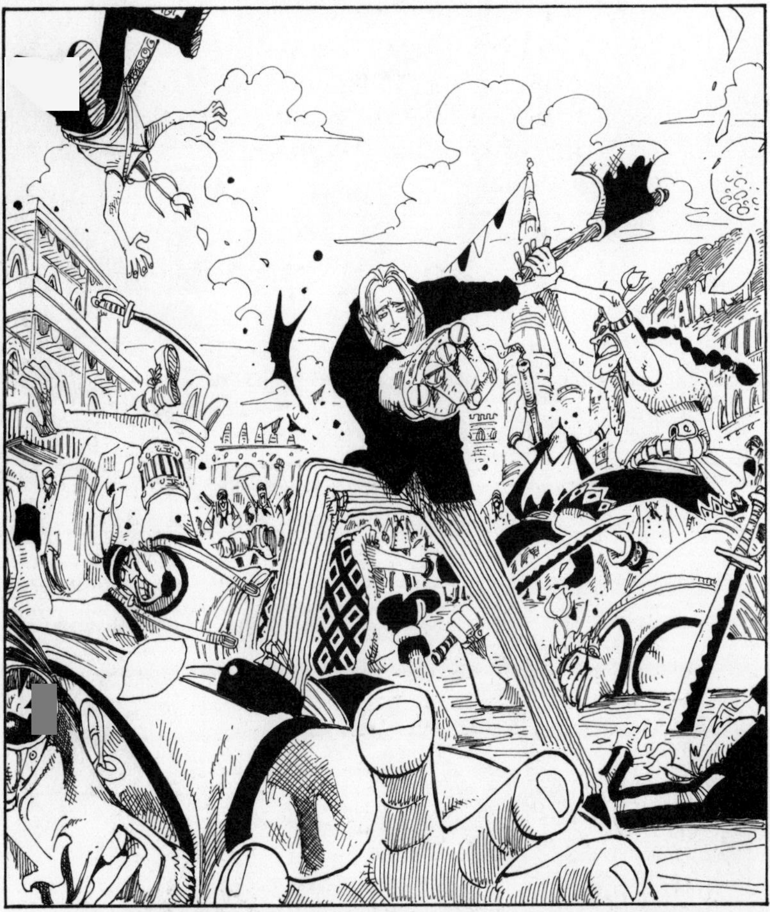

DJANGO'S DANCE HEAVEN, VOL. 22: "THE MIGHTY CAPTAIN OF THE NAVY'S MAIN FLEET"

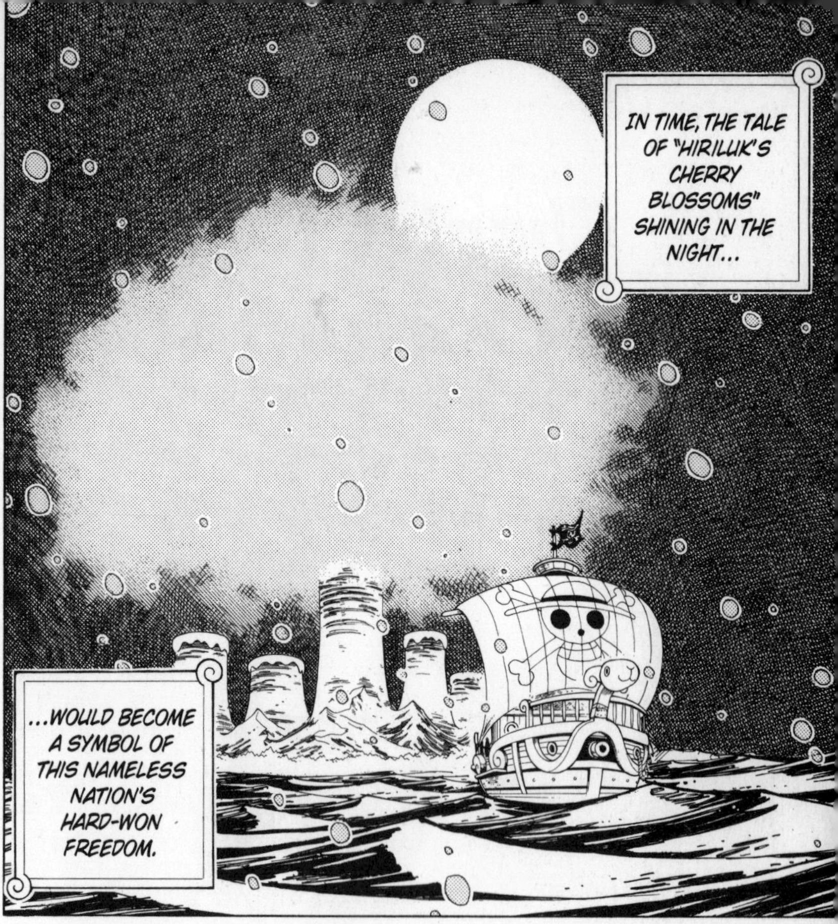
IN TIME, THE TALE OF "HIRILUK'S CHERRY BLOSSOMS" SHINING IN THE NIGHT...
...WOULD BECOME A SYMBOL OF THIS NAMELESS NATION'S HARD-WON FREEDOM.

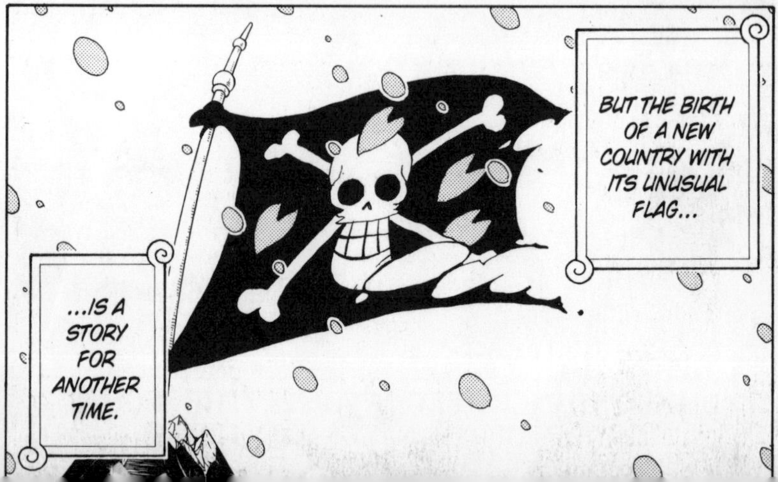
BUT THE BIRTH OF A NEW COUNTRY WITH ITS UNUSUAL FLAG...
...IS A STORY FOR ANOTHER TIME.

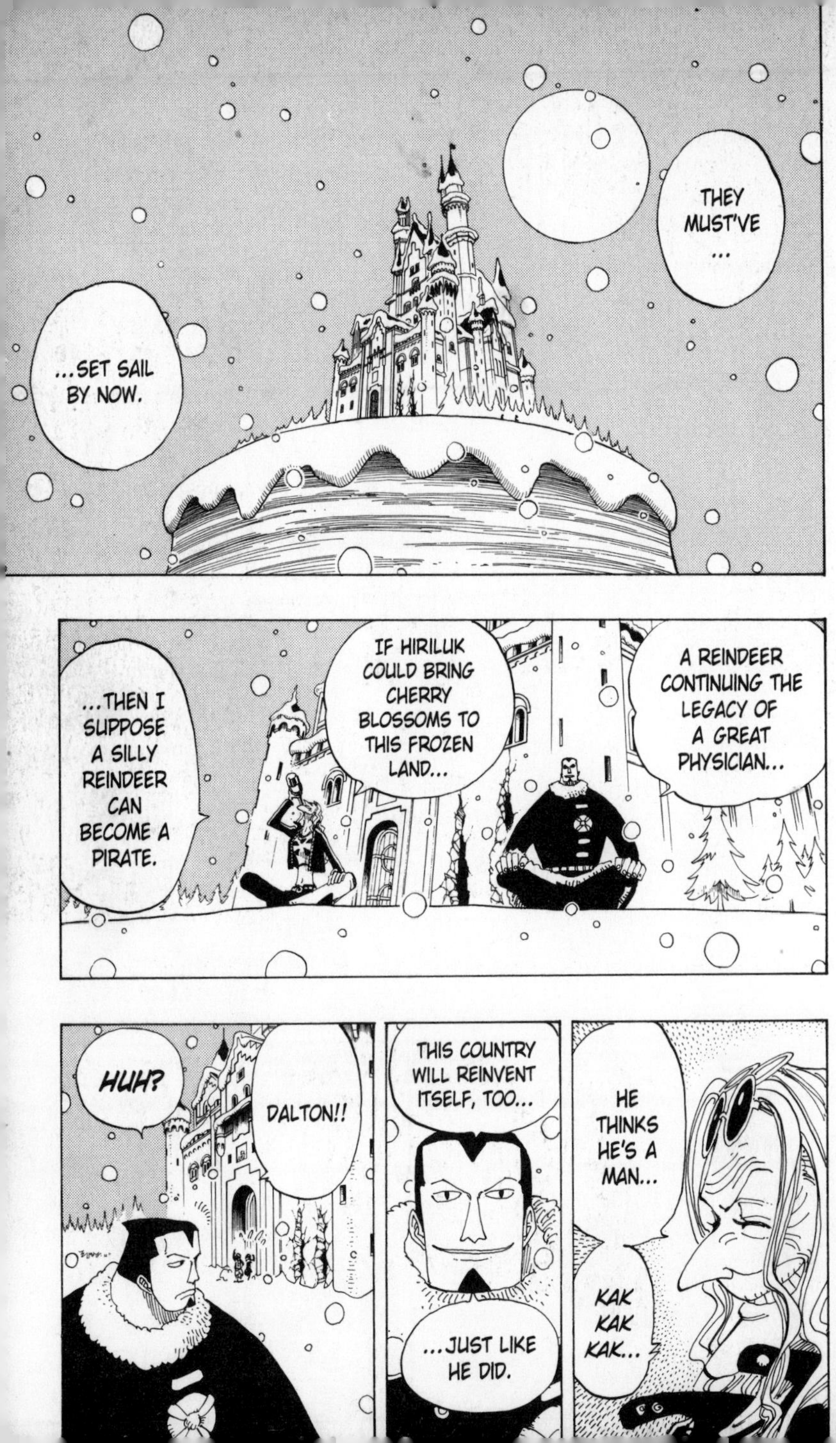
THEY MUST'VE ...
...SET SAIL BY NOW.
A REINDEER CONTINUING THE LEGACY OF A GREAT PHYSICIAN...
IF HIRILUK COULD BRING CHERRY BLOSSOMS TO THIS FROZEN LAND...
...THEN I SUPPOSE A SILLY REINDEER CAN BECOME A PIRATE.
HE THINKS HE'S A MAN...
KAK KAK KAK...
THIS COUNTRY WILL REINVENT ITSELF, TOO...
...JUST LIKE HE DID.
DALTON!!
HUH?

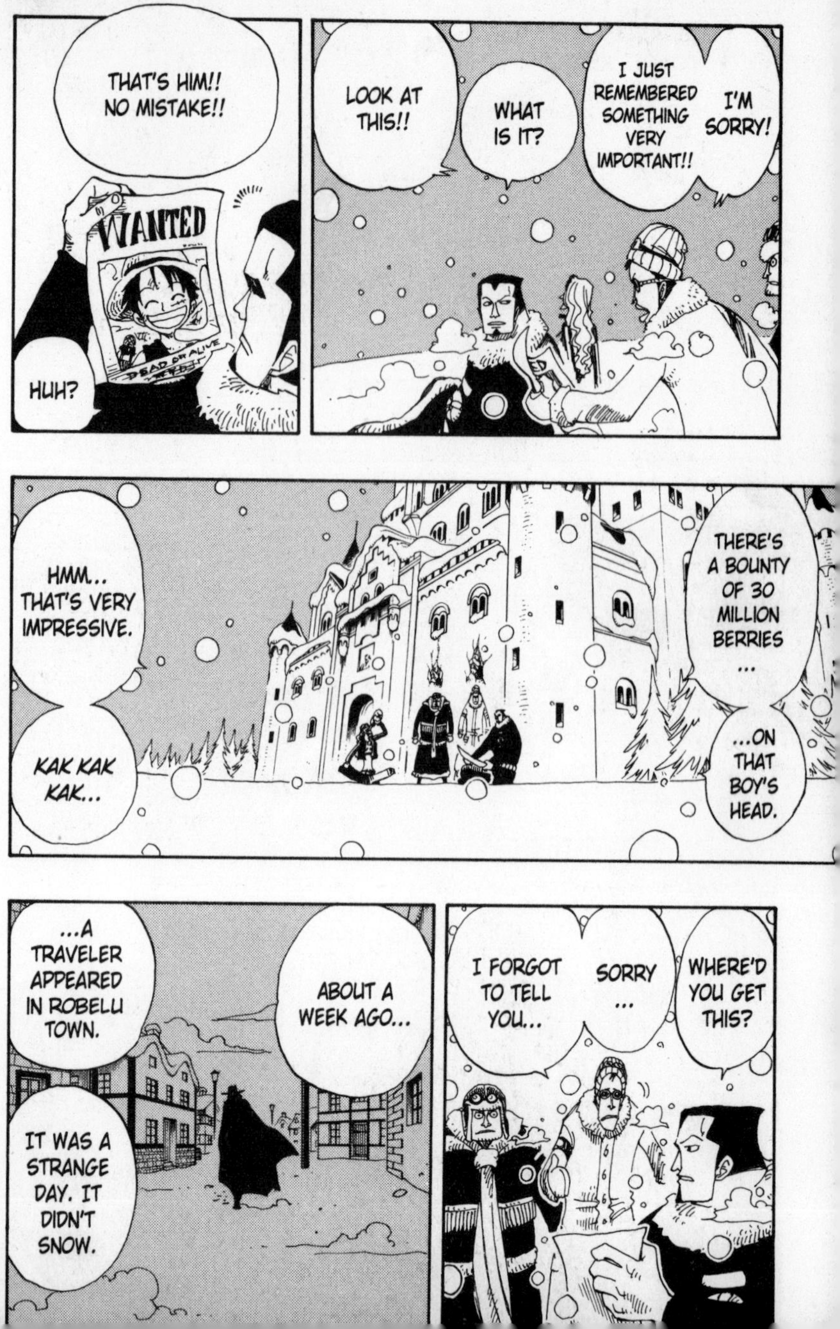
I'M SORRY!
I JUST REMEMBERED SOMETHING VERY IMPORTANT!!
WHAT IS IT?
LOOK AT THIS!!
THAT'S HIM!! NO MISTAKE!!
WANTED
DEAD OR ALIVE
HUH?
THERE'S A BOUNTY OF 30 MILLION BERRIES ...
...ON THAT BOY'S HEAD.
HMM.. THAT'S VERY IMPRESSIVE.
KAK KAK KAK...
WHERE'D YOU GET THIS?
SORRY ...
I FORGOT TO TELL YOU...
ABOUT A WEEK AGO...
...A TRAVELER APPEARED IN ROBELU TOWN.
IT WAS A STRANGE DAY. IT DIDN'T SNOW.

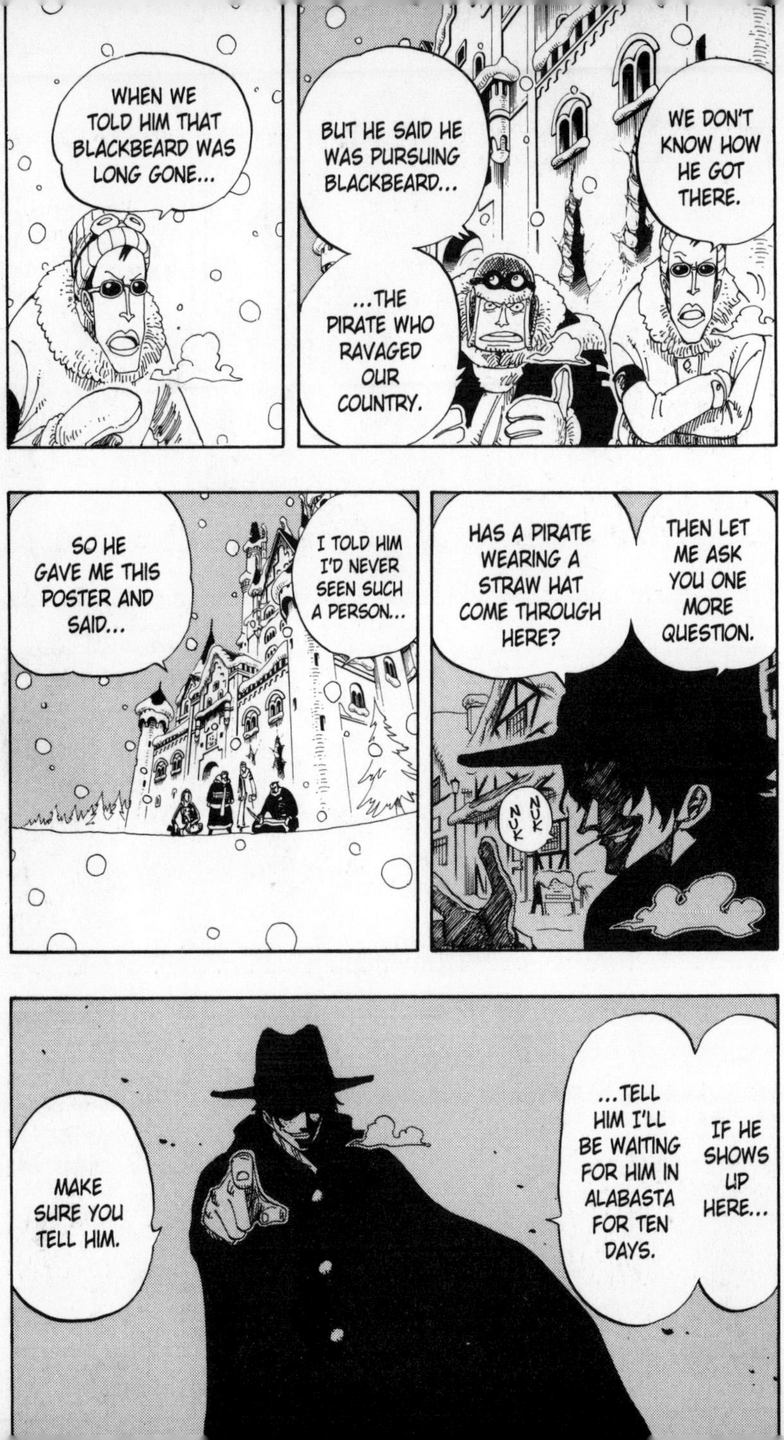
WE DON'T KNOW HOW HE GOT THERE.
BUT HE SAID HE WAS PURSUING BLACKBEARD...
...THE PIRATE WHO RAVAGED OUR COUNTRY.
WHEN WE TOLD HIM THAT BLACKBEARD WAS LONG GONE...
THEN LET ME ASK YOU ONE MORE QUESTION.
HAS A PIRATE WEARING A STRAW HAT COME THROUGH HERE?
NUK NUK
I TOLD HIM I'D NEVER SEEN SUCH A PERSON...
SO HE GAVE ME THIS POSTER AND SAID...
IF HE SHOWS UP HERE...
...TELL HIM I'LL BE WAITING FOR HIM IN ALABASTA FOR TEN DAYS.
MAKE SURE YOU TELL HIM.

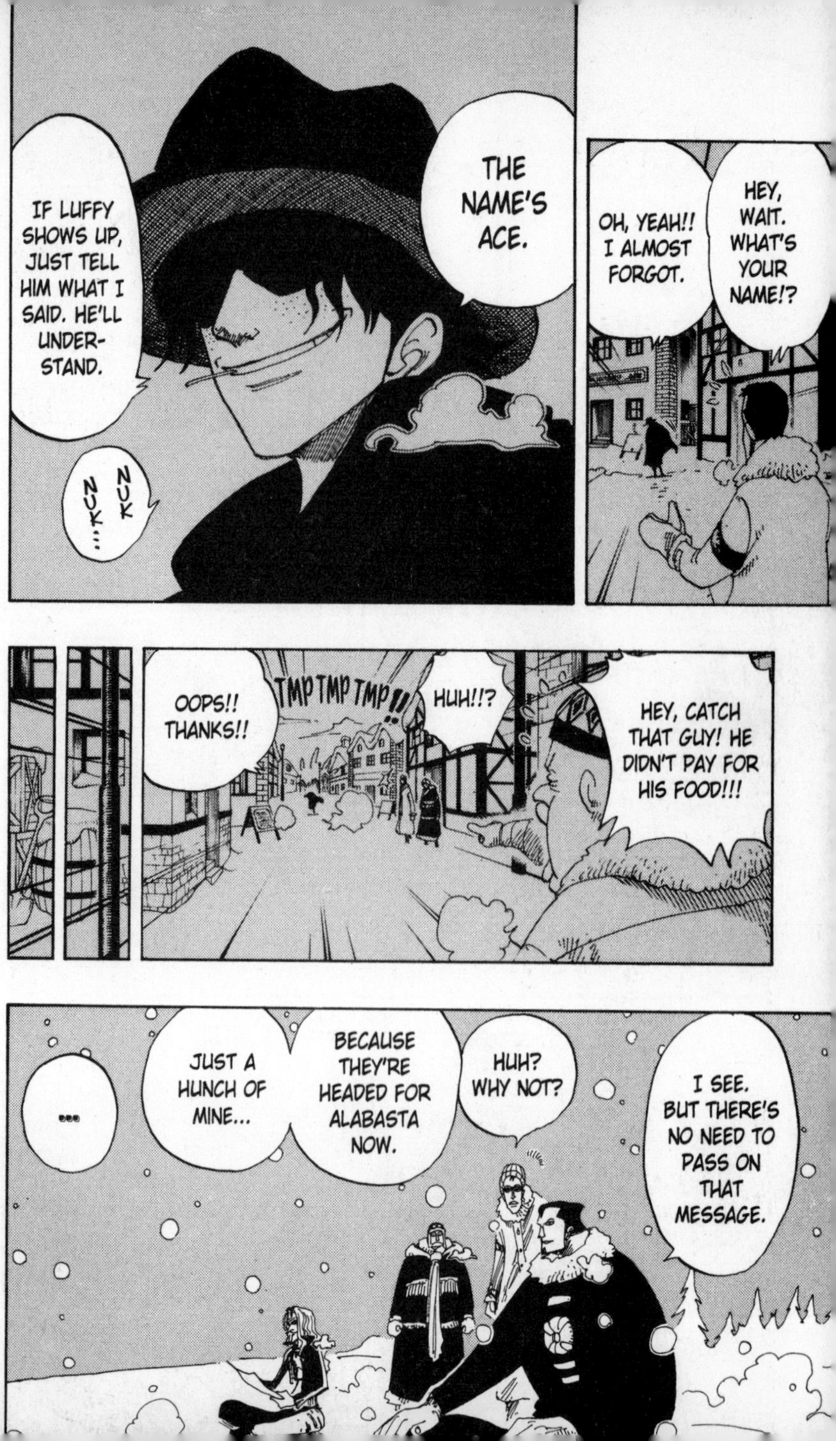
HEY, WAIT. WHAT'S YOUR NAME!?
OH, YEAH!! I ALMOST FORGOT.
THE NAME'S ACE.
IF LUFFY SHOWS UP, JUST TELL HIM WHAT I SAID. HE'LL UNDER-STAND.
NUK NUK...
HEY, CATCH THAT GUY! HE DIDN'T PAY FOR HIS FOOD!!!
HUH!!?
TMP TMP TMP!!
OOPS!! THANKS!!
I SEE. BUT THERE'S NO NEED TO PASS ON THAT MESSAGE.
HUH? WHY NOT?
BECAUSE THEY'RE HEADED FOR ALABASTA NOW.
JUST A HUNCH OF MINE...
...

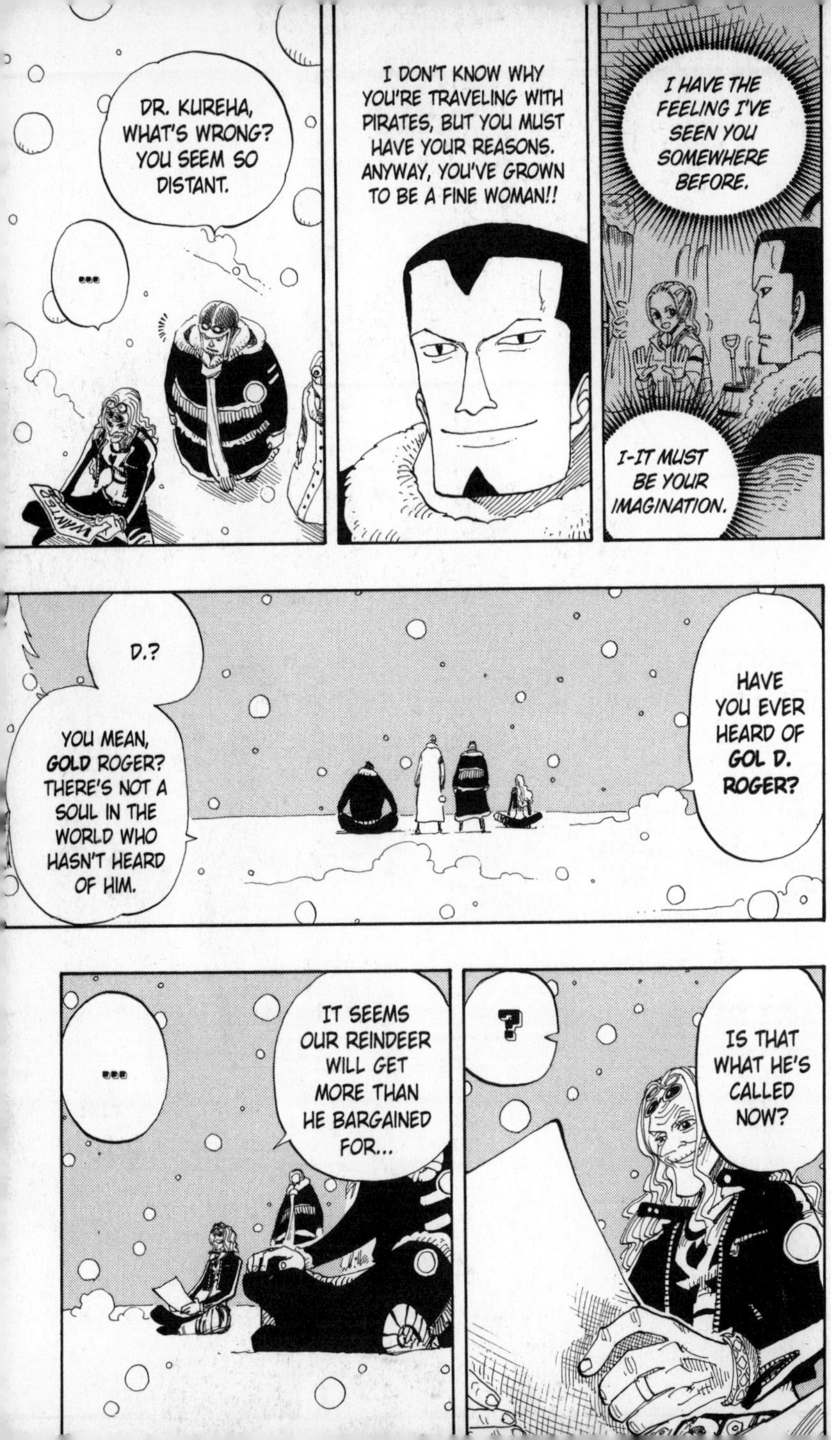
I HAVE THE FEELING I'VE SEEN YOU SOMEWHERE BEFORE.
I-IT MUST BE YOUR IMAGINATION.
I DON'T KNOW WHY YOU'RE TRAVELING WITH PIRATES, BUT YOU MUST HAVE YOUR REASONS. ANYWAY, YOU'VE GROWN TO BE A FINE WOMAN!!
DR. KUREHA, WHAT'S WRONG? YOU SEEM SO DISTANT.
...
HAVE YOU EVER HEARD OF **GOL D. ROGER?**
D.?
YOU MEAN, **GOLD ROGER?** THERE'S NOT A SOUL IN THE WORLD WHO HASN'T HEARD OF HIM.
IS THAT WHAT HE'S CALLED NOW?
?
IT SEEMS OUR REINDEER WILL GET MORE THAN HE BARGAINED FOR...
...

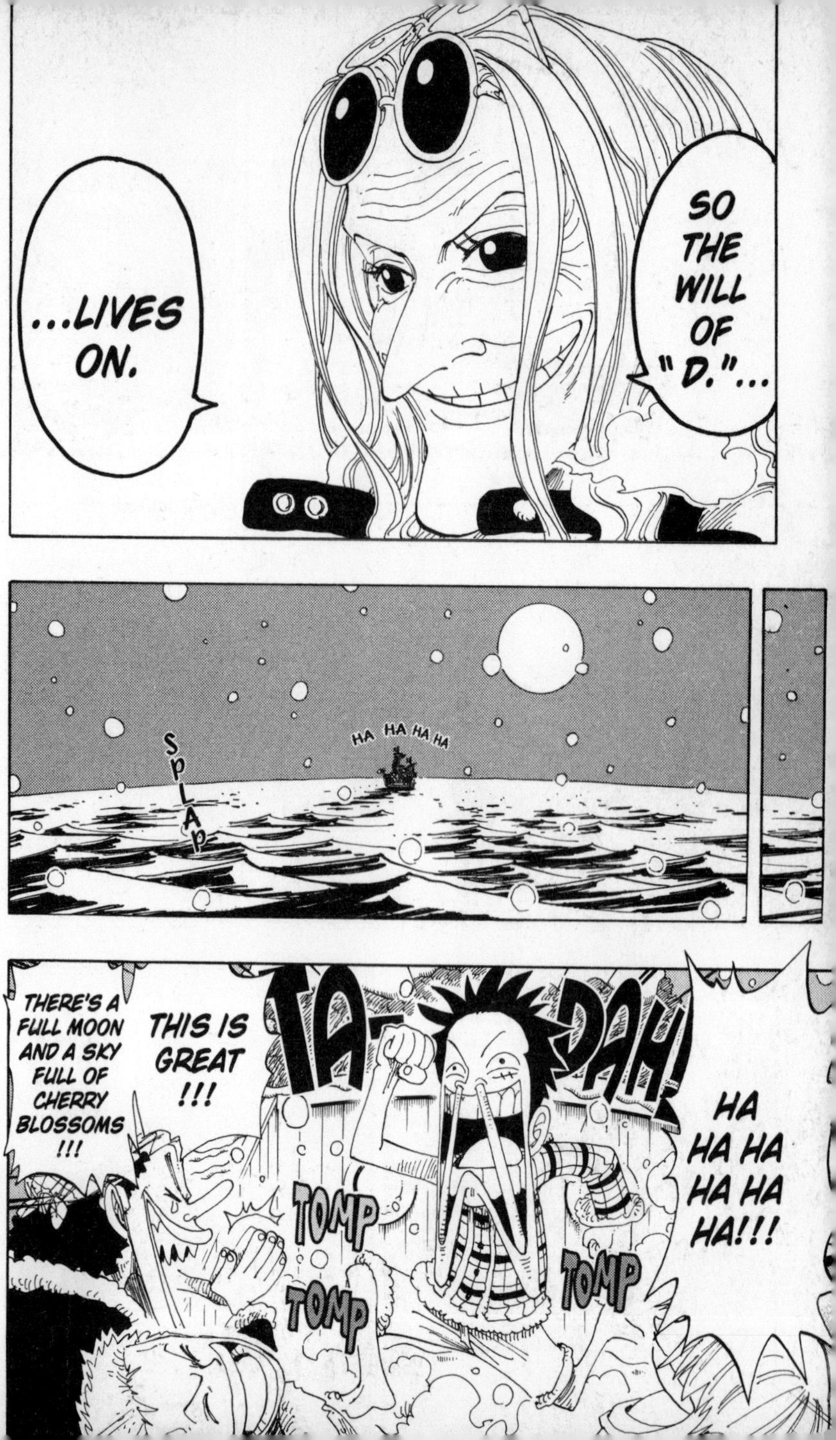
SO THE WILL OF "D."...
...LIVES ON.
SPLAp
HA HA HA HA
HA HA HA HA HA HA!!!
TA-DAH!
THIS IS GREAT!!!
THERE'S A FULL MOON AND A SKY FULL OF CHERRY BLOSSOMS!!!
TOMP
TOMP
TOMP

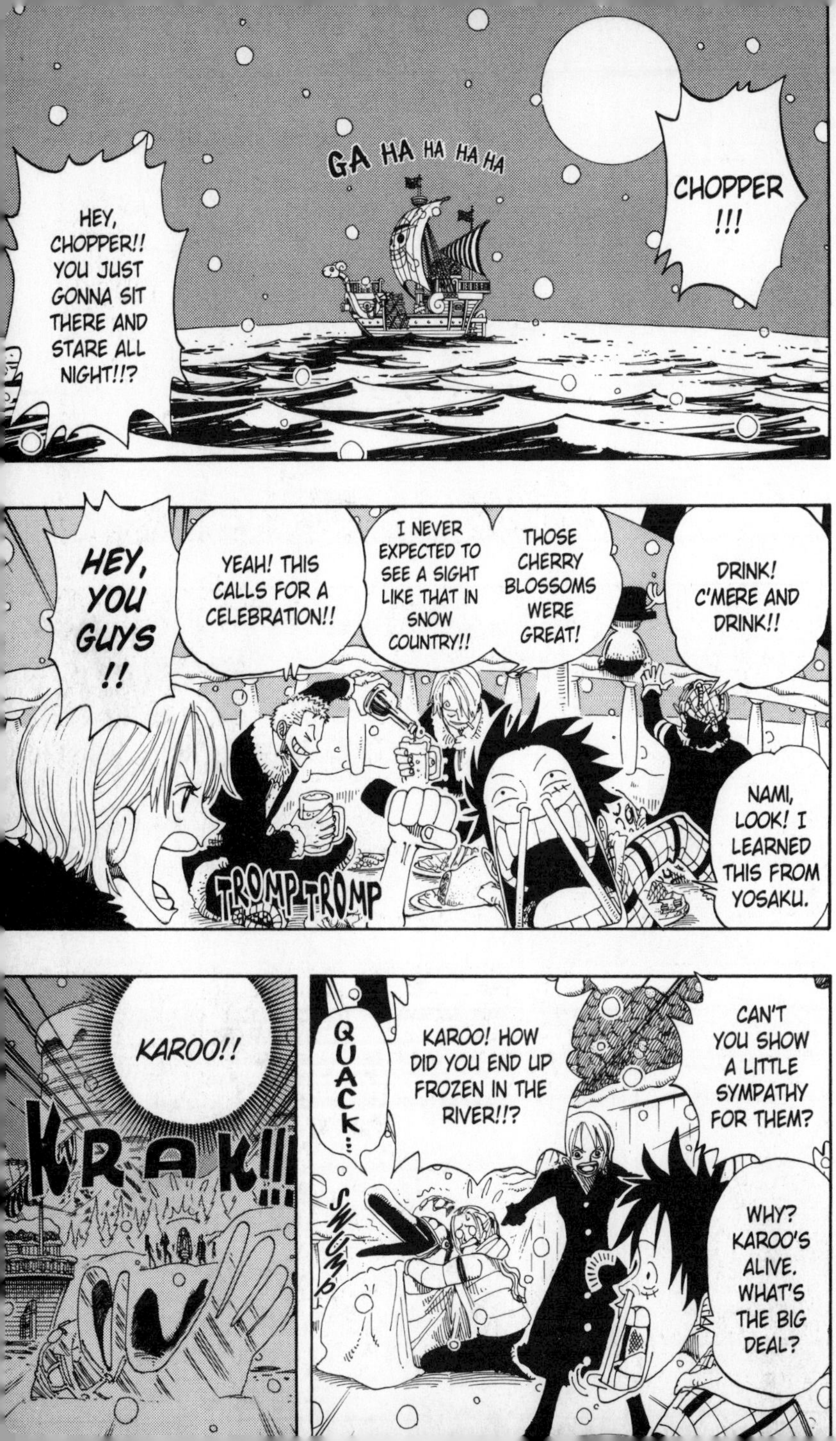
CHOPPER !!!
GA HA HA HA HA
HEY, CHOPPER!! YOU JUST GONNA SIT THERE AND STARE ALL NIGHT!!?
DRINK! C'MERE AND DRINK!!
NAMI, LOOK! I LEARNED THIS FROM YOSAKU.
THOSE CHERRY BLOSSOMS WERE GREAT!
I NEVER EXPECTED TO SEE A SIGHT LIKE THAT IN SNOW COUNTRY!!
YEAH! THIS CALLS FOR A CELEBRATION!!
TROMP TROMP
HEY, YOU GUYS !!
CAN'T YOU SHOW A LITTLE SYMPATHY FOR THEM?
KAROO! HOW DID YOU END UP FROZEN IN THE RIVER!!?
QUACK...
WHY? KAROO'S ALIVE. WHAT'S THE BIG DEAL?
SWUMP
KAROO!!
KRAK!!!

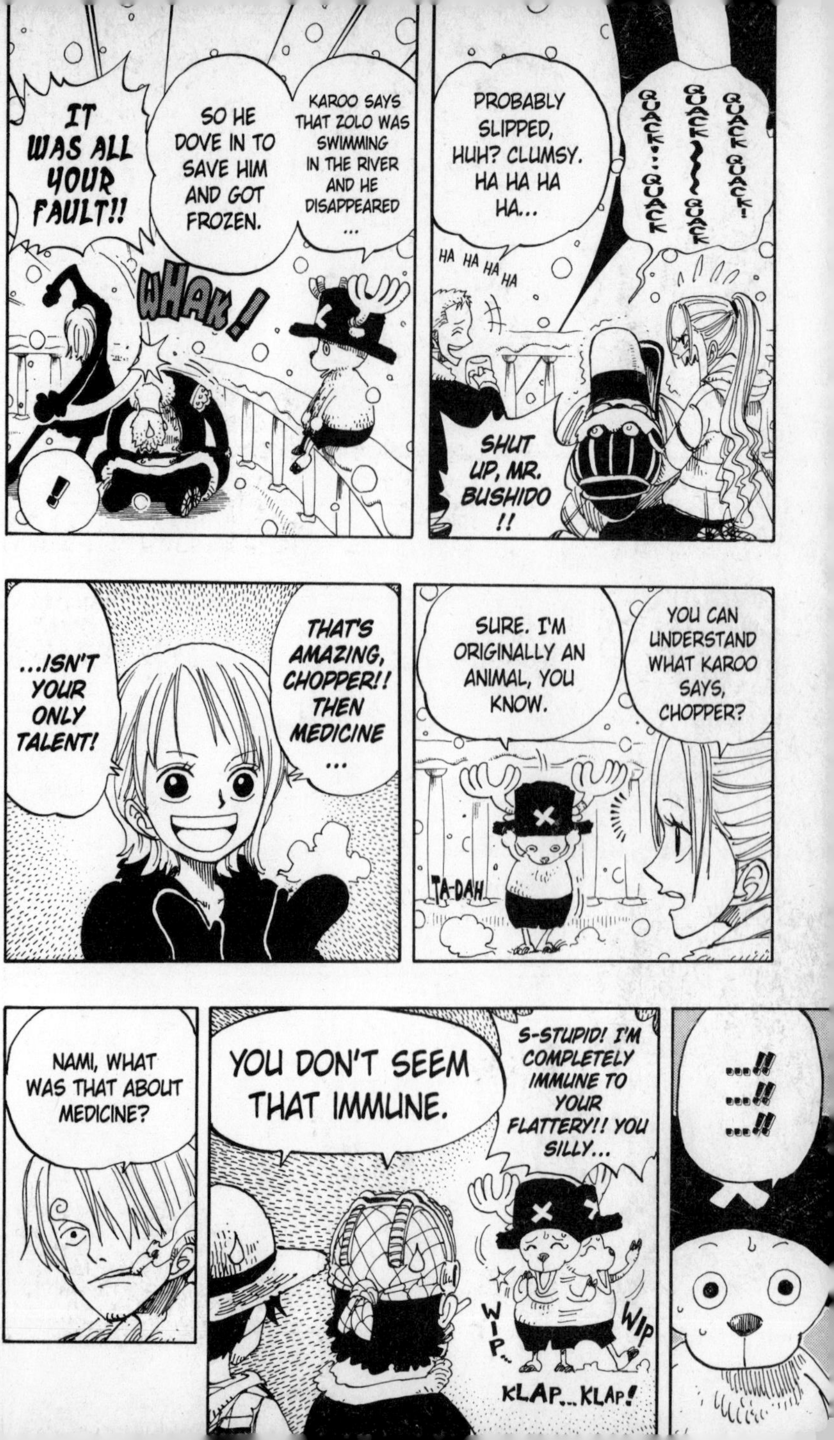
QUACK QUACK!
QUACK~~QUACK
QUACK!..QUACK
PROBABLY SLIPPED, HUH? CLUMSY. HA HA HA HA...
HA HA HA HA
SHUT UP, MR. BUSHIDO!!
KAROO SAYS THAT ZOLO WAS SWIMMING IN THE RIVER AND HE DISAPPEARED ...
SO HE DOVE IN TO SAVE HIM AND GOT FROZEN.
IT WAS ALL YOUR FAULT!!
WHAK!
!
YOU CAN UNDERSTAND WHAT KAROO SAYS, CHOPPER?
SURE. I'M ORIGINALLY AN ANIMAL, YOU KNOW.
TA-DAH
THAT'S AMAZING, CHOPPER!! THEN MEDICINE ...
...ISN'T YOUR ONLY TALENT!
...!!
...!!
...!!
S-STUPID! I'M COMPLETELY IMMUNE TO YOUR FLATTERY!! YOU SILLY...
WIP
WIP...
KLAP... KLAP!
YOU DON'T SEEM THAT IMMUNE.
NAMI, WHAT WAS THAT ABOUT MEDICINE?

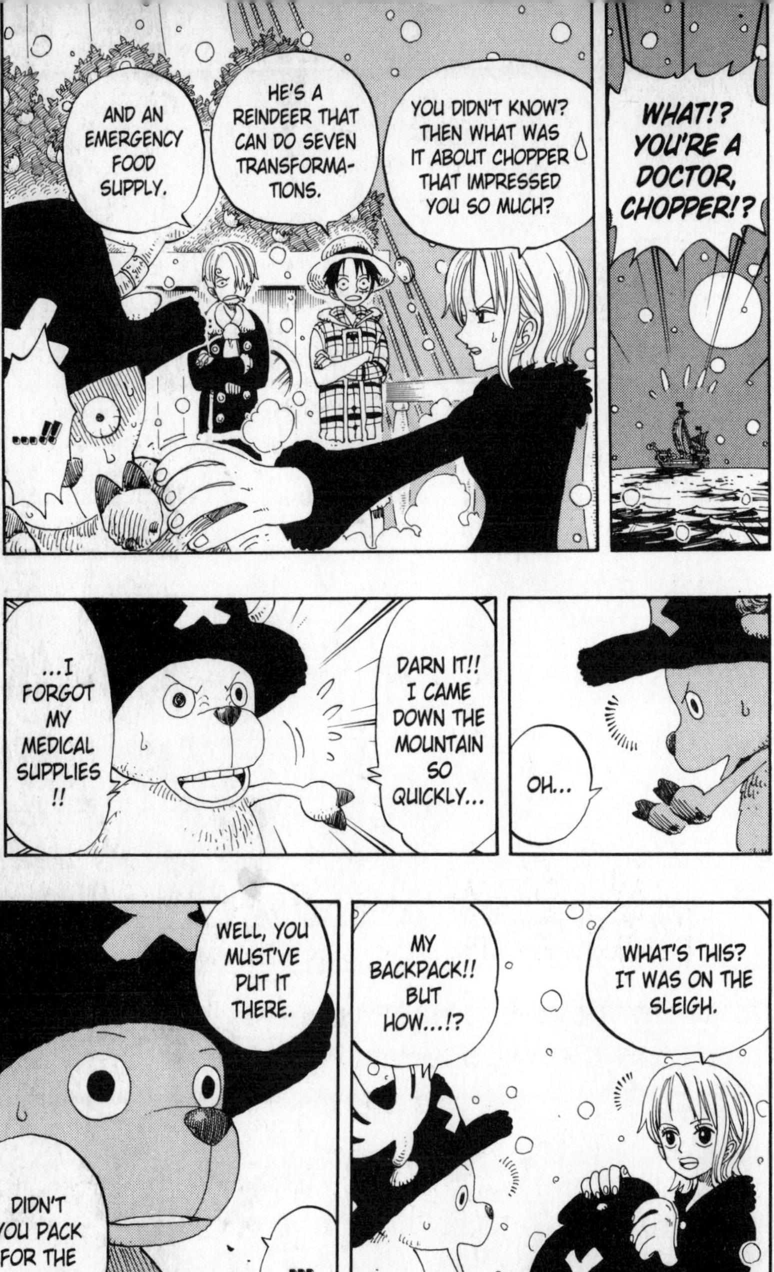
WHAT!? YOU'RE A DOCTOR, CHOPPER!?
YOU DIDN'T KNOW? THEN WHAT WAS IT ABOUT CHOPPER THAT IMPRESSED YOU SO MUCH?
HE'S A REINDEER THAT CAN DO SEVEN TRANSFORMA- TIONS.
AND AN EMERGENCY FOOD SUPPLY.
...!!
OH...
DARN IT!! I CAME DOWN THE MOUNTAIN SO QUICKLY...
...I FORGOT MY MEDICAL SUPPLIES!!
WHAT'S THIS? IT WAS ON THE SLEIGH.
MY BACKPACK!! BUT HOW...!?
WELL, YOU MUST'VE PUT IT THERE.
...
DIDN'T YOU PACK FOR THE JOURNEY?

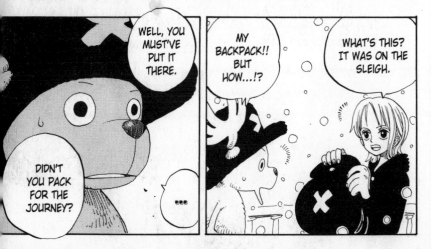

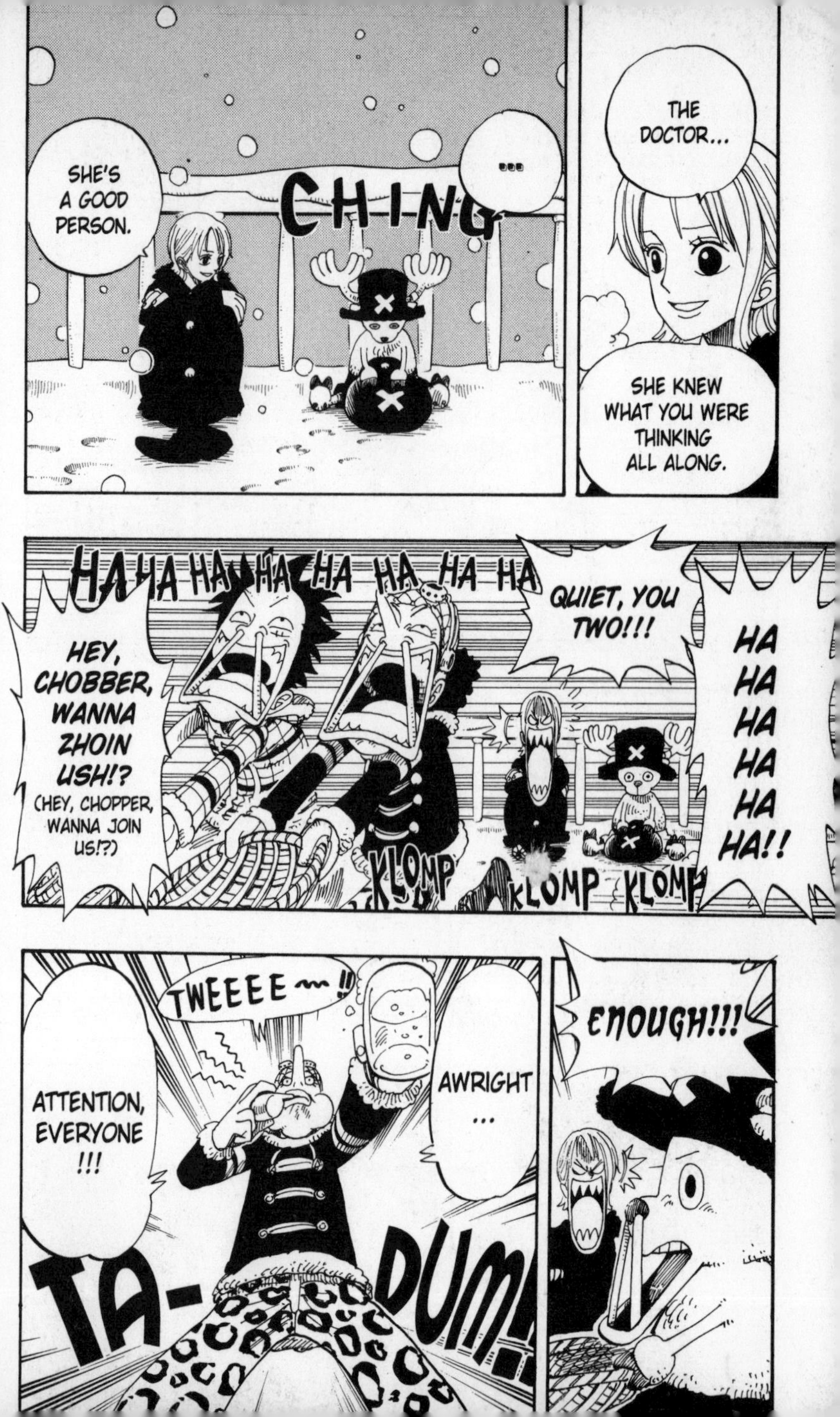
THE DOCTOR...
SHE KNEW WHAT YOU WERE THINKING ALL ALONG.
...
CHING
SHE'S A GOOD PERSON.
HA HA HA HA HA HA!!
QUIET, YOU TWO!!!
HA HA HA HA HA HA HA HA
HEY, CHOBBER, WANNA ZHOIN USH!?
(HEY, CHOPPER, WANNA JOIN US!?)
KLOMP KLOMP KLOMP
ENOUGH!!!
AWRIGHT ...
TWEEEE~!!
ATTENTION, EVERYONE!!!
TA-DUM!!

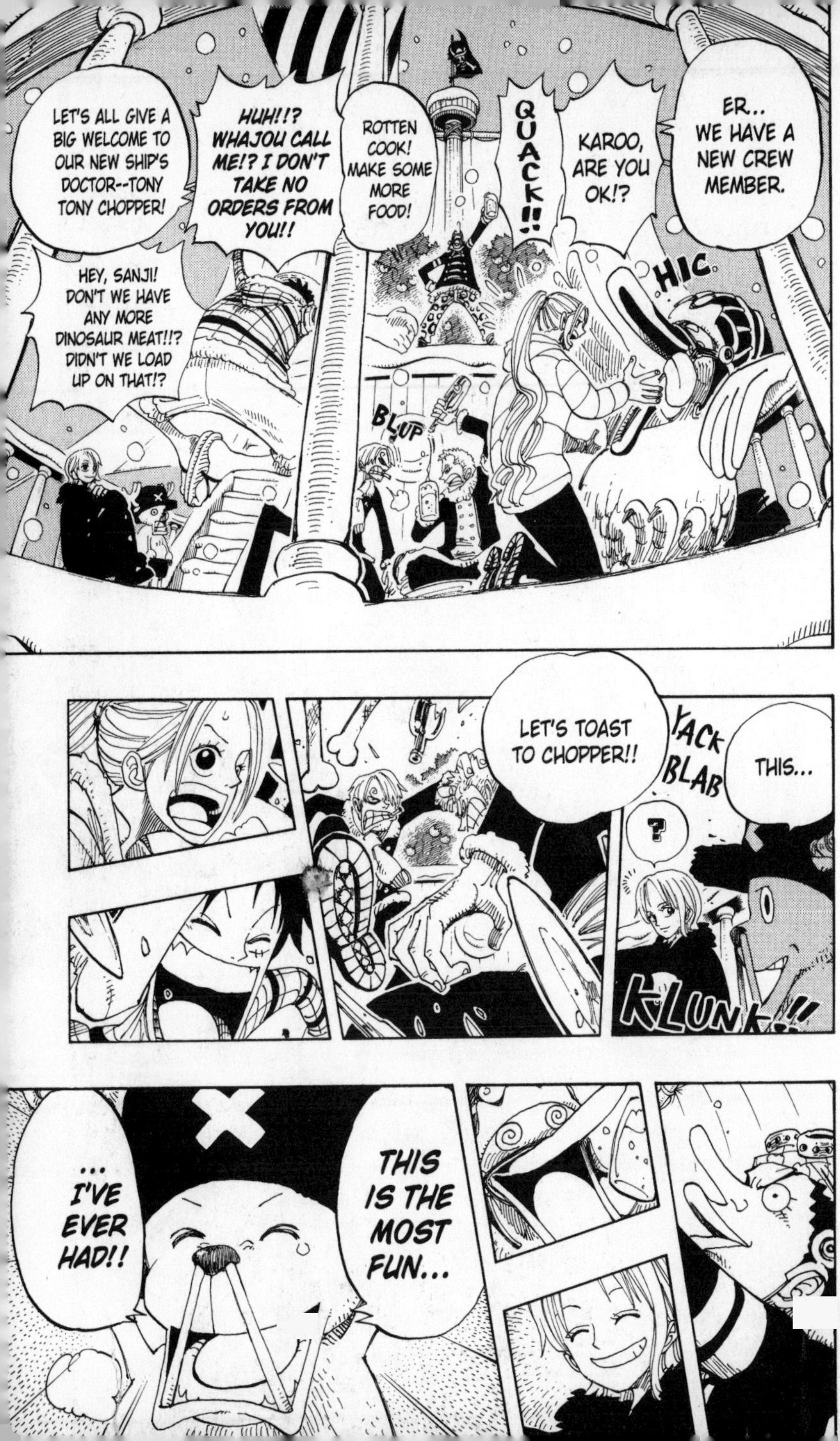
ER... WE HAVE A NEW CREW MEMBER.
HIC
KAROO, ARE YOU OK!?
QUACK!!
ROTTEN COOK! MAKE SOME MORE FOOD!
HUH!!? WHAJOU CALL ME!? I DON'T TAKE NO ORDERS FROM YOU!!
LET'S ALL GIVE A BIG WELCOME TO OUR NEW SHIP'S DOCTOR--TONY TONY CHOPPER!
HEY, SANJI! DON'T WE HAVE ANY MORE DINOSAUR MEAT!!? DIDN'T WE LOAD UP ON THAT!?
BLUP
THIS...
YACK BLAB
?
KLUNK!!
LET'S TOAST TO CHOPPER!!
THIS IS THE MOST FUN...
... I'VE EVER HAD!!

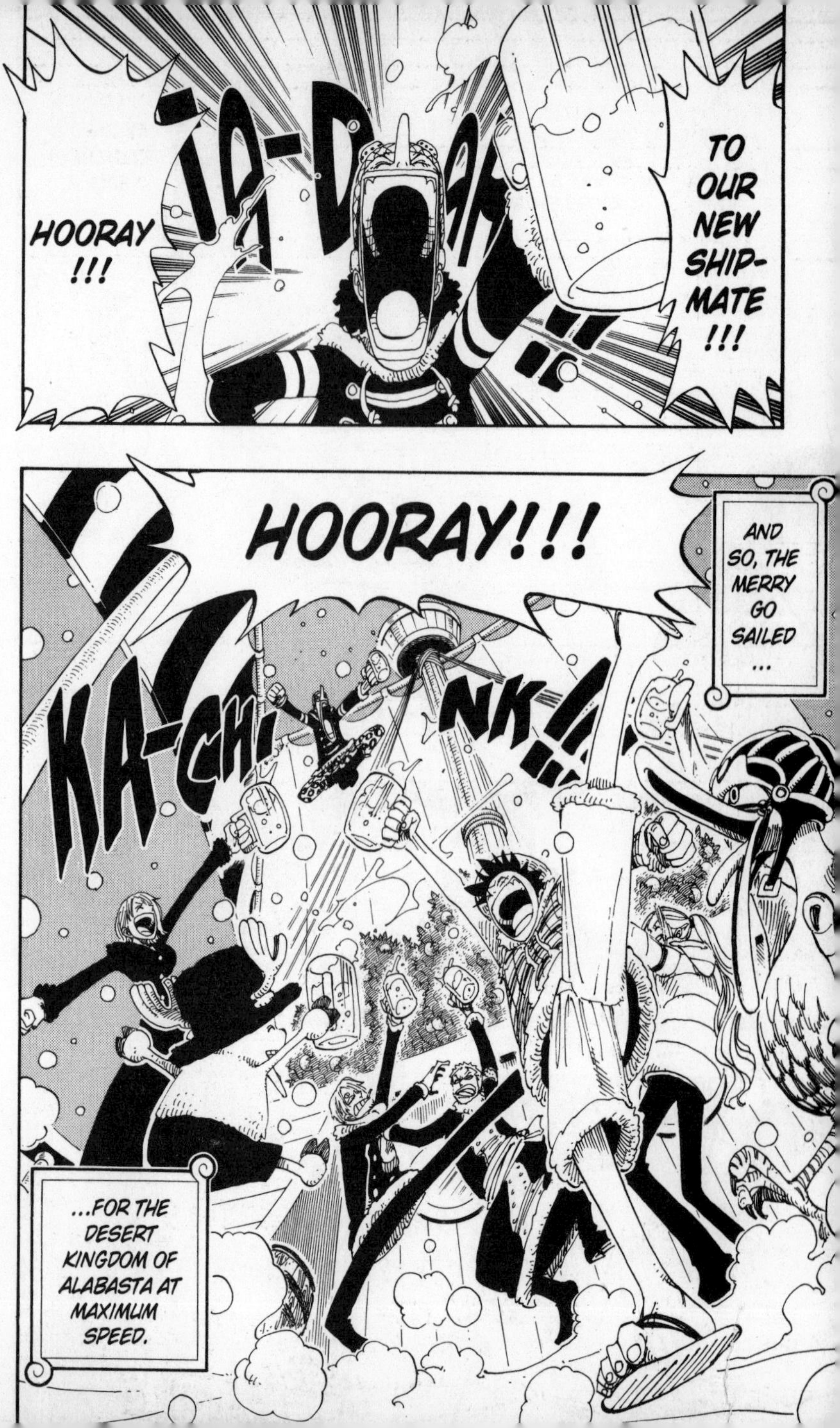
TO OUR NEW SHIP-MATE!!!
HOORAY!!!
HOORAY!!!
AND SO, THE MERRY GO SAILED...
KA-CHINK!!
...FOR THE DESERT KINGDOM OF ALABASTA AT MAXIMUM SPEED.

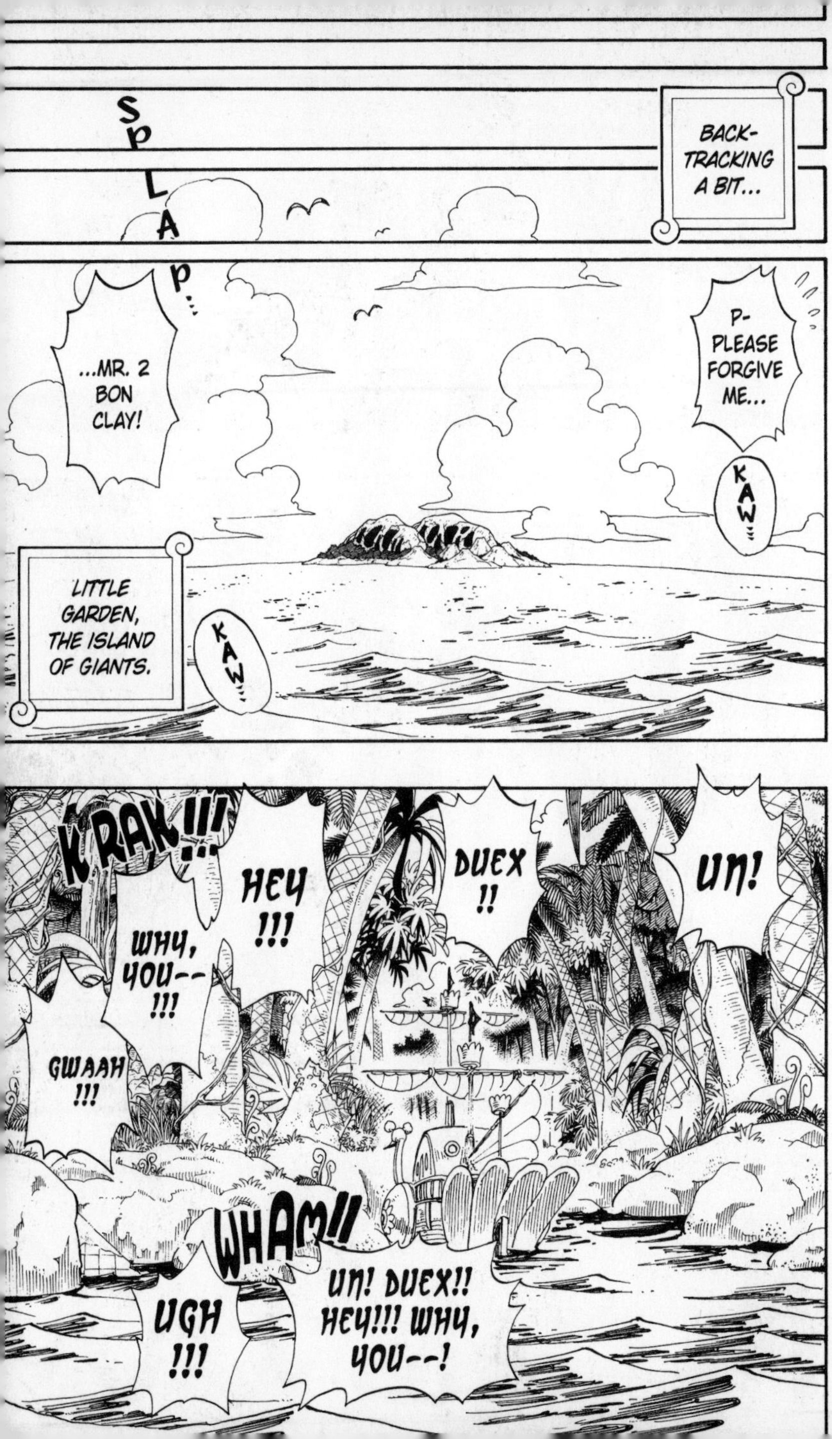
BACK-TRACKING A BIT...
SPLAP...
P-PLEASE FORGIVE ME...
KAW...
...MR. 2 BON CLAY!
LITTLE GARDEN, THE ISLAND OF GIANTS.
KAW...
UN!
DUEX!!
HEY!!!
KRAK!!!
WHY, YOU--!!!
GWAAH!!!
WHAM!!
UN! DUEX!! HEY!!! WHY, YOU--!
UGH!!!

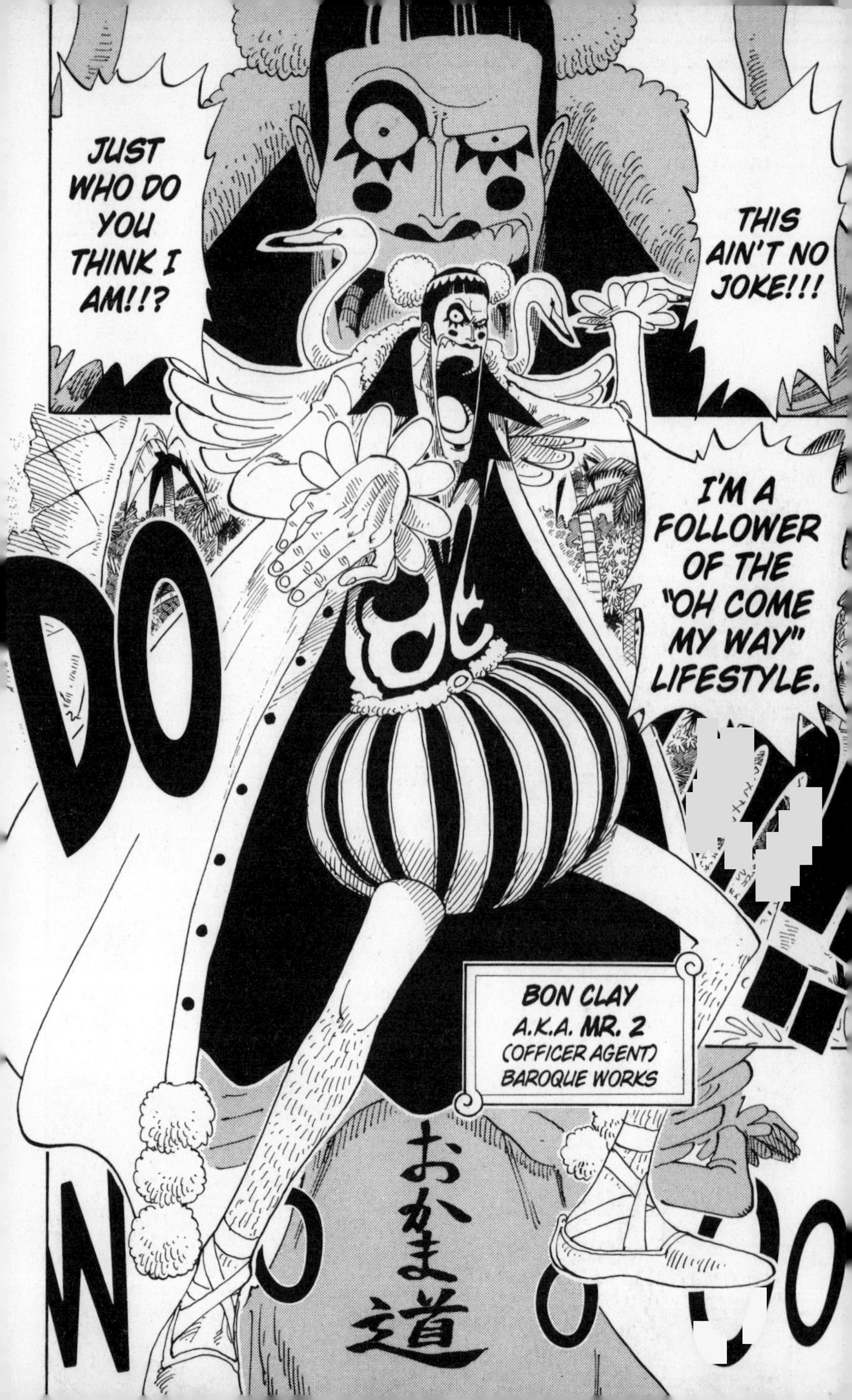
THIS AIN'T NO JOKE!!!
JUST WHO DO YOU THINK I AM!!?
I'M A FOLLOWER OF THE "OH COME MY WAY" LIFESTYLE.
DO
BON CLAY A.K.A. MR. 2 (OFFICER AGENT) BAROQUE WORKS
おかま道

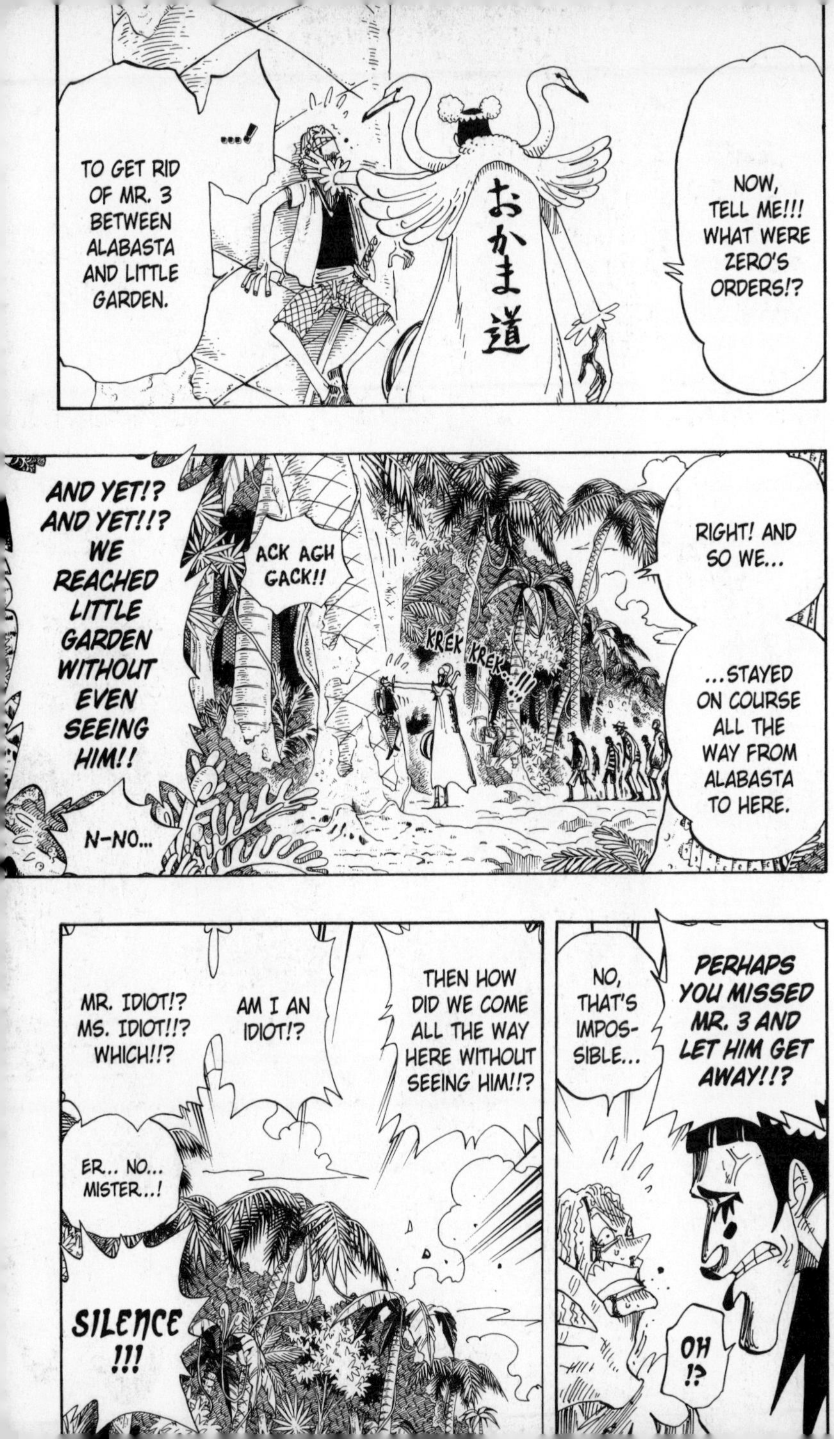
NOW, TELL ME!!! WHAT WERE ZERO'S ORDERS!?
...!
おかま道
TO GET RID OF MR. 3 BETWEEN ALABASTA AND LITTLE GARDEN.
RIGHT! AND SO WE...
...STAYED ON COURSE ALL THE WAY FROM ALABASTA TO HERE.
KREK KREK
ACK AGH GACK!!
AND YET!? AND YET!!? WE REACHED LITTLE GARDEN WITHOUT EVEN SEEING HIM!!
N-NO...
PERHAPS YOU MISSED MR. 3 AND LET HIM GET AWAY!!?
NO, THAT'S IMPOS-SIBLE...
OH!?
THEN HOW DID WE COME ALL THE WAY HERE WITHOUT SEEING HIM!!?
AM I AN IDIOT!?
MR. IDIOT!? MS. IDIOT!!? WHICH!!?
ER... NO... MISTER...!
SILENCE!!!

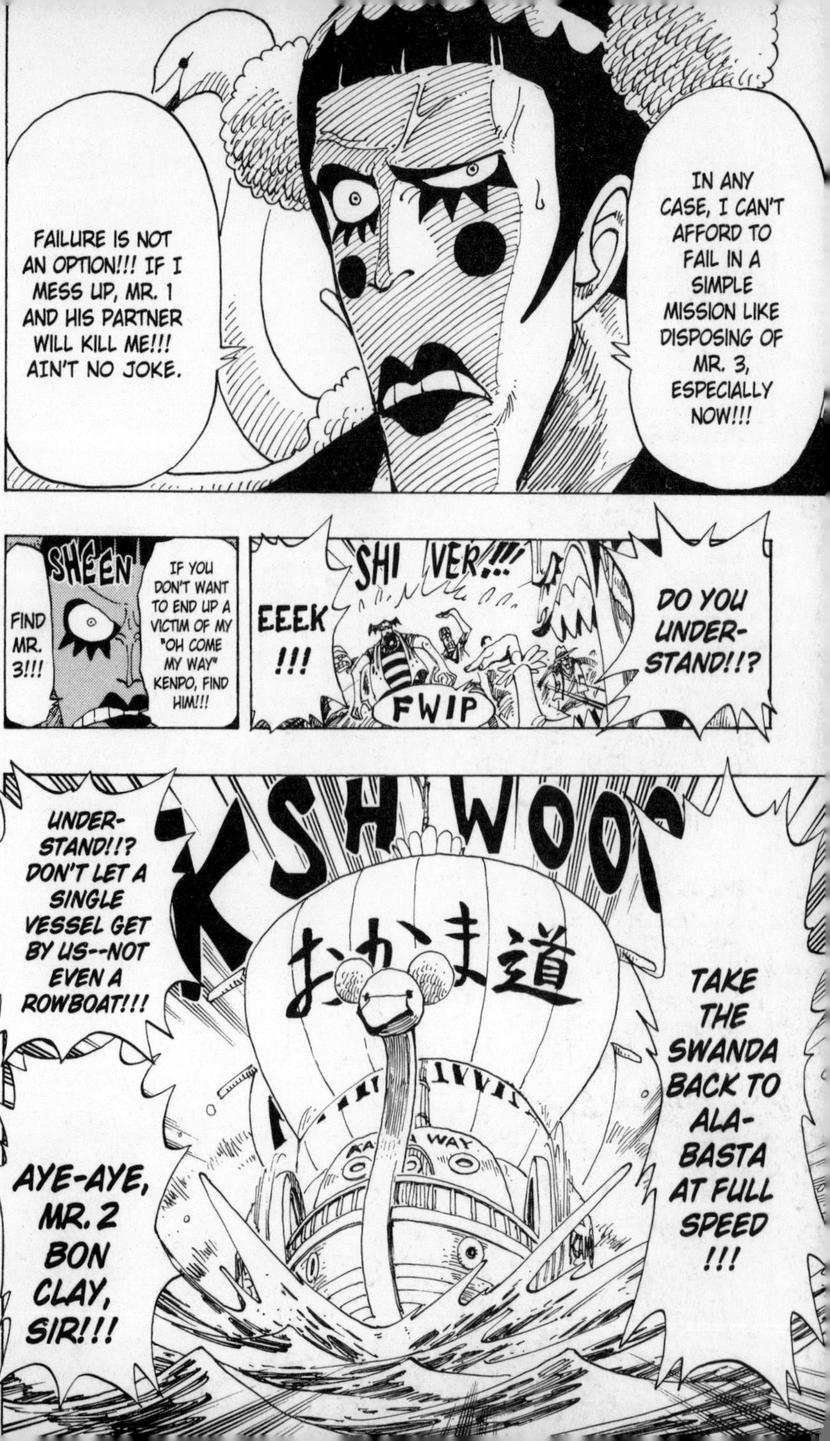
IN ANY CASE, I CAN'T AFFORD TO FAIL IN A SIMPLE MISSION LIKE DISPOSING OF MR. 3, ESPECIALLY NOW!!!
FAILURE IS NOT AN OPTION!!! IF I MESS UP, MR. 1 AND HIS PARTNER WILL KILL ME!!! AIN'T NO JOKE.
DO YOU UNDERSTAND!!?
SHIVER!!!
EEEK!!!
FWIP
IF YOU DON'T WANT TO END UP A VICTIM OF MY "OH COME MY WAY" KENPO, FIND HIM!!!
SHEEN
FIND MR. 3!!!
TAKE THE SWANDA BACK TO ALABASTA AT FULL SPEED!!!
KSHWOO
おかま道
UNDERSTAND!!? DON'T LET A SINGLE VESSEL GET BY US--NOT EVEN A ROWBOAT!!!
AYE-AYE, MR. 2 BON CLAY, SIR!!!

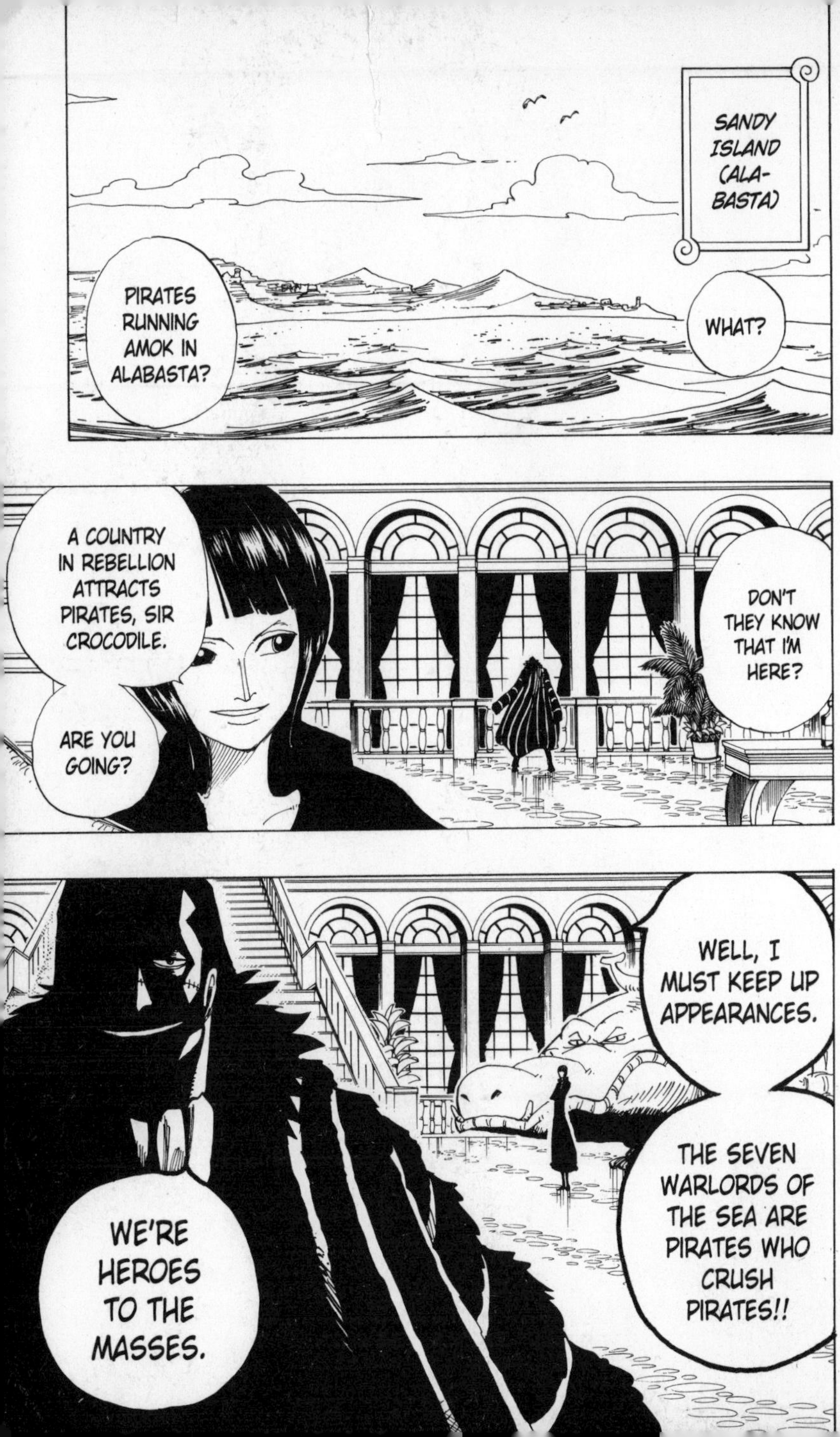
SANDY ISLAND (ALABASTA)
WHAT?
PIRATES RUNNING AMOK IN ALABASTA?
DON'T THEY KNOW THAT I'M HERE?
A COUNTRY IN REBELLION ATTRACTS PIRATES, SIR CROCODILE.
ARE YOU GOING?
WELL, I MUST KEEP UP APPEARANCES.
THE SEVEN WARLORDS OF THE SEA ARE PIRATES WHO CRUSH PIRATES!!
WE'RE HEROES TO THE MASSES.

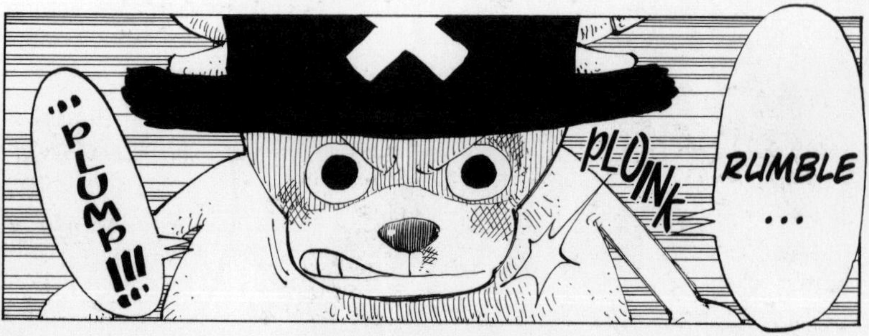
RUMBLE
...
PLOINK
"PLUMP!!!"

# Chapter 155:
# SIR CROCODILE, THE PIRATE

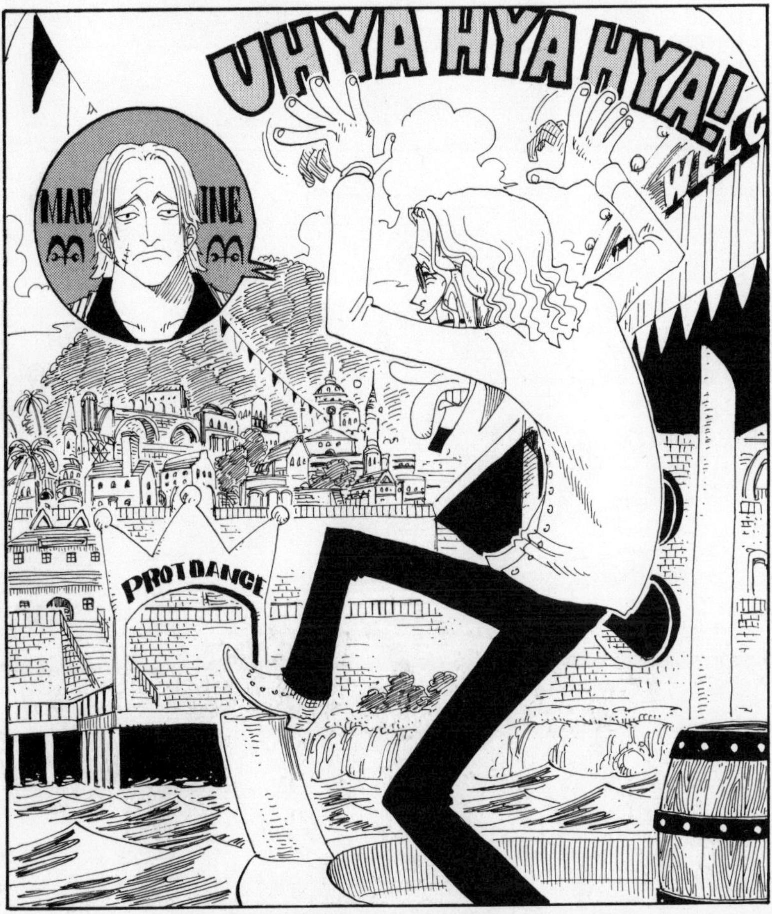
UHYA HYA HYA!
MAR INE
PROTDANCE

DJANGO'S DANCE HEAVEN, VOL. 23:
"SO LONG, YOU STUPID NAVY GUYS!!"

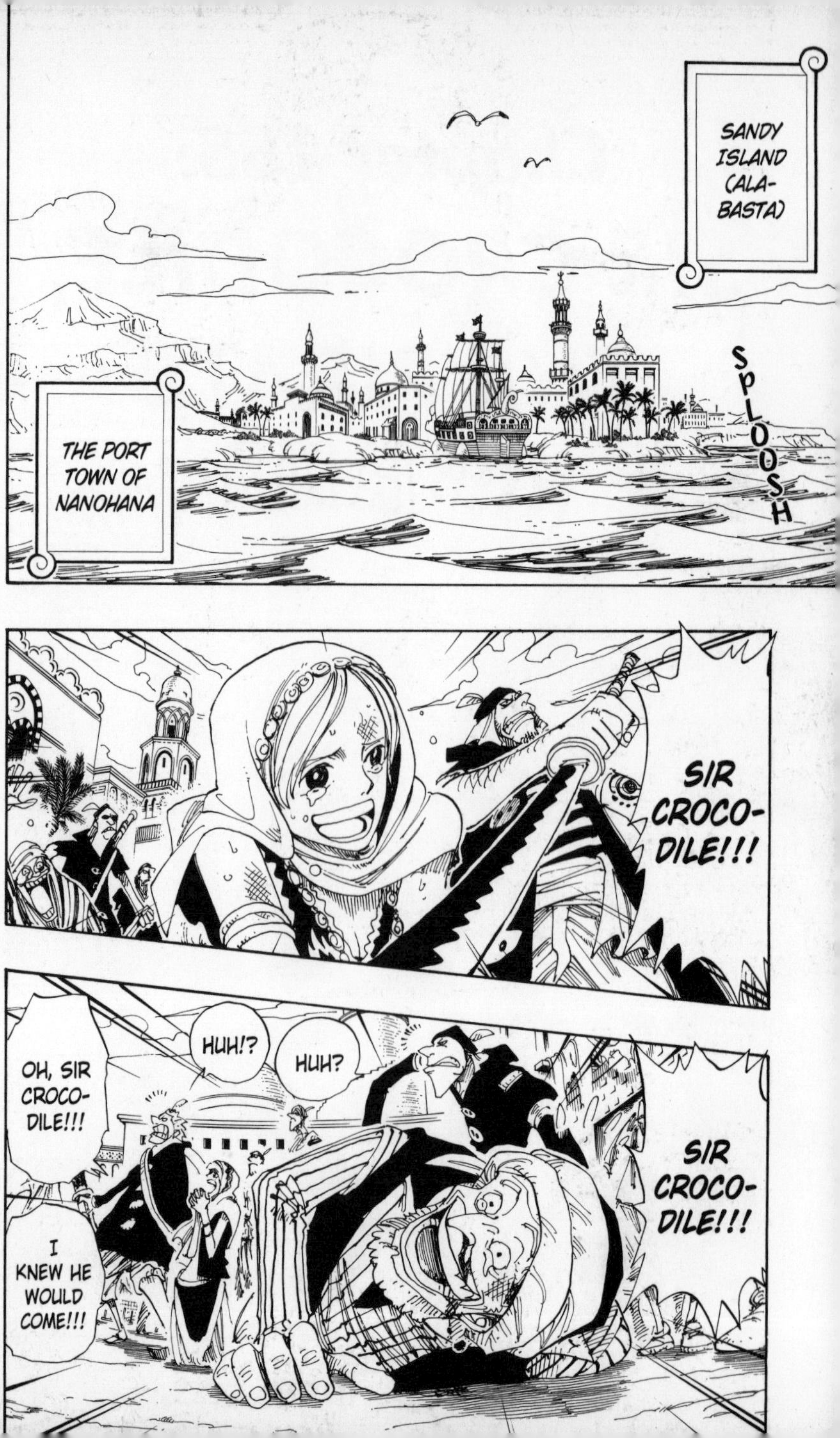
SANDY ISLAND (ALA-BASTA)
SPLOOSH
THE PORT TOWN OF NANOHANA
SIR CROCO-DILE!!!
SIR CROCO-DILE!!!
HUH?
HUH!?
OH, SIR CROCO-DILE!!!
I KNEW HE WOULD COME!!!

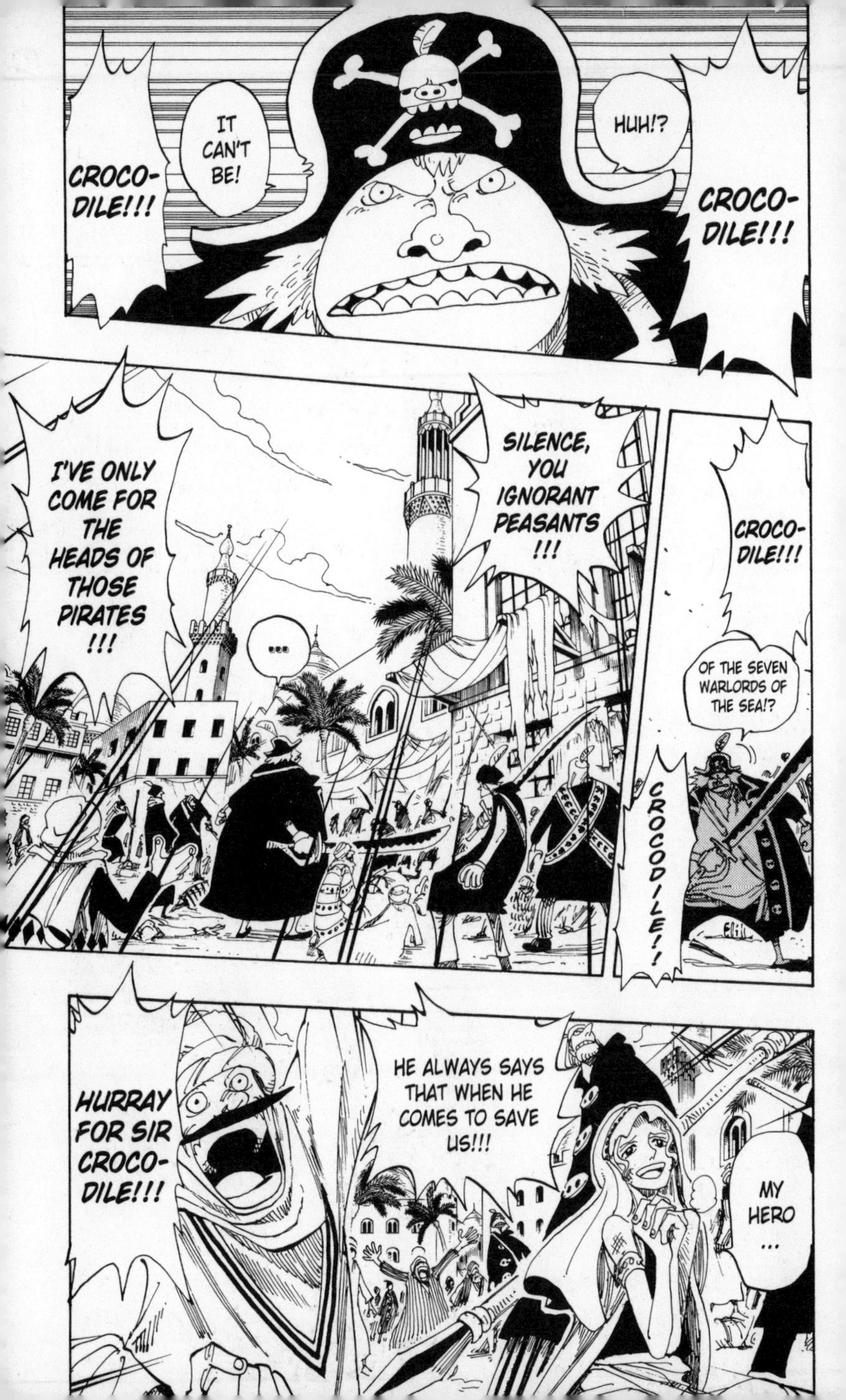
CROCO-DILE!!!
HUH!?
IT CAN'T BE!
CROCO-DILE!!!
CROCO-DILE!!!
OF THE SEVEN WARLORDS OF THE SEA!?
CROCODILE!!
SILENCE, YOU IGNORANT PEASANTS!!!
...
I'VE ONLY COME FOR THE HEADS OF THOSE PIRATES!!!
MY HERO ...
HE ALWAYS SAYS THAT WHEN HE COMES TO SAVE US!!!
HURRAY FOR SIR CROCO-DILE!!!

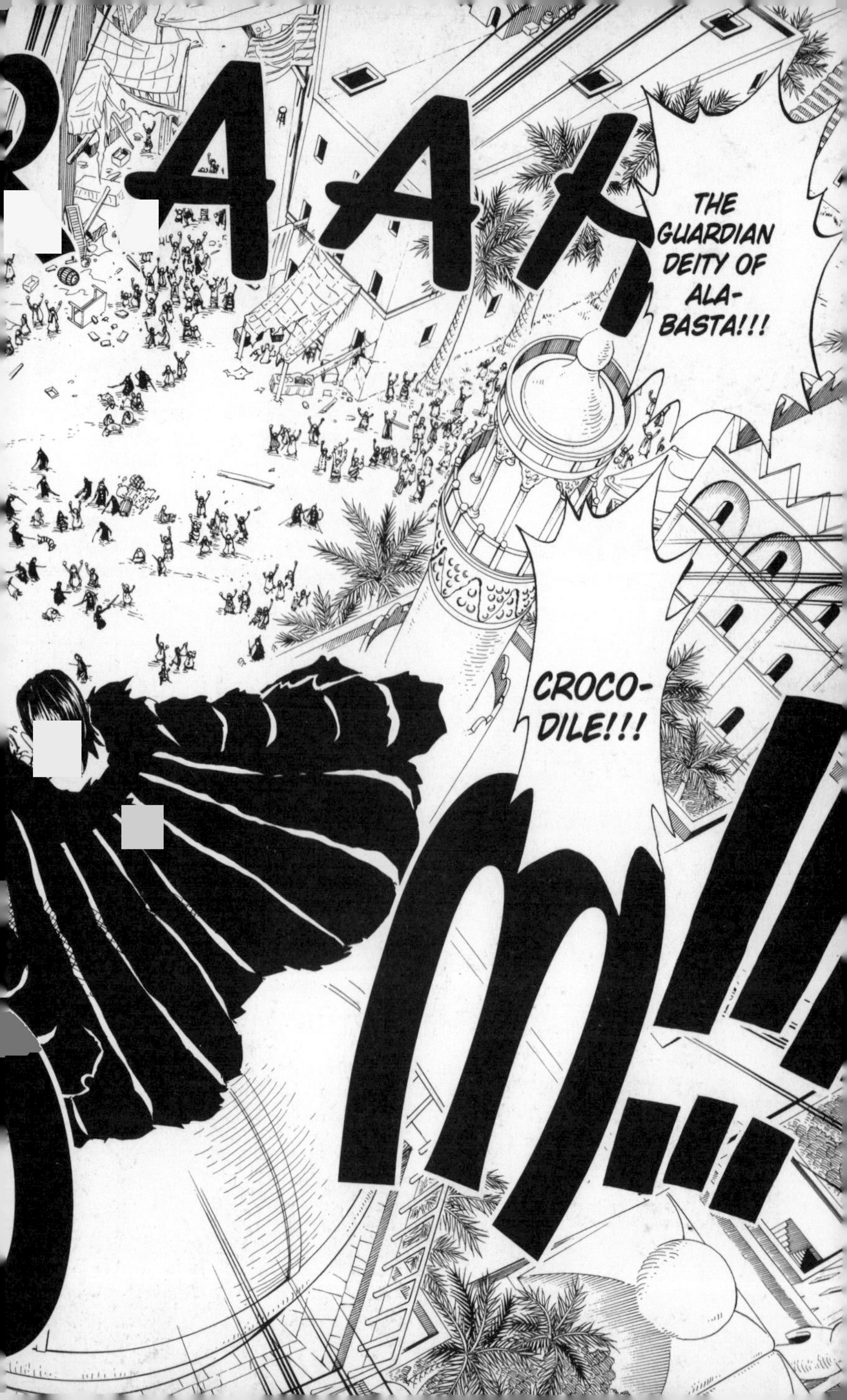
THE GUARDIAN DEITY OF ALA-BASTA!!!
CROCO-DILE!!!

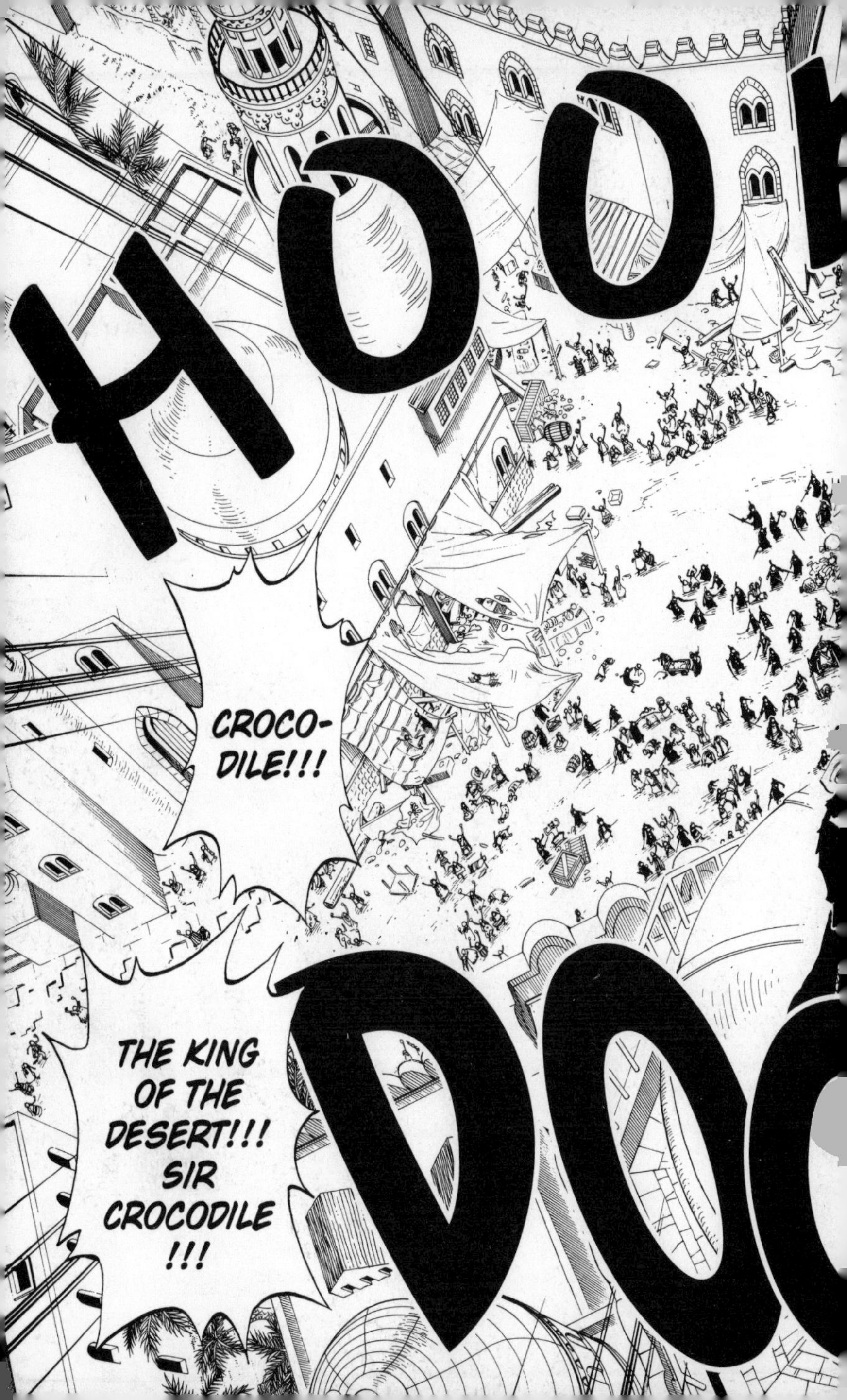
HOO
CROCO-DILE!!!
THE KING OF THE DESERT!!! SIR CROCODILE !!!
DOO

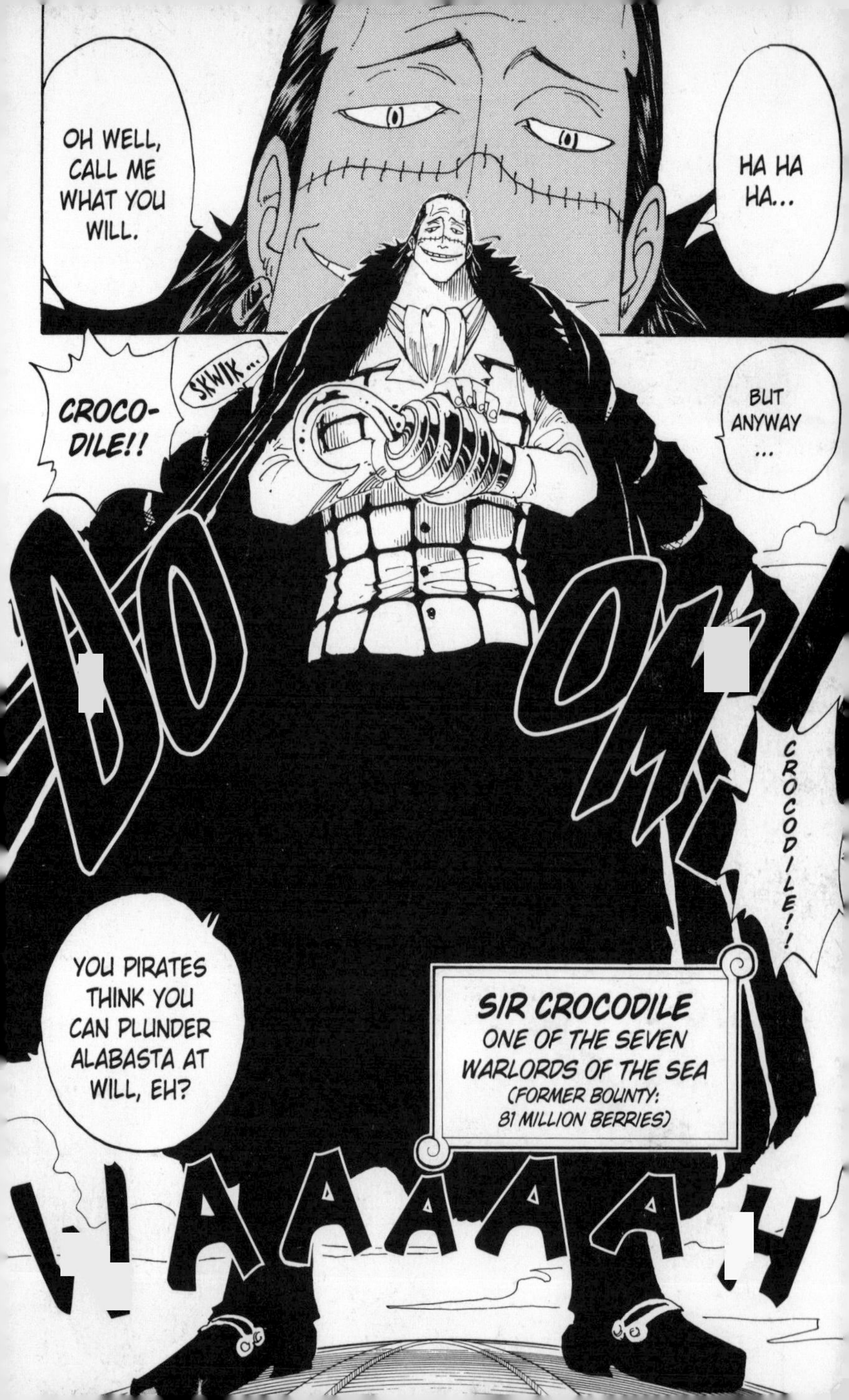
HA HA HA...
OH WELL, CALL ME WHAT YOU WILL.
BUT ANYWAY ...
SKWIK...
CROCO-DILE!!
DOOM
CROCODILE!!
SIR CROCODILE
ONE OF THE SEVEN WARLORDS OF THE SEA
(FORMER BOUNTY: 81 MILLION BERRIES)
YOU PIRATES THINK YOU CAN PLUNDER ALABASTA AT WILL, EH?
WAAAAAH

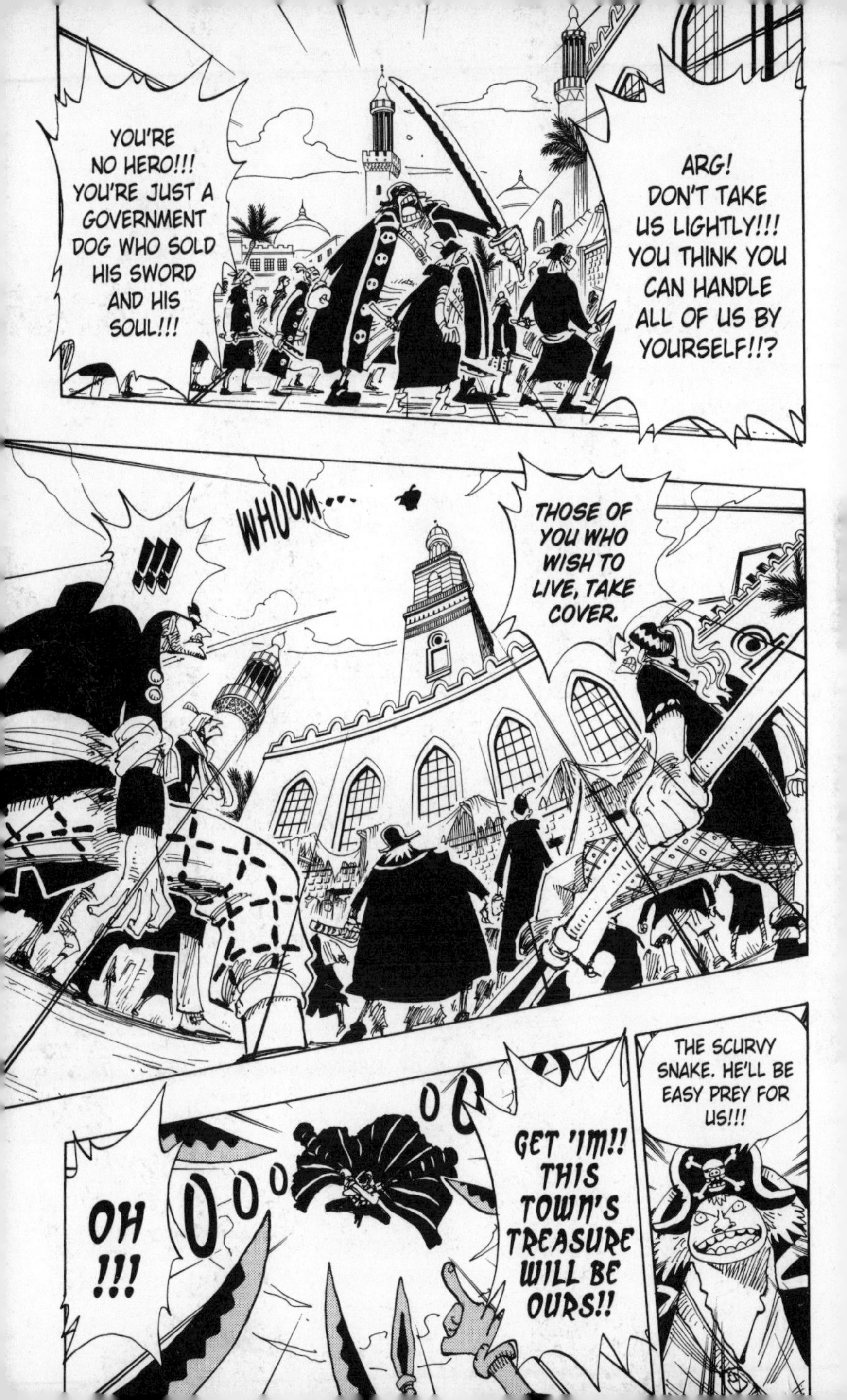
ARG! DON'T TAKE US LIGHTLY!!! YOU THINK YOU CAN HANDLE ALL OF US BY YOURSELF!!?
YOU'RE NO HERO!!! YOU'RE JUST A GOVERNMENT DOG WHO SOLD HIS SWORD AND HIS SOUL!!!
THOSE OF YOU WHO WISH TO LIVE, TAKE COVER.
WHOOM...
!!!
THE SCURVY SNAKE. HE'LL BE EASY PREY FOR US!!!
GET 'IM!! THIS TOWN'S TREASURE WILL BE OURS!!
OOOOOO
OH !!!

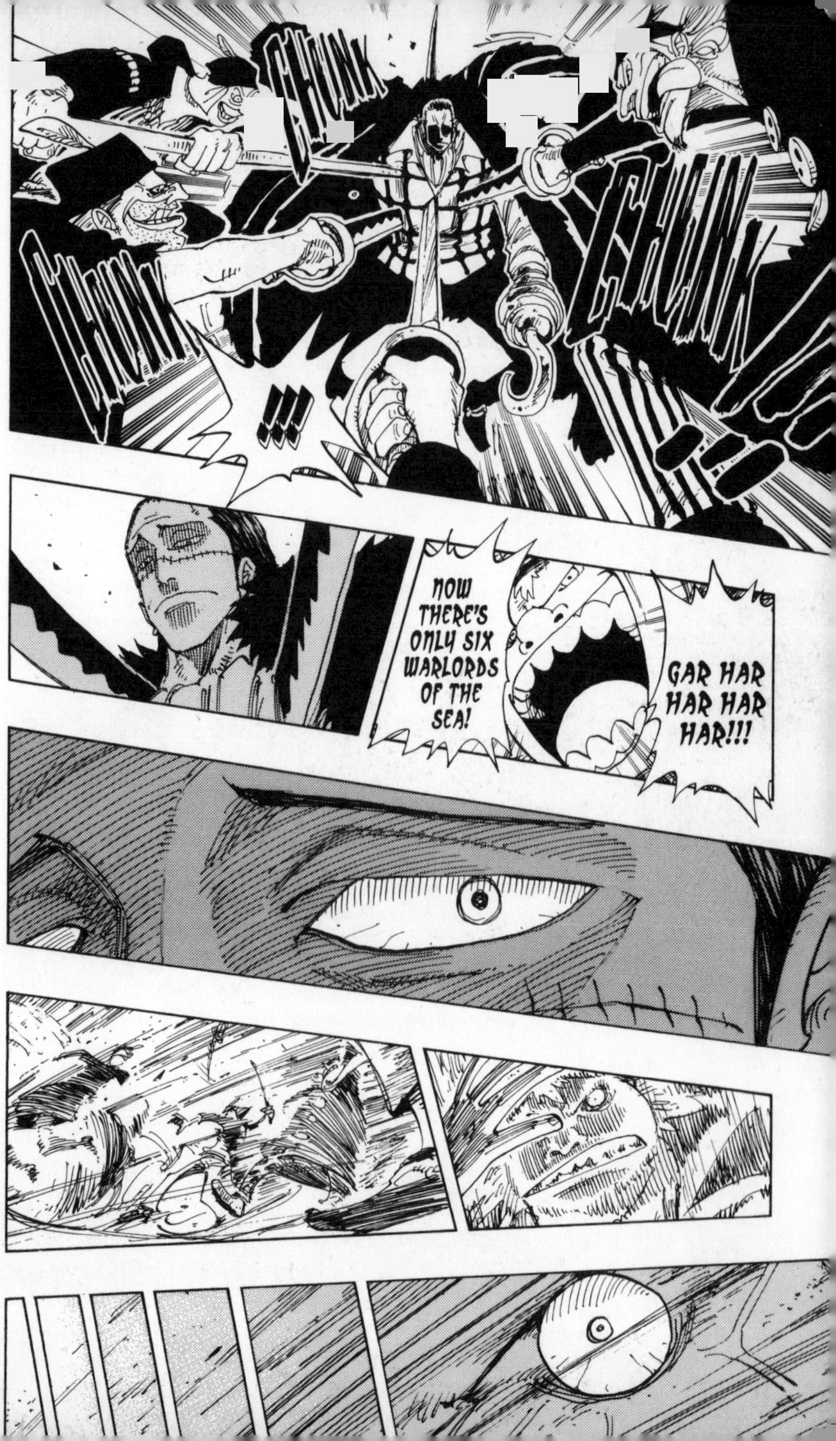
CHUNK
CHUNK
CHUNK
!!!
GAR HAR HAR HAR HAR!!!
NOW THERE'S ONLY SIX WARLORDS OF THE SEA!

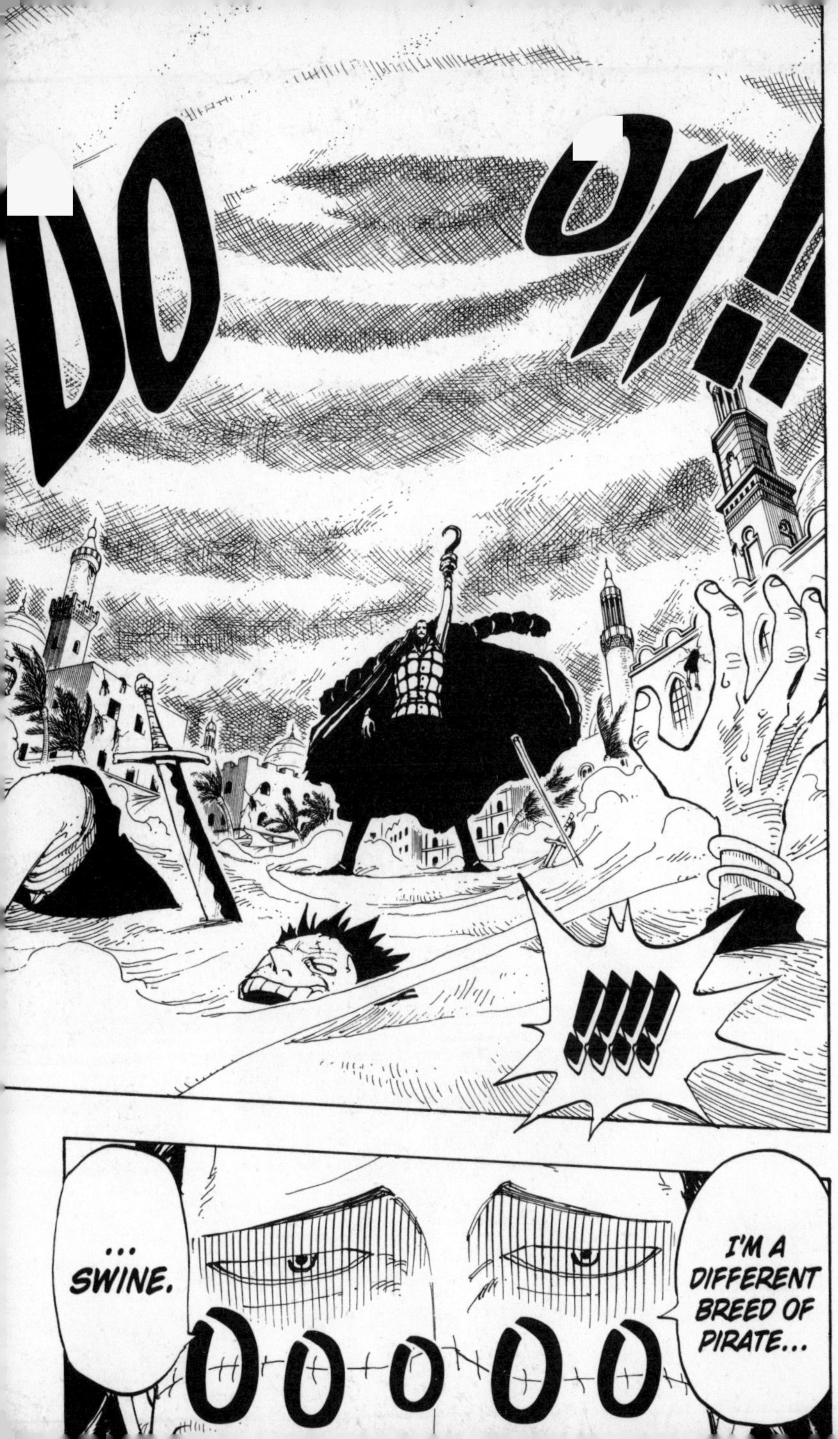
DOON!!
!!!!
I'M A DIFFERENT BREED OF PIRATE...
... SWINE.
OOOOOO

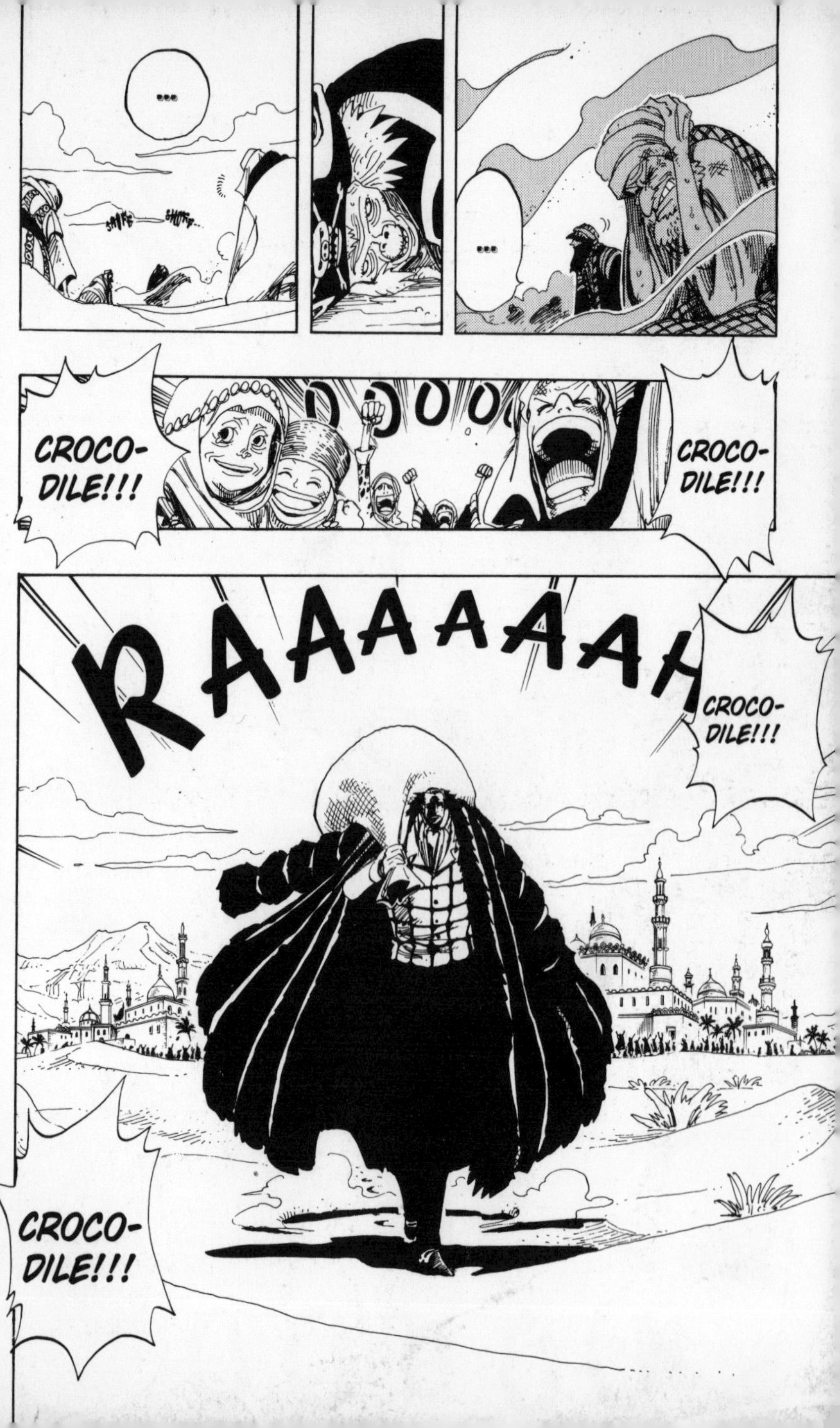
...
...
CROCO-DILE!!!
CROCO-DILE!!!
RAAAAAAH
CROCO-DILE!!!
CROCO-DILE!!!

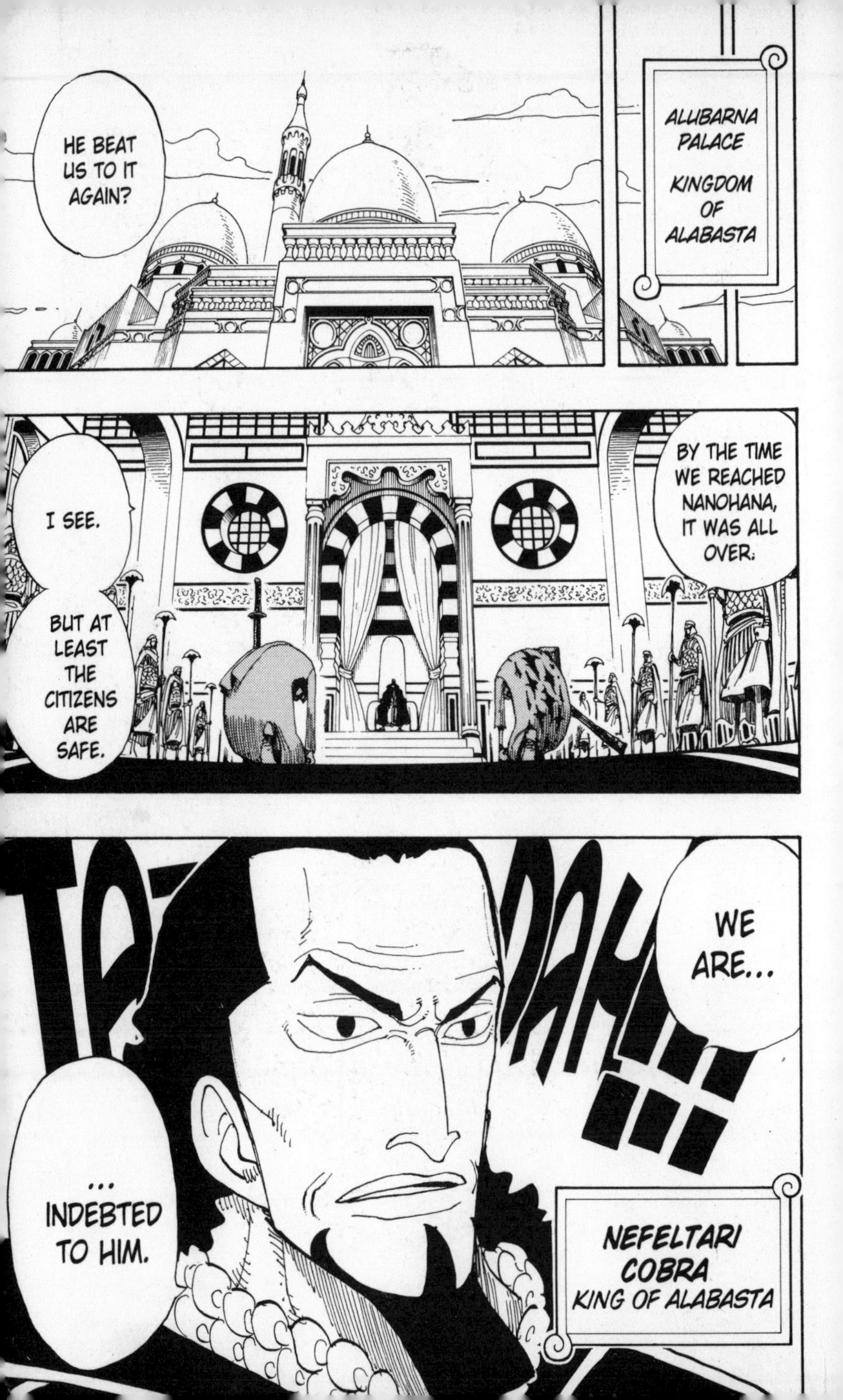
ALUBARNA PALACE
KINGDOM OF ALABASTA
HE BEAT US TO IT AGAIN?
BY THE TIME WE REACHED NANOHANA, IT WAS ALL OVER.
I SEE.
BUT AT LEAST THE CITIZENS ARE SAFE.
WE ARE...
...INDEBTED TO HIM.
NEFELTARI COBRA
KING OF ALABASTA

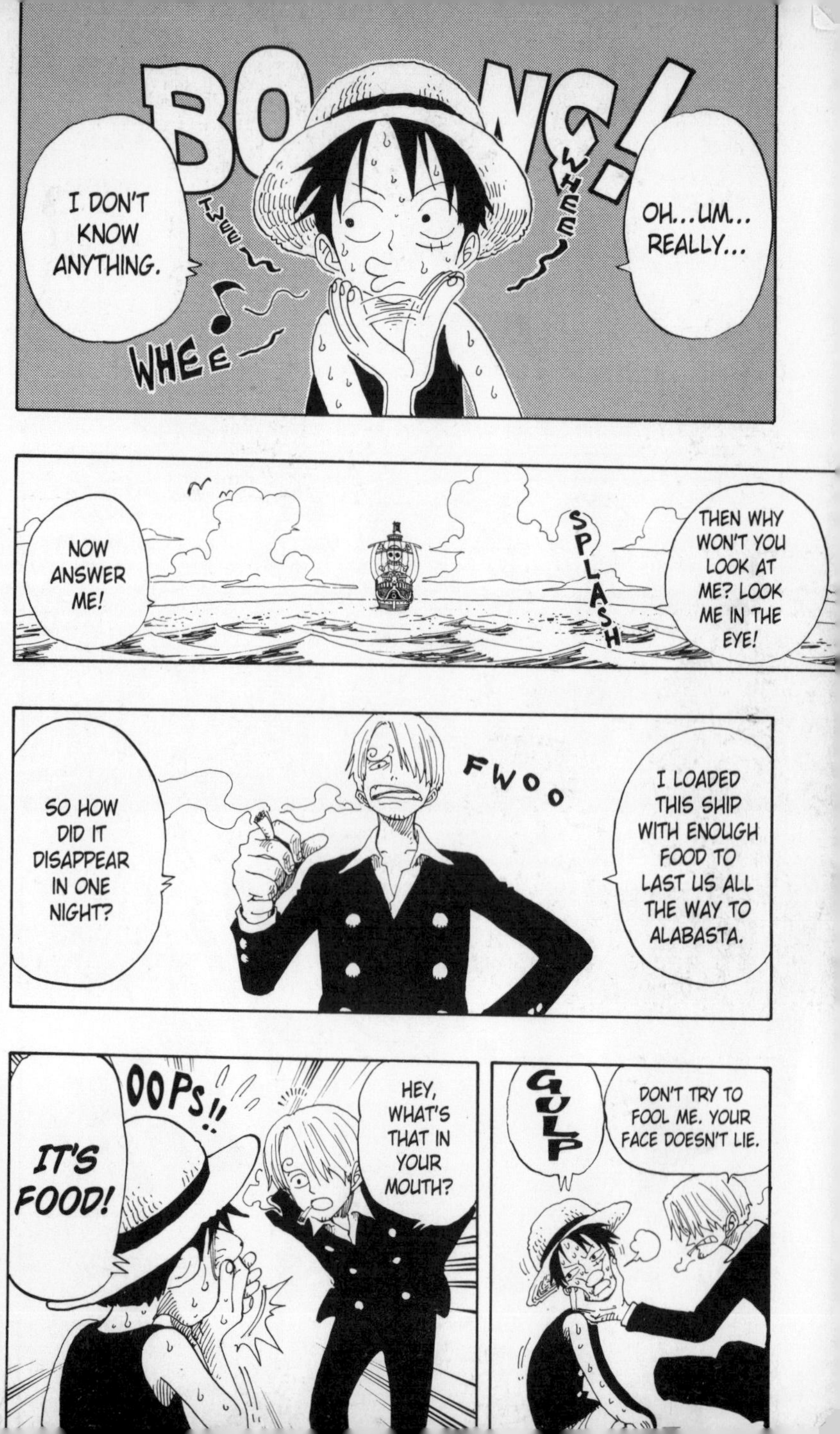
BO NG!
OH...UM... REALLY...
WHEE
TWEE
I DON'T KNOW ANYTHING.
WHEE
THEN WHY WON'T YOU LOOK AT ME? LOOK ME IN THE EYE!
SPLASH
NOW ANSWER ME!
I LOADED THIS SHIP WITH ENOUGH FOOD TO LAST US ALL THE WAY TO ALABASTA.
FWOO
SO HOW DID IT DISAPPEAR IN ONE NIGHT?
DON'T TRY TO FOOL ME. YOUR FACE DOESN'T LIE.
GULP
HEY, WHAT'S THAT IN YOUR MOUTH?
OOPS!!
IT'S FOOD!

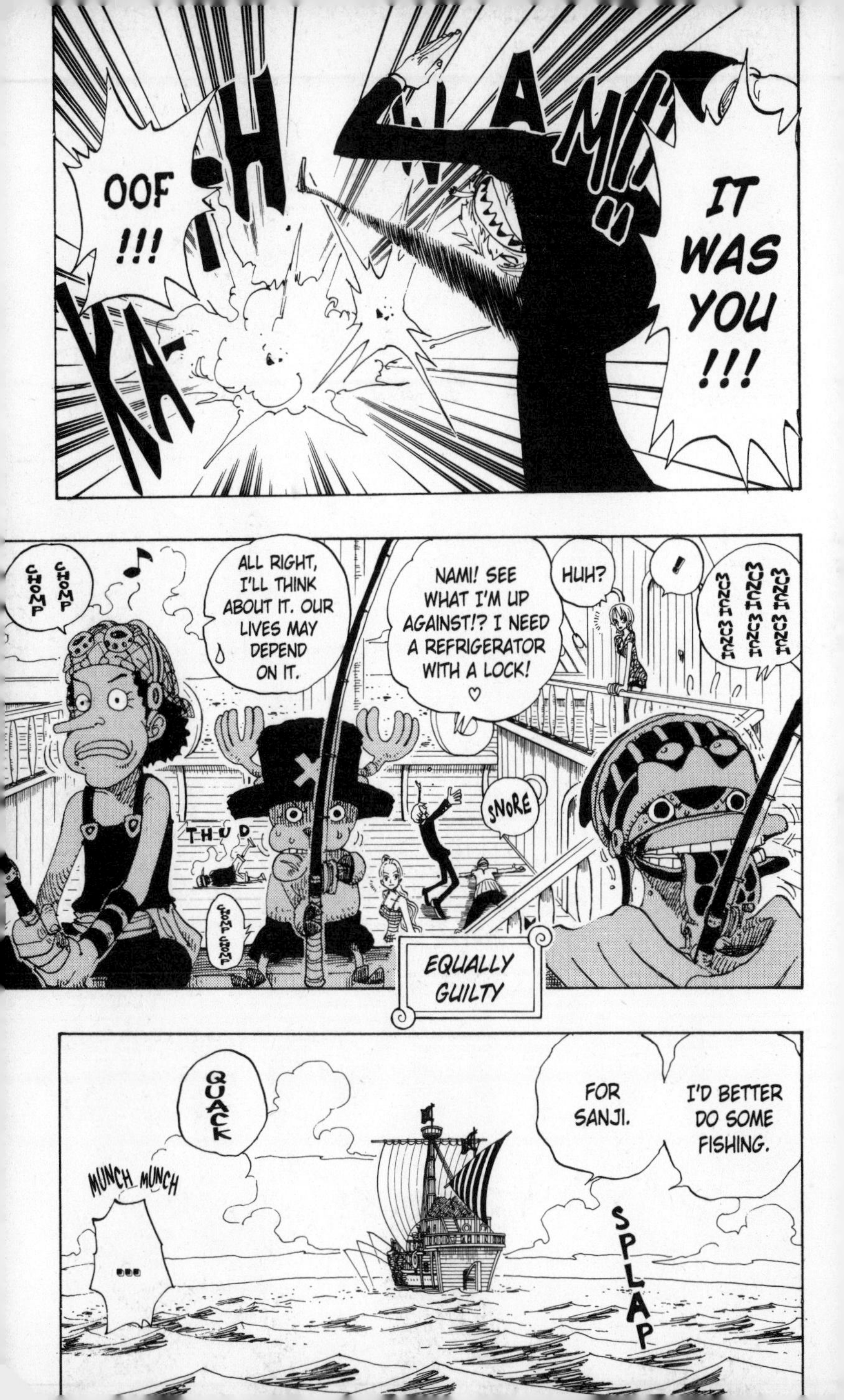
IT WAS YOU!!!
KA-WHAM!!
OOF!!!
MUNCH MUNCH MUNCH MUNCH MUNCH MUNCH
!
HUH?
NAMI! SEE WHAT I'M UP AGAINST!? I NEED A REFRIGERATOR WITH A LOCK! ♡
SNORE
ALL RIGHT, I'LL THINK ABOUT IT. OUR LIVES MAY DEPEND ON IT.
CHOMP CHOMP
THUD
CHOMP CHOMP
EQUALLY GUILTY
I'D BETTER DO SOME FISHING.
FOR SANJI.
SPLAP
QUACK
MUNCH MUNCH
...

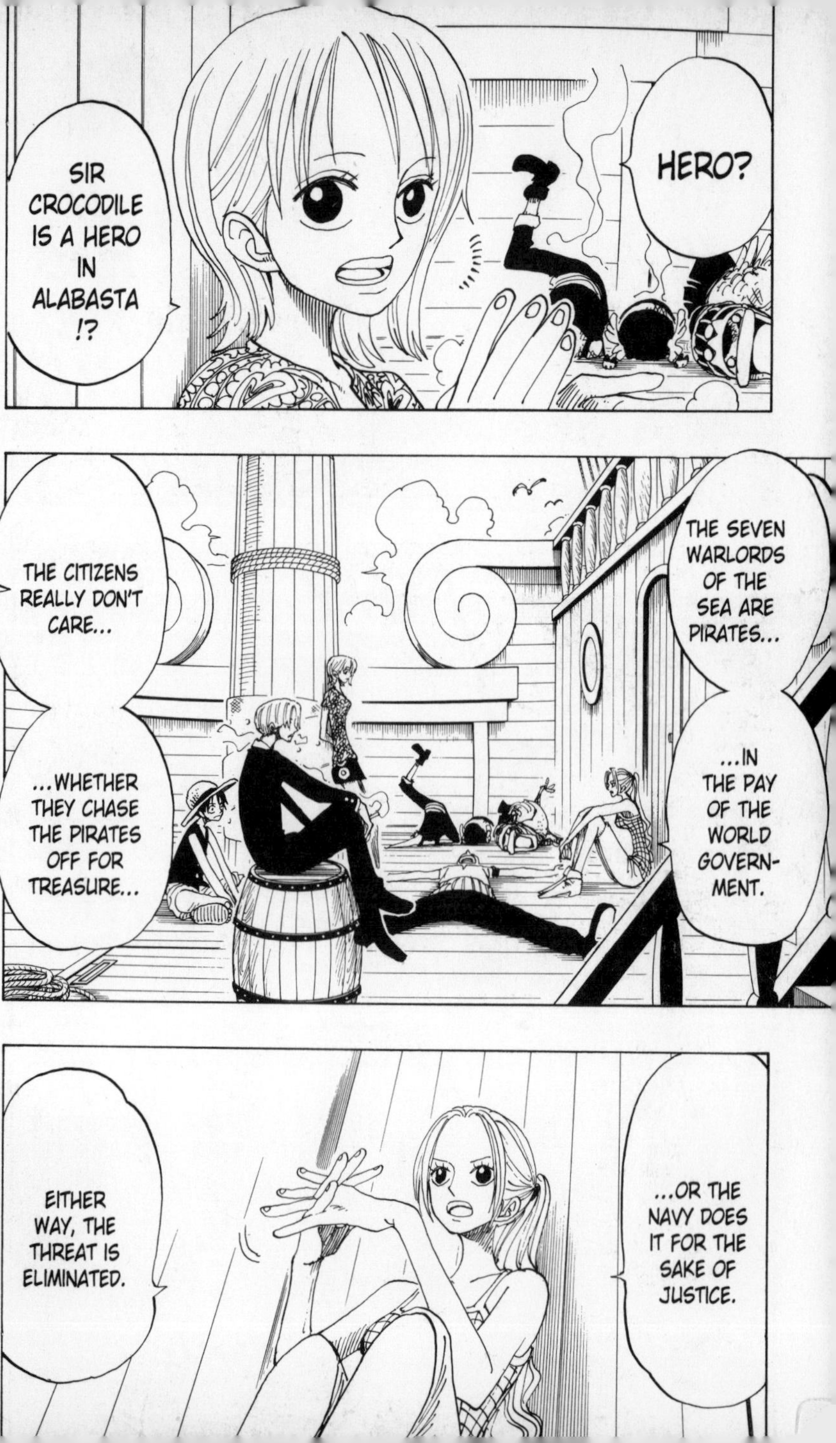
HERO?
SIR CROCODILE IS A HERO IN ALABASTA!?
THE SEVEN WARLORDS OF THE SEA ARE PIRATES...
...IN THE PAY OF THE WORLD GOVERNMENT.
THE CITIZENS REALLY DON'T CARE...
...WHETHER THEY CHASE THE PIRATES OFF FOR TREASURE...
...OR THE NAVY DOES IT FOR THE SAKE OF JUSTICE.
EITHER WAY, THE THREAT IS ELIMINATED.

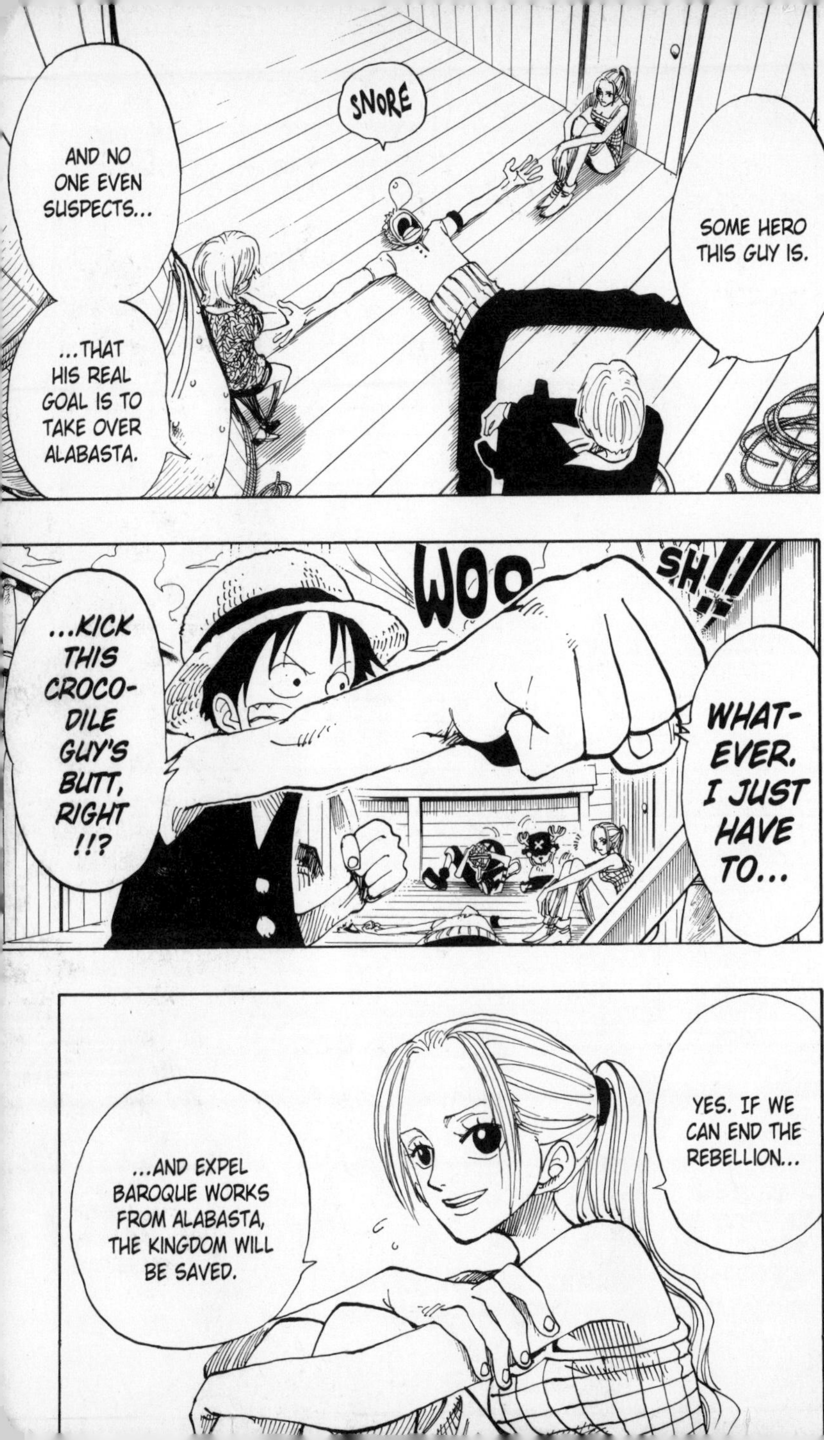
SOME HERO THIS GUY IS.
SNORE
AND NO ONE EVEN SUSPECTS...
...THAT HIS REAL GOAL IS TO TAKE OVER ALABASTA.
WHAT-EVER. I JUST HAVE TO...
WOOSH!!
...KICK THIS CROCO-DILE GUY'S BUTT, RIGHT!!?
YES. IF WE CAN END THE REBELLION...
...AND EXPEL BAROQUE WORKS FROM ALABASTA, THE KINGDOM WILL BE SAVED.

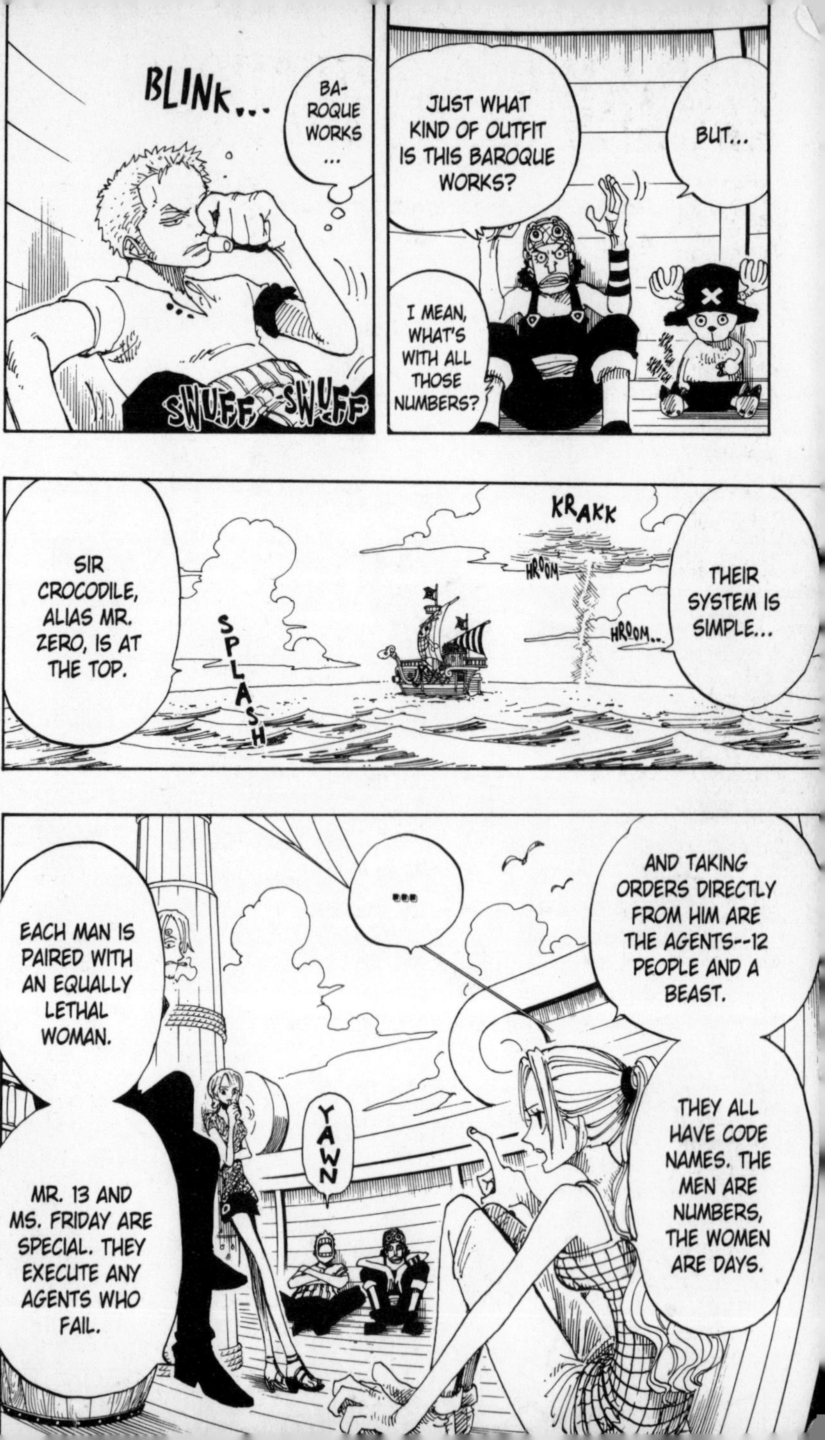
BUT...
JUST WHAT KIND OF OUTFIT IS THIS BAROQUE WORKS?
SKRITCH SKRITCH
I MEAN, WHAT'S WITH ALL THOSE NUMBERS?
BA-ROQUE WORKS ...
BLINK...
SWUFF SWUFF
KRAKK
THEIR SYSTEM IS SIMPLE...
HROOM
HROOM...
SPLASH
SIR CROCODILE, ALIAS MR. ZERO, IS AT THE TOP.
AND TAKING ORDERS DIRECTLY FROM HIM ARE THE AGENTS--12 PEOPLE AND A BEAST.
THEY ALL HAVE CODE NAMES. THE MEN ARE NUMBERS, THE WOMEN ARE DAYS.
...
YAWN
EACH MAN IS PAIRED WITH AN EQUALLY LETHAL WOMAN.
MR. 13 AND MS. FRIDAY ARE SPECIAL. THEY EXECUTE ANY AGENTS WHO FAIL.

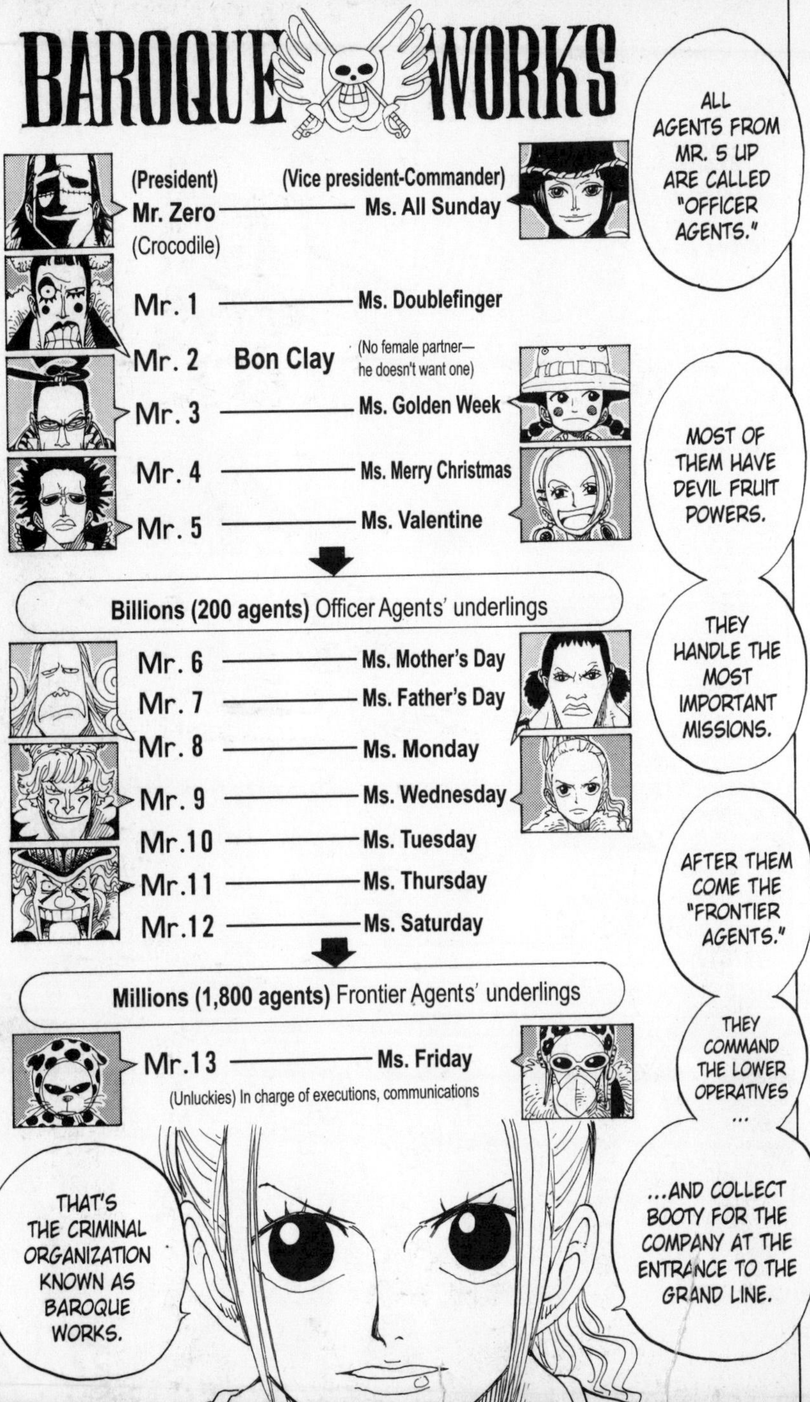
BAROQUE WORKS
(President) Mr. Zero (Crocodile) — (Vice president-Commander) Ms. All Sunday
Mr. 1 — Ms. Doublefinger
Mr. 2 Bon Clay (No female partner— he doesn't want one)
Mr. 3 — Ms. Golden Week
Mr. 4 — Ms. Merry Christmas
Mr. 5 — Ms. Valentine
Billions (200 agents) Officer Agents' underlings
Mr. 6 — Ms. Mother's Day
Mr. 7 — Ms. Father's Day
Mr. 8 — Ms. Monday
Mr. 9 — Ms. Wednesday
Mr.10 — Ms. Tuesday
Mr.11 — Ms. Thursday
Mr.12 — Ms. Saturday
Millions (1,800 agents) Frontier Agents' underlings
Mr.13 — Ms. Friday
(Unluckies) In charge of executions, communications
ALL AGENTS FROM MR. 5 UP ARE CALLED "OFFICER AGENTS."
MOST OF THEM HAVE DEVIL FRUIT POWERS.
THEY HANDLE THE MOST IMPORTANT MISSIONS.
AFTER THEM COME THE "FRONTIER AGENTS."
THEY COMMAND THE LOWER OPERATIVES ...
...AND COLLECT BOOTY FOR THE COMPANY AT THE ENTRANCE TO THE GRAND LINE.
THAT'S THE CRIMINAL ORGANIZATION KNOWN AS BAROQUE WORKS.

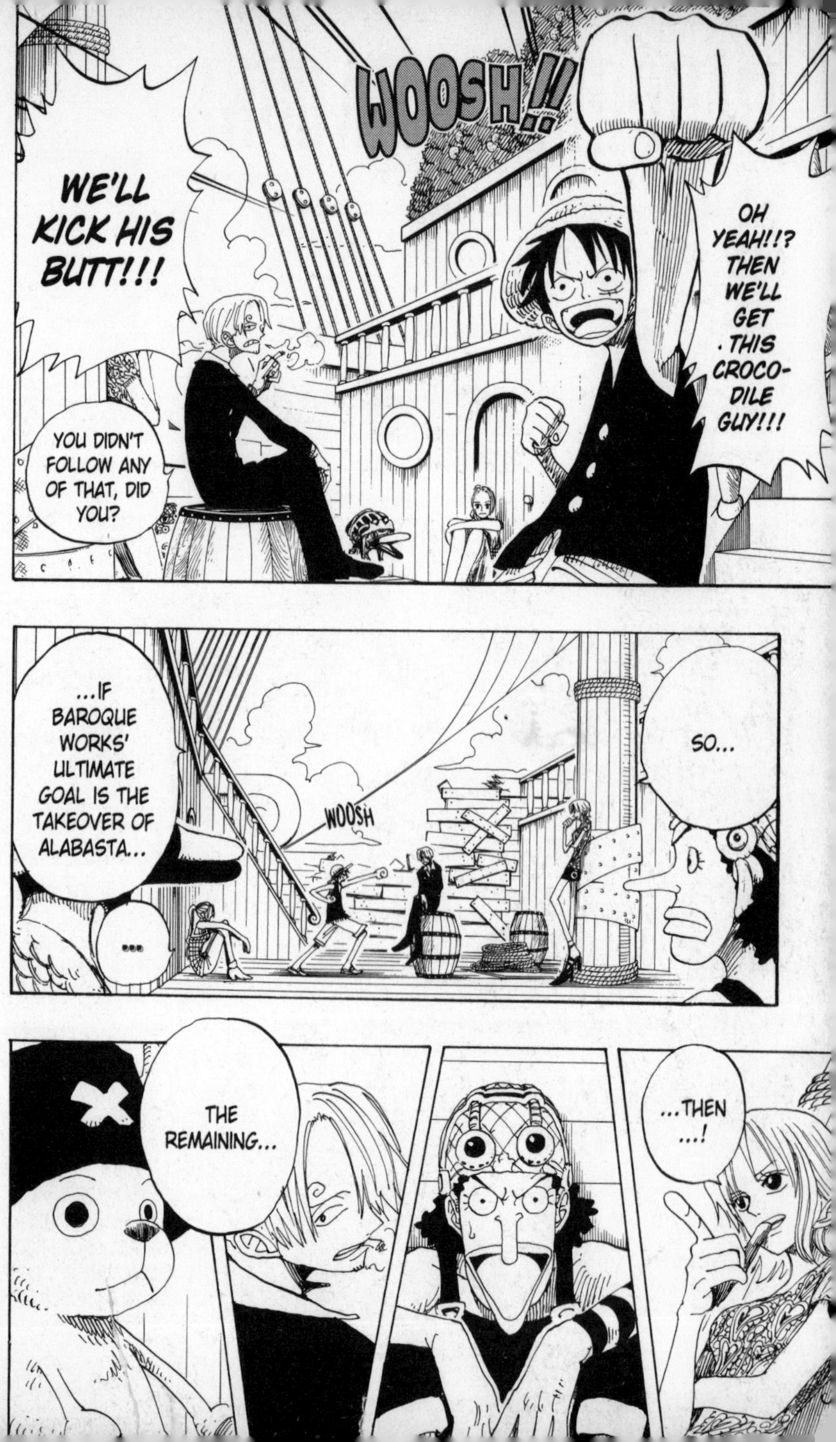
OH YEAH!!? THEN WE'LL GET THIS CROCODILE GUY!!!
WOOSH!!
WE'LL KICK HIS BUTT!!!
YOU DIDN'T FOLLOW ANY OF THAT, DID YOU?
SO...
...IF BAROQUE WORKS' ULTIMATE GOAL IS THE TAKEOVER OF ALABASTA...
WOOSH
...
...THEN ...!
THE REMAINING...

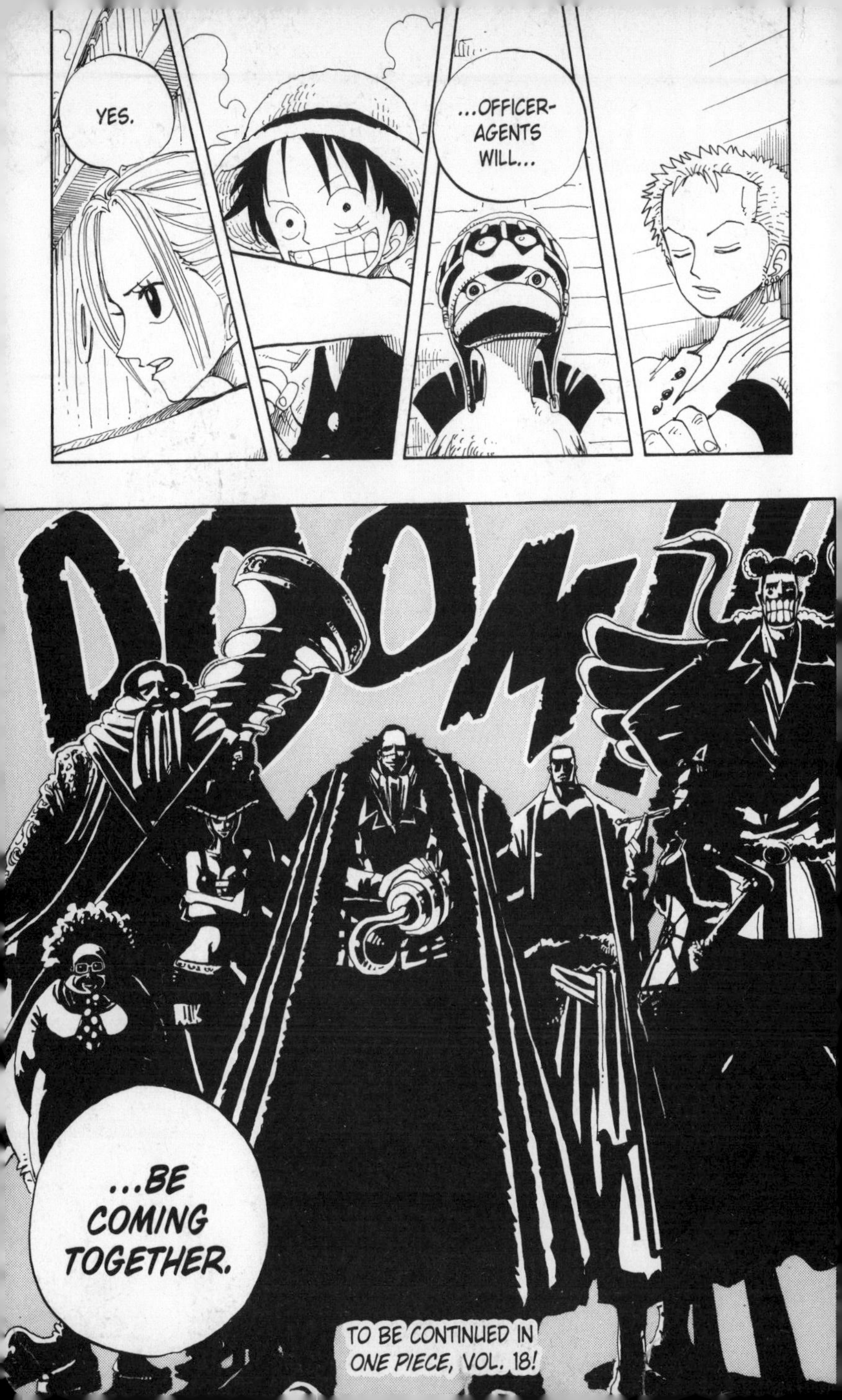
...OFFICER-AGENTS WILL...
YES.
DOOM!!
...BE COMING TOGETHER.
TO BE CONTINUED IN ONE PIECE, VOL. 18!

# COMING NEXT VOLUME:

The desert's hot! Real hot! Luffy and friends find out the
hard way as they take a long trek through the desert sun!
A half-baked Luffy falls prey to a group of scheming birds
and they relieve him of most of the team's supplies!
Traversing the desert fully loaded is hard enough, but
without any water?! Meanwhile the Baroque Works have
all gathered, and their main plot is at last revealed!

## ON SALE NOW!

*Read it first in SHONEN JUMP magazine!*

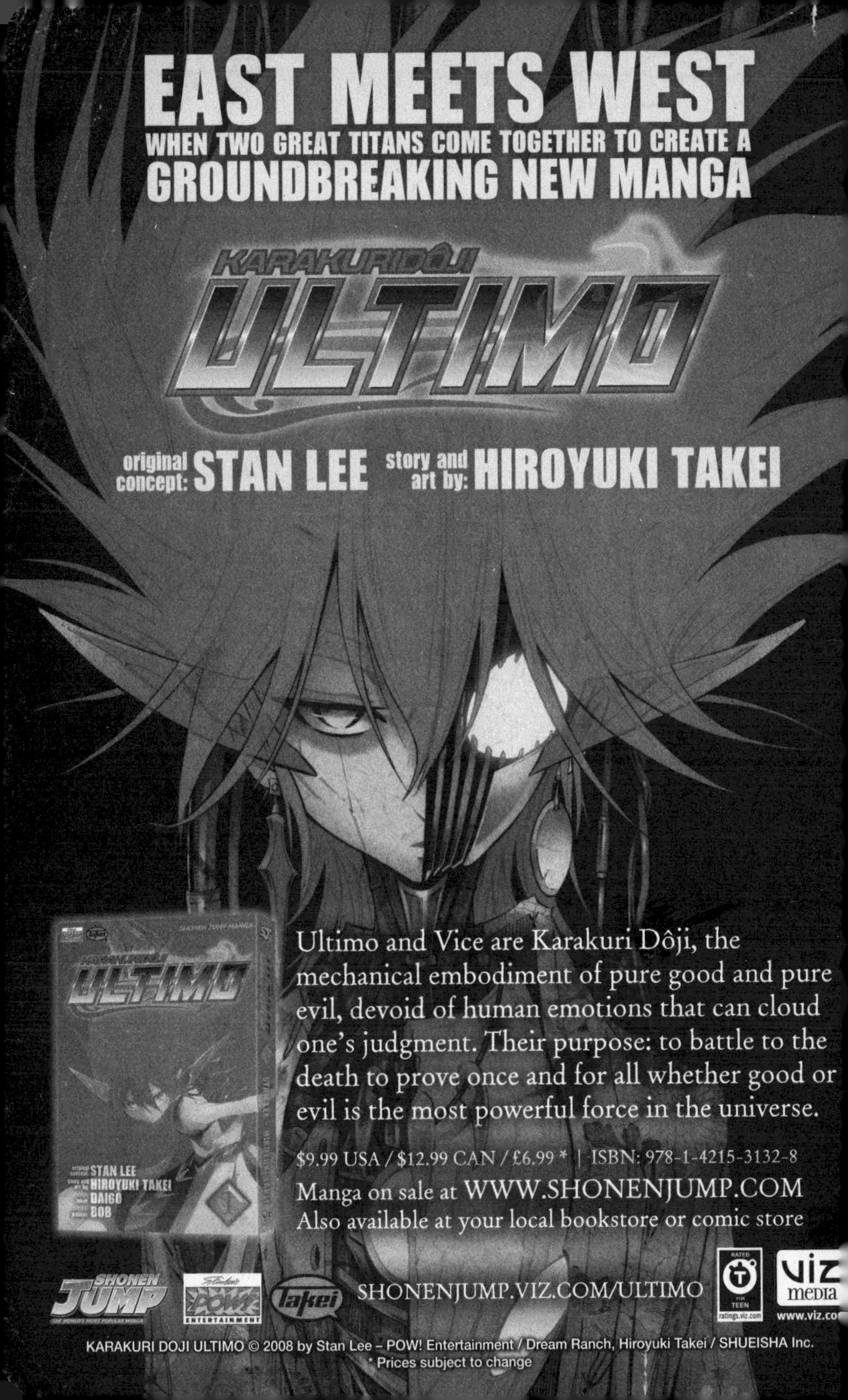
EAST MEETS WEST
WHEN TWO GREAT TITANS COME TOGETHER TO CREATE A
GROUNDBREAKING NEW MANGA
KARAKURIDÔJI
ULTIMO
original concept: STAN LEE story and art by: HIROYUKI TAKEI
SHONEN JUMP MANGA
ULTIMO
STAN LEE
HIROYUKI TAKEI
DAIGO
BOB
Ultimo and Vice are Karakuri Dôji, the mechanical embodiment of pure good and pure evil, devoid of human emotions that can cloud one's judgment. Their purpose: to battle to the death to prove once and for all whether good or evil is the most powerful force in the universe.
$9.99 USA / $12.99 CAN / £6.99 * | ISBN: 978-1-4215-3132-8
Manga on sale at WWW.SHONENJUMP.COM
Also available at your local bookstore or comic store
SHONEN JUMP
SHONENJUMP.VIZ.COM/ULTIMO
RATED T FOR TEEN
ratings.viz.com
viz media
www.viz.com
KARAKURI DOJI ULTIMO © 2008 by Stan Lee – POW! Entertainment / Dream Ranch, Hiroyuki Takei / SHUEISHA Inc.
* Prices subject to change

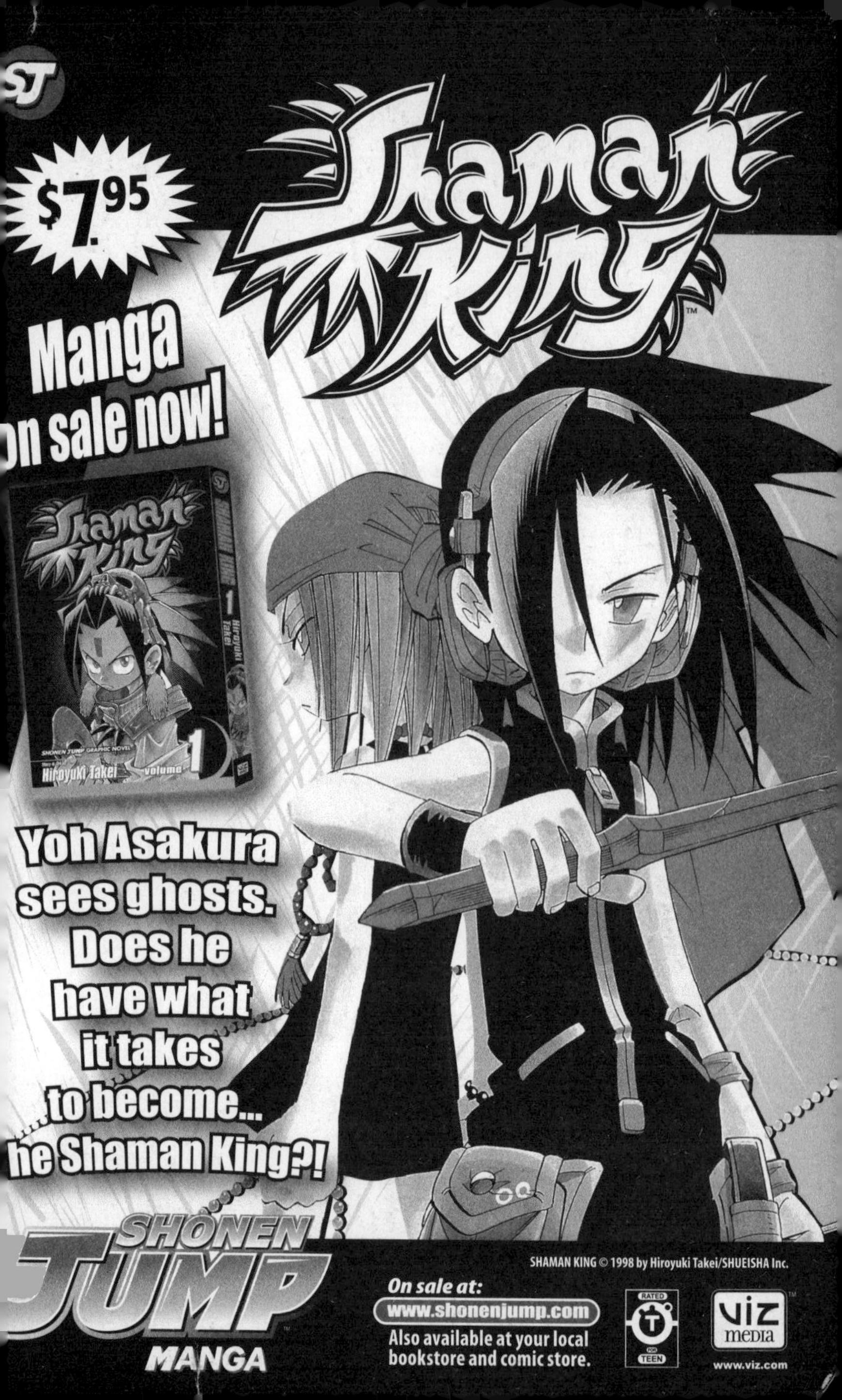

SJ
Shaman King™
$7.95
Manga
n sale now!
Shaman King
1
Hiroyuki Takei
SHONEN JUMP GRAPHIC NOVEL
Hiroyuki Takei volume 1
Yoh Asakura sees ghosts. Does he have what it takes to become...
he Shaman King?!
SHONEN JUMP MANGA
SHAMAN KING © 1998 by Hiroyuki Takei/SHUEISHA Inc.
On sale at:
www.shonenjump.com
Also available at your local bookstore and comic store.
RATED T FOR TEEN
viz media
www.viz.com

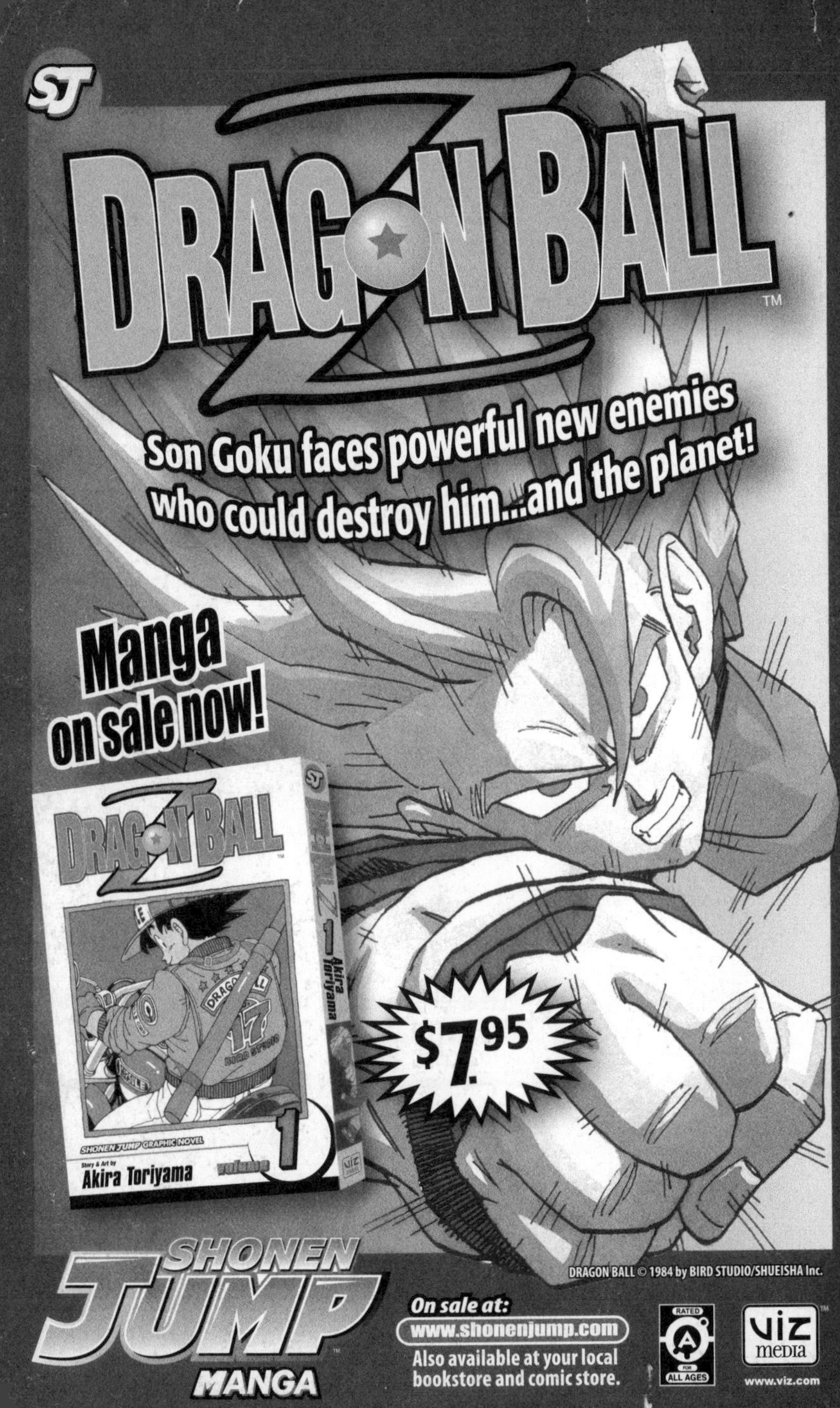

SJ
DRAGON BALL Z™
Son Goku faces powerful new enemies who could destroy him...and the planet!
Manga on sale now!
DRAGON BALL Z
SHONEN JUMP GRAPHIC NOVEL
Story & Art by Akira Toriyama
volume 1
$7.95
DRAGON BALL © 1984 by BIRD STUDIO/SHUEISHA Inc.
SHONEN JUMP MANGA
On sale at:
www.shonenjump.com
Also available at your local bookstore and comic store.
RATED A FOR ALL AGES
VIZ media
www.viz.com

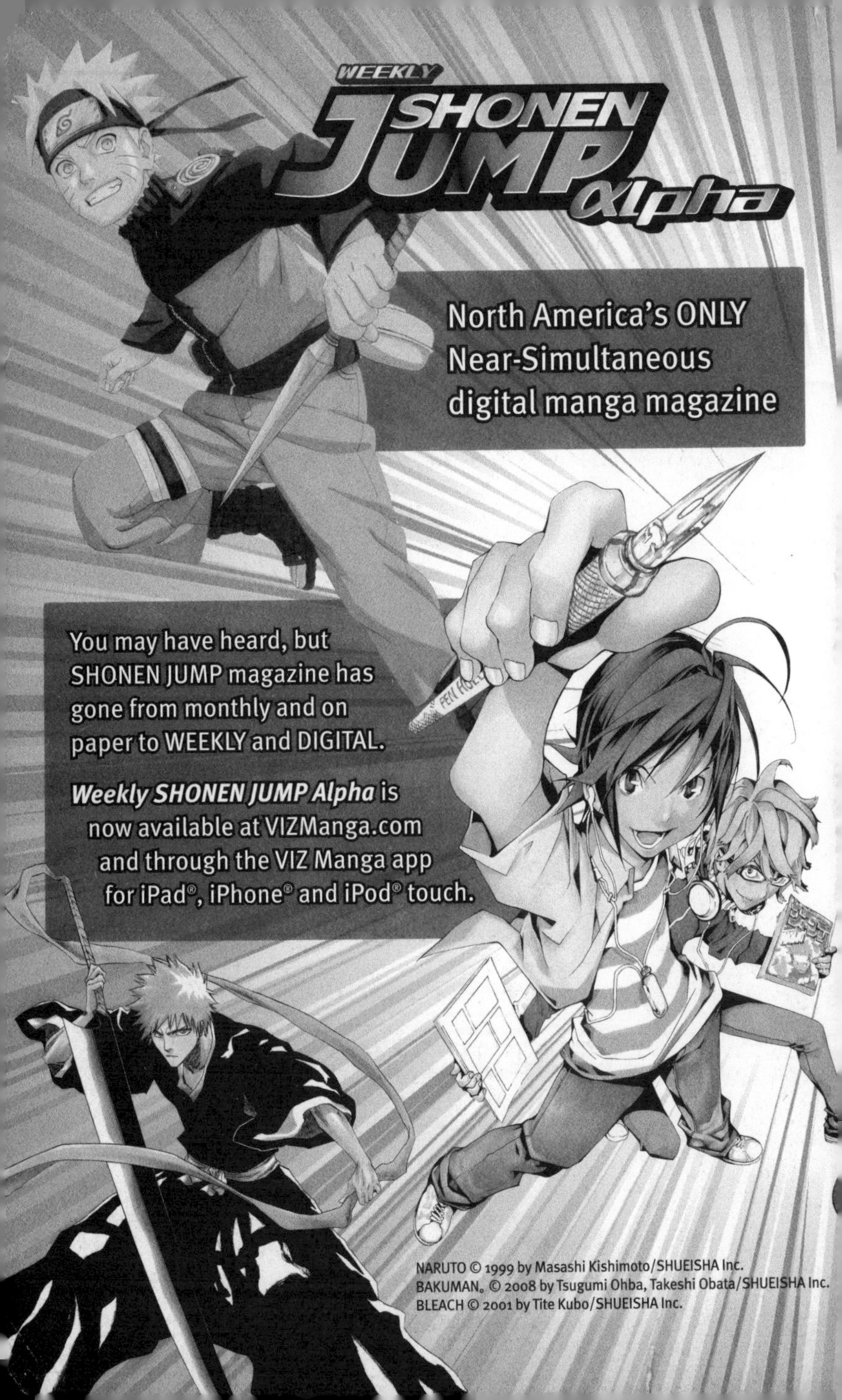
WEEKLY SHONEN JUMP Alpha
North America's ONLY Near-Simultaneous digital manga magazine
You may have heard, but SHONEN JUMP magazine has gone from monthly and on paper to WEEKLY and DIGITAL.
Weekly SHONEN JUMP Alpha is now available at VIZManga.com and through the VIZ Manga app for iPad®, iPhone® and iPod® touch.
NARUTO © 1999 by Masashi Kishimoto/SHUEISHA Inc.
BAKUMAN。 © 2008 by Tsugumi Ohba, Takeshi Obata/SHUEISHA Inc.
BLEACH © 2001 by Tite Kubo/SHUEISHA Inc.

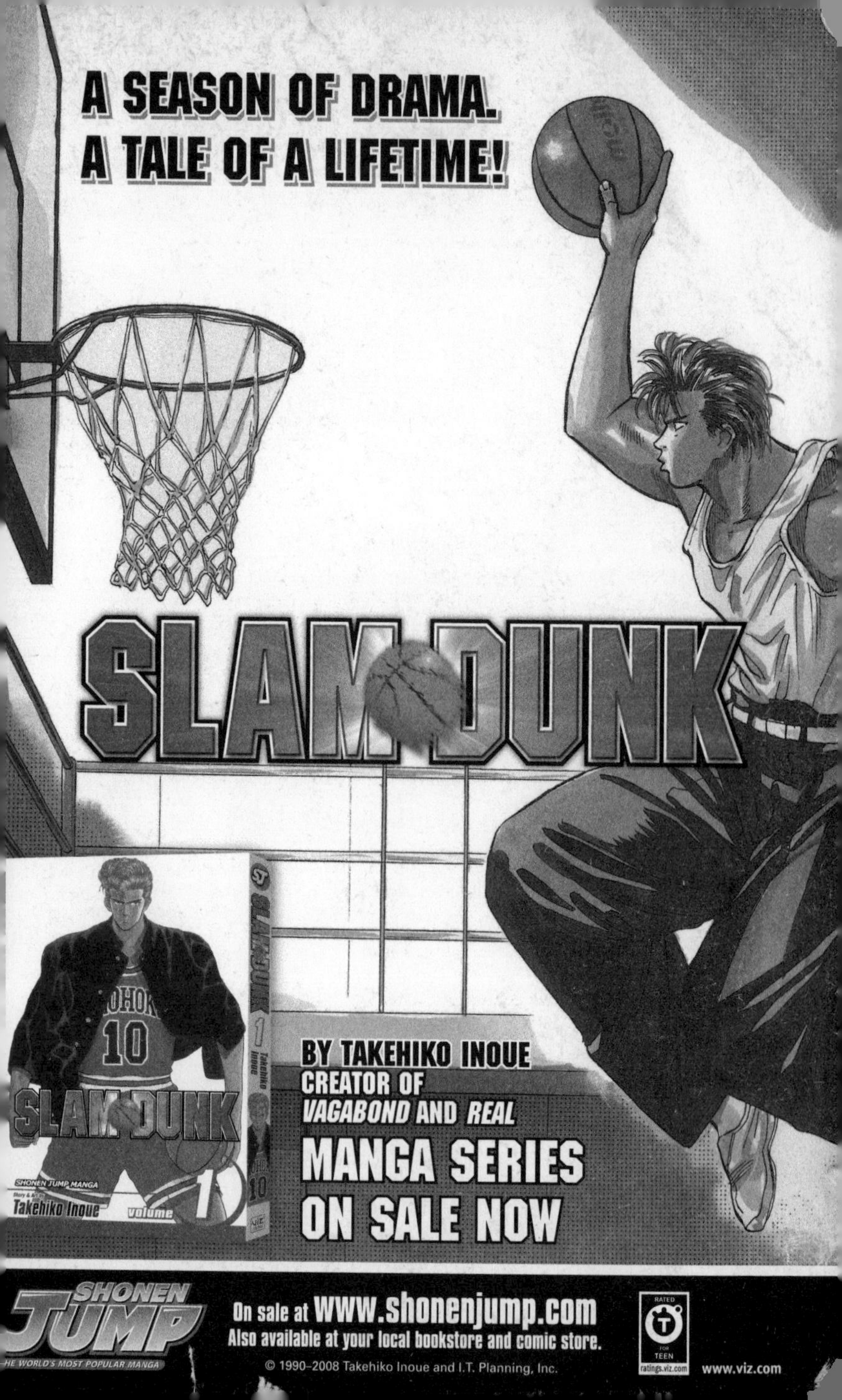

A SEASON OF DRAMA.
A TALE OF A LIFETIME!
SLAM DUNK
SLAM DUNK
SHONEN JUMP MANGA
Takehiko Inoue
volume 1
BY TAKEHIKO INOUE
CREATOR OF
*VAGABOND* AND *REAL*
MANGA SERIES
ON SALE NOW
SHONEN JUMP
HE WORLD'S MOST POPULAR MANGA
On sale at www.shonenjump.com
Also available at your local bookstore and comic store.
© 1990–2008 Takehiko Inoue and I.T. Planning, Inc.
RATED T FOR TEEN
ratings.viz.com
www.viz.com

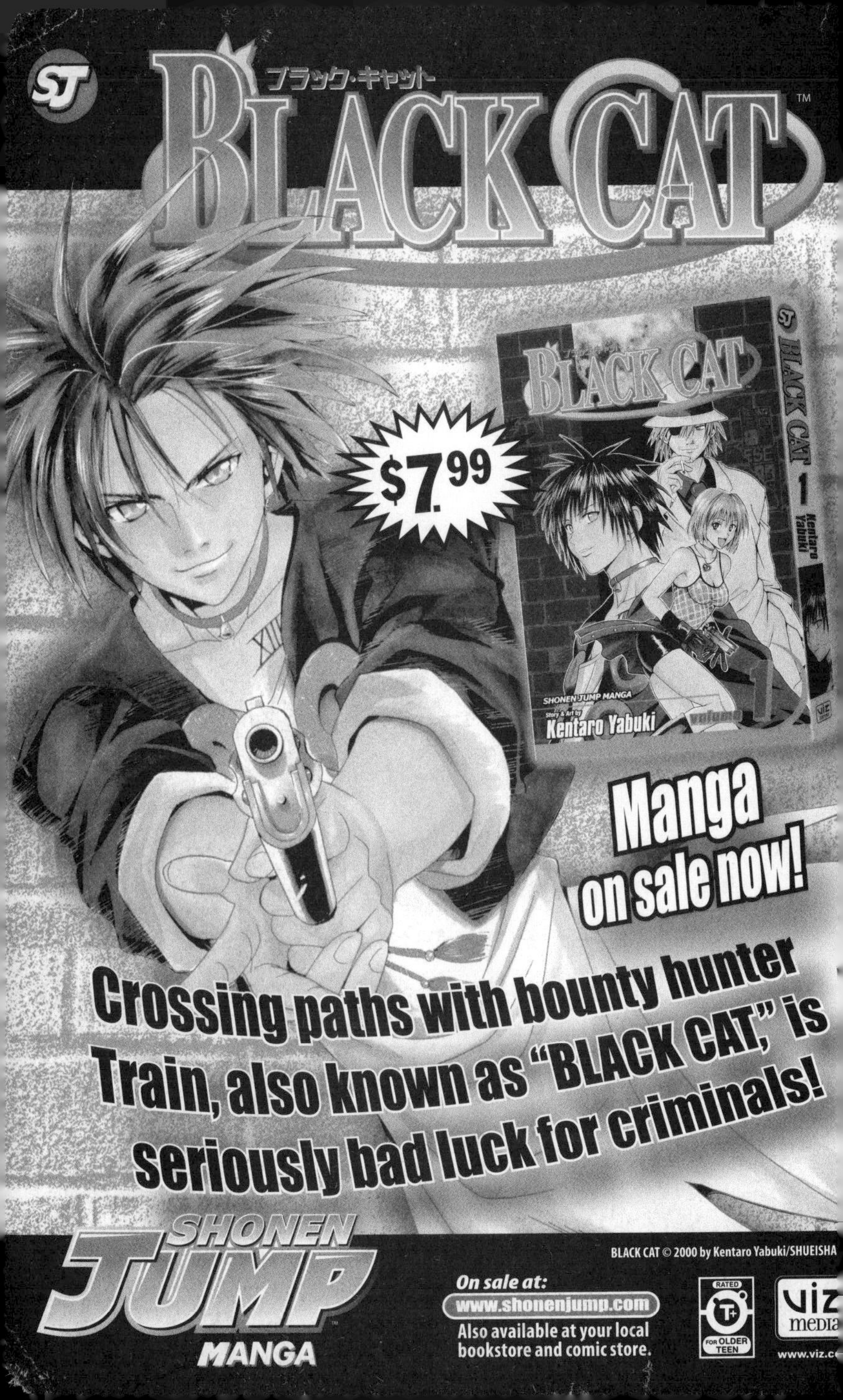

SJ
ブラック・キャット
BLACK CAT™
$7.99
BLACK CAT
SHONEN JUMP MANGA
Story & Art by
Kentaro Yabuki
BLACK CAT 1 Kentaro Yabuki
Manga
on sale now!
Crossing paths with bounty hunter
Train, also known as "BLACK CAT," is
seriously bad luck for criminals!
SHONEN JUMP
MANGA
BLACK CAT © 2000 by Kentaro Yabuki/SHUEISHA
On sale at:
www.shonenjump.com
Also available at your local
bookstore and comic store.
RATED T+ FOR OLDER TEEN
viz media

BAKUMAN。
1
STORY BY
TSUGUMI OHBA
ART BY
TAKESHI OBATA
SHONEN JUMP MANGA

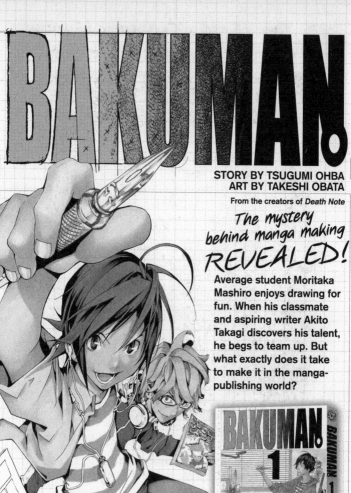

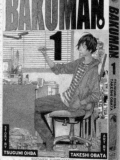

# The World's Greatest Manga
# Now available on your iPad

## Full of FREE previews and tons of
## new manga for you to explore

From legendary manga like *Dragon Ball* to *Bakuman*, the newest series from the creators of *Death Note*, the best manga in the world is now available on the iPad through the official VIZ Manga app.

- ## Free App
- ## New content weekly
- ## Free chapter 1 previews

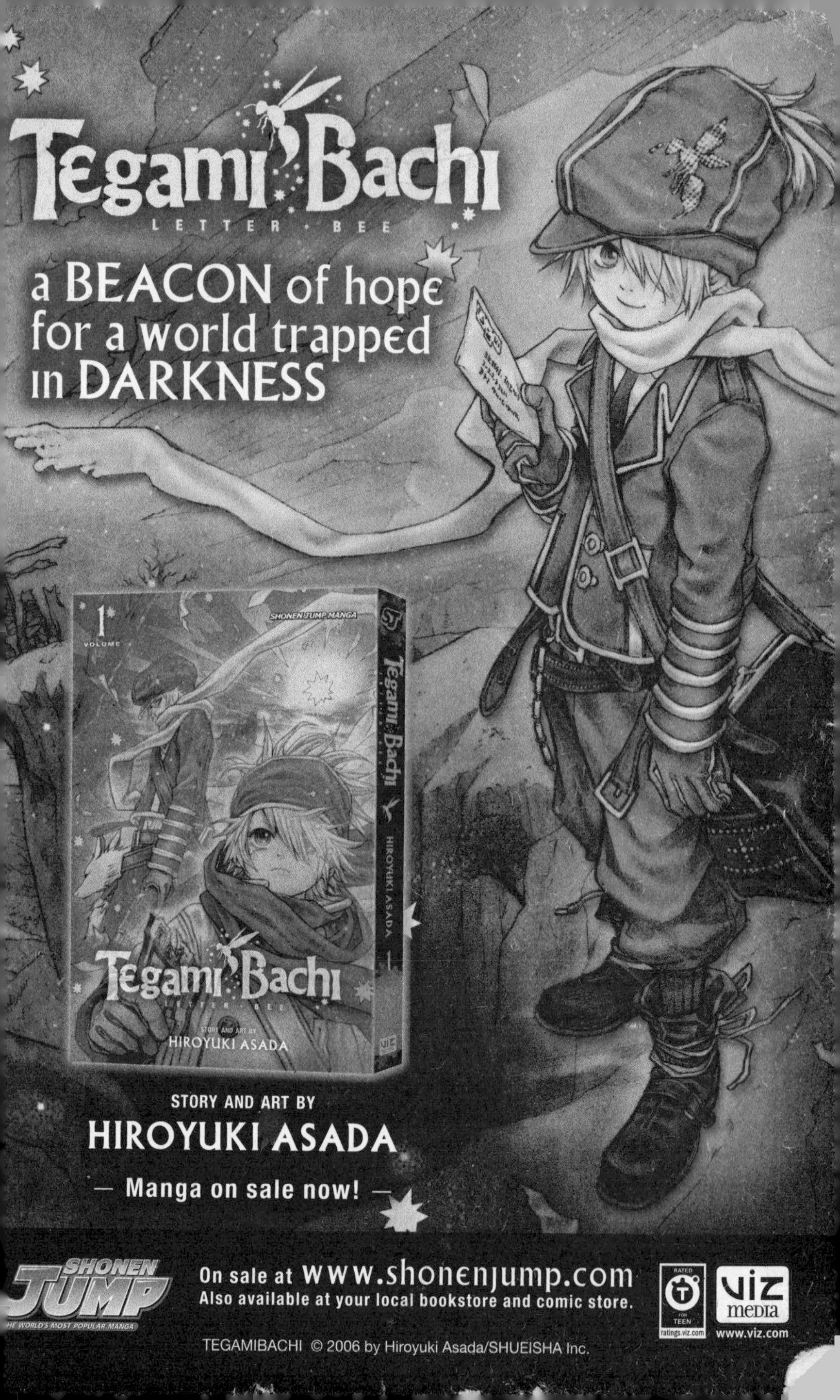

Tegami Bachi
LETTER • BEE
a BEACON of hope for a world trapped in DARKNESS
SHONEN JUMP MANGA
1 VOLUME
Tegami Bachi
LETTER • BEE
STORY AND ART BY
HIROYUKI ASADA
STORY AND ART BY
HIROYUKI ASADA
— Manga on sale now! —
SHONEN JUMP
THE WORLD'S MOST POPULAR MANGA
On sale at www.shonenjump.com
Also available at your local bookstore and comic store.
RATED T FOR TEEN
ratings.viz.com
viz media
www.viz.com
TEGAMIBACHI © 2006 by Hiroyuki Asada/SHUEISHA Inc.